Kangshung

Pethangtse
22080

Makalu II
25130

Barun

Makalu I
27790

REACHING THE SUMMIT

SIR EDMUND HILLARY'S LIFE OF ADVENTURE

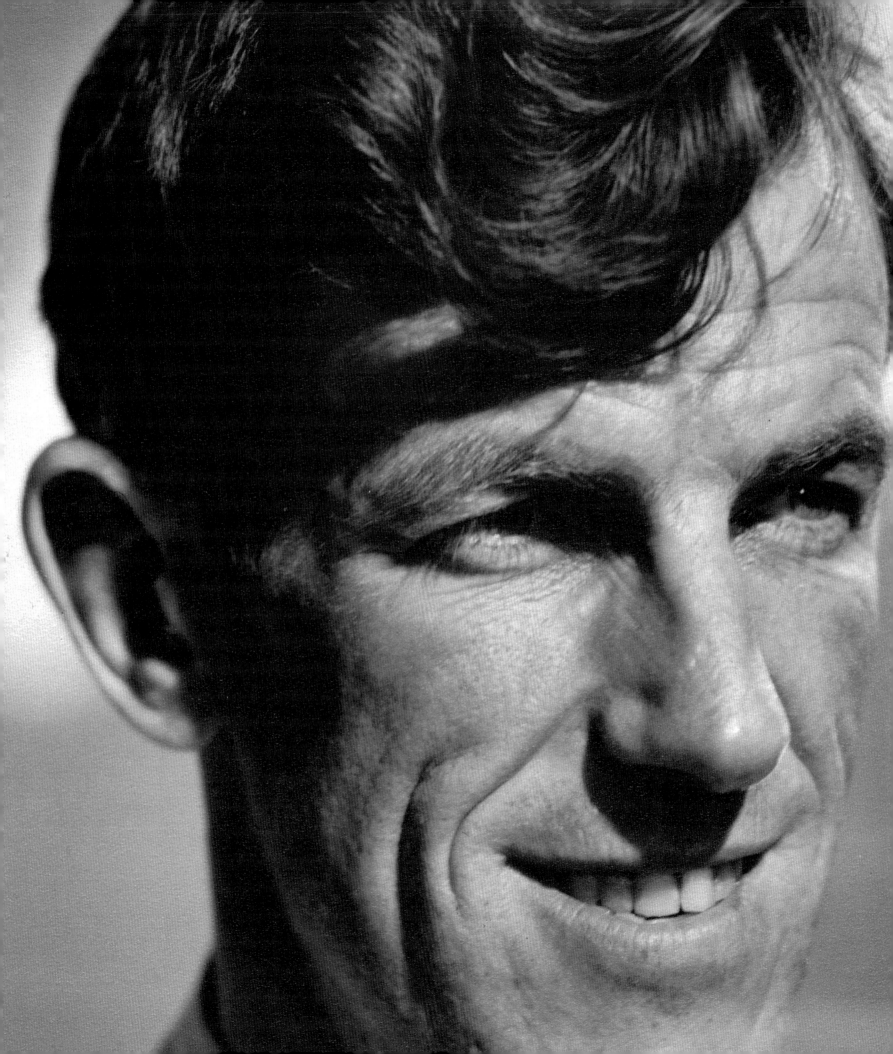

The authorised, illustrated biography by
ALEXA JOHNSTON

REACHING THE SUMMIT

SIR EDMUND HILLARY'S LIFE OF ADVENTURE

London, New York, Munich, Melbourne, Delhi

This book was first produced by
Penguin Group (NZ), cnr Airborne and Rosedale Roads,
Albany, Auckland 1310, New Zealand
(a division of Pearson New Zealand Ltd)

Dorling Kindersley Limited
Category Publisher Stephanie Jackson
Managing Editor Julie Oughton
Managing Art Editor Heather McCarry
Production Chris Avgherinos

First American edition, 2005
00 01 02 03 04 05 10 9 8 7 6 5 4 3 2 1

Published in the United States by
DK Publishing, Inc.
375 Hudson Street
New York, New York 10014

1974

A CIP catalog record for this book is available from
the Library of Congress.

ISBN 0-7566-1527-5

Designed by Inhouse design
Printed in China through Bookbuilders, Hong Kong
Maps by Terralink

Discover more at
www.dk.com

Endpapers: Maps of the Everest
region and Antarctica from a
Hillary family scrapbook

Previous pages: Sir Edmund
Hillary, August 1953
Baron Studios, Mayfair

Below: Storage boxes for the
Hillary family's 35mm slides
Jennifer French

Below: Ed, Sarah, Peter, Belinda
and Louise Hillary, c. 1962
Studio Holm, Johansen & Messenger, Whangarei

Ruapehu from Tongariro
National Park, August 1958
Edmund Hillary

I was
sixteen
before I ever
saw a mountain...
in the winter of
1935 I'd saved a
little money and
I was allowed
to join a School
Ski-ing Party
to Ruapehu –
one of our large
New Zealand volcanoes.
EDMUND HILLARY

CONTENTS

*For Malcolm and Paula and Malcolm
and for Sarah*

PROLOGUE

Edmund Hillary wanted to call his 1955 book about the Everest climb *Battle against Boredom*. It seems a modest motivation for the first ascent of Mount Everest – a feat that captured world headlines in June 1953 and became one of the great adventure stories of the twentieth century. In the end his book was published as *High Adventure*, a more stirring and saleable title. But Hillary's preference shows his signature gift for understatement – a trait which emerged during the frenzy of media attention after the climb and has remained an endearing hallmark of his public persona.

In fact his success was not unexpected. Climbing in New Zealand and the Himalayas had absorbed all of Ed Hillary's free time for more than fifteen years, and others took note of his ambition, determination and drive. After climbing with him in 1951 and 1952, leading British mountaineer Eric Shipton believed that Hillary had 'summit potential'. James Morris, the 1953 expedition's special correspondent, used more colourful language: 'He had a tremendous bursting, elemental, infectious, glorious vitality about him, like some bright, burly diesel express pounding across America.' When a few more steps needed cutting in a 'nasty bit' of a crevasse below camp, Hillary persuaded Morris to crawl out into stinging, driving snow on a horrid moonless night and provide a belay as Hillary, 'huge and cheerful', worked on the icy face. 'I first detected this strain of greatness in him that evening below Camp III,' Morris wrote, 'as the ice-chips flew through the darkness, his striped hat bobbed in the chasm, and I stood shivering and grumbling, all messed up with ropes, crampons and ice-axes, at the top.'[1] At more than 6000 metres (20,200 ft) most climbers find their energy flagging, but rather than lie in a tent with a book (a posture sometimes described as the 'Everest position') Hillary battled boredom with physical activity – and an intense focus on the progress of the expedition up the mountain.

'Relief and a vague sense of astonishment' were the words Hillary used to describe his feelings at 11.30 a.m. on Friday 29 May 1953, when with Tenzing Norgay, a Sherpa climber, he reached the summit of the world's highest peak. They were members of the 1953 British Everest Expedition, the ninth attempt on Everest by the British and the culmination of more than thirty years of expeditions to that mountain. With George Lowe, one of the support team for their summit attempt, Hillary and Tenzing returned to Advance Base Camp on the 30th, bringing the story to their leader, John Hunt, and a crowd of relieved and exhilarated companions. That afternoon correspondent James Morris and climber Michael Westmacott raced down through the icefall to Base Camp with news of the success, and on the morning of 31 May a Sherpa runner set off with Morris's dispatch to the village of Namche Bazar, 2000 metres below, and a long day's walk even for a Sherpa. From Namche it was radioed to the British Embassy in Kathmandu and from there to *The Times* of London. The truth was concealed in a cunning code devised by Morris:

```
Snow Conditions Bad.
Advanced Base Abandoned Yesterday.
Awaiting Improvement. All well.
```

Other media intercepted the radio transmission and quickly reported the failure of the summit attempt. But *The Times* decoded a triumphant message: 'Summit of Everest reached on 29 May by Hillary and Tenzing. All well.' It arrived in London on the eve of the Coronation of Queen Elizabeth II. Fifty years later the Duke of Edinburgh wrote, 'On 2 June 1953, the day of the Coronation, the Queen and I were woken with the news that Hillary and Tenzing had reached the summit of Mount Everest. It was a marvellous beginning to a wonderful day.'[2]

Crowds waiting in the rain for the Queen's coach to pass on its way to Westminster Abbey cheered when they heard the reports, and newspapers trumpeted 'The Crowning Glory – Everest is climbed!' A *New York Times* editorial rhapsodised over 'one of the most remarkable conjunctures of events in all history. Nothing less can characterize that wonderful combination of the conquest of the last unconquered spot on

earth and the dawn of a new Elizabethan era.' The enthusiastic writer went on to predict that Hillary and Tenzing would take their places in history alongside Sir Walter Raleigh and Sir Francis Drake.

In Nepal King Tribhuvan and Queen Kanti Rajya were particularly delighted that Tenzing Norgay Sherpa had reached the summit. All the climbers were granted a royal audience on their return to Kathmandu, and Tenzing, Hunt and Hillary were each presented with the Nepal Tara: 'The Most Refulgent Order of the Star of Nepal'. Indian newspapers carried the story and official welcomes and presentations were planned in New Delhi, Calcutta and Bombay.

At home in New Zealand, the acting prime minister interrupted the broadcast of the Coronation to announce that Hillary had 'put New Zealand...on top of the world. How proud we all are! And what a magnificent Coronation present for the Queen!' On a wave of euphoria, and without waiting to consult Hillary, Prime Minister Sid Holland, in London for the Coronation, accepted a knighthood for him. From now on, like it or not, Ed Hillary would be Sir Edmund Hillary KBE.

Fifty years later the lustre of that first Everest climb had not faded. On 29 May 2003 the *Guardian*'s leading article read: 'Hillary and Tenzing's ascent still shines like a peak, high in the sunlight. In a world that reduces so many human acts and aspirations to banality, their achievement remains a matchless pinnacle of genuine unselfish heroism.' In the years after Everest, Edmund Hillary's life took on a new shape. He arrived on the world stage as a climbing hero but his significance has extended far beyond the sport of mountaineering. He has become a highly respected citizen of the world, with tremendous mana in his own country. In 2003 New Zealand historian Michael King described Ed Hillary as 'our most loved national figure'. He embodies many of the qualities we most admire – he is strong, determined, adventurous, calm, quietly doing a power of practical good in the world and, despite honours and accolades, remaining approachable, good-humoured and down to earth: an extraordinary ordinary bloke.

Towering arrogantly above all else, on the crests and down the spurs, stood groups of the kauri, the giant timber tree of New Zealand, whose great grey trunks, like the pillars in the ancient halls of Karnak, shot up seventy and eighty feet without a knot or branch, and whose colossal heads, swelling up into the sky, made a cipher of every tree near.
JANE MANDER

Facing page: Wharves and shipping at Dargaville, the chief town of the North Auckland West Coast, c. 1910
P. A. Hillary

Top left: Kauri logs, Northern Wairoa, c. 1910
P. A. Hillary

Bottom left: Kauri tree, Northern Wairoa, c. 1910
P. A. Hillary

01 BORN IN NEW ZEALAND

Adventurousness, courage and daring appear often in Ed Hillary's family history, along with more settled achievements like writing, planning and community leadership. His New Zealand roots are in the Northern Wairoa, centre of the thriving kauri industry. In the 1890s, as the Thames and Waihi goldfields were worked out, the demand for kauri timber and kauri gum, the semi-fossilised resin of ancient, long-dead trees, sparked another gold rush. Millions of metres of timber were felled, sawn and loaded on to the sailing ships which crowded into the Kaipara Harbour, and from there shipped all over the world. The Northern Wairoa River flows into the Kaipara, and noisy mill towns sprang up along its banks. Itinerant loggers, mill workers and gum diggers, Maori, British and Dalmatian, lived in small encampments in the bush, coming to town to spend their pay or sell their kauri gum for gold. Respectable settlers mingled with rugged and sometimes desperate men of every class.[1] Ed Hillary's parents, Percival and Gertrude, grew up in this rough-edged but prosperous district.

12   Gertrude Clark's pioneer grandparents, Charles
and Dinah Clark, emigrated from Yorkshire in
1843. Seventeen years later, after working in
Nelson, Auckland and Northland, they were at
last able to achieve every settler's dream and
purchase their own land – sixty-two hectares
at Whakahara on the Northern Wairoa. Faced
with the task of moving there from Paradise,
a tiny settlement on the upper reaches of the
river, Charles built an enormous kauri raft
which drifted downriver with the tides, carrying
the family, their possessions and livestock to
their new home. At Whakahara the Clarks built
a house which looked out across the wide
expanse of the river. They broke in the land for
cattle, constructed a jetty, and opened a store
and post office.

    The family raft trip is often mentioned
in histories of the Kaipara, as is Dinah Clark's
adventure in the winter of 1853. She travelled to
Auckland with four companions – a journey of
over 180 kilometres – on foot and by open boat.
They were forced to wait for a break in the
weather, so camped for three days on wet sand
at the Kaipara Harbour mouth with 'not even a

Far left: Mrs E. Hillary, 1922.
Inscribed: Gertie and Percy
from Mum, May 1922
Wilbar Portrait, Auckland

Left: *Northern Wairoa
Gazette*, 16 September 1886

Below: *Northern Wairoa
Gazette*, 5 August 1886

roof to cover us or shelter us from the pitiless blast', then made it safely across the heads. They crossed the swollen Kumeu River on trees uprooted in the storm and reached Riverhead on Auckland Harbour. Dinah's only protective clothing, an outer petticoat made from an old blue blanket, was torn to shreds. The last stage of the trip was a long row down the harbour, during which they survived a total swamping. Ten days after leaving Paradise, they waded ashore at Auckland through knee-deep mud to the foot of Albert Street.[2]

Charles and Dinah were trusted figures in the Northern Wairoa community, and the Whakahara Store became a popular stopping place. Their two boats, the *Minnie Casey* and the *Kina*, met the Auckland train at Helensville, and delivered mail and took passengers and goods to and from Dargaville. George Clark, the youngest of their four children, worked alongside his parents and eventually took over the management of the store at Whakahara. According to family lore, a young seamstress named Harriet Wooderson came to make new summer dresses for Dinah and her daughters,

and stayed to marry George. Ed Hillary's mother Gertrude was the eighth of their eleven children. She grew up in a close and loving family with a busy mother and a cheerful, kind-hearted father who was widely respected for his upright character. George served on many local committees, and was a sportsman too, winning a £20 first prize with his fifteen-foot yacht *Demon* in one hotly contested race at Te Kopuru Regatta.

But in 1901, when Gertrude was only nine, George Clark was killed, kicked in the head by a horse as he was trying to free it from a strangling slip-knot. Harriet never fully recovered from the shock, and Gertrude's older sisters looked after her and the three younger ones. This strong family of women was also important for Gertrude's children, who as teenagers enjoyed many sociable gatherings at the Epsom home of their Clark aunts.

The first Edmund Hillary, Percy Hillary's father, was born in Staleybridge, Ashton-under-Lyne, Lancashire, in 1836. He was a watchmaker and jeweller who, despite his sedentary trade, had a varied and adventurous career. In the 1850s he answered a newspaper advertisement

for a position maintaining a collection of clockwork birds and animals for an Indian aristocrat; he went on to work for several other Indian collectors whose clockwork toys entertained visitors and demonstrated the wealth and modernity of their owners. After some years in India Edmund returned home in financial comfort, and in 1881 was in Wales with his mother and sister. Three years later he had come out of retirement, moved to the other side of the world and was firmly established in Dargaville. He opened a jeweller's and watchmaker's shop in Hokianga Road, and the *Northern Wairoa Gazette* records his marriage on 3 December 1884 to Annie Clementina Fleming, a young Irish woman.

Annie Fleming, who was always known as Ida, had sailed from Ireland to New Zealand with her family at the age of eight, and travelled across the Pacific to Hawaii while working as a governess before her marriage. Ed Hillary was enthralled by his grandmother's tales of these long sea voyages, and impressed by her boldness and self-reliance. He later wrote that making her marriage work required all her

Right: Hokianga Road, Dargaville, from the mast of a ship at Dargaville wharf, c. 1911
P. A. Hillary

Far right: Percival Augustus Hillary, (centre) aged about twenty-six, with two unidentified companions c. 1911
P. A. Hillary

Right: Aurega House, Dargaville, the Hillary family's home, c. 1907
P. A. Hillary

14 grit and resilience, but it began well. She was twenty-eight and had found a man of large personality and considerable charm. Edmund must have felt rejuvenated in his new country – he lowered his age from forty-eight to forty-four on their wedding certificate.

Edmund Hillary immersed himself in Dargaville life. He was an expert marksman and a foundation member of the Dargaville Rifle Volunteer Corps, which paraded in dashing red and gold uniforms and practised shooting every week. By May 1886 he had become secretary of the Dargaville Town Board and announced in the paper the establishment of a public dog pound. The *Gazette* ran an article about the problem of stray dogs attacking poultry and sheep, which was headed: Collarless Canines Cause Ceaseless Contention. Concerning Contumelious Culprits Councillor Coutts Commends Coercive Collection. Contemplated Court Cases.

In July the paper noted with wry approval that the Dargaville 'skiters', led by Mr E. Hillary, intended establishing a debating society: 'the world is topsy-turvy and calls aloud for an expression of an opinion from the Dargaville settlers!' Edmund was founding secretary of the society and provider of the first debate: 'Monogamy versus Polygamy'. The *Gazette* summarised his arguments for and against the topic: 'The speaker gave a very graphic description of the domestic economy of the Rajah of Mysore's household and the number of his wives and the perennial bliss pervading the *sanctum sanctorum* of that dignitary. This he brought forward as a pleasing side of polygamy. Upon the whole, however, he drew up his conclusions in favour of monogamy. The debate occupied just one hour and the division list showed in favour of monogamy 8, of polygamy 3.'[3]

Edmund's familiarity with the households of Indian aristocrats crops up again in a story he told his children. While attending to the clocks in a large palace, he rescued from the harem a young English woman who had been sold there by her soldier father. Edmund, using his watchmaking expertise, fashioned a key for the harem door and raced away with her on horseback. After eluding their pursuers by hiding among the roots of a huge banyan tree, they rode on to the British military encampment. The father of the rescued damsel was drummed out of the army, and she was safely restored to her family in England.[4] It's an exotic and heroic tale – worthy of the boyhood adventure stories enjoyed by Edmund's grandson, the young Ed Hillary.

In September 1885 Edmund and Ida's first child was born and named Percival Augustus. The family believed they were connected to Sir William Hillary, the distinguished and heroic founder of the Royal National Lifeboat Institution on the Isle of Man, who had called his son Augustus. This is no doubt the provenance of Percy's rather splendid name. There would be three other children: John Edmund, Leila Osberta and Clarice Irene. At home in Hokianga Road, Edmund sang as he worked on the watches. He was proud of his voice, having performed before Queen Victoria when he was eighteen with a Welsh choir at the Royal Albert Hall. The Hillarys were gardeners too, and in 1886 the *Gazette* noted that their garden had produced a natural marvel in the form of a 12.8-kilogram Savoy cabbage.

Left: Gertrude Clark in Auckland aged seventeen in 1909. She was about to begin studying at teachers' training college

Below: The Clark family in 1915, taken on George and Edwin Clark's final leave from army-training camp, before they went to war in France and Belgium.
(L–R) Back row: Ada, Mabel, Gertrude, Charles, Florence, Dorice, Edith
Front row: Helen, George, Harriet, Edwin, Annie

Edmund built a large two-storeyed family home on Victoria Street, overlooking the river. 'Aurega House' was named after Ida's family home in Ireland and had paddocks and stables for Edmund's racehorses. Kaipara residents were passionate followers of horse racing and the papers ran accounts of the numerous local meetings as well as the Auckland and Melbourne cups. Edmund was a player. One of his horses, Aurega, did reasonably well, but in the end racing was his downfall. Family tradition has it that in his sixties, ruined by gambling losses, Edmund took to his bed. Whether he was a genuine invalid or not, family loyalties are with Ida who, like many pioneer women, rose to the challenge of ensuring her children were properly raised and educated. All four had the full eight years at school, the girls leaving for 'domestic duties' and the boys for work.

Ida Hillary painted pictures for sale, took in dressmaking and did any work she could to keep the family together. Edmund occasionally emerged from his bedroom on the top floor of the house to paint a little, but the children helped their mother as soon as they were able.

In December 1898, at the age of thirteen, Percy was employed as a copy boy for the *Wairoa Bell and Northern Advertiser*. At school English had been his best subject and he was soon promoted to reporter. Ed Hillary remembers his father's delight in a favourite book on English usage and the book-rack he constructed – it was designed to hang over the back of a cow so he could read while milking. Percy taught himself photography, lugging his camera to the top of a mast to get bird's-eye views of Dargaville: clustered houses, hotels and churches, sailing ships at the wharves and timber mills working. Several of his photographs were accepted for publication in Auckland's *Weekly News*, the major illustrated newspaper of the time. By December 1911 he was printing and publishing the *Wairoa Bell* each week for its proprietor, local businessman A. J. Stallworthy. He was twenty-six.

Dargaville was a few hours up the river with the tide from Whakahara. Gertrude Clark was shopping there with her mother one day when Mrs Clark stopped to talk to a friend, a cheerful and pleasant Irish woman, Mrs Ida

Hillary. Her son Percy joined them and was introduced to Gertrude – and 'from that day he had eyes for no one else'.[5] Tall, slender, graceful and with elegant manners, Gertrude Clark loved poetry and music, was the family accompanist on the piano and, like several of her sisters, became a schoolteacher. She had also inherited the family's strength and resilience, qualities she would certainly need in the years ahead.

Gertrude Clark and Percy Hillary were engaged to be married. Percy was a sociable young man and his future wife's sisters enjoyed his company too. Those climbs up the masts of tall ships were proof of his daring and stamina, and all his life he would value physical fitness and a healthy diet. Tall, lean and wiry, he enjoyed rugby, cricket and tennis, and umpired the matches of the Dargaville ladies' basket-ball team.

Ed Hillary describes his father as 'a keen thinker', and a man whose family background moulded his character into 'a mixture of moral conservatism and fierce independence and pride'. Newspaper work kept him up to date with world events, and he was intensely interested

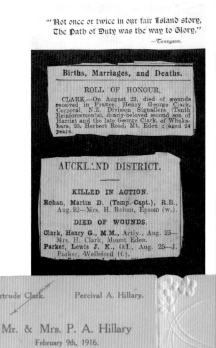

in social reform and in the nineteenth century's crop of religious and philosophical movements. In November 1909 the *Wairoa Bell* announced that a branch of the Theosophical Society would be established there 'to form a nucleus of the Universal Brotherhood of Humanity, to study comparative religion, philosophy and science and to investigate unexplained laws of nature'. Theosophists were exhorted to study religion in all its forms, to be tolerant, to work perseveringly and to 'Aim High'. Percy was attracted to such sentiments, and his son has often used the words 'Aim High' in book inscriptions.

By April 1914 Percy had left the *Wairoa Bell* to purchase its rival, the *North Auckland Times*, 'the only Press Association Paper on the North Auckland West Coast'. Six months earlier a notice had appeared in the paper announcing that Aurega House, 'late establishment of Mr Hillary…is now open as a private Boarding House run by Mrs Gilliard'. The house may have been sold to help fund the purchase of the newspaper or just to assist Ida with family finances. At any rate Percy's financial commitment was considerable and a month after he

bought the paper he joined up with a business partner, Archibald Hillier.

In Europe war was looming, and on Friday 7 August 1914 the paper began issuing 'complete and full WAR EDITIONS' at four p.m. each day. A double page of news kept Dargaville citizens abreast of developments across the Empire. The *North Auckland Times* set up a Patriotic Fund to help equip the New Zealand Expeditionary Force and made a generous opening donation of two guineas. All around New Zealand thousands of young men volunteered for the army, fired by war news and the patriotic mood of the country. At twenty-nine Percy Hillary was older than many other volunteers, but just as determined to be part of this great cause and adventure. His partnership with Hillier was legally dissolved in October 1914, and he enlisted with the New Zealand Expeditionary Force. He became a private in the Auckland Infantry Battalion, and left New Zealand in December 1914 for training in Egypt.

Unlike so many who sailed away to support Britain and the Empire, Percy Hillary returned home. (Of the 8556 New Zealand troops

who fought at Gallipoli, 2721 were killed and 4725 wounded.) But the gruelling and fruitless campaign in the Dardanelles left him physically and psychologically scarred. On 29 April 1915, just four days after the first ANZAC troops landed on the nightmarishly precipitous slopes of the Gallipoli Peninsula, Percy was wounded by a bullet through the nose. He returned immediately to duty and was soon promoted to acting sergeant. On 8 May he took part in a doomed attack across a notorious piece of ground known as the Daisy Patch. Eight hundred men from the New Zealand Brigade were lost. And months in the muddy trenches around Anzac Cove took a further toll. ANZAC troops were later to emerge as the heroes of the botched campaign, but they were infuriated by incapable commanders, constantly under Turkish fire, assailed by swarms of flies and the stench of bodies between the lines, and debilitated by inadequate rations and desperately low morale. Widespread dysentery added to their misery.

Late in July Percy Hillary collapsed with diarrhoea and exhaustion. After his condition

Far left: Birth notice for Edmund Percival Hillary, 20 July 1919

Left: Edmund Percival Hillary, aged about nine months, 1920

worsened he was transferred to Malta with 'nerves and breakdown', and from there was sent to Bristol for another month in hospital. He recovered enough to embark for New Zealand, arriving at Auckland on 2 February 1916. A week later, at St Matthew-in-the-City, he and Gertrude Clark were married. The witnesses were Gertrude's youngest sister Dorice, and her brother Henry, an army volunteer who was in training at Trentham Camp. Henry was later killed in France and another brother, Edwin, died at Passchendaele.

Gertrude had left Dargaville several years earlier. The timber industry in the Northern Wairoa was on the wane – seven large mills cutting kauri for forty years had effectively wiped out the enormous forests in the area, and dairy farming would take some years to become established.[6] The store was closed and cousins farmed the Whakahara block. Gertrude worked as a pupil-teacher at Te Kopuru School, then enrolled for teacher training at Ardmore Teachers' College in Auckland. She taught for a year before marrying Percy, but her training and her commitment to the importance of

education were a positive force in the upbringing of her family.

Percy was pronounced 'medically unfit' and officially discharged from the New Zealand Expeditionary Force on 5 May 1916. His war experiences, shared by so many in the military mess that was Gallipoli, left his temperament darkened, and he would not be an easy man to live with. Many years later his sister-in-law Ada Clark wrote to June Hillary that Percy returned from the war 'a changed man',[7] and his children had only rare glimpses of a positive and cheerful father. His vehement and principled opposition to war would later have a profound effect on his sons.

Ed was born Edmund Percival Hillary in Auckland on 20 July 1919. He had an older sister, June, who was born in 1917, and his brother Rex was born in 1920. Percy and Gertrude were by this time living in Tuakau, a small farming town sixty-five kilometres south of Auckland, where Percy had been allocated eight acres (3.2 ha) of land after the war. The elder Hillarys had moved there too, and Percy's sister Leila lived nearby; her

husband, Bert Sumner, managed the Farmers Cooperative stores in Tuakau and at Pukekohe, the largest nearby town.

Returned servicemen could learn beekeeping at an apiary and model bee farm at the Ruakura government farm in Hamilton, and Percy listed his occupation on the 1919 electoral roll as 'beekeeper'.[8] He had been unable to return to journalism immediately postwar – to his extreme irritation, his former Dargaville partner had not kept up payments on their printing press. Within a couple of years, however, he took up journalism again. He set up a printing office in George Street, the main street of Tuakau, and became founding editor of the *Tuakau District News*, a weekly paper owned by Northern Waikato Newspapers Limited. He also kept bees.

Gertrude Hillary, a warm and loving mother, was the heart of the family. Her children remember her as refined and ladylike – she received callers on Tuesday afternoons at three o'clock – but she worked hard in the garden and with the bees when Percy's other commitments got in the way. Gertrude read and enjoyed poetry all her life and her leather-bound copy of

18   *Palgrave's Golden Treasury* brought enormous
pleasure. In the early days in Tuakau, Percy
printed extracts from poems selected by Gertrude
before his leading articles in the newspaper.

Ed Hillary remembers his father doing
almost everything to get the paper out each
Thursday – attending rugby matches and
council meetings, writing them up, setting the
type, printing the newspapers, and at times
even delivering them himself. To record the
progress of a rugby game Percy would divide
his journalist's pad into three columns: he used
one for notes, and in the other two traced the
movements of the ball and the extent of
possession achieved by each team. The children
went with him to the rugby – they shared their
father's love for New Zealand's national game.
Percy admired Maori skill on the rugby field
and in the timber industry, and in December
1922 Tuakau saw one of the first performances
of Te Pou o Mangatawhiri, a touring concert
party set up by the visionary Maori leader
Princess Te Puea Herangi. This was an innovative venture to raise funds for the marae at
Turangawaewae, and as editor of the local

paper Percy could give it valuable support.
Princess Te Puea became a lifelong friend.

Ed Hillary's early years in this small
country town were happy. On family picnics Ed
and his brother Rex built rafts from driftwood
and floated down the Waikato River below
Tuakau. They were all excellent swimmers. The
best times with their father were spent sitting
on his knee in the evenings as he told them
stories about a character called Jimmy Job who
lived in a hollow tree at the bottom of the garden.
The children got on well together and spent many
hours playing in the fields around the house,
which Percy built but never quite completed.
There were too many other calls on his time. His
father's tendency to leave projects incomplete
worried Ed, and in his own career he would be
driven to see things through to the end – whether
climbing a mountain or travelling overland to
the South Pole or building a school in Nepal.

Just 800 metres from home was Tuakau
Primary, a three-room school. Ed had grown
from a bonny baby to a rather skinny boy –
he remembers being very small for his age and
enjoying the protection of an older Maori girl

who shared a desk with him. But he swept
through, skipping two classes and completing
the curriculum at eleven, two years earlier than
usual. He ascribes this to his mother's home
coaching and to his own ability to absorb
lessons intended for the older children in the
same classroom.

By the age of seven or eight Ed was also
a keen reader. He had few friends, apart from his
brother and sister, and books opened up new
landscapes and experiences. Against their
father's rules, he read at night with a torch
under the bedclothes, and his sister June
collaborated in an early-warning scheme to
protect him from discovery. The material for
this clandestine reading was a standard range
of boys adventures by writers like Edgar Rice
Burroughs, Rider Haggard and Zane Grey, whose
ripping yarns complemented the exciting films
screened each week at Tuakau War Memorial
Hall: romances on Tuesdays and the wild west
on Saturdays. As little boys, Rex and Ed were
determined to get to the pictures no matter
what, trailing around after their mother in tears
until she agreed to take them with June to the
Tuesday romance, much to June's irritation.
Once there, the boys sat at the front while June
and Gertrude went upstairs, and there was
always singing before the film began. Two of the
old songs, 'There's a Bridle Hanging on the Wall'
and 'Red River Valley', remain Ed Hillary's
favourites.

Walking in bare feet over prickly grass,
sharp gravel or hot and sticky asphalt, and
sloshing along streaming gutters in the rain –
Ed was a typical New Zealand schoolboy. And a
familiar walk can quickly become an adventure
if you imagine yourself galloping across fields
of purple sage, or swinging smoothly through a
steaming jungle. His longing for adventure grew.
After school and at weekends, once the chores
were done, Tuakau offered grassy fields, creeks,

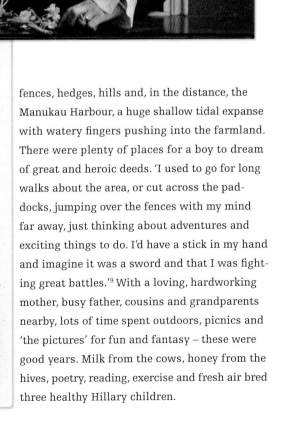

fences, hedges, hills and, in the distance, the Manukau Harbour, a huge shallow tidal expanse with watery fingers pushing into the farmland. There were plenty of places for a boy to dream of great and heroic deeds. 'I used to go for long walks about the area, or cut across the paddocks, jumping over the fences with my mind far away, just thinking about adventures and exciting things to do. I'd have a stick in my hand and imagine it was a sword and that I was fighting great battles.'[9] With a loving, hardworking mother, busy father, cousins and grandparents nearby, lots of time spent outdoors, picnics and 'the pictures' for fun and fantasy – these were good years. Milk from the cows, honey from the hives, poetry, reading, exercise and fresh air bred three healthy Hillary children.

The Tuakau District News

With which is Incorporated **THE FRANKLIN COUNTY ARGUS,**

TUAKAU, THURSDAY, OCTOBER 10, 1929.

PRICE, ONE PENNY.

120 MILES an hour!
or
2 MILES

A MINUTE AT
Average Separating Speed

To make it easy to run the Separator at this high speed (necessary for clean skimming) the McCormick-Deering Cream Separators are equipped with four ball bearing and a positive, automatic oiling system. The combination of ball bearings and plenty of oil make McCormick-Deering run so easily that a boy or girl can do the work easily.

CLOSE SKIMMING

EASY TURNING

Three Six Features make the McCormick-Deering So Much Better.

TENNIS NOTES

WHANGARATA CLUB.

The Whangarata Tennis Club opened its courts on Saturday, when the President, Mr. R. Furniss, welcomed the visitors and spoke of the value to the district of the club, especially as regards the social side of its activities. The membership numbered 20 and the work done in preparing and improving the court had been given voluntarily. Mrs Furniss hit the first ball over the net, and the President then declared the courts open for play. A tempting afternoon tea was dispensed, and the afternoon tea was devoted to most enjoyable games on the very fine court which is situated on the school grounds.

ONEWHERO COURTS.

The Onewhero Tennis Courts were opened in glorious weather on Saturday last. A large gathering of members and visitors enjoyed an ideal afternoon's tennis. The President, Mr R. J. Glasgow, made a telling speech and appealed for the keen interest of members. He urged that the achievements of the Club in past seasons should be excelled in the coming year.

The courts were in splendid condition. The ladies dispensed a tempting afternoon tea, and enjoyed the social side of the function as well as the active part on the courts.

MANGATAWHIRI CLUB.

A large gathering of tennis enthusiasts from surrounding districts attended the Mangatawhiri tennis courts on Saturday, when the official opening was performed by Mr Ken Murray. Mrs Murray hit the first ball over the net, and games were organised and an enjoyable time was spent by all. A delicious afternoon tea was dispensed by the ladies.

MERCER CLUB.

The Mercer Tennis Club is opening its two courts on Saturday next and a hearty invitation is extended to all surrounding clubs. The third court is waiting a little preparation before being opened and the Club anticipates a large membership. There was a membership last year of 47.

WOMEN'S INSTITUTE

The monthly meeting of the

FOOTWEAR SPECIALISTS
TUAKAU

Woods' Great Peppermint Cure
For coughs and colds, never fails.

Printed and published for the Proprietors, the Northern Waikato Newspapers, Ltd., by Percival Augustus Hillary, of Tuakau, journalist, at the Company's registered printing office, George Street Tuakau, New Zealand.

THURSDAY, OCTOBER 10 1929

Above: Tuakau Station before 1935. There were six trains from Tuakau to Auckland on week-days. The earliest departed at 7.01 a.m. and the journey took an hour and forty minutes
Harbett Photography

Facing page: *Tuakau District News*, Thursday, 10 October 1929, edited and printed by Percival Augustus Hillary

I had a considerable respect for my father. I admired his moral courage – he would battle fiercely against society or the powers-that-be on a matter of principle and he also had the ability when in the mood to make his children laugh – and there was nothing I enjoyed more in life than laughing. My mother had a more gentle disposition, although strongly principled too, and we relied on her for the warmth and affection that all families need.
EDMUND HILLARY

21

02 TOUCH OF SOIL AND WIND AND ROCK

Tuakau Museum still has a few copies of the *Tuakau District News* – a two-page broadsheet, price one penny, filled with accounts of community affairs. There is none of the international news or political commentary that Percy Hillary had provided in Dargaville. Local residents could find these in the large Auckland dailies, and on Thursday 10 October 1929 Tuakau had other concerns: spring was in the air. The paper is bursting with advertisements for pigs and chickens, milk cans and milking machines, cream separators and chain harrows, cattle drench and fertiliser, Chevrolet cars, 'splendid English cycles' and 'A Wonderful Selection of the World's Best Racquets'. At the Tuakau Pictures in the Memorial Hall the film is *Red Lips* – a 'Universal' starring Charles Rodgers and Marian Nixon. 'Local News' includes the Tuakau Presbyterian Ladies' Guild's Bring and Buy, and the Aka Aka group's securing the district's highest herd average of butterfat content per cow during August – 49.6 pounds. 'Local Information' has the town's statistics: population 632; saw mills, flax mills, bone mill, apiaries, fruit and whitebait canning factories; fourteen and three-quarter miles of streets, with eight and a quarter miles in formed footpaths; bowling green, tennis courts and a town hall. Tuakau had been wired for electricity since 1925. It was a lively place.

The Hillary children were growing up – Ed was nine now – and the household, the bees and the garden left Gertrude with less time for poetry. No poem appears in this copy of the paper, but Percy's interests and his contributions to community affairs are well recorded. The front page has 'Tennis Notes' from the three local clubs – Percy and Gertrude were keen players and Percy was president of the Tuakau Tennis Club. On the inside pages we hear about the 'brilliant success' of the Franklin Rugby Union's Annual Ball, held in the Tuakau Town Hall. Before presenting the trophies the president 'paid tribute to the work of the Secretary of the Union (Mr P. A. Hillary) and moved that a vote of thanks be accorded to him'. Descriptions of the beautiful ensembles worn by the ladies fill a whole column. At the Onewhero Ratepayers meeting the president of the Tuakau Chamber of Commerce, Mr P. A. Hillary, discussed the siting of the new Tuakau Bridge across the Waikato River – the old wooden bridge had collapsed in August 1929. When the new concrete 'bowstring' bridge opened in June 1933 the Hillarys were all there.

22

They were an active family. Percy knew that a healthy diet and regular exercise were vital for physical fitness, which he valued highly. Sport and outdoor work provided the exercise, and they always had enough to eat. But when they were sick Percy believed in fasting as a remedy for illness. This was to prove rather trying for his children. Books by nutrition and fitness gurus such as Bernarr Macfadden (who trained Charles Atlas) had been available in New Zealand from the 1890s, and Stanley Lief's magazine *Health for All* arrived from Britain each month. These publications promoted a very modern-sounding approach to nutrition and exercise: eat moderately and only when hungry; choose raw vegetables, fruit and whole grains; drink plenty of water; and exercise regularly in the fresh air. But their theories about fasting, without a scientific understanding of the way the body fights illness, were less well grounded.

The leading New Zealand proponent of this approach to health care was Dr Ulric Williams, an Edinburgh-trained physician based in Wanganui. Gertrude had a well-used

Three recipes from Gertrude Hillary's cookbook

HONEY BISCUITS
4 ozs honey
8 ozs butter
¾ lb wholemeal flour
Grated rind 2 oranges
1 egg
Beat butter and honey to a cream; add orange rind and flour. Mix with egg (do not use this if the mixture already seems thin); roll out quickly and cut into squares. Put on floured trays and bake slowly 20 to 30 minutes.

[Use New Zealand clover or manuka honey; New Zealand butter in the 1930s was always salted, so add a pinch of salt if you wish; 1 oz = 28 g; oven temperature should be 325°F, 160°C.]

EVERYDAY SALAD
Finely grate raw vegetables in any combination with either lettuce, spinach, dandelion leaves, silver beet leaves, turnip tops, etc., for the green element. For example: an excellent and inexpensive salad may be made of grated carrot, turnip, beetroot, apple, a few raisins and heart of white cabbage.

often in advanced cases, to Rheumatism, Goitre, Eczema, He Disease, Kidney Disorder, High and Low Blood Pressure, and m of the other symptoms we have wrongly looked upon as diseases.

Orthodoxy derides; but futile expedients, retailed often at fantastic figure, to deal with the effects while the cause is allowed continue, are, as in the economic world, being more and more clea "seen through."

Let the realisation sink in, that what we have been taught to dre as an attack by something likely to destroy, rightly apprehended frequently only a beneficent process whose purpose is to prote True, if through gross infraction of the Law the balance is heav against the sufferer, the healing crisis may become a disease crisis, a the possibility of recovery remote.

Orthodoxy, mistaking Nature's curative effort for an attack "germs," and not sufficiently familiar with natural therapeutic resourc uses every endeavour to frustrate. Instead of promoting eliminati and so facilitating the cleansing of the system, crisis after crisis attacked and suppressed by operations, sera, and drugs; under delusion that each of these cleansing efforts is a fresh disease. T operations, sera, and drugs, when not immediately fatal, by preventi Nature's cure, become themselves a cause of chronic disorder; and, infrequently, among the most destructive agents in the disease proce Thousands of sufferers are still wending their weary and expensive w from one medical man to another, from one futile expedient to the ne and NONE OF THEM IS EVER CURED. It is difficult visualise the extent of the folly into which by our blindness we a being betrayed.

VERY IMPORTANT. Remember that the two gr reasons for the occurrence and persistence of Chronic Disease are:—

1. Continuation of the Cause, with Shortage of Essentials, a Accumulation of Waste.

2. Suppression of Nature's Healing Efforts.

The body is a self-cleaning "machine"; and Nature's periodi attempts, which may utilise a variety of outlets to clear the system, m be respected and encouraged.

PRACTICALLY ALL ACUTE ILLNESS IS NATURE METHOD OF CURE.

Running to a medical man, after years of self-indulgence a wrong thinking, to have the healing crises suppressed, is little bet than suicidal folly.

26

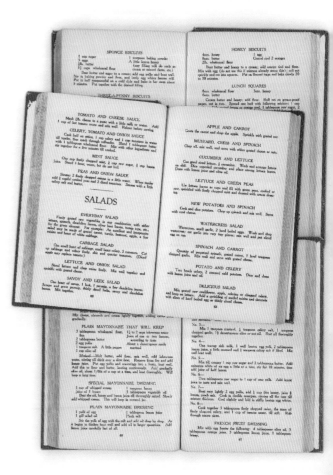

Disease, whether of body, mind, or soul, is mostly a degenerative process, due to failure to comply with the Law; and may be arrested and converted into a regenerative process through repentance and conversion to the Law. If symptomatic warnings of the presence of disease have been ignored and measures for dealing with the cause neglected, sooner or later, even though the cause continue, Nature will wage a reaction. There are surprising recuperative and regenerative resources in the body; and after a period of mistaken methods of living the eliminative process may be stimulated by Chiropractic, Osteopathy, and Manipulative Treatment generally; by Water Treatments, Eliminating Diets and Fasting; even by the adoption of the Standard Diet alone.

As in many other human concerns, critical periods recur in major and minor cycles of six and seven—days, weeks, months, years, decades, centuries, etc. Six is the figure of flux; and seven, fruition. Very commonly, though by no means invariably, in the 6th WEEK from the commencement of an improved regime, or course of stimulative treatment, a cleansing effort takes place; but so ingrained is the fear of disease as something attacking from without, that despite the most careful warnings, the significance of these acute disturbances is still frequently overlooked, and the customary suppressive treatment resorted to. When acute illness occurs, it is usually a sign that Nature is preparing to throw out in bulk poisons which hitherto she had been eliminating piecemeal.

THIS IS THE HEALING CRISIS.

The Healing Crisis is usually ushered in by an unexpected onset of acute illness—loss of appetite, dullness, shivering, furred tongue, assorted aches and pains, and general malaise. Particular symptoms such as raised temperature, catarrhal elimination, sore throat, exaggeration or recurrence of familiar symptoms, diarrhoea, biliousness, skin rash, or boils, may appear, corresponding to the channel or channels chosen by the "Directive Intelligence" for the elimination. The duration of the crisis is generally one to four days; but may extend to ten or twelve, or exceptionally even considerably longer. Where the system has been badly poisoned for many years, and specially where orthodox suppressive treatment in the form of operation or drugs has been carried out, a considerable period of time may elapse, punctuated by several healing efforts, before regeneration can become well advanced. It may easily be several years before the process is complete. Nature's methods are slow, which is one reason for the popularity still enjoyed by those who proffer a quick alternative.

Whenever a Healing Crisis occurs, A FAST MUST BE UNDERTAKEN IMMEDIATELY. NO FOOD WHATEVER should be given, not even milk. If it is, elimination will be

27

PLAIN MAYONNAISE DRESSING
1 yolk of egg
1 gill salad oil
½ tblsp lemon juice
Pinch salt
Stir the yolk of egg with the salt and add oil drop by drop. As it begins to thicken beat well and add oil in larger quantities. Add lemon juice carefully last of all. [One gill = ¼ pint = 150 ml. This recipe would have been unusual at the time since most New Zealanders made salad dressings from sweetened condensed milk, vinegar and powdered mustard.]

Ed's sister June Carlile still uses her mother's copy of the book these recipes come from: *Hints on Healthy Living* by **Dr Ulric Williams, Wanganui, New Zealand, c. 1934.** June remembers her friends' smiles of astonishment at the lunch she brought to university each day – a jar of raw vegetable salad. The Hillarys were healthy eaters.

copy of Dr Williams's book *Hints on Healthy Living*, in which he asserts that 'wrong habits of living' are the main cause of sickness. He was by all accounts a compassionate man but there is something of the 'puritanical Savonarola' about his combination of religious fervour with strict advice on diet and exercise.[1] In the front section of the book he warns sternly against 'Wrong Habits', which he defines as Wrong Thinking, Wrong Feeding – including Toxic Accumulations and Vitamin and Mineral Starvations – and failure to obey Christ's law of perfect love to God and our neighbour. With generous use of capital letters Dr Williams sets out his prescription for combating the onset of illness, which he calls 'The Healing Crisis': 'Whenever the Healing Crisis occurs, A FAST MUST BE UNDERTAKEN IMMEDIATELY. NO FOOD WHATEVER should be given, not even milk. If it is, elimination will be interfered with and Nature's purpose delayed and even prevented.'[2] He includes in his book a large selection of recipes which are reassuringly traditional, if mainly meat free, and many pages are devoted to the baking of healthy cakes and biscuits. This was an important skill, for tempting and attractive baking – usually provided by ladies bringing 'a plate' – was considered essential at most New Zealand social events. Since eating between meals was forbidden, however, the correct time to consume these treats remains a mystery.

Fasting tends to make young people irritable, and compulsory fasting did not help the relationship between Percy and Ed, who would desperately conceal any symptoms of a cold or the flu to avoid being condemned to a fast. But he wasn't often ill and he grew quickly. Modern nutritional thinking is that people can eat odd diets – and do so, all over the world – but if they exercise sensibly, their bodies will cope.[3] Certainly the Hillary children were lean, fit and healthy, with plenty of stamina for work and play, but Percy's strictness and short temper ensured that youthful high spirits were often suppressed. 'Like my father, I was very stubborn. He tried to break my stubbornness and this led to huge conflict between us as I grew up'.[4]

Bad behaviour always led to a beating – a discipline used in many families of the time, but seldom with the desired deterrent effect.

'I experienced a great deal of physical punishment both at home and at school but never became resigned to it,' Ed recalls. 'It was aggravated by the appalling fact that tears came easily to my eyes…from the embarrassment and indignity of the whole miserable proceedings. I have been involved in outbursts of violence in my own life but I have always regretted it afterwards. I have yet to see the occasion when physical punishment achieved a really worthwhile result even under the best of motivation.'[5]

Life was not always grim; there was plenty of laughter at home too, and by his teens Ed had a reputation in the family for humour and dry wit. But he was about to attend a school where caning was the accepted punishment for all misdemeanours – and he was regularly caned. The usual reason was inadequate homework. Ed saw this as unjust and resented it bitterly, but he kept the episodes to himself.

Ed's parents were unaware of his dislike of Auckland Grammar. It is a leading New Zealand school with a reputation for academic and sporting excellence and many high-achieving 'old boys'. It was founded in 1869 by Sir George Grey, and bears the stern motto: *Per Angusta ad Augusta* – 'Through trial to triumph'. Ed Hillary's four years there were a definite trial, but Gertrude was determined that Ed should go to a good school. Percy may not have agreed with the expense involved, but Gertrude was the educator and she had her way.

June had won a scholarship to Diocesan School for Girls and was boarding in Epsom with a school friend of Gertrude, who also had a daughter at Dio. But Ed was not to be a boarder – he took the morning train for Auckland each day, which meant cycling to the Tuakau Station before seven a.m. He arrived back at Tuakau after six in the evening and cycled home again – a long day for an eleven year old. For three and a half years, until the family moved to Auckland, these train journeys dominated Ed's days, and contributed both to his homework problems and his slide from star pupil to average student. He was small and shy, found it hard to make friends, and his confidence took an early battering from the sarcastic comments of a boorish gym teacher. 'I developed a feeling of inferiority about my physique which has remained with me to this day – it wasn't an inferiority about what I could achieve, but a solid conviction about how appalling I looked.'[6]

Commuting from Tuakau effectively barred him from after-school activities, but when he grew taller – 22.5 centimetres in two years – he took boxing lessons. He was not a natural fighter, but the lessons focused his strength, and he was regularly involved in scuffles with the other boys on the train. He loved running, and the train journeys gave plenty of opportunities: 'Leaping off while it was gaining speed, holding onto the handrails and running furiously alongside and then leaping tigerishly aboard at the last desperate moment – this was living!'[7] Adventure-struck boys such as Ed could get inspiration from Grammar's visiting speakers who showed lantern slides and told fascinating stories about exploits in many parts of the world. He arrived at the school too late to hear Robert Falla's talks about the Antarctic expeditions led by Sir Douglas Mawson, or Mr Cunningham of the Central China Mission talking about life in Tibet, but lecture topics during his years included the lives and customs of the peoples of China, India and the South Sea Islands. And Grammar also gave Ed Hillary his first sight of a mountain.

Every August holidays the school organised a sixth-form trip to Tongariro National Park in the centre of the North Island. In 1935, after much pleading with Percy, Ed went along and spent nine days racing about in the snow, learning to ski, snow fighting and building snowmen. 'I saw my first snow at midnight when we stepped off our train at the National Park Station. There wasn't much of it but it was a tremendous thrill, and before long snowballs, as hard as iron, were flying through the air. And as our bus carried us steadily up towards the Château, perched high on the mountain-side, its powerful lights sparked into life a fairyland of glistening snow and stunted pines and frozen streams. When I crawled into my bunk at two in the morning, I felt I was in a strange and exciting new world.'[8] That same year New Zealander Dan Bryant made a lasting impression on the famous British climber, Eric Shipton. The toughness and mountaineering skill that he observed in Bryant on the 1935 Everest Reconnaissance Expedition aroused Shipton's interest in New Zealand climbing expertise.[9] Sixteen years later Eric Shipton would be on Everest with Ed Hillary, the boy who was now getting his first taste of snow.

While Ed was still at Grammar the family acquired a bach at Orewa, a magnificent beach north of Auckland. It was a very modest holiday home, one of four original buildings in the area. Percy had some bees on a property nearby and after Christmas, once the honey harvest was complete, the Hillarys spent long summer days swimming, rowing and walking on the beach. They travelled up to Orewa in an 'Overland' car which had belonged to Uncle Bert, who had the luxury of a new car every two years. Percy took this one over, pulled it to bits and got it going again. It was at Orewa in the summer of 1934 that Ed received some great news. He opened the newspaper, scanned down a long list of names and could hardly believe it when he saw his own – E. P. Hillary. He had passed Matriculation, the main external examination for fifteen-year-olds in New Zealand. The excitement and relief were overwhelming and Ed's confidence received a much-needed boost. The Auckland Grammar *Chronicle* noted his success, but school had not given him any sense of his own value or potential.

In 1935, Ed's last year at Grammar, the family left Tuakau and moved to Auckland. June was attending Auckland University College and the Auckland Teachers' Training College, and came back home to live; Rex was at King's College. Percy had given up his job with the newspaper after a disagreement with the owners and now turned his full attention to beekeeping. He was founding editor and manager of the *N. Z. Honeybee: a Journal Devoted to the Interests of Beekeepers*, and become a force in the honey industry. Ed and Rex also worked hard – every weekend and all the school holidays were taken up with the bees. Gertrude made a major contribution to the family's finances by breeding and selling queen bees which were sought by apiarists around New Zealand and as far away as Australia and California. (Many years later Rex Hillary described the attributes of a good queen as: 'good colour, a good breeder and not too sting-ey'.[10]) Even George Lowe, who was to become Ed's closest climbing friend, knew of Gertrude Hillary's queens – from his father, a Hawke's Bay orchardist who kept bees. In the 1930s, the range of bee products produced and sold was far narrower than it is today, but the advantages of eating honey rather than refined sugar made sense to the Hillarys. And there were other benefits – ancient Greeks had first discovered the anti-inflammatory properties of bee venom, and Gertrude used bee stings to treat arthritis.

In Auckland they bought a substantial house in Remuera Road, where Gertrude made another beautiful garden. Beekeeping is a financial gamble in which the weather dictates a bumper crop or a failure, and important acquisitions in the Hillary household were planned around the arrival of the honey cheque in April. Ed has no idea how his parents afforded this house, since family finances had always been tightly stretched and the children received no pocket money or allowance of any kind. But the summer of 1934–35 had been a good season and the sale of the property at Tuakau must have helped too. Now it was Percy who did the commuting. He had over 1000 hives on farms around South Auckland and a honey house in Papakura where the honey was spun from the combs and packed into four-gallon tins

Left: The Hillary family outside their new house at 730 Remuera Road, Auckland, c. 1936. (L–R) Rex, Gertrude, Percy, June, Edmund

Below left: The *N. Z. Honeybee*, 20 November 1938. A monthly journal for beekeepers established, edited and managed by Percy Hillary

THE

N.Z. HONEYBEE

A JOURNAL DEVOTED TO THE INTERESTS OF BEEKEEPERS

EDITOR-MANAGER . . . P. A. HILLARY

ISSUED on 20th of Each Month:
Subscription: 3/6, post free.

The Only Beekeeping Journal Published in New Zealand.

VOL. 2, No. 4   NOVEMBER 20, 1938.   PRICE 4d.

News of General Interest

Manawatu Branch

At the monthly meeting of the Manawatu branch, N.B.A., over which Mr. F. J. Lewin presided, a provisional date was set for the middle of March, 1939, for a district field day to be held at Massey College. A committee consisting of Messrs. Lewin, H. L. Turnbull, H. F. Dodson and J. Dale was appointed to complete arrangements.

A discussion took place on the new marketing arrangements for honey, and they were recognised as being steps in the right direction. It was stated that it was now possible to consign honey in a liquid condition to grade stores. It was agreed to make inquiries concerning certain points in the initial policy of the Internal Marketing Department.

Mr. B. G. Goodwin, the newly-appointed district supervisor of the Horticultural Division, was introduced to those present.

Mataura Report

I am very pleased to see that the New Zealand Honeybee is gaining ground, and wish it every future success. The weather has been very dry except for an occasional shower. Good rains came at the end of October and in November, and the prospects for the coming season's honey flow are now quite satisfactory. It is going to be an early season. There were odd heads of clover out at the beginning of October.—G.C.

From Our Correspondents:

Our mail has contained many interesting letters from foreign countries, including U.S.A., Canada, South Africa, Australia, Egypt, Finland and England.

High Production Records.

Sir,—Perhaps I could get some idea of weights of honey taken from individual colonies through the "N.Z. Honeybee." Last season I took 310 lb from one colony that had been brought through the previous winter as a 3 frame nucleus. I took ½ ton from 12 colonies. There is no doubt, Mr. Editor, that this paper is filling a want among beekeepers and may it have every success.—"Amateur."

[We would be pleased to publish any replies to the above letter.—Ed.]

Books For Beginners.

"Sir,—Could you please tell me of books suitable for a beekeeper with six hives.—J.S., Auckland."

Answer: Beginners are advised to purchase the book published by the Department of Agriculture for beginners, and then "Practical Beekeeping" by the late Isaac Hopkins. The next step is to secure "The ABC and XYZ of Bee Culture," by Root, and "First Lessons in Beekeeping" by Dadant. As experience with the bees is obtained, the beekeeper should secure "Honey Production," by R. O. B. Manley, and "The Honey Bee," by Langstroth (revised by Dadant). Other excellent books are "A Thousand Answers to Beekeeping Questions," and "Fifty Years Among the Bees," both by Dr. Miller, "Out-Apiaries," by Dadant, "Beekeeping" by Phillips. There are many others.—Ed.

---

for export. Clover honey was the main crop, although with luck you could get early pohutukawa honey into the shops before Christmas.[11]

For Ed, the move to Auckland coincided with youthful questioning about the meaning of his life. He read a great deal and thought hard about the way political ideas intersected with his religious beliefs.

Ed Hillary's father was passionate about social justice and Ed's own political awareness sharpened during the economic depression of the 1930s. Like many other New Zealanders, Percy was appalled that hunger could exist in a farming country which produced more than enough to feed its small population. He vehemently condemned the government for refusing to intervene in the economy and help people who had no jobs and no money. Ed agreed with both his father's analysis and his determination to see justice done. 'I admired his moral courage – he would battle fiercely against society or the powers-that-be on a matter of principle'.[12] These determined traits appear in Gertrude's family too.

Gertrude's sisters Mabel, Helen and Ada lived in Herbert Road, Epsom. Mabel, the eldest, was the housekeeper, dressmaker and a wonderful cook; Ada and Helen were teachers. They often had nephews and nieces staying with them, and the sprawling wooden house with its large garden and tennis court was a focus for Clark family gatherings. On Sunday evenings, June, Ed and Rex would walk several kilometres to join in singing around the piano, laughing, arguing and listening to the radio. Ed never missed hearing the Reverend Colin Scrimgeour's programme, 'The Friendly Road'. By 1934 the government had banned political broadcasts but Uncle Scrim, the Methodist Church's Auckland city missioner and a determined activist, preached 'the message of the carpenter's son', exhorting people to help each other, and giving a mixture of practical encouragement and religious uplift.

Scrim brought hope to the desperate and gave a voice to the unemployed, the hungry and the homeless, but he didn't restrict himself to positive thinking and religious platitudes. Scrim used radio to focus attention on the plight of the urban poor. He worked unceasingly, introducing many schemes to alleviate their distress: reopen-

'The Friendly Road'

There's a new
day in view,
There's gold in
the blue,
There's hope in
the hearts of men.
All the world's
on the way
To a happier day
For the road is
open again.

From the theme song of the programme 'The Friendly Road' on radio 1ZR, Auckland.

On Sunday evenings during the early 1930s, the Rev. Colin Scrimgeour's 'Man in the Street' session on 'The Friendly Road' was listened to by thousands. 'He used the Sermon on the Mount to suggest that where there was meat and bread there should be no hunger, where there were wool fibre and idle mills none should be threadbare, that where the trees unaffected by the Depression still grew and sawmills were idle and carpenters were without jobs there should be no

homeless...He gave hope to the distressed...He was a voice for the unemployed, the hungry, the home-less, the poorly-clad." This message of social justice and responsibility for others appealed to Ed Hillary. He listened to Scrim's broadcast every week.

ing shops where donated meat was prepared by unemployed butchers for distribution to the hungry; setting unemployed cobblers repairing boots to save others from the stigma of cheap sand shoes – and he lobbied the government to take action. By 1932 the situation was far beyond the reach of charity. There were over 60,000 unemployed in April that year when despairing and hungry people rioted in Auckland, tearing pickets from the fence outside the City Mission and breaking shop windows in Queen Street. In his broadcast the following evening Scrim said that if this made authority act to help desperate people, then the church had given them the most outstanding service of its history.[13] The government came to fear his influence and his ability to ignite emotions and on the eve of the 1935 General Election his broadcast was jammed.

Political analysis, religious conviction and practical action seemed to come naturally to the Hillary family. Ed was among the many thousands who admired Scrim enormously, as did his Aunt Ada. A feisty spinster schoolteacher, who also gave years of voluntary work to organisations like the Flying Angel Mission to Seamen, she had been badly injured as a girl when her ankle was crushed between two kauri logs at Whakahara. Ada Clark fought medical opinion and kept her leg, but she was often in pain. Ada encouraged Ed's dreams of adventure and was always his champion. In 1957 when he was criticised for his drive to the South Pole she commented: 'Well if you'd finished your job and had always wanted to, wouldn't you have gone to the Pole? Of course we all prayed like anything!'[14] In 1965 Ada Clark was awarded an MBE for her work with the missions.

The election in November 1935 saw New Zealand bring in its first Labour Government. Thereafter life began to change for working people. It was a long road back to full employment and the creation of a welfare state which cared for its citizens, but the turbulent years

of the 1930s and the example of men like Scrim shaped Ed Hillary's political views.

The Hillarys had been members of St John's Anglican Church in Tuakau and the children had gone regularly to Sunday school and Bible class, but they gradually drifted away from the mainstream church. Ed's first religious disappointment came as a teenager when he was confirmed by the visiting Bishop of Auckland and the spiritual transformation he had expected failed to eventuate. Alternative forms of religious expression, encouraging healthy living and physical fitness within a framework of Christian commitment, better suited the family's approach to life.

By 1938, after two notably unsuccessful years studying mathematics and science at the University of Auckland, Ed decided to give up on formal education. He was unsure of the future direction of his life and the best option seemed to be full-time work with Percy. Rex had finished school, and both young men loved the activity and freedom of beekeeping. Ed recalled: 'We were constantly on the move from site to site – especially when all 1600 hives decided to swarm at once...all through the exciting months of the honey flow the dream of a bumper crop would drive us on through long hard hours of labour; manhandling thousands of ninety pound boxes of honey comb for extracting...and grimacing at our daily ration of a dozen, or a hundred, beestings. We were incurable optimists.'[15]

In 1938 Percy took the family to hear Dr Herbert Sutcliffe, proponent of a philosophy of physical and moral fitness called 'Radiant Living'. The idea was that positive thought and affirmation would encourage health, happiness and success. The *Radiant Living* journal gave advice on health and diet, and included inspirational writing of a liberal Christian cast.[16] Ed was impressed by Herbert Sutcliffe's lively and confident style of presentation, and the family all became foundation members of the Auckland School of Radiant Living. By March 1939 Gertrude Hillary was secretary and the journal published her description of the school's new meeting hall in Auckland's Wellesley Street. Although he eventually lost interest, Ed gained a great deal from his five-year association.

Left: Edmund and Rex Hillary aged eighteen and seventeen, wearing their first tailored suits, 1938

Right: Journals published by the Sutcliffe School of Radiant Living, a liberal Christian movement which emphasised positive thought and attitudes, and healthy living. The Hillary family were founding members of the Auckland school, established in September 1938

'I learned to speak confidently from the platform; to think more freely on important topics; to mix more readily with a wide variety of people.'[17] In 1940 he travelled to Gisborne as Herbert Sutcliffe's campaign assistant, and in 1941 sat his examinations to become a teacher of Radiant Living. Ed's test lecture topic was 'Inferiority – cause and cure'. He closed with the words 'I Can!' and gained a pass mark of 100 per cent.

But Radiant Living was only one of the determining factors in Ed's life story. He was extremely fit, and outdoor life was his real passion. He ran in to university every day rather than take the bus, and the main benefit of his time there was membership of the Tramping Club. 'I was adopted by a group of young trampers who spent their winter Sundays walking through the dense rain forest of the Waitakere Ranges. They were a cheerful, pleasant lot and I was thankful for their friendship and happy to carry any load, push anybody up hills, rush off on any reconnaissance, make any trail...I knew I had more physical energy than most and I revelled in driving myself to the utmost. I still found it difficult to believe that anyone in their right mind could get pleasure from my company.'[18] Climbing many of New Zealand's mountains in the 1940s brought him new friends – and real adventures at last.

Above: Rex, June and Ed Hillary on Waiheke Island in 1946 before June sailed for England

I was intoxicated with the whole experience, the hurling of our bodies uncontrollably down an almost vertical slope; skiing through forest and rocks to the Chateau, the magnificent food; even the freedom and the lack of regular tasks... I showed little natural skill at skiing but plenty of strength and energy and I returned home in a glow of fiery enthusiasm for the sun and the cold and the snow – especially the snow!
EDMUND HILLARY

03
TO THE DELECTABLE MOUNTAINS

Mountaineers are often asked why they climb. Why expose yourself to uncomfortable and dangerous situations, risking everything just to stand on the top of a mountain? In *Upon that Mountain*, one of Ed Hillary's favourite reads, Eric Shipton gives a fairly comprehensive reply: 'Mountaineering provides good exercise in pleasant surroundings, a sense of satisfaction in overcoming difficulties, the joy, akin to dancing, of controlled rhythmic movement, a stimulating contact with danger, a wealth of beautiful scenery and a release from the tiresome restrictions of modern life.' As well as all that, many climbers speak of a spiritual lift or sense of heightened awareness – Shipton calls this 'rare moments of intellectual ecstasy which occur perhaps on a mountain summit, perhaps on a glacier at dawn or in a lonely moonlit bivouac.'[1] Ed Hillary talked about the 'constant battle against rain and weather and sheer misery' in climbing, but he told the photographer Yousuf Karsh, 'It is an act of worship just to sit and look at a high mountain.'[2]

Needham's Apiary
September 1946.

The Waikato River in flood
September 1946.

Southern Alps - Jan. 1946

Self on summit of Mt. Hamilton.
(9,915'). in Malte Brun range.

Malte Brun
10,421' from
Tasman Glacier
at Malte De la
Beche corner.

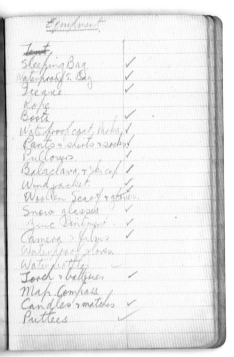

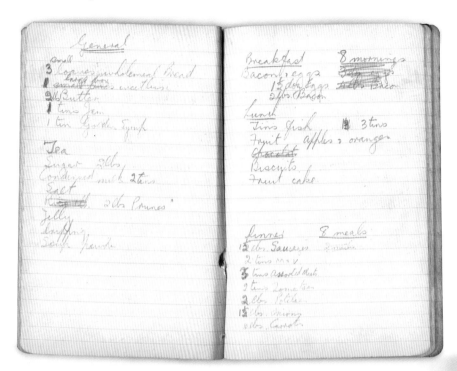

In the 1940s Ed did a lot more than sit and look.
He was young, strong and energetic, and for ten
years he tramped and climbed as often as he
could. Carefully labelled photographs in his
album show sparkling snow slopes, broad
glaciers, remote huts, dense bush, a few summits
and many happy young people. Ed had at last
found companions who shared his enthusiasms:
'people like Harry Ayres and George Lowe
became the first real friends I'd ever had'.[3] His
accounts of these early days of climbing, both
on his own and with others, are sprinkled with
superlatives: 'the happiest day I had ever spent';
'I'd climbed a decent mountain at last'; 'I kept
my mind occupied by giving forth a great
speech to the elements. You should have heard
the speech – it was a beauty'; 'We went across
the hills like a tornado – it was terrific fun!'; 'It
had been one of the wettest but most enjoyable
days we had spent'; 'My tiredness meant
nothing – for me it had been a day of triumph.'
Climbing in New Zealand usually meant
carrying heavy loads long distances before
even getting near the snow, but at the end of a
gruelling day there was always the tent to look

forward to: 'Before long our primus stove was
humming fiercely and there was plenty of time
to cook ourselves an excellent meal. Full and
contented we pulled on every piece of clothing
and wriggled into our sleeping bags.'[4] And when
morning brought miserable weather high on a
mountain, fellow climber Mick Sullivan described
the perfect breakfast: 'A breath of fresh air and
a good look around.'[5]

At the start of World War II, Ed was in
the mountains whenever he could be spared
from the bees. Like many climbers, he had
always wanted to fly, so in 1939 he applied to
join the air force. There was, however, a long
delay before training could start and he began
to have doubts about the morality of being in
the armed forces. His father's opposition to war
influenced him too. 'I was greatly troubled over
the approach a Christian should have to killing
– and I regarded myself as an enthusiastic
Christian at the time. I wasn't too impressed with
the arguments put up by some clergymen and
Christians to justify the support of war and I had
no doubt that equally devout people in Germany
were convinced that God was on their side.'[6]

And pacifism was an essential tenet of Radiant
Living. After 'much agonising reflection' Ed
decided to withdraw his air-force application
and both he and Rex registered as conscientious
objectors. Percy successfully applied to have Ed
exempted from conscription since beekeeping
was a reserved occupation, like farming, but
when Rex's call came a second Hillary exemption
was not approved. Rex spent four long years in
a detention camp at Strathmore, near Reporoa –
one of the 800 conscientious objectors the New
Zealand Government confined in camps. It was
a miserable time. The Hillarys' position was
noticed and frowned upon – they were already a
family apart from the mainstream – and by 1942
Ed had had enough. His religious convictions
were diminishing and he persuaded Percy to
apply to have him released for service. Early in
1944 he was called up by the Royal New Zealand
Air Force.

The air-force training camps in Marl-
borough and New Plymouth were both within
striking distance of some good climbing, and
Ed made the most of the new luxury of free
weekends. He made friends, did well in his

Below: Royal New Zealand
Air Force Catalina flying boat
crew, Fiji, 1945; Ed Hillary
centre of back row

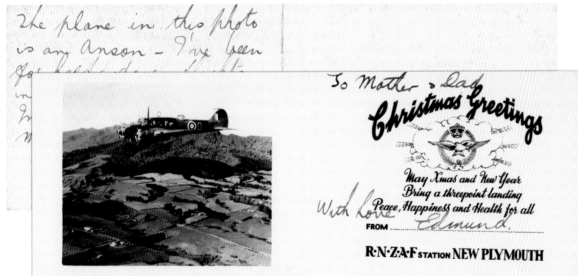

The plane in this photo
is an Anson – I've been
for holidays ... light
in ...
...

So Mother & Dad

Christmas Greetings

May Xmas and New Year
Bring a threepoint landing
Peace, Happiness and Health for all

With Love

FROM Edmund

R·N·Z·A·F station **NEW PLYMOUTH**

Above: Christmas card from
Ed Hillary to his parents,
December 1944

Right: Ed Hillary with
crocodile, Solomon
Islands, 1945

exams, qualified as a navigator and that summer
spent his first Christmas away from the family.
Percy had employed others to help with the bees
and Ed couldn't resist trying some climbing
near Mount Cook, New Zealand's highest peak.
He planned carefully, compiling precise lists of
food and equipment, but his journal of a solo
climb in the delectable mountains is far from
prosaic – there is something of a youthful
Pilgrim's Progress about it. He was mulling over
the idea that the decisions faced in climbing
could be a metaphor for the ones he faced in
life: finding the right route on a mountain
sometimes means choosing a narrow, difficult
way, not a broad and easy path; and the wisdom
of others who have gone before can help us
make these hard choices. Then, having scaled
the heights and learned the way, we can retrace
our steps with ease, face new challenges with
increased composure and pass on our knowledge to others. These are themes to which Ed
Hillary has often returned, advising young
people to look for guidance from those with
more experience; to 'Aim High'; to remember
that there is no virtue in easy victory – and to
hope that luck will go your way.

His posting to Fiji and the Solomon
Islands early in 1945, navigating a Catalina
flying boat, brought more adventures – sailing,
climbing, crocodile shooting and larking about
with friends. But for the first time he was away
from New Zealand and confronted by the reality
of poverty and hardship in remote communities.
Although impressed by dedicated people
working in mission hospitals, he was no longer
sure that Christianity offered the only path to
spiritual truth. An evening spent discussing
religious ideas and Indian politics with a
Muslim teacher left him feeling 'incredibly
narrow minded and insular'.[7]

He was a thoughtful young man, but
finding adventure was still the main thrust of
Ed's life. Streaking across limpid blue water in
a yacht he had built with his friend Ron Ward
was almost as much fun as climbing, and they
graduated to an old motor boat. Then one sunny
Sunday morning disaster struck. The petrol tank
exploded and both men were burnt – Ed severely
so. They managed a long swim to shore, walked
to the nearest habitation and were ferried to the

31

Above and facing page, far right: The *New Zealand Alpine Journal*, June 1948, vol. XII, no.35
Jennifer French

Ed Hillary and Harry Ayres on the summit of Mount Cook, (3754m; 12,316ft), 30 January 1947
Steve Brockett

Harry Ayres 1912–87
A master of snow and ice

Harry Ayres had a long association with the Mount Cook area as a climber and guide, and eventually head ranger for the Mount Cook National Park. Ayres was originally included in the 1953 British Everest expedition with Ed Hillary and George Lowe, but his selection was reversed when John Hunt replaced Eric Shipton as leader. In 1956–58 Ed Hillary invited him to be part of the New Zealand team on the Commonwealth Trans-Antarctic expedition where he worked with a dog team, making sledging trips surveying the mountains of Victoria Land. Jim Wilson described an Antarctic incident which illustrates Ayres's mastery of ice: 'An entire dog team fell down a crevasse in an isolated area far from base and was held only by the sledge which jammed across the lip. Nine times Harry jammed his way down that crevasse, back against one wall, feet braced against the other, several hundred feet of cold air beneath the seat of his pants; and nine times he inched his way back up with a struggling, half-crazed dog snapping in his arms.'* Ayres rescued them all.

Ed wrote in his foreword to the book *Harry Ayres: Mountain Guide*: 'Of moderate size but incredibly wiry and strong he had the toughness and endurance to tackle any problem. His great ice axe cut innumerable safe steps in solid green ice and his arms seemed tireless... His remarkable flair for route-finding in badly crevassed areas carried him through where many others failed. He left a trail of half-smoked cigarette butts up the mountainside behind him but it never seemed to affect his strength and agility... I regard myself as very fortunate to have shared adventures with him when he was in his formidable prime.'† Ed Hillary and Harry Ayres made a Grand Traverse of Mount Cook with Mike Gill, Jim Wilson and Graeme Dingle in 1969 to celebrate Ed's fiftieth birthday. Harry Ayres died in 1987.

American hospital at Guadalcanal. Both recovered well and had excellent medical care, but doctors were surprised at the speed with which Ed got back on his feet. His back had been severely burned, but he soon began nagging his doctor to let him leave. 'After three weeks I emerged from the hospital still swathed in bandages, a bit shaky and a lot thinner...All I wanted now was to return home...I found it infuriating to be kept waiting several weeks for observation and treatment'.[8] In December 1945 he was flown back to Auckland and discharged from the air force with sick leave. The inactivity of hospital life had simply been too boring.

Back in New Zealand Percy didn't need him immediately; besides, he was supposed to be taking it easy and convalescing. So Ed took off for the mountains again. This was to become the pattern of the next few years: every spare moment was spent climbing, tramping and skiing with friends, as well as with Rex and sometimes June, who was now a schoolteacher. Ed could plan for expeditions, carry heavy loads and sometimes lead a group, but he still wanted to learn the more advanced techniques of

mountaineering. 'And then [in 1946] I met Guide Harry Ayres. Harry was New Zealand's outstanding climber, with a tremendous reputation for brilliant ice-craft. He took me under his wing, and for three marvellous seasons we climbed the big peaks together.'[9]

Ed admired Harry's philosophy of safe but forceful mountaineering, his speed, skill and decisiveness on ice. High on mountains Harry was relaxed, at ease with himself and always good company.[10] They made a good team. 'I learned a lot from Harry. I learned how to cut a step and when to cut it; and I learned a little of that subtle science of snow- and ice-craft that only experience can really teach.'[11] They climbed Mount Cook together in January 1947, and the following year decided to attempt a very difficult, unclimbed route on the mountain, described as 'one of the great challenges in the Southern Alps'.[12]

On 6 February 1948, with Ruth Adams and Mick Sullivan, they made a successful and historic ascent of the South Ridge of Mount Cook, but three days later, on an adjacent peak called La Perouse, Ruth Adams slipped, a rope

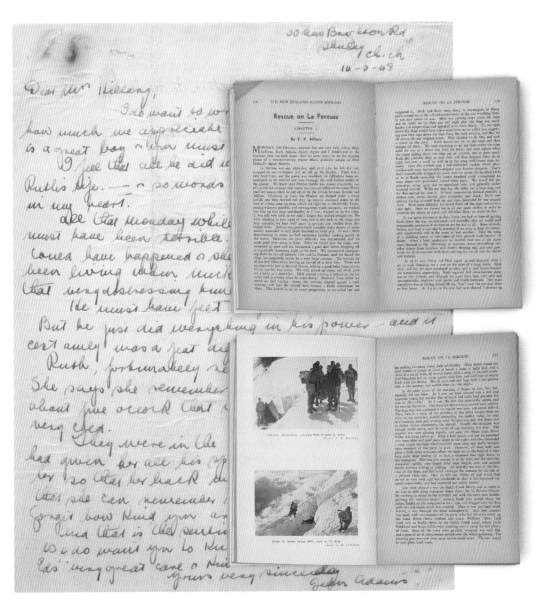

broke, and she fell some distance and was injured. It was early in the morning. Ed stayed with Ruth while the others went for help; he dug out a snow cave, made her as comfortable as he could and kept her spirits up. Mick Sullivan arrived back after dark with food, a cooker and a sleeping bag for Ruth from their last hut, and the next day after a chilly night some supplies were airdropped to them. A day later, Harry Ayres and the rescue party reached them, with chief guide Mick Bowie in charge. Their arrival was a huge relief. Ed recalled: 'Mick Bowie was a powerful man of tremendous personality and experience and with his arrival everything seemed to come under control…his quiet presence welded us into an effective team.'[13] Bowie decided that the safest way to carry Ruth out was over La Perouse ridge and 3000 metres down the other side across glacial moraine through the dense West Coast bush. The nerve-wracking, arm-stretching journey took five days and it remains a famous New Zealand mountaineering rescue. It is a dramatic story of selfless courage, determination and grit and, best of all, it has a happy ending: Ruth emerged safely. Near the end of their ordeal the hungry rescuers were delighted when a plane dropped them a large box. In his account of the rescue, Norman Hardie described the contents: 'a giant fruitcake. What a joyful sight! Ruth's father, Ernest Adams, runs New Zealand's main cake bakery.'[14]

Norman Hardie, Earle Riddiford and Bill Beaven were all on the La Perouse rescue and were among New Zealand's strongest climbers. Ed had not climbed with them before: he wasn't free until after the summer honey harvest and by then most amateur climbers were back at work or studying. For these young men, the Himalayas were the great dream. The Southern Alps gave them the perfect training ground and within a few years all of them would climb Himalayan peaks over 7000 metres (23,000 ft). Earle Riddiford would be the driving force behind the 1951 New Zealand expedition to the Garhwal Himalaya in northern India; Bill Beaven and Norman Hardie were both on the New Zealand Alpine Club Barun Valley expedition in 1954; and Norman Hardie was on the first ascent of Kangchenjunga in 1955. Ed saw a lot more of them in the years to come.

Above: Letter from Jean Adams, Ruth Adams's mother, to Ed Hillary's parents, thanking them for his part in her daughter's rescue, 14 March 1948

Above: La Perouse rescue party, January 1948.
(L–R) Front row: 'Snow' Mace, Ed Hillary, Ruth Adams in stretcher with sunglasses, Mick Bowie, T. Newth, Dr Gerald Wall

Second row: Bill Beaven, J. Sullivan, Frank Gillett, Doug Dick, Harry Ashworth
Third row: Norman Hardie, R. Johnson, Harry Ayres, J. Glasgow, (Guide Mount Cook) **J. N. Hamilton**

Right: La Perouse rescue: lowering the stretcher down an ice face.
(L–R) Front: Norman Hardie, Ruth Adams in stretcher, Harry Ayres
Back: J. Glasgow, Ed Hillary, Bill Beaven, Mick Sullivan
J. N. Hamilton

Ed joined the New Zealand Alpine Club, and wrote several articles for the club's journal, including an account of the South Ridge climb. Through his association with the club he met Jim Rose and Roland Ellis, experienced older climbers who encouraged his ambition and treated him as an adult – something Percy found hard to do. Roland Ellis was president of the club and Jim Rose would become president in 1953. Both were mentors for Ed Hillary and made him welcome in their homes in Auckland and Dunedin. Again Ed sought out experience, wisdom and sound judgement – steadiness as well as vigour.

By all accounts the young Ed Hillary was a fairly unpolished diamond. He was strong, enthusiastic, kind and funny, but still not socially at ease – particularly with women. Nevertheless, he developed a 'considerable enthusiasm' for Jim and Phyl Rose's daughter, Louise. She was twelve years younger than him – a laughing, vivacious teenager, a talented musician and, like her parents, very keen on outdoor life. In 1950 Ed took her with some friends to Mount Ruapehu on a training climb and Louise's brave reaction to a frightening fall clinched his interest. On a steep ice slope Ed was below, calling up instructions, when Louise slipped and came hurtling down towards him on her back. 'She was coming straight at me and I had two alternatives – to receive the ten points of her crampons in my stomach or to step aside. I glanced quickly downwards; the route below was rough but she would probably survive… I stepped calmly backwards and watched her shoot by. I rushed down to join her and she lay smiling up at me, bruised but undamaged and only a little mortified… I determined that I would get to know her better.'[15]

George Lowe's friendship was the other boon of these years. Tall and lanky like Ed, he began tramping and climbing while at teachers' training college, took holiday work as an assistant guide in the Mount Cook area, and climbed Mount Cook, Mount Tasman and other high peaks in the summer of 1946–47. George and Ed first met on a bus taking climbers and tourists up to the Tasman Glacier. Lowe described his first impressions: 'I noticed a

34

Right: Ski-mountaineering in winter. Fred Edwards, Ed Hillary, Rex Hillary and Bert Barley at the Godley Hut, Mount Cook National Park, August 1948

Louise Rose on Terra Nova Pass, on a summer holiday expedition around the Godley Glacier with her father and other friends, Christmas 1951

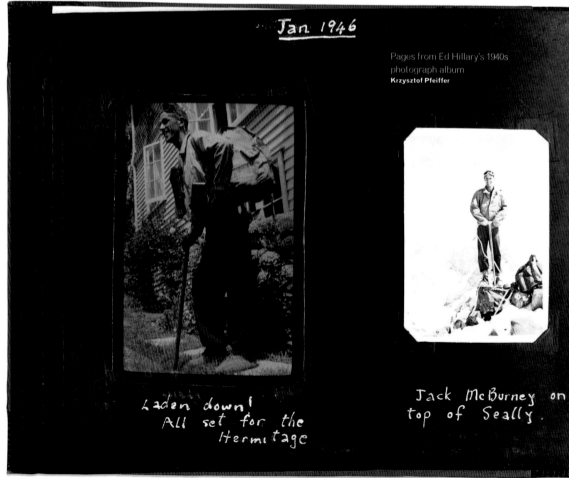

Jan. 1946

Pages from Ed Hillary's 1940s photograph album
Krzysztof Pfeiffer

Laden down!
All set for the Hermitage

Jack McBurney on top of Sealy.

George Lowe

In the preface to *High Adventure,* Ed Hillary wrote: 'I have gained much from the mountains, and not least has been the companionship and friendship of so many fine mountaineers.' He dedicated the book to four men – Harry Ayres, Eric Shipton, John Hunt and 'to my old friend George Lowe, for so many years of cheerful comradeship.'* Twenty years later Ed wrote: 'Whenever I think of my early days in the Himalayas, George Lowe automatically comes to mind. George was a primary school teacher in New Zealand and a born entertainer. I have never laughed longer and louder than I did in his company. He was tall and strong and a formidable climber with an effective ice-axe and bouncing energy.'†

As a boy of nine living in Hastings, George Lowe broke his left elbow and, despite several operations, it remained in a right-angled position. Lowe became an accomplished climber despite this handicap. He met Ed Hillary in 1949 while working as an assistant guide in the Mount Cook area during the holidays from teachers' training college, but they first climbed together on Mount Elie de Beaumont in January 1951, in preparation for the New Zealand Alpine Club expedition to the Garhwal Himalaya. The two men became fast friends. In 1952 they were on the Cho Oyu expedition with Eric Shipton, and Lowe and Hillary were the two New Zealand members of the 1953 British Everest expedition. George was best man at Ed's wedding to Louise Rose, and they lectured together in Europe and America. They also wrote a book together: *East of Everest: An Account of the New Zealand Alpine Club*

Himalayan Expedition to the Barun Valley in 1954.‡ George Lowe was official photographer and film cameraman for the 1957–58 Antarctic-crossing party with Dr Vivian Fuchs, and published a book about his expedition experiences, *Because It Is There.*§ George Lowe's first marriage was to Susan Hunt, daughter of John Hunt, and they had three sons. His climbing achievements include the highest peak in the Russian Pamirs, and the highest in Ethiopia; his teaching career took him to Santiago, Chile, where he was a school principal for eight years and travelled with Eric Shipton in Patagonia.

In Britain George Lowe was an HMI (Her Majesty's Inspector of Schools) as was his second wife Mary, and in 1989 when George retired the Lowes established the Sir Edmund Hillary Himalayan Trust, UK. George had been with Ed Hillary on the 1960–61 Silver Hut expedition when the idea of a school for the Sherpas first arose. The Himalayan Trust UK raises funds for the schools in the Solu Khumbu region of Nepal and supports in particular the teacher-training programmes, which have made a vital contribution to the schools' continuing success. George and Mary Lowe live in England and visit New Zealand each year.

George Lowe was awarded the OBE by New Zealand in 1954 and was made a companion of the New Zealand Order of Merit in 1997. In January 2005 he was made an Honorary Doctor of the University of Derby in recognition of his work with young people.

Left: George Lowe drawing a map of the routes he and Ed Hillary followed around the northern side of Mount Everest on the Cho Oyu expedition in 1952

Right: Ed Hillary and George Lowe cutting an Everest cake on board the flying boat *Aotearoa II*, from Sydney to Auckland, 8 August 1953. The cake was provided by the New Zealand manager of TEAL (Tasman Empire Airways Ltd) G. N. Roberts

long-limbed, keen-faced young man sitting alone on the rear seat. Dressed in old tweed trousers with puttees around the ankles, a tartan shirt with a sweat rag circling his neck, all topped by a battered brown ski-cap, he carried an ice-axe and a small rucksack, and his green eyes roved with a curious excitement over the scenery.'[16] They were heading in different directions this time but decided to do a climb together when they could, and two years later they bumped into each other at the Haast Hut. While a storm raged outside, they played draughts using chunks of parsnip and carrot as draughts-men, and talked about the Himalayas. They were determined to do whatever they could to get there.[17] Both had something to prove in the mountains. A doctor had told George he would always be partially crippled after a broken arm was badly set, and the ridicule of the Auckland Grammar gym teacher had not faded from Ed's memory. Both those doomsayers would soon be proved wrong.

After several years teaching, June Hillary travelled to England to complete an Honours degree at University College, London. At Percy's insistence she joined the Royal Commonwealth Society, where she met Jimmy Carlile, a young Norwich doctor. They became engaged, and Percy and Gertrude sailed to Britain to attend the wedding on 14 May 1949. Gertrude was keen to see something of the world while they were there, but Percy was reluctant to drive in Europe, so Ed was summoned to be his parents' chauffeur after the wedding. He packed his ice-axe and boots, and booked his passage in a six-berth cabin on the lowest deck of the ageing P & O liner *Otranto*. The ship was filled with young people heading overseas for the first time, and Ed found himself enjoying the social whirl. The ship stopped at Colombo and Aden, passed through the Suez Canal and carried on to Southampton. Ed met his parents in London, and they set off to drive around France, Italy, Switzerland, Germany, Austria and Holland, visiting churches, galleries, museums, monuments and gardens everywhere. The weather was perfect; Percy was happy; Gertrude loved

market shopping and experimenting with new languages; and rather to Ed's surprise they had a wonderful holiday together. Back in Britain he went exploring by bus and train but was still keen to do some climbing. 'I boarded the train at Victoria Station in company with hundreds of holiday makers. I was surprised how many of them were laden with backpacks, ice-axes and ropes and suspected they were heading for a mass invasion of the north face of the Eiger.'[18] It quickly became clear that most were intending to tramp in France or camp on the Riviera, whereas Ed and his New Zealand companions Cecil Segedin and Bruce Morton were heading for Innsbruck and the Stubai Alps in Austria. After climbing several peaks they moved on to Switzerland and tackled the Jungfrau (4158 m; 13,642 ft). 'It was a thrill when we finally set foot on the summit – a picture of the Jungfrau had been a treasured possession when I was a child – and now I was standing on top of the mountain!'[19] The view of the Matterhorn from Zermatt was another highlight of this brief climbing holiday, and although they didn't attempt that famous peak Ed was well satisfied.

36

Above: Gertrude Hillary, June Hillary, Rex Hillary and his son John, on board the *Port Hobart*. June was about to sail for England, 3 January 1947

A letter from George Lowe arrived as he was about to leave Switzerland: Earle Riddiford had moved forward with plans for a Himalayan expedition, and Ed and George were invited to join the party.

After persevering through endless red tape, in early 1951 Earle Riddiford succeeded in getting permission for a New Zealand expedition to the Garhwal Himalaya in north-west India. The Himalayan Club in Calcutta suggested that they attempt two unclimbed peaks: Nilkanta, (6595 m; 21,640 ft) and Mukut Parbat, (7240 m; 23,760 ft). There was a huge amount of preparation to do, and Ed was impressed with Riddiford's persistence. 'At times it seemed that we'd never get away, but Riddiford never lost heart. He was a man of tremendous enthusiasm and considerable organising ability.'[20] There were four climbers in the party and they decided to do a test climb with another experienced mountaineer, Bill Beaven. They would attempt the first ascent of Mount Elie de Beaumont by the difficult Maximilian Ridge at the head of the Tasman Glacier. 'We backpacked seventy pounds over high and difficult passes, weathered a torrential northwest storm, and established a base camp on the remote Burton Glacier,' Ed recalled. 'I was quickly learning to appreciate the qualities of the others; Ed Cotter's whimsical humour; George's boisterous competence; Earle's cool intellect. In one glorious day we battled our way up the magnificent Maximilian Ridge and reached the summit of the mountain. George and I had teamed up for the first time and George led most of the climb in impressively calm and confident fashion.'[21]

Bill Beaven became ill with chickenpox on the day they were heading for the top and nobly insisted he would look after himself while the others charged on. Ed caught chickenpox too, but by 3 May 1951 he was well recovered, and a fit and cheerful group boarded the flying boat to Sydney. Their thirty-four cases of food and equipment only just made it out of New Zealand before the waterfront lockout closed New Zealand ports for five months.[22] Again it was Riddiford's persistence that saw them through.

On the P & O liner *Orion* the four young adventurers were a popular group – Ed Cotter's trick of walking on his hands along the ship's rail in rough seas attracted much admiring attention – and they disembarked with some reluctance at Colombo. But the first New Zealand-organised expedition to the Himalayas was under way at last.

In the stifling heat of May they negotiated the complications of Indian railways, chartered a bus for all their gear, and eventually arrived at the famous hill station of Ranikhet at 2000 metres. 'We broke through the pine forests onto the crest of the ridge, and there were the mountains – Nanda Devi, Trisul and a host of others. Our hearts were filled with wild enthusiasm…I felt a rush of emotion at this first sight of the Himalayas and wandered off by myself in the dust to revel in the great peaks lining the horizon.'[23] It was an overwhelming moment. Eric Shipton had linked the 'exquisite joy that any mountaineer must experience in treading new ground' with his first sight of a legendary peak: 'Out of the centre of the basin rose the wonderful spire of Nanda Devi, 13,000 feet above its base, peerless among mountains, always changing and ever more lovely with each new aspect, each fresh effect of colour and cloud.'[24] Ed Hillary could not look at the Himalayas without thinking of Eric Shipton, and hearing his words.

They met the Sherpas Pasang Dawa Lama, Thondup, Nima and Tenzing for the first time too, and soon formed a congenial team. Twelve weeks later Ed, Lowe, Riddiford and Cotter trekked back into Ranikhet, tired and dirty, but fit and well satisfied. They had coped with the new challenges of working with Sherpas and porters, learned to pace themselves at altitude, acclimatised well and scaled five peaks over 6000 metres. Riddiford and Cotter had reached the summit of their main objective, Mukut Parbat, by pushing on despite intense cold and fading light. Ed and George, who had been coping with frozen feet, did not persist, and deteriorating weather precluded another attempt. As Riddiford had not been well, his achievement demonstrated that 'a tremendous will could dominate most bodily weakness'.[25]

Facing page: Wedding of Dr James Carlile and June Hillary, St Martin-in-the-Fields, Trafalgar Square, London, 14 May 1949. Gertrude Hillary provided her daughter's wedding dress. It was made by Mrs Blair of Meadow-bank, Auckland, and it fitted perfectly

Right: Ed Hillary on the ridge across to Wilczek from Mount Elie de Beaumont (3117 m; 10,226 ft) at the head of the Tasman Glacier, Mount Cook National Park, 31 August 1948
Bert Barley

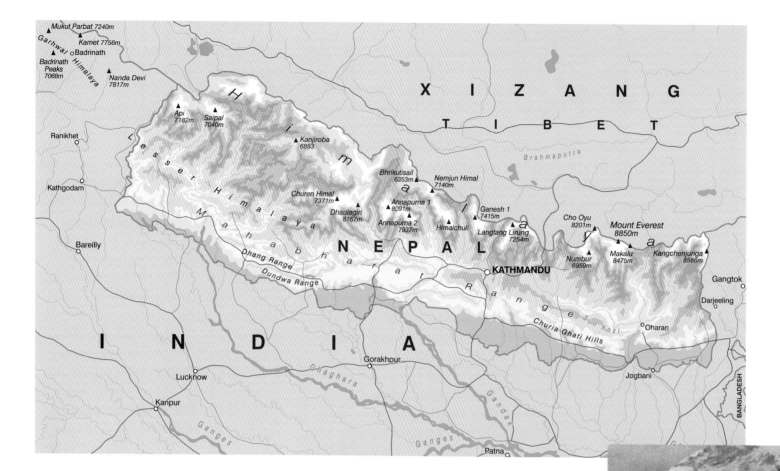

successfully climbing Garhwal Himalaya being included forthcoming Everest expedition… excellent type climbers who through being acclimatised should prove useful adjuncts.'[28] Ed had also written to Scott Russell a few weeks earlier after a friend sent them a press clipping about Shipton's plans.

Ed had learned an important lesson. In the pile of mail that awaited them they found a telegram addressed to the New Zealand Garhwal Expedition – amazingly, it was from Eric Shipton himself. With three younger British climbers he was heading off on a reconnaissance of the southern side of Mount Everest and he wrote:

ANY TWO CAN JOIN US. GET THEIR OWN PERMISSION. BRING THEIR OWN FOOD AND CATCH US UP.[26]

George Lowe described the effect: 'It was like getting a telegram from mountaineering's Angel Gabriel.'[27]

The offer had been triggered by a telegram from the New Zealand Alpine Club to Scott Russell, a New Zealand botanist who had climbed with Shipton and was on the British Himalayan Committee. At the suggestion of Ed's old friend Roland Ellis, the president of the club, Harry Stevenson had written: 'Any possibility one or more NZ party…at present

Eric Shipton later said that he would have been quite happy if all four had turned up, but, as it was, his message shattered the relaxed and positive mood of the group.[29] Ed Hillary was an obvious choice – he was powerfully fit and could afford to stay on. Ed Cotter quickly withdrew from the bitter wrangle – he was also very fit and an excellent climber, but he disliked the

Above left: Ed Hillary, Ed Cotter, George Lowe and Earle Riddiford about to sail from Sydney to Calcutta in May 1951 on the New Zealand Alpine Club expedition to the Garhwal Himalaya in north-west India

Above: Ed Hillary climbing the rocky section between Camps II and III on Mukut Parbat

Top: Map of Nepal

turn of events and he couldn't afford to have more time away from New Zealand. Of the other two, George Lowe was more robust than Earle Riddiford, but Riddiford was an aggressive climber, he had climbed Mukut Parbat, had played the largest part in organising the expedition, and he had the money. In the end Hillary and Riddiford were the fortunate ones, but the conflict affected them all. Ed wrote later: 'I can still remember George's accusing face as he watched us depart by bus for the railhead.'[30] Lowe himself recalled, 'Ed Cotter and I were riddled with envy, flatness and disappointment…we sailed home to New Zealand…a joyless couple.'[31] Ed Hillary's competitive drive was now at full strength.

The 1951 Everest Reconnaissance was suggested to the Himalayan Committee in London by a young British climber and doctor, Michael Ward. It was autumn, after the monsoon, and an actual attempt on Everest was not part of the plan. The idea was to see if there was a climbable route to the summit from the southern side in Nepal, since the northern approach through Tibet had defeated numerous expeditions. The party was Shipton, Ward, leading Scottish climber Bill Murray, and Tom Bourdillon, a tall and strong British mountaineer.

Ed and Earle Riddiford raced across the top of India by bus, stopped to buy supplies at Lucknow and almost missed their train to Jogbani on the India–Nepal border where they were to meet Shipton. 'We leapt into a second class carriage containing two Indian passengers, and then, to their utter horror, we commenced piling in tents, bags, and boxes of food, tins of kerosene, and all the various paraphernalia of an expedition. A wild scattering of coins to our coolies, a sudden jerk that nearly threw us on the floor and another expedition had started.'[32]

Below: Eric Shipton before a fluted ridge after making the first crossing of the Ama Dablam Col with Ed Hillary and three Sherpas, October 1951 **Edmund Hillary**

Bottom: Eric Shipton in the Karakoram in 1939

Eric Shipton 1907–77

A quiet and modest man, Eric Shipton was one of the world's greatest mountain explorers. His companions included leading Himalayan climbers H. W. Tilman and Frank Smythe. With Smythe he made the first ascent of Kamet (7756 m; 25,447 ft) in 1931 – the highest peak to be climbed at that time. With Tilman in 1934 he explored the approaches to the remote and beautiful Nanda Devi (7817 m; 25,646 ft) and he mapped and explored the glaciers and mountains north and west of K2. Over two decades from 1933 he took part in four expeditions to Everest from Tibet, and was originally appointed to lead the 1953 expedition. But after the 1952 Cho Oyu expedition, the Himalayan Committee of the Royal Geographical Society and the Alpine Club decided to replace him with John Hunt. Ed Hillary, Tom Bourdillon, Charles Evans and George Lowe all fought to keep Shipton, but he was perceived as an explorer rather than a driving leader, and his preference for small, lightly equipped expeditions counted against him. Despite his disappointment, Shipton was generous in his congratulations of the successful team.

Eric Shipton was a brilliant lecturer and wrote six highly acclaimed books about his mountain travels. Ed Hillary wrote: 'In my younger days Eric Shipton was a hero to me. He did all the things I wanted to do – exploring remote areas, crossing unknown glaciers and passes, and forcing a way through incredibly rough and unknown country. When I was invited to join his British Everest Reconnaissance in 1951 it was like the answer to a prayer. And Eric lived up to what I expected of him – tough and determined, incurably inquisitive about unvisited remote areas, and yet gentle and kind to young companions. He was a great explorer and a great man.'[*]

They were old India hands now. But they arrived at Jogbani to find that Shipton had already gone. There followed a mad rush north across monsoon-swollen rivers – to the consternation of their porters, they used the New Zealand bush technique of clinging on to a long pole – and finally reached the village of Dingla on 8 September. Ed was nervous about meeting Eric Shipton at last – meeting heroes is always a risky business – but his fears of finding Englishmen who shaved every day and were 'sticklers for the right thing' proved unfounded. 'I have rarely seen a more disreputable looking bunch, and my visions of changing for dinner faded away forever.'[33]

From the English corner, Ward described his first sight of Hillary and Riddiford. They were wearing sunhats with flaps and 'carrying immense Victorian-looking ice-axes...gaunt figures in patched clothes. From the way they bounded up the hill and the ease with which they wolfed down a horrid meal of boiled rice and indeterminate green vegetables they were both in training and used to the squalid aspects of Himalayan travel.'[34] After the expedition, the

40

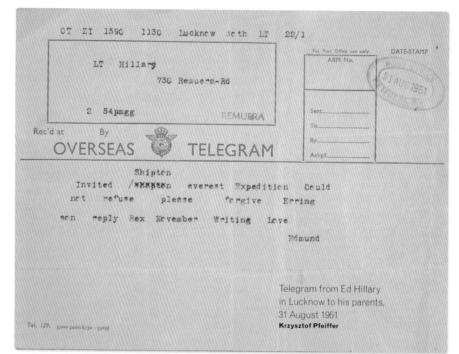

Telegram from Ed Hillary in Lucknow to his parents, 31 August 1951.
Krzysztof Pfeiffer

Below: Map of the Everest region

Above: Members of the Mount Everest Reconnaissance Expedition 1951, sponsored by the Joint Himalayan Committee of the Royal Geographical Society and the Alpine Club, Dingla, 9 September 1951. (L–R) Eric Shipton, Bill Murray, Tom Bourdillon, Earle Riddiford; Michael Ward and Ed Hillary seated in front

Ang Tharkay
1909–81

A legend among Sherpas and
European climbers, Ang Tharkay
was born in the village of Kunde.
In 1931 he moved to Darjeeling to
seek expedition work and quickly
established a reputation as a
strong climber and an excellent
organiser. Ang Tharkay was one
of the first Sherpas to receive a

Tiger Medal from the Himalayan
Club in Darjeeling, which helped
expeditions recruit Sherpa guides
and porters. The Tiger Medal was
a prized recognition for those who
had carried loads to the highest
camps – a feat beyond the powers
of most European climbers. Ang
Tharkay carried to Camp VI on
Everest in 1933, and was sirdar
(head Sherpa) many times for
Eric Shipton, who saw him as
'a shrewd judge of men and of
situations, and absolutely steady
in any crisis…modest, unselfish
and completely sincere, with an
infectious gaiety of spirit.'*
Ed Hillary gave his impressions
of Ang Tharkay after first meeting
him on the 1951 Everest Reconnaissance Expedition: 'Small
and compact and with a fiery
enthusiasm [he] had great
vitality and I warmed to him
immediately.'† They remained
friends and after Ang Tharkay
retired with his wife Ang Yangzen
to Kathmandu, the Hillary family
regularly put up their tents and
camped in his garden on their
way to and from the Khumbu.

honorary treasurer of the Alpine Club in London
rejected Ed's and Riddiford's receipts for expenses,
which included numerous cups of tea from way-
side tea shops, with the comment: 'Gentlemen
are expected to pay for their own cups of tea.'
Their speedy rejoinder was that they were not
'gentlemen' but New Zealanders.[35]

Their sirdar Ang Tharkay and the
other Sherpas grew progressively more excited
as they neared home. On the afternoon of
22 September they arrived at Namche Bazar
(3440 m; 12,200 ft), the trading centre for the
Sherpa villages tucked into the steep hillsides
of the Khumbu region. Further up the Dudh
Kosi valley, surrounded on all sides by snowy
peaks of utter loveliness, is Tengboche Monastery, the spiritual heart of Sherpa life. Shipton
had longed to visit this area for more than
twenty years: 'it had become a kind of Mecca,
an ultimate goal in Himalayan exploration'.[36]
Ed was in heaven. He described the astonishing
peaks all around them: 'mighty ice-fluted faces,
terrific rock buttresses, and razor-sharp, jagged
ice ridges soaring up to impossible summits…
I found it hard to believe they would ever be
climbed.'[37] And Tengboche, in its glorious
setting, was 'wrapped in an aura of peace and
meditation'.[38] The party enjoyed generous
Sherpa hospitality and felt fortunate indeed to
be among the first European visitors to the Solu
Khumbu. It seemed like Shangri-La.

Their Base Camp was below the 600-
metre (2000 ft) barrier of the Khumbu Icefall,
in Shipton's description: 'a wild labyrinth of
ice walls, chasms and towers'. While the others
reconnoitred the lower part of the icefall, Shipton
and Hillary climbed a ridge on a nearby peak –
Pumori – and saw that there was a route up
the glacier of the Western Cwm to the South Col
of Everest. It was a charged moment: two men
whose names would always be linked with that
mountain standing together and seeing the route
that would eventually lead to the summit.

But first the icefall had to be negotiated,
and therein lay the rub. The whole party
eventually got through to the top, and although
a huge crevasse blocked them from progressing
further up the Cwm they were confident it was
bridgeable. The real problem lay in making the
icefall itself safe for laden Sherpas. Every part

41

A southern route to Everest

As Everest continued to defeat successive expeditions approaching from the north through Tibet, mountaineers hoped there might be an alternative route to the summit from the southern side. On the 1921 Everest reconnaissance George Mallory climbed from the Rongbuk Glacier to the Lho La (6006 m), the distinctive col between the west shoulder of Everest and Lingtren, looked over into the Western Cwm, took photographs and gave the Cwm its name, but could not see to the top. And the icefall at the base of the Cwm looked an insuperable barrier. On the 1935 Everest expedition New Zealander Dan Bryant took a more detailed photograph from the same point. In it the floor of the Cwm could be seen – split with crevasses, but reasonably level. Until Nepal opened its borders to Europeans in 1949, there was no way of investigating further, except by air. In April 1933, with Nepalese government approval, two flights were made around the southern side of Everest by British aircraft. The photographs from these flights were converted into a map by the secretary of the Royal Geographical Society, A. R. Hinks, but the map went into the society's archives and was forgotten.'

In March 1950 H. W. Tilman and Charles Houston, a leading American mountaineer, were the first Europeans to walk into the Khumbu and up towards the icefall. Tilman climbed Kala Pitar (5545 m; 18,192 ft) and looked into the Cwm from the south. He wrote: 'In spite of our height and our distance from it – about seven miles – we could not see the high col [South Col] between Everest and Lhotse . . . A shoulder of Nuptse cut across the south ridge of the mountain, hiding the whole length of the western cwm and this col at its head. We could see at most the upper 3,000 ft. of the south ridge which looked so steep that we dismissed at once any idea of there

Ed Hillary looking from a ridge on Pumori into the Western Cwm. The first view of the southern route to Mount Everest, 30 September 1951
Eric Shipton

being a route, even supposing the col could be reached.'[†] But Michael Ward, a young English climber, was convinced that there must be a southern approach. He spent hours in the Royal Geographical Society, poring over the aerial photographs from 1933 and others from 1945 and 1947 flights – and he discovered the map. Ward put all the information together and persuaded a reluctant Himalayan Committee that a reconnaissance expedition should go to Everest from Nepal. Michael Ward, Tom Bourdillon, Bill Murray and their leader Eric Shipton left for Nepal in August 1951. Early in September they were joined by New Zealanders Earle Riddiford and Ed Hillary.

Ed Hillary described the next part of the story in his book *High Adventure*.

'On the morning of September 30th it was fine and clear. Four men left to examine the icefall – Riddiford, Bourdillon, Ward, and Pasang, who had proved himself a forceful climber in Garhwal. Shipton wanted to climb to a position where he could get a look into the Western Cwm, and invited me to accompany him. We left camp and scrambled onto the bottom of a ridge which came down off Pumori (23,190 ft). At 19,000 feet [5790 m] we stopped for a short rest and admired the wonderful views that were opening up around us. Then we pushed on up the last pitches. We scrambled up a steep rock bluff, chipped a few steps over some firm snow, and collapsed with relief on a little ledge at 20,000 feet [6096 m]. Almost casually I looked towards the Western Cwm, although I didn't expect to see much of it from here. To my astonishment the whole valley lay revealed to our eyes. A long, narrow, snowy trough swept from the top of the icefall and climbed steeply up the face of Lhotse at the head of the Cwm. And even as the same thought was simmering in my own mind, Shipton said, "There's a route there!" . . . I returned down the ridge in a daze of excitement – I'd been one of the first men to look into the Western Cwm, I'd seen a new route up the mountain, and I'd had the old classic route explained to me in detail by one of its most famous characters. What more could I ask!'[‡]

A few days later, when the team pushed through to the top of the icefall, it was clear that although fraught with difficulties, this was a feasible route to the top of Everest. Michael Ward's determination had paid off.

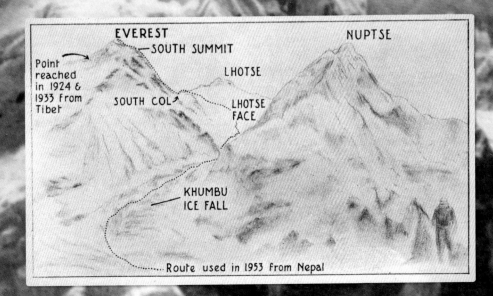

EVEREST
—SOUTH SUMMIT
Point reached in 1924 & 1933 from Tibet
SOUTH COL
LHOTSE
LHOTSE FACE
NUPTSE
KHUMBU ICE FALL
······ Route used in 1953 from Nepal

of the route was menaced by unstable ice towers and the possibility of crevasses opening up as the glacier ground its way slowly downwards. Back at Base Camp they discussed the problem for hours, and in the end there was only one thought: a way would have to be found. They would be back next year, in the spring of 1952.

Between stints of tackling the icefall, the party split into two groups to explore the area. Shipton invited Ed to go with him on an unforgettable fortnight's expedition looking around the south-east side of Everest. The character of Shipton made a huge impression on Ed Hillary: 'his ability to be calm and comfortable in any circumstances; his insatiable curiosity to know what lay over the next hill or around the next corner; and, above all, his remarkable power to transform the discomfort and pain and misery of high-altitude life into a great adventure.'[39] These were qualities which others would observe in Ed himself in the years ahead.

Riddiford and Ed had to get back to New Zealand – they had both been away for longer than they originally planned – and so raced back down ahead of the others, crossing

a difficult high pass to arrive in Kathmandu on 17 November. But the comfort of the British Embassy was no consolation for the news they heard there: the Swiss had been given permission to attempt Everest the next year. All their hopes could come to nothing.

The Himalayan Committee in London was not about to give up yet. They applied for permission to try again in 1953 and meanwhile planned another expedition for 1952 – to Cho Oyu (8190 m; 26,870 ft) about thirty-two kilometres west of Everest. This would give them a fit and experienced team if the Swiss were not successful, and they could test the oxygen equipment which was being increasingly seen as essential for high-altitude climbing. Shipton was again the leader. Ed and Earle Riddiford had impressed Michael Ward with their acclimatisation, their fitness and mental stamina, and their ability to carry heavy loads while finding routes. He attributed this to New Zealand's more 'pioneering' style of climbing. Shipton agreed with him, and invited them and a third New Zealander to join the Cho Oyu party. It was Ed who had the happy task of sending a telegram to George Lowe at the Hermitage: 'Come to the Himalayas.'[40]

In fact they didn't succeed in climbing Cho Oyu: the attempt was abandoned when Shipton and Bourdillon were unwilling to venture into Chinese-controlled Tibet. The party retreated back to Namche Bazar to regroup – Earle Riddiford had left earlier after injuring his back. The others, who included Bourdillon, Alfred Gregory, Charles Evans and the physiologist Griffith Pugh, split into three groups to do more climbing and to test the oxygen systems. George and Ed had been climbing brilliantly together, scaling seven peaks, mostly over 6000 metres (20,000 ft), so with Shipton's blessing they set off on another adventure. Convinced that the Chinese Army would not be patrolling above 5000 metres, they negotiated another massive icefall, and crossed the Nup La, a high pass into Tibet. 'We turned the corner into the East Rongbuk valley – the old pathway to Everest. On the far side of the valley we could see a few stone walls rapidly falling into disrepair. We crossed over and examined them. This was Camp I. It gave me an eerie feeling to look at it, as though ghosts of Mallory and Irvine and Smythe were still flitting amongst the ruins.' They pushed on until they could see the route taken by mountaineers who had been

Right: Some members of the Cho Oyu expedition; sirdar Dawa Tenzing fourth from left, back row.
Front row: Eric Shipton, Charles Evans, George Lowe
Edmund Hillary

Ed's climbing inspiration. 'There was Everest again, proud and aloof against a wind-streaked sky. And the East Rongbuk Glacier was a shining pathway of clear blue ice sweeping up to the foot of the mountain.'[41] It was a thrilling sight.

Ed and George raced back to Namche, where the rest of their team was camped, as was the Swiss expedition. They had not reached the summit this time, but Ed was mightily impressed with their courage and daring. In India on their way out they heard that the Swiss were planning to try again in autumn, but for now they held fast to the knowledge that the way was still open.

Left: Ed Hillary weighing Eric Shipton at the beginning of the 1952 Cho Oyu expedition, probably at Chisapani where they sorted and weighed loads for the porters

Below: Some of Ed Hillary's slides of the Cho Oyu expedition
Edmund Hillary

The Sherpas of the Himalayas

The Sherpa people came into Nepal over the Himalayan passes from eastern Tibet more than 500 years ago. The name Sherpa comes from the Tibetan language – *shar* meaning east and *wa* meaning person – and the Sherpa language is a dialect of Tibetan. They settled in the high valleys of Khumbu and Solu below Chomolungma, and in other valleys further south. Their religion is the oldest form of Tibetan Buddhism, Nyingmapa (ancient people), and its compassionate philosophy is significant in all aspects of their lives. The religious centre of the Khumbu is Tengboche Monas-

tery, an offshoot of the famous Rongbuk Monastery on the north side of Everest.

Sherpas were originally farmers and traders. They grew crops that would survive the short summers at altitude – barley at first and then potatoes; they bred and kept yaks, and traded tea, salt and yak products with Tibetans and Nepalese. They were employed as load carriers and general assistants on the first British reconnaissance to Everest in 1921, and their name has since been inextricably connected with Himalayan climbing, and synonymous with adaptability to altitude, endurance and cheerfulness.

The hill town of Darjeeling in the northern Indian province of Sikkim

was the starting point for most early Himalayan expeditions, as Nepal's borders were closed until 1951. Many young Sherpas moved to Darjeeling to find expedition work with the *feringhi* – foreigners. Being paid in cash for climbing and carrying was an attractive, if dangerous, alternative to subsistence farming. They were well used to carrying loads as Sherpa villages are connected by narrow, often precipitous walking tracks and all goods not carried by yak must be carried on the back of a person. In the years after the successful Everest climb the economy of Sherpa communities changed, and working for expeditions – both climbing and trekking – is now a regular source of income.

Ed Hillary dedicated his book *Schoolhouse in the Clouds* to three of his Sherpa friends: Mingma Tsering, Ang Temba and Pemba Tarkay. He wrote in the preface: 'The name Sherpa does not mean mountaineer, guide or porter – it is simply the name of a race of people, Tibetan in origin, who inhabit the southern flanks of the Himalayan range. They are good and bad, strong and weak, honest and dishonest like the rest of us. But few of those who visit them can remain indifferent to their loyalty, affection and charm or unimpressed with their remarkable toughness and courage.'

04 THE TALLEST PEAK

Ed Hillary and George Lowe made the long
journey home – Ed to beekeeping with Rex,
and George to a final term of school teaching
in Hawke's Bay. Their thoughts and conversation turned constantly to the Himalayas
and Everest. Although the Cho Oyu trip had
not been a total success, both were fairly
confident of being selected for the 1953
expedition. They had shown impressive fitness at altitude and skill in tackling difficult
ice conditions, and were now well known to
Eric Shipton and the leading British climbers.
Their last stop was Sydney, where Ed resumed
his good-humoured, self-effacing courtship
of Louise Rose, now studying viola at the
Sydney Conservatorium. He had written to
her often, but agonised about ever finding
the courage to propose.

**On March 10th we left
Kathmandu to start a
leisurely march to the
foot of Everest. For
seventeen days we
walked up hill and down
dale across the lovely
Nepalese countryside
in almost perfect
weather. We swam in all
the rivers, ate enormous
meals, and slept out
under the stars. By the
time we reached the
Monastery of Thyang-
boche we were a very
fit party, and as was
obvious by now, a very
happy one. It was a
tremendous thrill to see
once again the great
bulk of Everest thrust-
ing high over the
Nuptse–Lhotse wall,
and we were eager to
get to grips with it.
EDMUND HILLARY**

On Saturday 11 August the flying boat landed in Auckland and Ed rushed to open a letter from Eric Shipton. They were in! And so was Harry Ayres. Ed passed the great news on to Harry with some typical Hillary teasing. After describing the travel arrangements, how much money he would need and the usefulness of formal wear for evening functions in Kathmandu, Ed wrote: 'George and I would like to get out with you some time and give you a few pointers on technique – smarten up your step cutting and so on. Unless you can cut with one hand you're no good to us... I'd better warn you that you have a colossal reputation to live up to. Whenever George and I saw a particularly difficult ice peak we'd tell the party that we were "saving it for Harry".'[1] George Lowe signed off the letter with 'Wacko! for the hills'. Murray Ellis, honorary secretary of the Otago section of the New Zealand Alpine Club, sent Harry Ayres heartiest congratulations for a 'well-deserved honour'.[2]

But in London changes were afoot. After eight expeditions and five summit attempts, the British desperately wanted to be the first to climb Mount Everest. Everything now depended on the 1953 expedition – if it failed, another country would probably succeed. Raymond Lambert and Tenzing Norgay had climbed above the South Col with the Swiss in May and would try again in the autumn; there could be only two attempts each year, and the French had already booked spring 1954. Eric Shipton preferred small, lightly provisioned expeditions, and the Himalayan Committee thought the 1953 attempt should be quite the opposite: a full-on assault with the latest equipment and a big team of climbers.

A few weeks after his first, another letter from Eric Shipton arrived at the Hillary household. The news was bad. Shipton was out and the Himalayan Committee had decided to ask John Hunt to lead the expedition. Shipton wrote, 'I don't know what led up to this and it was a considerable and somewhat painful surprise to me... I will do my damnedest to see that it doesn't affect the selection of you three, but I suppose the final word will rest with Hunt.'[3] Hillary sent a copy of the letter to Harry Ayres: 'I feel thoroughly depressed about the whole thing as Everest never will sound quite the same without Shipton.'[4]

In early November it was looking as though Everest would be without Ayres too. Ed sent John Hunt an impassioned plea on behalf of his old friend and climbing mentor. 'Harry Ayres is New Zealand's outstanding mountaineer... His outstanding technical ability, his fine judgement, and great determination give him a record that has been but rarely equalled and never surpassed in our mountains.' He wrote to Harry, 'I feel thoroughly depressed about the whole business...this has been quite a bombshell...perhaps the Swiss will get to the top and all our worries will be for nothing.'[5] By mid-November all was confirmed. John Hunt felt he should know all the team personally – and preferably have them in London to help with the planning and preparation. Other British climbers had supported Hillary and Lowe, despite their inconvenient location on the other side of the world, but Ayres was out. Hunt sent sympathy and regrets. Ed wrote to Harry: 'It's going to be a great disappointment to me not to see you bashing your way up the icefall to the West Cwm...all I can say is how much I regret it all.'[6] For Ed Hillary it was a confused and inauspicious start to the great expedition.

Then came news from the Swiss. Tenzing and Lambert had again climbed high, but again had been forced to retreat. The way was open – but there was a lot to be done. From a small office at the Royal Geographical Society in London, John Hunt directed operations, working long hours himself and delegating wisely. His skill as a leader would be confirmed over the next six months and his organising secretary, Charles Wylie, took on an enormous workload. Clothing, tents and equipment of all kinds were tested; food was selected and packed; quantities of donated goods from companies and supporters all over Britain were prepared for shipping to India. Oxygen apparatus was vitally important, and Tom Bourdillon was leading the development and testing of a new closed-circuit system in addition to the more widely accepted open circuit.

In New Zealand Hillary organised goosedown double-layer sleeping bags from Arthur Ellis and Co. in Dunedin. He and George Lowe sent their measurements to London for expedition clothing, and Rex's wife Jenny made Ed a new sunhat from blue and white striped

Above: Everest expedition stores at Bhimpedi, 8 March 1953. Everything was transported from here by overhead ropeway into the valley of Kathmandu, including an enormous round sackcloth package described by Wilfrid Noyce as 'the bane of all who tried to handle it'. It contained the New Zealand sleeping bags and they would soon be grateful for them

linen – with the flap he liked to protect his neck from sunburn. In London Joy Hunt and other volunteers sewed the name tags into everyone's gear.

The whole 1953 Everest team assembled at the British Embassy in Kathmandu in the first week of March. Most had sailed to Bombay before escorting the 473 expedition packages on Indian trains and lorries in stifling heat to the Nepal border. They had then loaded everything on to the ropeway which swung over the mountains into the valley of Kathmandu. George Lowe met the main party of climbers at Bombay, but Ed sailed to Calcutta on a later boat – February is a busy month for beekeepers – and flew to Kathmandu. Twenty high-altitude Sherpas walked down from the mountains to meet their new employers.

Ambassador Sir Christopher Summerhayes and his family made everyone welcome, and in the Embassy garden, among piles of boxes, packages and cases, Ed finally met John Hunt. He was definitely impressed, despite his inevitable disappointment at Shipton's absence. He also met the famous Tenzing Norgay, their

Above: L. V. 'Dan' Bryant looking at the north face of Everest on the 1935 Everest Reconnaissance Expedition
Eric Shipton

Right: The creation of Sagarmatha, Lhotse and Nuptse, by Lama Geshe, 2002. The painting illustrates Sherpa stories which tell of these mountains emerging from the sea

Chomolungma / Mount Everest / Sagarmatha
A history

Sixty-five million years ago when the Indian and Eurasian continents slowly collided, the earth's crust was forced upwards, creating the Himalayan mountain range and the Tibetan Plateau. The highest summits in the Himalayas are sedimentary rock that originally formed beneath the sea, and they are still rising about one centimetre each year. Sherpa origin stories tell about a primeval ocean whose currents and waves joined particles of earth together. They emerged from the sea as the first mountains: Sagarmatha, Lhotse and Nuptse.

In 1808 the British began the Great Trigonometrical Survey of India, a detailed survey of the sub-continent. Through a complex series of triangular grids, the surveyors produced scientific proof of the earth's curvature, and a means of calculating the height of the tallest Himalayan peaks. The survey lasted almost fifty years, using giant theodolites so heavy that it took twelve men to carry them. In 1849 survey officer James Nicholson observed a peak more than 150 kilometres distant, which his sightings showed was the highest in the world, but for many years it was

referred to simply as 'Peak XV'. Nicholson's calculations were confirmed by the survey's 'chief computer' Radhanath Sickdhar, a Bengali mathematician, and the British surveyor-general Andrew Waugh decided that the peak should be given a name.[*] The Indian survey had generally used local names, but Waugh wanted to call this one Mount Everest after his predecessor Sir George Everest, surveyor-general from 1830 until 1843, in acknowledgement of his considerable contribution to accurate geographical research. In 1865, a year before Sir George's death, the Royal Geographical Society officially adopted Mount Everest as the name of the world's highest mountain. The mountain already had a Tibetan name, Chomolungma, which can be translated as 'Goddess Mother of the World'; and in 1961 it was given the Nepalese name Sagarmatha, from *sagar* meaning sky and *matha* meaning forehead.[†]

All three names are used today. The Survey of India gave the height of Everest as 29,002 feet (8839 m) and this remained the agreed figure for almost 100 years. In January 1921, the Royal

Geographical Society and the Alpine Club of Great Britain formed a Mount Everest Committee to send a reconnaissance expedition of nine men to Everest. Their aim was to find the best way to the mountain through unknown Tibet, and to identify, if possible, a route to the summit. George Leigh Mallory resigned from his teaching position at Charterhouse to take part and succeeded in climbing to the North Col (7010 m; 23,000 ft). It was Mallory who answered a question about why he wanted to climb the mountain with the famous phrase: 'Because it is there.' He took part in the 1922 expedition, and led the 1924 expedition on which he and Sandy Irvine disappeared. Mallory's body was found on Everest in 1999. The British sent expeditions to Everest from Tibet in 1933, 1935, 1936 and 1938. New Zealand mountaineer Dan Bryant was on the 1935 expedition led by Eric

Shipton. Bryant's skill in climbing on ice and snow alerted Shipton to the Southern Alps of New Zealand as an excellent training ground for Himalayan climbers. In 1950 he asked Bryant to suggest New Zealand climbers who might be useful on the 1951 Reconnaissance Expedition. Bryant recommended a young Auckland climber who had the right qualities – his name was Edmund Hillary.

In the 1950s Indian surveyors, using higher observation points, revised the height of Mount Everest to 29,028 feet (8848 m). On 5 May 1999 American and Sherpa climbers placed GPS equipment on the summit, and from this data American cartographer Brad Washburn produced a new figure: 8850 metres; 29,035 feet.

Left: Tenzing wrapped four flags around the shaft of his ice-axe before leaving Advance Base with Ed Hillary on 25 May, the start of their attempt on the summit. They were the flags of the United Nations, Nepal, India, and the Union Jack
Alfred Gregory

Tenzing Norgay

'I was eager to meet Tenzing Norgay. His reputation had been most impressive even before his two great efforts with the Swiss expeditions the previous year – and I certainly wasn't disappointed. Tenzing really looked the part – larger than most Sherpas he was very strong and active; his flashing smile was irresistible.'[*] Tenzing was raised in the village of Thami in the Khumbu, at an altitude of 3800 metres. His parents were yak herders and had moved there from eastern Tibet to find work. Tenzing's biographer Ed Douglas wrote: 'Put together with the resourcefulness that managing a herd of yaks, often alone, engendered and the physical toughness of life in a country with no modern amenities, Tenzing's genetic advantage made him well suited for high-altitude climbing before he'd ever set foot on a mountain.'[†] And unlike most of his Sherpa peers, he wanted to climb. Tenzing's mother Kinzom had called Chomolungma 'The Mountain

Right: Tenzing Norgay and Raymond Lambert, May 1952. On the Swiss Everest expedition, these two men climbed to within 300 metres of the summit. They remained close friends, and on the 1953 summit climb Tenzing wore a red scarf given to him by Lambert
Norman G. Dyhrenfurth

So High No Bird Can Fly Over It' and it was the name he liked best for the mountain.
In 1932 Tenzing moved to Darjeeling to find work on expeditions. He was a high-altitude porter on British Everest expeditions in 1935, 1936 and 1938. In 1934 he married Dawa Puti, also from Thami, and they had a son, Nima Dorje, and two daughters, Pem Pem and Nima. When World War II began, climbing expeditions ceased and Tenzing went to work in Chitral in north-west India, but late in 1939 he learned that his four-year-old son had died from dysentery. Tenzing brought his remaining family to Chitral to be with him, and then in 1944 Dawa Puti also died – a bitter blow. Tenzing returned to Darjeeling

with Pem Pem and Nima in 1945.[‡] Eventually he married Ang Lhamu, a widow who had been working as a nanny for British families in Darjeeling. A devoted wife and loving mother to the girls, she supported the family when Tenzing could find only occasional work. After the war the expeditions returned and Tenzing, who had been awarded a Tiger Medal in 1938, was again in demand. He became a climbing member of the 1952 Swiss Everest expedition and, with Raymond Lambert, reached 8595 metres (28,200 ft). By 1953 Tenzing had become something of a legend, able to acclimatise fully and stay fresh and vigorous at great heights. The Swiss joked that he had three lungs – the higher he went, the better he felt.
After the Everest success Tenzing was honoured by the governments of Nepal, India, the UK and USA.

In response to his achievement, then prime minister of India, Pandit Nehru, opened the Himalayan Mountaineering Institute (HMI) in Darjeeling in November 1954. Tenzing was appointed director of field training, a position he held until 1976, introducing many hundreds of young people to the experience of climbing. His life story, *Man of Everest*, was published in 1955. Like Ed Hillary, he used the earnings from his first book on a house for his family. Tenzing retired from HMI in 1976, but continued to work for several years as an expert guide for trekking expeditions. He died in 1986, leaving his third wife, Daku, seven children and many grand-children.

50

Sherpas and sahibs

Sherpas were an indispensable part of the 1953 Everest team. Their ready laughter even in trying circumstances was appreciated and Ed Hillary always enjoyed their company. Wilfrid Noyce observed: 'From previous expeditions Ed had picked up enough Urdu to make his needs known to the Sherpas, who responded to his cheerful address and warm laugh. Any story, capped with the laugh, would receive an ovation.' On most Himalayan expeditions climbers were paired with a Sherpa whose job it was to look after them. Some men resisted this approach at first, but they generally succumbed to having tea brought to their tents in the morning and help in carrying their gear. After his first Himalayan expedition in 1961 Mike Gill wrote: 'The term sahib sounds like an undesirable relic of the British Raj. In effect it simply means any foreign member of an expedition as distinct from Nepalis or Sherpas or Tibetans. Sherpas use it all the time with no underlying suggestion of class distinction and the word is too convenient to be discarded. Attached to each sahib was a Sherpa to act as personal assistant and interpreter, for most have a smattering of English and some speak it well. One might criticise this undemocratic relationship as being demoralising to sahib or Sherpa or both; in practice it had the effect of establishing a strong bond of affection and loyalty between the two.'†

strong and capable sirdar, veteran of two Everest attempts the previous year and the most experienced Himalayan climber in the team. No one knew who would be in the eventual summit attempt – that would be Hunt's decision once they were all on the mountain – so cameraman Tom Stobart was extremely relieved to find at the end of the expedition that he had filmed this first smiling meeting of the summit pair. Ed wrote to Jim Rose from Kathmandu: 'I am very impressed with our team this time and I think it will be a formidable one.'[7]

About twenty kilometres out of Kathmandu, the road ended at Bhadgaon, and their eight tons of equipment was sorted into several hundred sixty-pound loads. On 10 March the first long winding crocodile of laden porters, climbers and Sherpas began the journey to Tengboche Monastery at 3876 metres (12,717 ft). They walked along rocky paths through a wonderland of spectacular views – terraced hillsides, trees loaded with fragrant flowers, brilliantly coloured birds, green forests and dark valleys – past rocky bluffs, and across milk-blue glacial rivers on horrifyingly precarious swing bridges. The climbers took photographs, caught butterflies, practised breathing through oxygen masks, read, swam, wrote in their diaries and settled into the expedition routine. And their excellent cook, Thondup, kept everyone well fed.

After two weeks they reached the valleys of Solu and Khumbu below Everest. The Sherpas' Buddhist beliefs were evident everywhere in stone *chortens*, fluttering prayer flags and walls of *mani* stones inscribed with the invocation '*Om Mani Padme Hum*' – 'Hail to the Jewel in the Lotus' – similar in intention to 'Hallelujah, Praise the Lord'. Families of expedition Sherpas came out to greet the sahibs, smiling and offering potatoes and *chang* – Sherpa rice wine. Ed Hillary loved being back among these people and these mountains.

The 1953 Everest team in the Western Cwm, 30 May 1953.
(L–R) Standing: Tom Stobart, Dawa Tenzing, Charles Evans, Charles Wylie, Edmund Hillary, John Hunt, Tenzing Norgay, George Lowe, Michael Ward, Tom Bourdillon, George Band, Griffith Pugh, Alfred Gregory, Wilfrid Noyce

Sitting: Topkie, Thondup, Chhangju, Annullu, Ang Tsering, Norbu, Balu Tensing, Mingma Tsering, Dawa Thondup, Ang Nyima, Da Namgyal, Thakto Pemba, Pasang Dawa, Nawang Gombu, unknown, Gyaljen, Phu Dorje, Nanje Kanchha, Ang Temba, Ang Dorji, Kirken, Ang Dawa. Michael Westmacott is not in the photograph – he was working in the icefall. (Identification of the Sherpa climbers courtesy of George Band and Nawang Gombu.) **Alfred Gregory**

Getting used to altitude, Tengboche, 29 March 1953

'We are camped in a grassy glade surrounded by pines and rhododendrons and only a few hundred yards from the monastery,' Ed wrote. 'In the morning I can poke my head out of my tent and see Everest to the north, with its great plume of snow towering over the Nuptse Lhotse wall. A little to the right is the fantastic shape of Amadablam. On every side are amazing peaks...It's a remarkable spot.'[8] They met the Head Lama of Tengboche, exchanged gifts and shared a meal. The monks offered prayers for the party's safe return from Chomolungma, and John Hunt wrote to his wife Joy: 'The old Abbot was very interesting about Yetis, leaving no doubt whatever in my mind about their existence.'[9]

Hunt's plan included three weeks of acclimatisation climbs to allow their bodies to adapt to the reduced oxygen available at altitude. They split into groups to tackle some of the peaks near Tengboche. Ed was with Charles Wylie, Michael Ward and Wilfrid Noyce, but had to stay behind at first. 'I, as usual, had my early bout of fever and general misery so could not go off with my party. However after a couple of days I had my usual rapid recovery (probably boredom) and caught them up in time to lead most of the best climb done by any party during this period – a nice ice peak of 20,100 odd.'[10]

Facing page: Mount Everest
from Tengboche, 29 March 1953
Edmund Hillary

Edmund Hillary's sizing sheet
for the expedition's high-
altitude boots

Right: Ed Hillary putting on
his high-altitude boots
Alfred Gregory

The boots they wore

For the walk from Kathmandu most of the climbers wore canvas sand shoes. On the mountain they were issued with mountaineering boots, with a double layer of freeze-proofed leather and fur between the layers, and specially designed high-altitude boots. Although very large – Wilfrid Noyce said they made the wearer look like 'an elephant footed biped' – these boots were warm, light and comfortable.[*] Thirty-three pairs were made to measure for the climbers and the high-altitude Sherpas – the Himalayan Club sent diagrams and measurements of the Sherpas' feet from Darjeeling. John Hunt described them: 'The more specialized boot for high-altitude climbing had uppers insulated with almost one inch of "Tropal" (an unwoven web of kapok fibres) contained between a very thin layer of glacé kid and an inner waterproof lining. The sole, instead of being made of the normal heavy-treaded rubber, was made from a micro-cellular rubber, much lighter in addition to having better insulation properties. The weight of an average pair of these boots was about 4 lb 4 oz. [1.9 kg].'[†] The thin outer layer suffered from crampon rips and tears, and ice steps had to be made very large to accommodate them, but no one suffered from frostbitten feet – a regular problem on earlier expeditions.

COLONEL JOHN HUNT, CBE, DSO, AGED 42

Expedition leader. Served during World War II as chief instructor (under Frank Smythe) at the Commando Mountain and Snow Warfare School, then in Egypt, Italy and Greece, commanding the Infantry Brigade of the 4th Indian Division. Hunt selected the members of the Everest expedition from a long list of candidates.

Expert in complex planning and in the leadership of men, John Hunt was prepared to do whatever he asked of his team. He carried a load of oxygen and supplies to 8335 metres (27,350 ft) to assist Hillary and Tenzing in the summit assault. His book *The Ascent of Everest*, written immediately after the return to Britain, gives an account of every aspect of the expedition. He was knighted in 1953, retired from the army in 1956 and spent the remainder of his life in public service. He was created a Life Peer and a Knight of the Garter. Lord Hunt died in 1998.

Photo: Alfred Gregory

CHARLES EVANS, FELLOW OF THE ROYAL COLLEGE OF SURGEONS, AGED 33

Deputy leader. Began climbing in Wales. Qualified as a doctor during World War II and served in Burma, then combined learning surgery with alpine and Himalayan climbing. He was on Eric Shipton's Cho Oyu expedition in 1952. Evans was quartermaster, organising all the stores and equipment and the loads to be carried from Base Camp to the higher camps on the mountain. He was in the first summit-assault party with Tom Bourdillon. Using closed-circuit oxygen equipment they reached the South Summit of Everest on 26 May 1953, one of the outstanding feats of the expedition. Evans led the expedition which succeeded in climbing Kangchenjunga (8586 m; 28,169 ft) in 1955, became a neurosurgeon, and was principal of the University of Wales, Bangor, from 1958 to 1984. He died in 1995.

Photo: Alfred Gregory

GEORGE BAND, AGED 24

A member of the climbing team, he was also in charge of wireless equipment and helped with the food. A graduate in geology and former president of the Cambridge University Mountaineering Club, he had climbed in Britain and the Alps since 1948. His national service was with the Royal Corps of Signals.

A member of the climbing team, he was also in charge of wireless equipment and helping with the food. Sugar and sweet lemon drinks were consumed in large quantities, and tinned peaches were particularly popular. Band was one of the expedition's humorists, concocting in conversation *The Hunt Manual of Man Management* and *Everest Exposed* – but neither was published. In 1955 George Band with Joe Brown made the first ascent of Kangchenjunga, the world's third-highest peak. Band worked in the oil industry and since his retirement has led many treks in the Himalayas. He wrote *Everest: The Official History*, published in 2003 for the fiftieth anniversary of the expedition.

Photo: Alfred Gregory

TOM BOURDILLON, AGED 29

In charge of the expedition's oxygen equipment. Served in Greece and Egypt during World War II, then worked as a physicist with the Ministry of Supply. An outstanding rock climber, Bourdillon was on the 1951 Everest Reconnaissance and the 1952 Cho Oyu expedition.

Tom Bourdillon and his father, Dr R. B. Bourdillon, developed the closed-circuit oxygen system which recycles exhaled air by removing carbon dioxide. It was still at an experimental stage in 1953. With Charles Evans, Bourdillon climbed 900 metres above the South Col in one day, to be the first on the South Summit of Everest. Tom Bourdillon was killed in 1956 while climbing in the Bernese Oberland.

Photo: Alfred Gregory

ALFRED GREGORY, AGED 39
Expedition photographer. In charge of travel to and from Kathmandu, and postal arrangements on the mountain. Gregory was an officer in the Black Watch Regiment and served in North Africa and Italy during World War II. He had extensive climbing experience in the Lake District and the Alps, and was on the 1952 Cho Oyu expedition.
Alfred Gregory's black-and-white photographs created an indelible record of the expedition and he assisted Tom Stobart with filming. Gregory had great stamina, and with George Lowe and Ang Nyima carried oxygen bottles and a stove to Camp IX at 8500 metres (27,900 ft) where Hillary and Tenzing spent the night on 28 May 1953. He became a full-time photographer and led several expeditions to the Himalayas. His 1993 book *Alfred Gregory's Everest* includes many of his most famous photographs. He lives in Australia.
Photo: Alfred Gregory

EDMUND HILLARY, AGED 33
Responsible for maintaining twenty-two primus stoves on the mountain and for obtaining the expedition's double-layer sleeping bags from Arthur Ellis and Co. in Dunedin. A beekeeper from Auckland. Served in the RNZAF during World War II, began climbing in the New Zealand Alps and was in the foremost rank of New Zealand mountaineers. Took part in the 1951 New Zealand expedition to the Garhwal Himalaya, the 1951 Everest Reconnaissance and the 1952 Cho Oyu expedition.
Eric Shipton had forecast Hillary as a strong contender for an Everest summit party, and Hunt described him as 'Quite exceptionally strong, abounding in a restless energy and possessed of a thrusting mind which swept aside all unproved obstacles...'* With Tenzing Norgay he reached the summit of Mount Everest at 11.30 a.m. on Friday 29 May 1953.
Photo: George Lowe

GEORGE LOWE, AGED 28
Teacher in a rural primary school in Hawke's Bay, New Zealand. He had extensive climbing experience in the New Zealand Alps and was a master of climbing on ice. He was on the 1951 New Zealand expedition to the Garhwal Himalaya and took part in the 1952 Cho Oyu expedition.
George Lowe's work in breaking a path on the difficult Lhotse Face was a turning point in the expedition. John Hunt described Lowe's performance as 'an epic achievement of tenacity and skill'.† Lowe did most of the high-altitude filming for Stobart. He climbed with Gregory, Ang Nyima, Hillary and Tenzing to establish Camp IX and, like George Band, he kept the expedition laughing. George Lowe photographed and filmed the 1957–58 Commonwealth Trans-Antarctic Expedition, and continued to climb in many parts of the world.
Photo: Alfred Gregory

WILFRID NOYCE, AGED 35
Responsible, after a short training course, for repairing the expedition's boots. He had a classics degree from Cambridge, and was a schoolmaster at Charterhouse, where George Mallory had taught. A leading British climber who served as an instructor at the Aircrew Mountain Centre in Kashmir during World War II, he had climbed in the Garhwal Himalaya and in Sikkim. Noyce led one of the parties of high-altitude Sherpas and played a vital role on the assault on the Lhotse Face. With the Sherpa Annullu, he broke the final path to the South Col on 21 May. A week later he returned to the South Col and, with George Lowe, welcomed Hillary and Tenzing after their summit climb. Wilfrid Noyce's book *South Col* gives a lively and personal account of the expedition and includes some of his own poetry. After the expedition he became a full-time writer. He was killed in 1962 on Mount Garmo in the Pamirs.
Photo: Alfred Gregory

DR GRIFFITH PUGH, AGED 43
Physiologist responsible for monitoring the fitness and acclimatisation levels of the group, sponsored by the British Medical Research Council. He was an Olympic-class skier and a physiologist at the Mountain and Snow Warfare Training Centre in the Lebanon during World War II, and was on the 1952 Cho Oyu expedition.

Pugh worked with Charles Evans selecting the expedition's diet and rations. He was a back-up medic for Michael Ward and carried out numerous experiments on the climbers. The results gave valuable new insights into high-altitude physiology. He continued to work in this area and led the scientific team on the 1960–61 Himalayan Scientific and Mountaineering Expedition. He wrote and published extensively on human physiology in extreme conditions. He died in 1994.

TOM STOBART, AGED 35
Film cameraman, sponsored by Countryman Films. A zoology graduate who had climbed in the Alps, Carpathians and the Himalayas, and photographed the Norwegian–British–Swedish Antarctic expedition, 1949–52. On Everest he used 16 millimetre cameras and dug a snow cave at Base Camp to store his film at a constant temperature.

To demonstrate the scale of the mountain, Stobart took an astonishing vertical panning shot from the Western Cwm which he described in his book *Adventurer's Eye*: 'By the time I had finished – holding my breath until it burst – I was almost lying under my tripod, tilting the camera up at the fabulous walls that loomed above.'* Premiered in October 1953, *The Conquest of Everest* won best documentary in the 1954 British Film Awards and was shown to great acclaim all over the world. He continued to work as a writer and filmmaker. He died in 1980.

TENZING NORGAY, AGED 39
Sirdar, in charge of all the Sherpas working on the expedition. He had many years of experience on five Everest expeditions. After reaching Camp VI in the 1938 expedition with Frank Smythe and H.W. Tilman, he was awarded a Tiger Medal by the Himalayan Club. Tenzing participated in the 1951 French expedition to Nanda Devi and in May 1952, on the Swiss expedition, climbed to within 300 metres of the summit of Everest with Raymond Lambert.

In *The Ascent of Everest* John Hunt described Tenzing as 'not only the foremost climber of his race, but a mountaineer of world standing'.† Tenzing bore his considerable management responsibilities cheerfully, but was always happiest when climbing. He acclimatised well and throughout the expedition remained fresh and exceptionally strong. His example encouraged the high-altitude Sherpas to make the final push carrying loads to the South Col on 22 May. He reached the summit of Chomolungma, Mount Everest, with Ed Hillary on 29 May 1953. Tenzing became director of field training at the Himalayan Mountaineering Institute in Darjeeling. He died in 1986.

DR MICHAEL WARD, AGED 27
Expedition doctor and experienced climber. Ward suggested and took part in the reconnaissance of the south side of Everest in 1951. Although expected primarily to care for the health of the other climbers, he was a reserve for the climbing party and led many groups of Sherpas through the icefall and as high as Camp VII.

Headaches, sore throats, nausea, loss of appetite and sleeplessness are the price of staying for too long at high altitude, but the expedition had a good supply of pharmaceuticals, many of them very effective, although Ward remarked dryly to one sufferer 'Try some of these – they do no good at all.' Ward assisted Pugh in the study of acclimatisation on Everest and on the Himalayan Scientific and Mountaineering Expedition. A consultant surgeon, he has continued to research and write on high-altitude medicine. His most recent book is *Everest: A Thousand Years of Exploration*.

All photos: Alfred Gregory

MICHAEL WESTMACOTT, AGED 28

Responsible for structural equipment and tents. A former president of the Oxford University Mountaineering Club and a mountaineer of first rank with alpine experience. He served in Burma during World War II with the Indian Army Engineers and was employed in statistical investigation at Rothamstead Experimental Station. Westmacott managed the disposition of the tents at each camp for the climbers and Sherpas likely to need them. While the main party was at Advance Base and the two summit assaults took place, daytime temperatures increased. Westmacott worked to keep open the route through the rapidly changing Khumbu Icefall, lengthening bridges and finding new routes where the old had become dangerous. On 30 May 1953 he escorted James Morris through with the news of the successful climb and his work ensured that the rest of the party descended safely. Westmacott worked in agricultural research and with Shell International. He continued to climb in many parts of the world, becoming president of the Alpine Club and developing the Himalayan Index, a database listing attempts and successful ascents of Himalayan peaks over 6000 metres.

MAJOR CHARLES WYLIE, AGED 32

Organising secretary and transport officer for the expedition. Wylie had climbed since boyhood in the United Kingdom, the Alps and the Himalayas. He was British pentathlon champion in 1939 and spent much of the war in a Japanese prisoner of war camp. A serving officer with the Brigade of Gurkhas, Charles Wylie spoke fluent Nepali and was seconded from the War Office to assist in the preparations for the expedition. Wylie paid meticulous attention to every aspect of the expedition's organisation. He managed the development of the high-altitude boots, and the selection and modification of tents, windproof cloth, wireless sets, cookers and bridging equipment. Tireless in maintaining morale and supporting the summit assault, Wylie led one of the two parties of high-altitude Sherpas, and climbed with Hillary and Tenzing to establish Camp VIII on the South Col. He continued to climb and after retiring from the army worked for many years for the Britain–Nepal Medical Trust and was chairman of the Britain–Nepal Society.

JAMES MORRIS, AGED 27

Special correspondent for *The Times*, attached to the expedition. Morris graduated from Oxford after serving in the army during the war, and worked as a journalist in England and Egypt before joining the editorial staff of *The Times* in 1951.

With no mountaineering experience, Morris climbed up to Camp IV to report on the expedition's progress. His frequent dispatches to *The Times* were carried by runner to Kathmandu – the fastest covering 240 kilometres in six days. When Hillary and Tenzing returned from the summit Morris raced down the mountain, accompanied by Westmacott, and radioed a brief coded message from Namche Bazar on 31 May. Despite intense media interest, his code was unbroken and the story became 'the scoop that crowned a Queen'. His book *Coronation Everest* was published in 1958. After forty years of considering himself female by gender, although male by sex, Morris completed a change of sexual identity in 1972. Since then she has been Jan Morris, a highly acclaimed writer.

The fever was probably a recurrence of the malaria Ed contracted when he was in the air force in the Solomon Islands; but, always a competitive mountaineer, and described by Shipton as 'a terrific goer', Hillary was keen to test his strength and fitness right from the start. He described himself as 'a glutton for leading', since he liked to set the pace. Wilfrid Noyce took the lead several times when climbing with him and noted another climber's comment: 'I try to get into the lead with Ed. It's more restful.'[11]

For the second acclimatisation climb Hunt asked Ed to lead a group of Sherpas with Lowe, Band and Westmacott to set up the main Base Camp below the Khumbu Icefall. Pugh and Stobart came too. Tom Stobart often felt that his bulky camera gear was a trial to the other climbers, but on this trip he saved the day by fashioning sun goggles from adhesive tape and celluloid for snow-blinded Sherpas. Ed was extremely grateful for this resourcefulness. Later Stobart noted that the special low-temperature adhesive tape he had for sealing his film canisters 'seemed to be sticking half the expedition together'.[12] Crampons are famous for puncturing everything within reach, and fifty years after the expedition a patch of Stobart's tape was still successfully covering a crampon gash in Ed Hillary's blue Everest windproofs.

58

Tackling the Khumbu Icefall, 13–17 April 1953

With Base Camp established, the real assault began, starting with the Khumbu Icefall – still a towering obstacle for climbers approaching Everest from the south. The Khumbu Glacier slides down between Everest and Nuptse, then turns a corner and falls over 600 metres. Its surface layer creaks, cracks and shatters as the glacier moves, forming massive seracs, or ice towers, which can topple onto a passing climber and bury them. Hillary wrote to Jim Rose: 'The first time I saw the icefall I was absolutely appalled. It was a thousand times worse than in 1951 and really looked quite hopeless. I've never seen such a mass of twisted seracs and contorted crevasses…Actually, Jim, we wouldn't dream of climbing in this sort of country in N.Z. – or anywhere else, but as it's Everest you just seem to push on and hope for the best.'[13] Their task

was to find and flag a safe route for the Sherpas and climbers to follow – fixing rope ladders, cutting big bucket steps around leaning towers of ice and into and out of crevasses. In the end they found a way through. Hillary, Band, Westmacott and Lowe forced a route to Camp II in the middle of the icefall and then on to the top. 'I personally am going like a bomb and seem to be able to bash about with the old ice axe almost indefinitely. Give us another week and we'll have the icefall an easy day for a lady – well almost!'[14]

Into the Western Cwm, 18 April–2 May 1953

They had a couple of days' rest at Lake Camp, where Ed was delighted to find chatty letters from family and copies of the *Weekly News*. He wrote to his parents: 'I'm perched behind some rocks…whenever I look up I can see straight above the howling wind whipping the snow off Everest and Nuptse – it looks very unpleasant up there. However it's very early in the season yet…and much will happen in the next month… Look after yourselves and send me any news. I'm extremely interested to know how the South African cricket team did in NZ. Love, Ed'.[15]

Right: In the Khumbu Icefall, 17 April 1953 **John Hunt**

Below: Reading the *Weekly News* at the Lake Camp at Lobuje, now known as Gorak Shep, 17 April 1953 **George Lowe**

Above: Carrying stores up the Khumbu Glacier to establish the expedition's Base Camp, 9 April 1953 **Alfred Gregory**

SUMMIT
SOUTH SUMMIT

IX

VIII

VII

VI

To V

IV

III

II

BASE

Above: Sherpas carrying loads
through the icefall
Edmund Hillary

On 21 April Sherpas began ferrying supplies through to Camp III at 6157 metres (20,200 ft). Just beyond it, their entry to the gigantic, snow-floored trench of the Western Cwm was still blocked by the yawning blue crevasse – five metres across at its narrowest – they had seen in 1951. The Swiss used ropes to cross it in 1952, but Hunt wanted a sturdier solution. Back in Britain, Charles Wylie had tested walking across a standard, heavy-duty builder's aluminium ladder: 'the sag was considerable over a 25-foot gap, but it held the manager, the works foreman and myself... without signs of collapse'.[16] They brought several lengths of this ladder with them, and Hunt, Evans, Noyce, Tenzing and Hillary took three sections to attempt a bridge. Ed recalled: 'On the edge of the crevasse we bolted them strongly together and then lowered the eighteen-foot ladder carefully into place. It spanned with a couple of feet to spare, but it looked a frail link across the deep gash. I crawled over it to try it out, and although it swayed a little it seemed stable enough.'[17] At last they were through into the Cwm itself. Aluminium ladders are still used on the southern approach to Everest.

On 26 April Tenzing and Hillary roped together for the first time to work on the route to the site of the Swiss Camp IV at 6462 metres (21,200 ft). This would be their Advance Base Camp, and the hot sun that day turned the Cwm into a glittering white inferno. In Ed's favourite book about Everest, *Camp Six*, Frank Smythe described the airless, blinding glare of a glacier which drains your energy 'like liquid through a funnel', yet Hillary and Tenzing plugged on strongly through deep, loose snow and had their reward – a stash of biscuits, cheese, porridge, bacon and jam that the Swiss had left behind. That afternoon they decided to return down the Cwm and through the icefall to Base Camp. George Lowe was with some Sherpas at Camp II and Ed promised to say hello on the five o'clock radio link-up from Base. 'That'll be the day,' George replied, and the race was on – an hour back to Base from Camp II would be a record.

They jogged through what they called the 'Atom Bomb' area of the lower icefall, and instead of using the snow bridge over the last crevasse Ed leapt across. He landed safely, but the overhanging edge snapped off and he went down with it. 'I only knew that I had to stop being crushed against the ice by the twisting block, and I threw my cramponed feet hard against one wall and my shoulders against the other. Next moment the rope came tight and the block dropped away beneath me. Tenzing's reaction had been very quick. I cut my way to the surface without too much difficulty and thanked Tenzing... He seemed to regard it as a rather good joke.'[18] Back at Base, Ed managed a breathless 'hello' to George and told the others, 'Without Tenzing I would have been finished today'.[19]

After this the two men regularly climbed together, developing the trust and familiarity they would need if they were selected for the summit assault. Frank Smythe had noted how disturbing it would be to make an attempt on the world's highest mountain with someone with whom he had never climbed before:

'A party must move as one man to stand a chance of success.'[20] Each relied on the other's judgement, alertness and pace. Ed wrote home with a progress report on 28 April: 'Actually I am going extraordinarily well and Tenzing (the famous Sherpa) and I have teamed up as the Tigers of the party. I hope I can keep it up. However everyone is in pretty good form so we have a strong party.'[21]

The formidable Lhotse Face, 2–15 May 1953

While Hillary and Tenzing rested at Base, the other climbers and Sherpas had been stocking Advance Base in the Western Cwm. On 2 May Ed persuaded Hunt to let him and Tenzing run a test on the open-circuit oxygen equipment – and on themselves – by attempting a fast climb from Base to Advance Base and back again. Both were extremely keen to be selected for the summit assault – Tenzing had got close twice before – so they needed to show John Hunt what they were capable of. They left at the crack of dawn and returned that same afternoon in a blizzard. They were tired but certainly not

Camp III at the top of the icefall, 6157 metres (20,200 ft) below the huge crevasse. Ed Hillary is on the left near the pyramid tent, John Hunt in the centre with braces and Sherpas are unloading stores they have carried from Camp II. New Zealand-made sleeping bags are draped over tents and the flags are for marking the next part of the route, 24 April 1953
Alfred Gregory

60

Ed Hillary with three
Sherpas in the Western
Cwm; at the head of the
Cwm is Lhotse, four kilo-
metres away. 10 May 1953
George Lowe

Ed Hillary clearing steps
on the lower Lhotse Face,
15 May 1953
Wilfrid Noyce

exhausted and Ed described the oxygen as
'bloody marvellous'. They had climbed 1200
metres in just over four hours, instead of the
usual nine hours spread over three days. It was
a considerable feat and a confirmation of the
benefits of supplementary oxygen. When John
Hunt announced everyone's role in the final
assault plan, their perseverance was rewarded.
There would be two attempts on the summit:
first Charles Evans and Tom Bourdillon using
the closed-circuit oxygen, then Hillary and
Tenzing using open-circuit. Other climbers would
take on the Lhotse Face, and establish camps on
the South Col and high on the south ridge.

Sections of aluminium ladder
were used to bridge the
worst crevasses in the
icefall. This one, between
Camps I and II, was prefer-
able to 'Hillary's Horror',
another crevasse further
to the right which had a
six-metre ice wall on its
upper side

Left: Ed Hillary and John
Hunt at Lake Camp
George Lowe

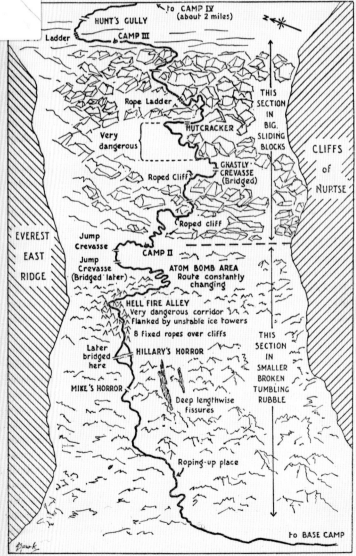

1953. A plan of the route through the Khumbu Icefall.

A. Spark

Some 1.5 kilometres from Advance Base, the Lhotse Face is a steep slope of snow and ice, rising 1200 metres and blocking the top of the Cwm. It is the approach to the saddle called the South Col, where the expedition needed a fully stocked camp for the summit attempts. Hunt hoped the route could be made in a few days, but as both altitude and climbing difficulty increased, everything began to slow down. Evans and Bourdillon made an initial foray up the Lhotse Face, testing the closed-circuit oxygen sets, and on 11 May Hunt sent George Lowe, 'a master of ice-craft', to lead the push on Lhotse. His work with Ang Nyima became a legend of the 1953 climb. Hillary recalled: 'In shocking weather conditions these two men worked under great difficulties, cutting innumerable steps on the steep ice-slopes, putting in fixed ropes on the more dangerous stretches, and generally transforming this highly technical route into one that a heavily laden man could follow.'[22]

While this struggle was going on Hillary worked in the Cwm, conducting parties of Sherpas from Camp III to Camp IV, and the weather kept getting worse. It snowed every afternoon, often a portent of an early monsoon, and the party was acutely aware if that happened their efforts would come to nothing. Glaciers warm up during the monsoon, and avalanches and collapses are frequent, making climbing impossible. On 15 May Wilfrid Noyce came up the Lhotse Face to give Ang Nyima a break and pushed on further with George Lowe, but Lowe, battered by the wind and the altitude, had run out of steam. Spending eleven days above 7000 metres was an extraordinary test in itself and Griffith Pugh, their physiologist, was worried about Lowe's health. Lowe returned to Advance Base where Tenzing and Wylie had now arrived with the last of the stores. To everyone's delight, Thondup the cook was in residence too.

The South Col at last, 21–22 May 1953

All eyes were on Camp VII which was visible from the Cwm, but most of the Sherpas who had carried supplies up there were utterly spent and unable to push on with Noyce to the Col. On the morning of 21 May, Hunt saw only two black dots emerge from the camp – Noyce and Annullu. Charles Wylie was on his way up with more Sherpas but even so the situation looked bad. Ed Hillary knew that desperate measures were called for. 'I went over to John Hunt's tent and literally pleaded with him to let me and Tenzing go up to Camp VII and spur on the major lift the next day. I was absolutely sure that Tenzing and I could go to the South Col and return and still be fit for our assault on the summit.'[23] Hunt had to agree – everyone was either in an assault team or recovering after work on the Lhotse Face. It was a crucial decision, and the correct one, for Tenzing's presence and example stimulated the exhausted Sherpas to one last mighty effort. At 8.30 a.m. on 22 May John Hunt saw two climbers followed by a string of seventeen Sherpas emerge from Camp VII: 'The entire caravan was on its way, carrying our vital stores to the foot of the final peak. The Assault was on.'[24]

The first summit attempt, 26 May 1953

At almost 8000 metres (26,000 ft) the South Col is a barren, icy, rubble-strewn plateau between Everest and Lhotse, which offers no shelter or respite from the shrieking, freezing wind that tears across it. Charles Evans and Tom Bourdillon supported by Hunt, Da Namgyal and Ang Tensing struggled for more than an hour to put up two tents that would have taken a few minutes to erect lower down the mountain. The altitude was badly affecting them all. They crawled into sleeping bags, wearing all the clothing they had, started the primus and brewed up. There was lemonade, soup, tea and cocoa, and they drank four mugfuls each – heeding Griffith Pugh's warnings about dehydration. The next day was spent sorting out the muddle of gear and oxygen equipment until Camp VIII was at last in place.

John Hunt and Da Namgyal left early on 26 May, carrying heavy loads of supplies that Hillary and Tenzing would need for their high camp two days later. Evans and Bourdillon followed in their steps and eventually climbed past them. Hunt wanted this first assault team to reach the South Summit, assess the difficulty of the climb beyond it and continue only if all

Facing page, left: Charles Evans looking at the summit ridge from the South Summit of Everest. To the right of Evans's head is the vertical rock step, later to be known as the 'Hillary Step'
Tom Bourdillon

Oxygen equipment on Everest in 1953

By 1953 it was generally accepted that supplementary oxygen would assist climbers to reach the summit of Everest. Griffith Pugh had established on Cho Oyu that earlier Everest expeditions had not been using enough oxygen to improve their performance, allowing for the weight of the equipment. At high altitudes on Everest, Pugh proposed flow rates of four litres per minute when climbing and two litres when sleeping. The expedition took three types of oxygen equipment – open circuit, closed circuit and sleeping sets. With the open-circuit set the climber inhales air enriched by added oxygen and exhales into the atmosphere. The closed-circuit set has no opening to the outside air. The climber inhales oxygen through a breathing bag, and exhales through a soda-lime canister which absorbs the carbon dioxide and allows exhaled oxygen to return to the breathing bag. The closed-circuit system was still somewhat experimental and proved less reliable on the mountain, but both systems were prone to having valves ice up, leaving the climber struggling to restore the flow. Tom Bourdillon had the unenviable task of keeping the equipment in good order and juggling the disposition of oxygen cylinders among the high camps. The sleeping sets were very successful, as sleeplessness is very common at altitude; oxygen helped the climbers feel warmer and more rested.[*] Ed Hillary quickly mastered the use of the open-circuit system. His careful management of their oxygen supplies contributed greatly to the success of his climb with Tenzing Norgay to – and from – the summit of Everest.

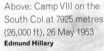

Above: Camp VIII on the
South Col at 7925 metres
(26,000 ft), 26 May 1953
Edmund Hillary

63

Sherpas carrying loads up
the Lhotse Face from Camp
VII, 7315 metres (24,000 ft),
with Charles Wylie leading,
22 May 1953

conditions – including their oxygen supply – were favourable. After pushing as high as they could, Hunt and Da Namgyal dumped their loads at 8300 metres (27,350 ft) and returned exhausted to the Col. Tenzing and Hillary had arrived from Advance Base and helped them into the tents for oxygen and a hot drink. George Lowe and Alf Gregory had come up with Ang Nyima, Pemba and Ang Temba, the support team for the second summit attempt. Camp VIII was getting crowded.

Early in the day Evans and Bourdillon were spotted going strongly past the South Summit and out of sight, but there was no sign of them again until 3.30 p.m. when they emerged from the mist, staggering with exhaustion. They had climbed higher than

anyone had been before, but had neither enough time nor enough oxygen to continue to the summit and return safely. Tenzing and Hillary raced out to meet them with hot soup as they stumbled across to the tents, and George Lowe recorded their progress. It made dramatic viewing in the expedition film.

That night at the Col the tents were packed, the wind relentless, the temperature well below freezing, and sleep almost impossible. Hillary described the situation in the pyramid tent: 'I looked into a scene of utter confusion. Greg was lying stolidly full-length on his air mattress…Lowe was struggling with a half-inflated air mattress, a sleeping bag and some bottles of oxygen…Tenzing, sitting cross legged, effectively occupied the rest of the room as he watched with an inscrutable air a vast yellow flame, three feet high, which was surging from a kerosene stove between his knees … I forced my

way inside, keeping a wary eye on the flaming cooker and giving a few helpful suggestions as to how to get it going properly.'[25] Eventually they were all squeezed in, the stove was working well and they had a meal of biscuits, jam, honey, sardines, dates, chocolate, cheese, tinned fruit, soup – and lashings of hot lemonade. The next day the wind was still too fierce to attempt a climb, but Hunt, Evans, Bourdillon and Ang Temba – all completely drained – lurched unsteadily back down to Advance Base. There was no radio contact between the Col and Advance Base; they would have to sit there and wait for news.

Three Sherpa climbers

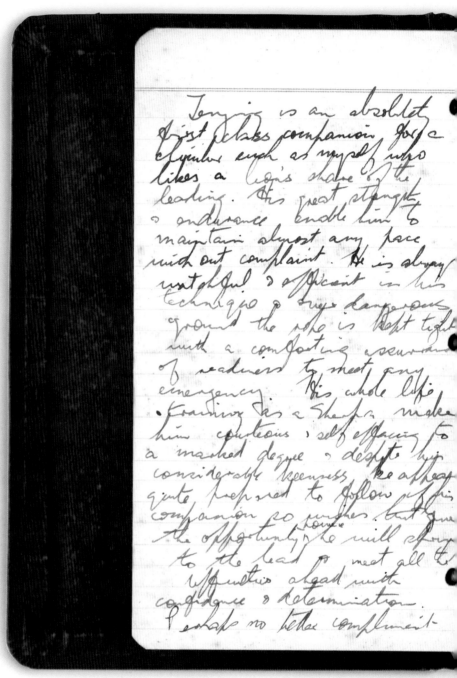

DAWA THONDUP
Took part in Himalayan expeditions from 1933, and was decorated by Hitler for his gallantry during a storm on **Nanga Parbat**, when six Sherpas and three Germans lost their lives. He was the forty-ninth Sherpa to be awarded the **Himalayan Club's Tiger Medal**; he climbed on Annapurna in 1950; and to the **South Col of Everest in 1952 and 1953**. In his late forties, he was the veteran of the 1953 team but out-performed many younger men.

ANG NYIMA
Climbed and carried to the **South Col of Everest** with the 1952 Swiss expedition. In 1953 he worked alongside George Lowe in terrible wind and snow conditions breaking a path across the **Lhotse Face**, and carried an eighteen kilogram (forty lb) load to **Camp IX** at 8504 metres (27,900 ft), where Hillary and **Tenzing Norgay** spent the night on 28 May. He climbed on many Himalayan expeditions and reached the summit of **Annapurna II** (7937 m; 26,040 ft) in 1960. Later he served with the **Gurkha Rifles** in Malaya and Borneo.

DA NAMGYAL
Climbed to the **South Col of Everest** with the Swiss in 1952. On 26 May he and John Hunt carried a tent, food, fuel and oxygen to 8340 metres (27,350 ft), for Hillary and **Tenzing** to use on their summit climb, then returned to the **South Col** without oxygen themselves. Ed was at **Camp VIII** when they returned. 'I looked at **Da Namgyal**. Faithful and strong, he is a magnificent type of Sherpa, and as he had looked after me in the earlier part of the expedition I had a particular affection for him. His cheerful and determined smile showed he still had a little strength in reserve.'*

Left: Ed Hillary's camera – a Type 118 Kodak Retina with a Zeiss Tessar lens and Compur shutter, made in 1935 and purchased second-hand in Auckland
Krzysztof Pfeiffer

64

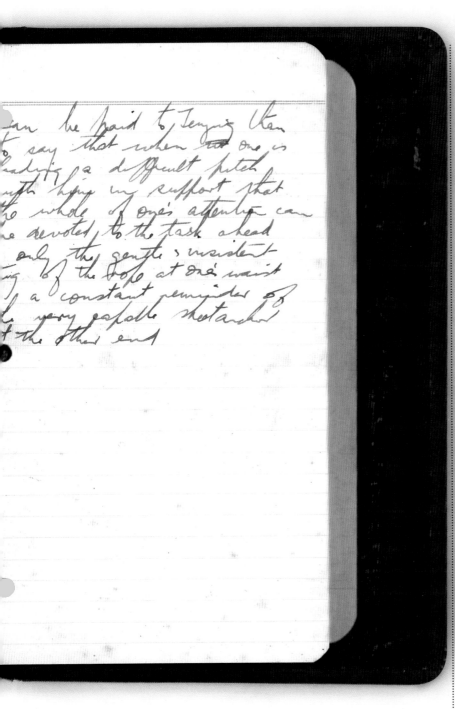

Tenzing Norgay
**FROM EDMUND HILLARY'S
1953 EXPEDITION DIARY**

Above right: Hillary and Tenzing
just below Camp IX at 8504 metres
(27,900 ft). Hillary is now carrying
more than twenty-eight kilograms
George Lowe

Tenzing is an absolutely first
class companion for a climber
such as myself who likes a
lion's share of the leading.
His great strength & endurance enable him to maintain
almost any pace without
complaint. He is always
watchful and efficient in his
technique & over dangerous
ground the rope is kept tight
with a comforting assurance of
readiness to meet any
emergency. His whole life and
training as a Sherpa make him
courteous, self-effacing to a
marked degree and despite his
considerable keenness he
appears quite prepared to
follow if his companion so
wishes. But given the opportunity he will spring to the
lead & meet all the difficulties ahead with confidence &
determination.

Perhaps no better compliment
can be paid to Tenzing than to
say that when one is leading
a difficult patch with him
in support that the whole of
one's attention can be devoted
to the task ahead & only the
gentle and insistent tug of
the rope at one's waist is a
constant reminder of the very
capable sheet anchor at the
other end.

The Carry to Camp IX, 28 May 1953

George Lowe set off first with Alf Gregory and Ang Nyima, cutting steps for Hillary and Tenzing to follow. All were carrying heavy loads and breathing oxygen at four litres a minute. Into a light cloth bag Hillary forced an extensive array of essentials: a sleeping bag, an air mattress, spare socks and gloves, down socks, a spare pullover, two spanners for the oxygen sets, two masks and tubes for sleeping oxygen, a pencil and paper, two boxes of matches, sticking plaster, two packets of dates, two tins of sardines, a half-used carton of honey, a few packets of lemon crystals, a tin of apricots in syrup, his camera and exposure meter. 'My cloth bag was almost bursting at the seams under this load, and although cold reason told me that most of this food wasn't really essential, I couldn't summon up the courage to part with any of it. I had already checked my oxygen set with its two light alloy cylinders of oxygen, and onto this I tied my bulging bag. I eyed it all gloomily. Including my camera and exposure meter, it must weigh nearly 50 lb.'[26]

After climbing 450 metres (1500 ft) they reached the stores carried up by John Hunt and Da Namgyal two days before: 'an impressive pile of oxygen bottles, a tent, food and fuel, and all of it essential for our high camp. We sat down on the ridge and looked at it ... We didn't even know if we *could* carry it.' After some discussion Ed agreed to take the 14.5-pound Meade tent if George would make the route ahead. They shared out the rest of the gear. 'I squatted down ... and gradually eased the weight on to my back. Grunting with the effort, I slowly tottered to my feet. I felt as though I was being crushed into the earth, I'd carried 63 lb. and more many times in New Zealand – it was never any fun, but we did it because we had to – but carrying such a load at 27,400 feet made quite a difference ... it was encouraging to find that I could move at all.'[27] This was a superhuman effort in the face of the general wisdom that fifteen pounds (6.8 kg) is a full load at altitude. They pushed on slowly, desperately tired, and at last found a small sloping shelf – just workable as a site for Camp IX. They were now at 8504 metres (27,900 ft).

The support group had to start back down, and as Ed farewelled them he struggled to control his emotions. These three men – his old friend George, the tough and nuggety photographer Alf Gregory, and cheerful Ang Nyima – forcing themselves on under enormous loads, were the embodiment of the effort which had brought him and Tenzing to this final point. In the pocket of his windproofs was the little cross that John Hunt had given him down on the Col and in his ears Hunt's words about the thousands of people who had pinned their hopes on this venture: 'Ed, the main thing is to get down safely, but I know you'll get to the top if you possibly can.'[28] Tenzing and Hillary watched the others descend, feeling intensely lonely on their little ledge. Now it was all up to them.

Camp IX, 28 May 1953

Without using oxygen, and working in ten-minute spells, they scraped away the surface snow and in the frozen rubble beneath managed to create two small terraces barely two metres long and a metre wide. One was fifteen centimetres higher than the other. Over these they put the Meade tent, securing the guy ropes somewhat precariously with oxygen bottles buried in snow and a network of ropes up to the rocks above them. Just below the tent the slope became a sheer rock face. While Tenzing got the stove going, Ed checked their oxygen for the next day. They didn't have enough left for the recommended four litres a minute, but with lighter loads they might be able to manage on three. That left enough for four hours of sleeping oxygen at one litre a minute. Inside the tent Tenzing made chicken-noodle soup, and they had biscuits, dates and the usual hot lemonade. The apricots were the luscious finale to the meal – once they had thawed out the frozen cylinder that slid from the tin. Tenzing decided to keep his boots on for the night and struggled into his sleeping bag on the lower ledge. It was very cold and they had brought only their outer bags from the South Col to save weight. Ed couldn't resist taking off his boots and putting on some dry socks. He then worked himself into his sleeping bag, but couldn't lie full length, so twisted across the airbed and

66

Hillary and Tenzing starting up
the Lhotse Face, 25 May 1953
Alfred Gregory

Food on
the mountain

Reduced appetite is a common complaint at altitude, so the climbers had to be strongly encouraged to eat to maintain their fitness. In an appendix to John Hunt's book *The Ascent of Everest*, Griffith Pugh and George Band wrote: 'Some men may become intolerant of fatty foods; some hanker after special foods which may not be available. High up on Everest in 1933 Shipton had a craving for a dozen eggs; Smythe wanted Frankfurters and Sauerkraut; in 1924 Somervell's favourite diet was strawberry jam and condensed milk; on Cho Oyu Hillary wanted pineapple cubes ... In general, men prefer to eat nothing rather than something that is distasteful to them, and if they do not eat they deteriorate all the more rapidly.'* Rice, potatoes, eggs and some meat were purchased locally; everything else was shipped from Britain and many firms donated supplies. At Base Camp and at Advance Base they ate in the mess tent, and the expedition's cook, Thondup, was a key contributor to group morale. Wilfrid Noyce wrote in *South Col*: 'The day was memorable for the most delicious scones. Thondup at his best could turn out something delectable, to be remembered for days; and any-

thing like bread was especially welcome. The addition of butter and jam raised the scones to one of the spheres of Paradise.'† The weight of supplies was reduced by vacuum packing, a new technique in 1953, so they had a reasonable variety of foods. A standard daily ration pack for two men at a high camp weighed four pounds (1.8 kg). It contained rolled oats, milk powder, sugar, jam, sweet biscuits, a mint bar, cheese, boiled sweets, salt, cocoa, tea, soup and lemonade powder. Climbers were able to substitute items in the packs with food from 'luxury' boxes they had selected themselves. Luxuries included tinned fruit, sardines (particularly popular), sweetened condensed milk, chutney, orange juice, ham, cheddar cheese, saucisson, brandy and rum. Sherpas at the high camps had the same rations with an allowance of *tsampa* – the roasted barley flour which is a staple of the Sherpa diet. *Tsampa* is eaten dry or mixed into a porridge with water and butter.

67

Left: Ed Hillary's 1953
expedition mug
Krzysztof Pfeiffer

poked his feet into the lower corner of the tent, across Tenzing's legs. It was not a comfortable night. The wind kept sweeping over them in roaring gusts and Ed braced himself against the upper corner of the tent, waiting for the whole camp to take off down the mountain. He was amazed at Tenzing's calmness on the lower ledge. With oxygen they managed to sleep from nine until eleven, but woke up cold. More hot, sugary lemon drinks passed the time until one a.m. They turned on the oxygen for another two hours, woke at three, shivered until four, then heaved themselves up to look out of the tent. It was 32°C below zero and a beautiful morning.

Tenzing pointed to Tengboche in its lovely setting 5000 metres below, where the monks would be performing their early-morning devotions – 'perhaps, as they had promised to do, they were at this moment turning their eyes up towards us and praying for our well-being'.[29] Again Tenzing got going on the primus while Ed knocked the ice off the oxygen sets and checked that everything was working. The sets were fine, but his boots were another story. They were

frozen solid. 'Obviously drastic measures were called for, so I put the stove between my knees and started to cook my boots in its fierce heat. Refusing to be cowed by the smell of burning leather and rubber, I persisted with this strong treatment and finally ended up with a pair of boots that were somewhat singed but at least malleable enough now to go on to my feet.'[30] They put on all the clothing they had – string singlet, woollen underclothes, woollen shirt and pullover, down trousers and jackets, windproofs over everything, three pairs of gloves, snow goggles. Around Ed's neck, tucked under his jacket, was his little Kodak Retina camera with a new roll of colour film.

To the summit, 29 May 1953

They set off at 6.30 a.m., crampons and oxygen sets strapped on, ropes attached and ice-axes in hand. Tenzing led at first since Ed's boots were still pretty inflexible, and they alternated the lead from then on. They encountered the 'mountaineer's curse' – breakable crust. But struggling for balance, and heaving themselves

out after each step, they were heartened to find two oxygen bottles, left by Evans and Bourdillon, with enough in them to ensure some oxygen at least for the downward journey. On one very steep slope the surface broke away and carried Hillary more than a metre downwards before it slithered out of sight and left him standing. 'My whole training told me that the slope was exceedingly dangerous, but at the same time I was saying to myself "Ed, my boy, this is Everest – you've got to push it a bit harder!" My solar plexus was tight with fear as I ploughed on.'[31]

From the South Summit at 9 a.m. they looked across to the vital ridge leading to the summit. Evans and Bourdillon had described its difficulty, and it certainly looked impressive. 'In the narrow crest of this ridge, the basic rock of the mountain had a thin capping of snow and ice – ice that reached out over the East face in enormous cornices, overhanging and treacherous, and only waiting for the careless foot of a mountaineer to break off and crash 10,000 feet to the Kangshung glacier.'[32] They cut themselves ledges to sit on and shared a drink from

The view from the summit of Chomolungma/Mount Everest (8850 m; 29,035 ft), at 11.30 a.m. on Friday 29 May 1953
Edmund Hillary

Tenzing's water bottle. Hillary checked their oxygen again. It was time to move on to their second bottles. He continued with his mental arithmetic and decided that, at the worst, they could reduce to two litres a minute on the way back. On the next stretch they found hard, crystalline snow, perfect for cutting steps. 'It was exhilarating work – the summit ridge of Everest, the crisp snow and the smooth easy blows of the ice-axe all combined to make me feel a greater sense of power than I had ever felt at great altitudes before.'[33] But their most formidable obstacle still lay ahead.

In 1951 on the Everest Reconnaissance Hillary had seen this great rock step through glasses from Tengboche, and it was visible in aerial photographs too, but no one knew quite how difficult it would be. Climbing steep rock at this altitude is fiendishly hard and dangerous, and crampons are made to grip ice and snow, not rock. At first Hillary could see no way around it. Then at the right-hand edge of the rock he saw a possibility. 'Overhanging the precipitous East face was a large cornice. This cornice, in preparation for its inevitable crash down the mountainside, had started to lose its grip on the rock and a long narrow vertical crack had been formed between the rock and the ice.'[34] It was worth a try, but first the arithmetic had to be done again: '– 2,550 lb. pressure. (2,550 from 3,300 leaves 750. 750 over 3,300 is about two-ninths. Two-ninths off 800 litres leaves about 600 litres. 600 divided by 180 is nearly 3½.) Three and a half hours to go.'[35] This kind of calculation is impressive enough at sea level.

Tenzing made a good belay and Hillary stepped into the crack. 'I took a hold on the rock in front and then jammed one of my crampons hard into the ice behind. Leaning back with my oxygen set on the ice, I slowly levered myself upwards...Constantly at the back of my mind was the fear that the cornice might break off, and my nerves were taut with suspense.'[36] Eventually, gasping for breath, he hauled himself out on top and the rope came tight – its twelve metres had been just enough. Once he had recovered, Hillary leaned over and waved to Tenzing who jammed his way up too. 'For the first time in the whole expedition I really knew I was going to get to the top.'[37]

But there was still more step-cutting to do around the undulating ridge, which bore away to the right, giving them no idea where the top was. They were both tired now, and their confidence was fast evaporating. 'And then I realised that this was the last bump, for ahead of me the ridge dropped steeply away in a great corniced curve, and out in the distance I could see the pastel shades and fleecy clouds of the highlands of Tibet.'[38] Hillary had been haunted by the idea that the summit might be the top of a precarious cornice, but with a strong belay from Tenzing he cut his way to the top of this last ridge and saw ahead a firm, rounded, snowy dome. They had done it. 'A few more whacks of the ice axe, a few very weary steps, and we were on the summit of Everest.'[39] And in Tenzing's words:

'We stepped up. We were there. The dream had come true.'[40]

We didn't feel that
we had conquered
Everest, we felt
that Everest had
relented.
EDMUND HILLARY

Tenzing Norgay on the
summit, 29 May 1953
Edmund Hillary

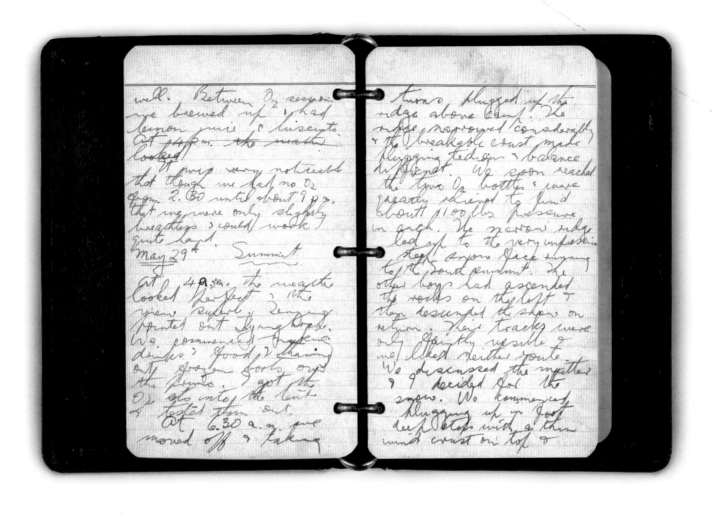

Above: Ed Hillary's 1953
expedition diary, summit
pages
Krzysztof Pfeiffer/Shaun Higgins

Left: The world's highest
snack – Kendal Mint Cake,
still made by George Romney
Ltd in Kendal, Lancashire,
England, and supplied to
expeditions since 1918
Jennifer French

05
AFTER
THE
CLIMB

Those fifteen minutes Hillary and Tenzing spent on the summit became the defining moments of their lives. They would never escape the effects of that particular dream coming true. So what did they do on the summit? They both told the story many hundreds of times. Ed went to shake hands with Tenzing, who threw his arms around Hillary's shoulders in utter delight. Hillary admitted being a little embarrassed, but nevertheless they thumped each other on the back in mutual congratulation. Ed took off his oxygen set, fumbled in his jacket for his camera and photographed Tenzing standing on the summit, ice-axe aloft, flags fluttering. Then he photographed all the ridges leading to the summit – and thought ahead to his next climbing challenge, noting a possible route up Makalu, a difficult adjacent peak.

Tenzing said prayers and buried in the snow some sweets and a special coloured pencil from his daughter Pem Pem. Remembering the cross John Hunt had given him, Ed put it beside Tenzing's offering: 'Strange companions, no doubt, but symbolic at least of the spiritual strength and peace that all peoples have gained from the mountains.'[1] They sat down and shared some Kendal Mint Cake, its icy flavour perfectly suited to the location. And they looked out across the vast expanse of the Himalayas: snowy peaks, valleys and plains reaching to the far horizon. It was a glorious day.

Then they heaved up their oxygen packs, clamped masks on to their faces and set off down the mountain. Hillary picked up and put in his pocket a few small rocks to take home. It was a tiring journey – along the summit ridge, back down the rock step, to the oxygen bottles left by Bourdillon and Evans. They stopped at the little camp for a hot drink, then loaded up again and, moving carefully, dropped down and down and down, to the last steep couloir above the South Col and the ragged little cluster of tents that was Camp VIII.

That night Hillary, Lowe and Noyce squashed into the two-man Meade tent on the Col, enjoying the warm fug from the primus, drinking the ubiquitous hot lemonade, and mulling over the summit climb and the whole team's effort on the mountain. Tenzing and Pasang Phutar were ensconced in the other small tent.

The next day they headed back to Advance Base. No one there knew the outcome of the climb, and the uncertainty had everyone on edge. Tension hung in the air. Just after two o'clock, five small figures appeared plodding down the Cwm, giving no sign of jubilation, and John Hunt's heart sank. They were all alive, thank heavens, but his feet felt leaden as he walked up to meet them. Then George Lowe gestured vigorously upwards with his ice-axe, and Hunt broke into a run, rushing to envelop first Ed, then Tenzing in his arms, pounding them on their backs and weeping with joy. 'The relief and the release of tension was like nothing I've ever felt, before or since.'[2] Tom Stobart filmed the ecstatic scene as Hillary and Tenzing, thin and tired, but with the broadest of grins, received

the congratulations of their fellow climbers and Sherpas: at last they were the triumphant Everest team.

Ed's conscientious attention to fluid intake and careful management of the oxygen supply had contributed greatly to the resilience of the summit pair. Griffith Pugh and Michael Ward, whose medical research set new guide-lines for surviving at high altitude, had drilled the climbers well. That afternoon James Morris raced off down through the icefall with Michael Westmacott to send his coded message to *The Times* and to the world. The climbers heard the announcement of their success on the BBC when they got back to Base Camp, and the realisation began to dawn that some tumultuous scenes lay ahead.

After the first flush of excitement, everyone rested before the long walk down to Kathmandu. George Lowe described the scene in a letter home: 'don't imagine our band of thirteen rolling and rollicking in an ecstasy brought on by victory. If you were at Base Camp now you would see nine sahibs and about fifteen Sherpas lying listlessly around the tents with bloodshot and glazed eyes, thin, dirty and bewildered. Ed is now sleeping as he has done for hours and hours, Charles is just smoking and tired; the talk is very desultory and dull; everyone is quite played out…Two days ago we were on the South Col urging ourselves to the limit – and now like pricked balloons all our reserves are gone.'[3]

The physical strain of going above 8000 metres is so extreme that it can take many weeks to recover completely, but Ed woke up eventually and wrote an aerogramme to his mother. (Mail runners were regularly taking letters from Base Camp to Kathmandu.) He opened in a self-deprecating tone: 'Dear Mother, Well, I may not have produced much joy and happiness in the world but at least I've helped make the Hillary name a bit famous.' He ended: 'What a lot I'll have to tell you on my return. John Hunt fully expects us to be introduced to the Queen and heaps of important people so it should be great fun…Love to Dad, Ed'.[4] Thirty-three-year-old Ed sounds like an excited boy as he breaks the great news. Percy and Gertrude's joy, and pride, at their son's success can only be imagined.

Right: Tenzing Norgay and George Lowe at Camp VIII on the South Col
Alfred Gregory

Below: George Band, Ed Hillary, Charles Evans and Michael Ward listening to a broadcast of the Coronation of Queen Elizabeth II, 2 June 1953
Alfred Gregory

Another letter went to Louise Rose. Ed was in love with her, but still plagued by that adolescent conviction of his own unattractiveness. Louise's interest in him had been clear before he left for Everest, but even now, writing to 'Dearest Darling Louise', he didn't assume she was his. To Louise's father Jim he wrote: 'Well all the flurry and bustle is over, all the hard work is finished and at long last we've climbed the jolly mountain. Now Himalayan climbing can settle down into a more normal routine and the "Everest" sense of values can be put aside.' This was followed by a climber's account of the last ten days of the expedition and the summit, with many references to the work done by the whole team. But John Hunt's prediction was looking accurate: 'We've just heard by radio that the Queen and Winston Churchill have sent messages of congratulations to us at Kathmandu so we are understandably excited. Also old Sid Holland [New Zealand prime minister] has said some kind words. What a business!' He signed the letter 'a somewhat confused Ed'.[5]

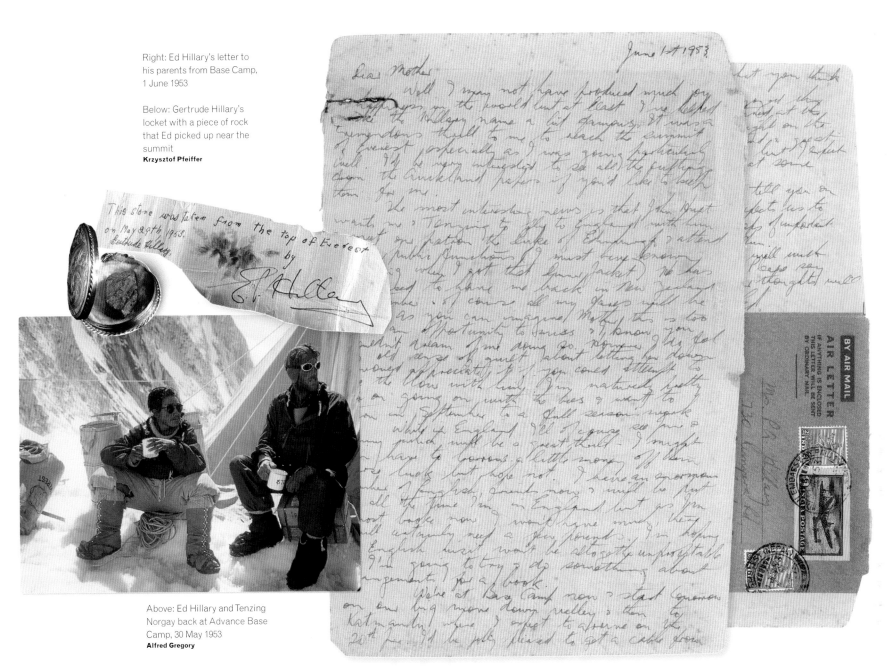

Every person who climbs the southern route on Everest today knows they are treading in Edmund Hillary's footsteps. His name is for ever associated with the mountain and with that steep rock step near the top – now called the Hillary Step. In 1953 Ed too was conscious of other, earlier footsteps on Everest. Recalling his feelings on reaching the summit, he wrote: 'My first sensation was one of relief ... But mixed with the relief was a vague sense of astonishment that I should have been the lucky one to attain the ambition of so many brave and determined climbers.'[6] As a young man he had immersed himself in Eric Shipton's lucid and evocative mountaineering books, and had been enthralled by *Camp Six*, Frank Smythe's brilliant account of the 1933 Everest expedition: 'With

Smythe I climbed every weary foot of the way up the North side of Everest. I don't think I have ever lived a book more vividly. I suffered with Smythe the driving wind and the bitter cold and the dreadful fight for breath in the thin air. And when he was finally turned back at 28,000 feet, I didn't regard it as a defeat, but a triumph.'[7]

Ed Hillary's comments to friends immediately after the climb reflect this awareness of finishing something others had begun. When the summit pair returned to the South Col and George Lowe asked, 'How'd it go, Ed?' Hillary replied with his usual wide grin and in a tone of some surprise, 'Well, George, we knocked the bastard off.'[8] His words were jokingly repeated among the climbers, and Alf Gregory recalls Ed being a bit worried that they might

get back to New Zealand and to his family: 'They wouldn't like their Ed saying "bastard".'[9] The famous line did get back of course and, whether he likes it or not, has clung to Ed Hillary's story ever since. Many years later John Hunt commented wryly: 'I wasn't altogether surprised, because it was so typical of Ed to say something slightly jocular and down-to-earth like that. I possibly had hoped that he would send some message of very high spiritual value and so on to the world at large – but it wasn't to be.'[10] Wilfrid Noyce recalled Ed suddenly saying, in that tent high on the South Col, 'Wouldn't Mallory be pleased if he knew about this!'[11] Frank Smythe would have been pleased too – and particularly pleased that a Sherpa was one of the summit pair. Smythe knew that attempts on Everest would not be possible without Sherpa support, courage and fortitude, and hoped that when the struggle was finally won their names would stand out 'in letters of gold'.

When the party reached the Sherpa summer village of Pheriche at some 4245 metres, they were at last below the snow line. George Band described their delight in again seeing 'trees, forest, rhododendrons, grass and little running streams – and drinking tea that was really hot'.[12] Water boils at a lower temperature at altitude, so the climbers had been enduring less-than-hot tea – a particular trial for Englishmen and New Zealanders. After seven weeks of striving on that huge mountain, they were all longing for ordinary life – and real food. In an early letter home Hillary wrote: 'You've no idea how I've been pining for a rip-roaring old roast dinner',[13] and he and George Lowe had wondered if the New Zealand Alpine Club might put on a meal for them. They were still assuming that life would return quite quickly to normal.

Eric Shipton, on learning that the expedition had succeeded, knew that the flurry and bustle was far from over. He wrote to a friend acknowledging his own regrets, but saying, 'Of course I'm really delighted that it was Ed Hillary who pulled it off – he is a grand mountaineer and a delightful person: he is one of the few I know who has the strength of character to withstand the avalanche of public acclamation that is coming to him. And *nothing* could have been more fitting than that Tenzing should have been there to represent the Sherpas.'[14]

No one, however, was prepared for the controversy that erupted as the expedition neared Kathmandu. There was, of course, great rejoicing in Nepal – and in India, since Tenzing lived in Darjeeling – that a Sherpa had reached the summit of Chomolungma, dwelling place of the gods. But the climbers' euphoria evaporated when they were besieged by reporters asking, 'Who got there first?' Tom Stobart wrote later: 'It never entered any climber's head to even ask who was first. It just did not matter.'[15]

Hillary and Tenzing were not in a race – they were roped together and neither could have been there without the other. Both found the

questions embarrassing and distressing, and it was galling for Hillary to see painted banners showing Tenzing hauling him up to the summit. In Kathmandu itself the atmosphere was more positive, and after discussion with John Hunt, Hillary and Tenzing signed a statement that they had reached the summit 'almost together'. But the newspapers were not satisfied and in India the question kept coming. Two years later, in his 1955 autobiography, Tenzing wrote the following: 'A little below the summit Hillary and I stopped. We looked up. Then we went on. The rope that joined us was thirty feet long, but I held most of it in loops in my hand, so there was only six feet between us. I was not thinking of "first" and "second". I did not say to myself, "There is a golden apple up there. I will push Hillary aside and run for it." We went on slowly, steadily. And then we were there. Hillary stepped on top first. And I stepped up after him.'[16] But in interviews, both men refused to discuss the matter. In Hillary's words: 'We shared the work, the risks and the success – it was a team effort and nothing else is important.'[17]

They were welcomed back to hot baths, good food, beds they found too soft to sleep on, and endless parties in Kathmandu. Then it was on to Calcutta, Delhi and Bombay for more tumultuous crowds at airports and at official welcomes. The avalanche of presentations began, awards and tributes of all kinds,

BRITISH MOUNT EVEREST EXPEDITION, 1953
(Himalayan Joint Committee of the Royal Geographical Society and the Alpine Club)

Rongbuk Monastery.
17th June.

Dear Mr & Mrs. Hillary,

The walk out from Everest is nearly completed & as each day comes & goes the excitement & pleasure, that we receive by being flooded with waves of goodwill from the world, daily increases.

At first the satisfaction of the successful ascent seemed great enough reward. Now, after reading the Times & other papers of India, America & England we realise what a fillip this has given to British prestige & with Ed & John receiving knighthoods the wonders & excitements never cease. For all these things we are delighted & righteously proud.

You will be feeling indescribably proud of Edmund, I am too, & can assure you you have every reason for being so. Throughout the expedition he was a most prominent driving force in the activity on the mountain & very early on we all looked on him as the most likely 'summit hope.'

BRITISH MOUNT EVEREST EXPEDITION, 1953
(Himalayan Joint Committee of the Royal Geographical Society and the Alpine Club)

During the final few days of the climb his efforts became somewhat legendary & I was lucky to be with him on all except the final day. I went up, alone, above South Col to welcome them down expecting to see two wrecks but they walked in in a matter of fact way tired but grinning like pleased cats.

The floods of cables received have given us all great pleasure & here I would like to thank you both for the cable of goodwill & congratulations that you kindly sent to me.

Three days ago when Ed received a note, addressed Sir Edmund Hillary K.B.E, he nearly fell flat & was most embarrassed. Everyone here was delighted at the honour & along with John he will carry it most worthily.

With the kindest regards to you both & sincere thanks for the many kindnesses you have shown me since I have known Ed.

Yours sincerely
George Lowe.

Above: George Lowe's letter to Ed Hillary's parents, 17 June 1953

Above left: 'Official' portrait of the successful summit team at Base Camp
Alfred Gregory

74

Above: Hillary and Tenzing in Kathmandu, June 1953

pa 100

British Embassy,
KATMANDU.

16th June, 1953.

Dear Mr & Mrs Hillary

This is to thank you most sincerely for your generous telegram of congratulations; I have picked it out of many hundreds we have received because I was so touched by your kind thought.

It may seem superfluous to add anything to the tremendous volume of praise which has been poured out over Ed's wonderful achievement. I would like to add my small word, however, as leader of the Expedition, to tell you what a tower of strength he has been within the team throughout. I always knew that we had a match-winning pair in Hillary and Tensing, provided that the rest of us could do our small bit in placing them high enough on the mountain for the final bid.

Yours sincerely,

John Hunt.

Above: John Hunt's letter to Ed Hillary's parents, 16 June 1953

Left: Pandit Jawaharlal Nehru, Prime Minister of India, greeting Tenzing Norgay, John Hunt and Ed Hillary in Delhi, 28 June 1953

but also the chance to meet the first prime minister of India, Pandit Jawaharlal Nehru, whom Hillary described as 'an enormously impressive person'.[18]

Tenzing was deeply impressed too. Tenzing's wife Ang Lhamu and their two daughters travelled with him and stayed at Rashtrapati Bhavan, the prime minister's residence in Delhi. The *Times of India* asked Ang Lhamu if Tenzing had special lungs. She replied: 'Why special lungs only? He has everything special – lungs, heart and smile. As for determination – I have never seen a more determined smile.'[19] Later, in one of the 'Nehru suits' that Nehru had given him from his own wardrobe, Tenzing – and his smile – were a sensation at London receptions.

The other climbers were surprised, bemused, occasionally irritated and eventually resigned to the lionising of two members of their party. Their responses were hardly surprising, as the British had put a great deal into Everest expeditions and had come to see it as 'their' mountain – it had certainly been their money, their research, their planning and

organisation. But Ed and Tenzing were both well liked, and everyone was impressed with their achievement. Wilfrid Noyce, an outstanding climber, wrote: 'Even from that first, fragmentary account, full of mountaineering understatement, it was easy to judge that it had been a superb climb, by two companions worthy of it and climbing as a rope of two should.'[20] Two weeks later George Lowe, himself the hero of the Lhotse Face, wrote to Percy and Gertrude Hillary from Rizingo Monastery on the way down to Kathmandu. 'You will be feeling indescribably proud of Edmund. I am too, & assure you you have every reason for being so. Throughout the expedition he was a most prominent driving force in the activity on the mountain & very early on we all looked on him as the most likely summit hope. During the final few days of the climb his efforts became somewhat legendary and I was lucky to be with him on all but the final day. I went up alone above the South Col to welcome them down expecting to see two wrecks but they walked in in a matter of fact way tired but grinning like pleased cats.'[21]

From Kathmandu John Hunt was moved to answer a congratulatory telegram he received from Ed's parents: 'I would like to add my small word...as leader of the Expedition, to tell you what a tower of strength he has been within the team throughout. I always knew we had a match-winning pair in Hillary and Tenzing, provided that the rest of us could do our small part in placing them high enough on the mountain for the final bid.'[22] For John Hunt, Tenzing Norgay and Ed Hillary, the Everest aurora would be permanent; for the other team members the glare of success was more thinly spread and hence more manageable – they could withdraw from the limelight when they'd had enough. All went on to excel in their various fields, and to continue climbing without having every step and every slip recorded. On another Himalayan climb in 1957, Wilfrid Noyce looked back at Everest and pronounced it 'splendid as a corporate venture but illuminated in retrospect by "a light that never was, on sea or land".'[23]

Rex Hillary the hardworking beekeeper, with the blessing of his wife Jenny, took out a mortgage on their house and flew to London to

Right: Tenzing Norgay wearing the Nepal Tara, George Medal, Coronation Medal and other decorations, Darjeeling, 1953

Far right: Pasang Phutar's eldest child wearing his father's Coronation Medal, presented by Charles Evans at Tengboche Monastery in 1954. Pasang Phutar was away with another expedition **George Lowe**

Above: June, Ed and Rex Hillary at Heathrow Airport, 2 July 1953

Above: Sir Edmund Hillary KBE wearing the Nepal Tara, Coronation Medal and other decorations, London, 16 July 1953

be there when Ed arrived. June and her husband Jimmy Carlile were at the airport too. When the group of tall, smiling Everest heroes finally emerged from the aircraft (other passengers on the flight had been asked to scurry off first) they met a barrage of cameras and cheering well-wishers – and the three Hillary siblings were reunited. Eric Shipton was there too, with a congratulatory bunch of bananas for Ed, who polished them off in the taxi back to London.

Ed and George Lowe stayed with New Zealand climbing friends, Norman and Enid Hardie. Norman was working as an engineer but had assisted with Everest expedition preparations at the Royal Geographical Society, and Enid taught at Saint Christopher's School for Girls. Ed and George gave a talk at the school – the first of many. They became a highly entertaining double act, although Ed always said that George's wit got everyone rolling in the aisles, so it was easy for him to follow up with the serious stuff.

The media gave a speedy assessment of the climbers' entertainment value at press conferences. A reporter from the *Glasgow Herald* wrote: 'It soon became obvious that Sir Edmund

Hillary is going to be a box-office draw when the Royal Geographical Society begins its series of lectures on Mount Everest…Sir Edmund has a happy turn of phrase – "the summit of Everest is a nice cone and does not rise to a particular point. At least, we sat down on it and ate some food, which would indicate that it was not very pointed." ' The reporter was delighted to note that Ed looked like a Scot or an Irishman with his 'long bony face, lean jaw and wide grin (Sir Edmund never succeeds in merely smiling).'[24] The grins kept getting broader as Ed and George enjoyed their 'wild colonial boy' image, and commented that their diet was now restricted to champagne and smoked Scottish salmon.

The whole team, including Hillary family members, was invited to Buckingham Palace, where Hunt and Hillary were knighted; Tenzing Norgay was awarded the George Medal; and the climbers received special Coronation Medals. There were medals for the high-altitude Sherpas too, and Charles Evans presented these at Tengboche the following year.

Gertrude Hillary's comment that 'There should have been 14 knighthoods' was quoted approvingly by a writer to the *Statesman* in

Calcutta as the summit controversy raged.[25] In fact, it was Ed's next achievement that was dearest to her heart. On 12 July he wrote to her with exciting news. He had been complimented by editors at *The Times* for his two articles describing the ascent, and best of all: 'Your greatest wishes for me appear to be coming true as it rather looks as though I'll be writing a book.' The publishers had offered him 'a deposit of £5,000 on account – just imagine it!' He would be home for August, then back in London for six lectures at the Royal Festival Hall, followed by a world lecture tour. 'What a life Mother! It's been very nice having Rex here, and great fun greeting June and Jimmy again. The children are great fun too and we are old friends already.'[26] June and Jimmy's home in Norwich was a

Right on the dot of 3.40 there was a roar in the western sky and <u>Aotearoa II</u> came diving low over the waiting crowds. It was then, Mr Lowe said later, that Sir Edmund turned from the window and remarked 'Gosh, this is going a bit too far.'

New Zealand Herald,
10 August 1953

welcome retreat. They spent many hours driving to and from London to attend receptions and functions for the climbers, and June wrote long, chatty letters to Percy and Gertrude to keep them in the picture.

Sir Edmund Hillary and George Lowe flew in to Sydney on 5 August 1953 hoping for three quiet days. Instead they were welcomed with a civic reception and constantly pursued by reporters. It was widely assumed that the newly knighted bachelor must be in want of a wife and Ed fielded media questions on this important matter. He had had a number of proposals of marriage since he and Tenzing climbed Everest: 'Many aspirants sent along their photographs…One asked me to return her picture if I were not interested. I did.'[27] The only woman he wanted was Louise Rose, and he was delighted to see her again in Sydney, but still couldn't find the confidence to propose – even as Sir Edmund Hillary, the hero of the day. Their future together remained uncertain until he was back in Auckland. There, after more euphoric welcomes, official speeches and receptions, he was reunited with Percy and Gertrude, and spent time with his old friends Jim and Phyl Rose. He confessed to Phyl that he wanted to marry Louise, but didn't have the courage to ask her. 'Would you like me to ring her?' asked Phyl. And she did: 'Louise, Ed wants to marry you.' Louise was delighted to accept.

Ed and George Lowe spent the next three weeks touring the country, giving lectures in packed halls and making New Zealand hearts swell with pride. They were told what people had done when they first heard the news: some Maori university students broke into an impromptu haka on the platform of Gisborne Railway Station,[28] climbers at Arthur's Pass wrote in the hut book, 'Ed Hillary climbed EVEREST', and followed it with a cartoon of Ed and Tenzing flying down the mountain on the back of an enormous bee – umbrella aloft.[29] There was a huge pile of mail to deal with too. All the children at a tiny sole-teacher school in Arero, near Gisborne, signed a letter to Percy and Gertrude: 'We just want you to know how happy we all are that your son and his brave companion are safe, and to express our joy at hearing of their accomplishment. Present and future school children will draw inspiration from this event, which shows so clearly, how the greatest of obstacles can be overcome by team-work and confidence, and by hard individual work.' Meanwhile, Rex had returned to the bees and resigned himself to an absent partner for another season.

Left middle: Leaving Mechanics Bay on Saturday afternoon – Sir Edmund, his mother, Mrs P. A. Hillary and Mr George Lowe.

New Zealand Herald,
10 August 1953

Left bottom: At a civic reception in the Town Hall, the Mayor of Auckland, Sir John Allum, presented Sir Edmund with an 'Everest' chair on behalf of the citizens of Auckland.

Below: Ed Hillary on a jungle gym with schoolchildren, August 1953. Ed Hillary and George Lowe met and entertained thousands of New Zealanders on a three-week lecture tour around the country

Auckland Star

AUCKLAND, N.Z., MONDAY, AUGUST 10, 1953 (One Shilling and Threepence a Week Delivered) — **PRICE 3D**

A Knight in bed

It was a tiring week-end. A triumphant homecoming and civ[ic] reception on Saturday; broadcast and reception at home yeste[r]day, as well as a dozen and one things an Everest conquero[r] must do. Bed came after midnight. So this morning Sir Edmun[d] Hillary was a late riser. But there's no rest—even in bed—f[or] the famous. Hundreds of telegrams were waiting to be rea[d] when he awoke.

Letters and press clippings from family scrapbooks. Percy and Gertrude Hillary were inundated with letters of congratulation. The letters on this page are from Ed's fellow climber Earle Riddiford and from Noel Odell, who was with George Mallory on Everest in 1924 and on the 1938 expedition led by Harold Tilman. He became professor of geology at the University of Otago, Dunedin

"I like musicians!"
EVEREST KNIGHT TO MARRY YOUNG N.Z. VIOLA PLAYER

SIR EDMUND HILLARY.
(By Radio Telephone from N.Z.)

Everest conqueror, Sir Edmund Hillary (34) announced today that he would marry 22-years-old Auckland music student, Louise Rose.

In an exclusive interview Sir Edmund told the Daily Mirror that the marriage would be in Auckland on September 2 or 3.

Miss Rose, who is in Sydney studying the viola at Sydney Conservatorium, will leave for New Zealand on Saturday.

When in Sydney last week Sir Edmund and Miss Rose saw each other frequently.

He and Miss Rose have been friends for years.

Speaking from his bee-farm at Papakura,

a suburb of Auckland, Sir Edmund said today: "We'll be married on . . . er . . . the first Tuesday in September. No that can't be right. Hang on a minute . . . September 2 or 3.

"Then we'll have our honeymoon on my lecture tour of En-land.

"Louise doesn't know anything about bees, but she's interested in mountain climbing.

"Am I a musician?" Sir Edmund chuckled.

"No, but I like musicians."

Everest 13/8/53

Sir Edmund Hillary
Conquistador del Everest
Auckland
Nueva Zelandia

Box 776
Wellington
8th June

Dear Mr & Mrs Hillary

May I join with thousands of others in saying how delighted & proud I was to hear the wonderful news of Ed's magnificent achievement & of the honours bestowed on him so well deserved. Knowing some of the difficulties involved I find it difficult to express my admiration of Ed's supreme effort. I have happy memories of your kind hospitality before we went away in 1951.

Yours sincerely
Earle Riddiford

P.O. BOX 56   Dept. of Geology
University of Otago
DUNEDIN, N.Z.

7 June 1953

Dear Mr & Mrs Hillary

In view of the second instalment of the wonderful news from Everest, as announced today, I feel that I must write you a note of warmest congratulation on the honour bestowed by the Queen on your son Edmund, who has at last achieved the summit of that wonderful Mountain. It really is grand to know that by his arduous preparation, & by his skill in mountain-craft he has been enabled to make this outstanding contribution to the success of the British party. I may add that on hearing the news last Tuesday, I sent your son & Tensing, a cable of congratulation, as well as one to my old friend John Hunt, now also suitably decorated. I am indeed proud to know all three of them, since Tensing Bhutia was one of our party to Everest in 1938. Incidentally, you may know of Tilman's comments on "Purba Tensing" (as he was then known) in Mount Everest, 1938, p. 30: he was then a promising 'lad' of 21 years, but since had become technically probably the best of all the Sherpas. It is gratifying to know that one of those grand hill-men, who have served us so well on all these Expeditions, was with Edmund in the crowning achievement.

With kind regards & renewed congratulation
Yours sincerely
N. E. Odell

Stuttgart 1
504 a
Einschreiben Zu

Edmund Hillary
breeder of bees (beefarm)
& conquest climber of the Mount Everest"
Neuseeland

Louise Rose

Growing up in a family who enjoyed life in the outdoors, **Louise Rose** was an enthusiastic walker and loved being in the mountains. Vivacious and with a ready sense of humour, she attended **Diocesan School for Girls** in Auckland and went on to study music at **Auckland University** – she was a gifted viola player. **Ed Hillary** was a regular visitor at her parents' home. 'Louise was a musician, friendly, cheerful and very energetic, and she was quite a bit younger than me. But we had much in common and I guess there was some significance in the fact that she was also the daughter of the president of the **New Zealand Alpine Club.** I had known **Jim Rose** well for several years before I really became aware of the bright young thing who seemed to rush in and out of his house on odd occasions.'* **Louise** won a scholarship for the **Diploma Course**

at the **Sydney Conservatorium of Music.** She sailed for **Sydney** at the end of 1952, and when **Ed** saw her off at the boat it felt like the end of the world. But **Louise** insisted that he visit her on his way to Everest, and the following March they spent two happy days together. 'We sat on the grass in the **Sydney domain** and listened with great pleasure to outdoor musical concerts. We walked hand in hand across the **Sydney Harbour Bridge** and halfway across I kissed **Louise** for the first time. This was a major breakthrough for me.'[†] From Singapore **Ed** wrote to **Louise:** 'Here I am on a trip that I suppose any **New Zealand** climber would be mad keen

to go on and I spend all my time thinking of something quite different – in fact you!... As long as I can keep you thinking of me now and then it will be a start.'[‡] **Ed Hillary** and **Louise Rose** were married in the chapel of **Louise's** old school just a month after **Ed** returned from **Everest.** Accepting that her husband would often be away from home, she became the much-loved centre of the family for him and for their children, **Peter, Sarah** and **Belinda.** She played the viola in the **Auckland String Players** and later in the **Auckland Symphonia,** was an active member of the **Himalayan Trust** and worked hard raising funds for the trust's projects with the **Sherpas.**

Left: Louise Rose on a climbing holiday in the Southern Alps, 1952

Far left: Louise Rose with her viola, c. 1950

Phyllis and Jim Rose

Archibald Clark, Jim Rose's grand-father, emigrated from **Scotland** in 1849, becoming the first mayor of **Auckland** in 1851 and a member of the **Provincial Council. Jim Rose** also contributed greatly to the life of **Auck-land.** A lawyer by profession, he was on the council of the **Auckland Institute and Museum Committee** from 1951 to 1970 and president from 1959 to 1961. A very keen climber, he served several terms as chair of the **Alpine Club's Auckland** section, and in 1953 was chairman of the **New Zealand Alpine Club. Ed Hillary** greatly valued **Jim** and **Phyl Rose's** intelligence, experi-ence, good humour and frank common sense, and their support for **Louise** when he was away from home.

Above: Phyllis and Jim Rose, Louise's parents

82

Sir Edmund Hillary and Louise Rose were married at the Diocesan School Chapel on 3 September 1953 – Louise's twenty-third birthday. George Lowe was best man. As they left the church they walked under an arch of crossed ice-axes held by New Zealand Alpine Club members. They emerged into the sunshine to be met by a barrage of press cameras, and by crowds waiting outside the school gates to cheer the hero and his bride. Among the hundreds of telegrams they received was one from Tenzing Norgay. It read: 'Heartfelt wishes for a happy marriage. May God bring you a long life together. Your Everest comrade, Tenzing.' And it was to be an extremely happy marriage: 'I quickly learned how fortunate I was to have such a wife. Louise was warm and loving, yet very independent, with a great love of the outdoors and a multitude of good friends...'[30]

The morning after their wedding, Ed and Louise flew out of Auckland with George Lowe for a five-month lecture tour around England and on to France, Scandinavia, Belgium and Italy. Charles Evans and James Morris joined them in North America, and they told the Everest story twelve to fifteen times a week. Their audiences were exhilarated, but Ed found the constant lecturing tiring – he was now unmistakably a public face and a focus of attention. Louise could always tease him into good spirits, but he was met with high expectations on many fronts. 'I read your comments Mother in your last letter with some despair... not only do I realise that I'm far from perfect in the social graces but as long as I'm being rushed madly about as at present I'm not likely to remember people's names. I fear your standards are too high for me...Would you mind telling Rex that the financial arrangements have not yet been finalised but I anticipate forwarding some money in the next week or so and will write then. Love, Ed'.[31]

Finances were definitely a worry. Ed had borrowed to pay Louise's airfare to Britain; he had to pay Rex for help with the bees; and although he was often told that he would 'never have to work again', he was working hard. The climbers were paid £25 for each lecture they gave, and the remaining proceeds established the Mount Everest Foundation to support future expeditions.

The New Zealand Alpine Club had already received permission from the Government of Nepal to send an expedition to the Barun Valley, east of Mount Everest in 1954. There were many fine peaks in the area, including the giant Makalu (8475 m; 27,804 ft) which Ed had assessed from the summit of Everest. He was to be the expedition's leader. Ed was reluctant to let the Alpine Club down, but had written to Jim Rose from Everest, before the summit climb, to say that he felt he could not afford to return to the Himalayas in 1954. 'Every year for the last four years I've rushed off from the bees, leaving Rex to clear up all the tag ends. Even though he is compensated financially for this it is small recompense for the worry, trouble and nuisance he has to put up with...it's certainly not fair to Rex and if I want to make a reasonable thing out of the bees I've no alternative but to stop this now yearly habit.'[32] From Calcutta on 27 June he wrote again to Jim: 'Irrespective of my participation or not, all my gear etc. is of course available for use and naturally anything I can do to assist in raising money will be done.'[33]

Right: Ed and Louise Hillary boarding the flying boat for Sydney, 4 September 1953

Far right: Louise Rose leaving her parents' house for her wedding, accompanied by her father, Jim Rose, 3 September 1953

Press clipping in a Hillary family scrapbook
Jennifer French

Conqueror of Everest Weds Auckland Girl

Sir Edmund and Lady Hillary leaving the chapel under an archway of ice axes.

The bride in her wedding frock of white nylon marquisetto over old gold satin.

The crowd surrounding the car after the ceremony.

But staying home for a year after he had climbed Everest proved impossible, and in the end he agreed to go. The advance on his book helped a little, but Ed's guilt about leaving Rex to cope persisted until 1959 when he finally acknowledged that his beekeeping days were over.

Ed and Louise returned from America on 15 March 1954, but only had a week together, and for the first time in his life Ed felt 'a strong reluctance to leave home'.[34] On 25 March he and George Lowe were off to the Himalayas again.

They remembered the beauty of the Barun Valley – and the tempting array of unclimbed peaks that encircle it – from their 1952 explorations. An American party had been given permission for an attempt on the Makalu climb, but the New Zealanders hoped to tackle Baruntse (7184 m; 23,570 ft), Chamlang (7319 m; 24,012 ft) or Ama Dablam (6856 m; 22,494 ft) – once they had mapped and explored the area. Three of the ten climbers, Hillary, Lowe and Evans, had been on the Everest expedition the previous year, and Norman Hardie and Jim McFarlane were both civil engineers with surveying experience. It was a very experienced team. The burden of organisation had been undertaken by the Alpine Club Committee in Dunedin, and in London, New Zealand climber Bill Packard negotiated some excellent deals on equipment – a vital part of any expedition's preparations. *The Times* was providing some money and in return the expedition's leader would write stirring articles for readers keen to hear about Hillary's next climbing exploit. Frank Smythe described the task of writing dispatches after a hard day's climbing as 'one of the penalties of leadership'.[35] Of course articles are particularly riveting if things go wrong, and on this expedition there would be two casualties – one of them Ed Hillary himself.

They travelled overland from India with the usual long caravan of porters through the rugged Himalayan foothills, across the Arun River and over a snowy pass into the Barun Valley. Their Sherpas included several from the Everest expedition, including the sirdar, Dawa Tenzing, whom Ed described as 'magnificent'; and a young man, Mingma Tsering, who would become Ed Hillary's closest Sherpa friend and fellow worker in the years ahead. Their Base Camp was at 4720 metres (15,500 ft), under the dramatic ice-clad face of Makalu. Evans and Lowe each led surveying groups which headed off with photo-theodolites they had been lent by the Royal Geographical Society, while Ed, Jim McFarlane and Brian Wilkins went on a four-day reconnaissance of the Barun Glacier.

On the last day Ed returned to their camp to get things organised – they intended to join the others lower down that afternoon – while Wilkins pushed on a little further with McFarlane, who was keen to look over a nearby pass to Tibet. The afternoon drew on and Ed was becoming worried at their lateness, then Wilkins, exhausted and bleeding from his face, staggered into camp with the news that they had both fallen into a crevasse. Jim McFarlane was injured and still trapped.

Ed rushed out into the gathering darkness with some Sherpas to attempt a rescue, but couldn't manage to extricate Jim, and cracked several of his own ribs while he was being lowered into the crevasse. The Sherpas were frightened and Ed desperately concerned, but it was now pitch dark and all he could do was

84

Above and right: Ed Hillary's photographs of Louise in the gardens of Government House, Singapore; in Iceland; and at an airport in America. Ed and Louise Hillary at Val d'Isere ski resort in France, on their lecture tour/honeymoon
Edmund Hillary

Left: Ed Hillary recording the introduction to Queen Elizabeth II's 1953 Christmas broadcast.

My wife and I are spending Christmas Day with my sister's family in just about the flattest place in England: in Norfolk, not so very far from the Queen's home at Sandringham while the Queen is spending her Christmas Day in Auckland, my home town...I'm very proud to have been chosen to send you New Zealand's Christmas greeting and the greetings of the whole Commonwealth... A Happy Christmas Your Majesty. Welcome to New Zealand.

N.Z. team bound for Himalayas

Four members of Sir Edmund Hillary's 1954 Himalayan expedition aboard the *Wairata* before she sailed for India today. From left: B. J. Wilkins (Dunedin), G. Harrow (Christchurch) C. J. McFarlane (Invercargill), C. M. Todd (Dunedin).

Left: Press clipping showing four members of the New Zealand Alpine Club Himalayan Expedition to the Barun Valley, about to sail to India, 13 February 1954. (L–R) Brian Wilkins, Geoff Harrow, Jim McFarlane and Colin Todd
Jennifer French

Below: Ed Hillary in Nepal, April 1954
Colin Todd

Above: Return to Auckland, March 1954

lower down some sleeping bags and insist that Jim get into them for the night. At five o'clock the next morning, fortified by sleep, Ed and Brian Wilkins started back up. They called down into the black depths of the crevasse and were overjoyed to hear a faint reply – Jim was still alive, but very weak and cold. Wilkins climbed down to attach a harness to him and eventually, after several attempts, they brought him safely to the surface. But Jim hadn't managed to get into his sleeping bags, and his hands and feet were badly frostbitten. There followed the nightmarish task of bringing the injured man down, on a stretcher made from three pack frames and an air mattress. Five Sherpas carried him over the rocky glacial moraine, with Ed and Wilkins taking turns being the sixth on the stretcher. But at 5800 metres the effort was enormous. 'My chest was hurting me abominably and Wilkins seemed at the end of his tether,' Ed recalled.[36] They stopped to make camp and Ed went on for help, arriving at Base Camp the following day, where 'George Lowe's strong, confident figure came towards me and I felt a lifting of my burden.'[37] Jim McFarlane was

eventually carried back to Base Camp – sixteen kilometres in four days. The expedition doctor Mike Ball, with help from Charles Evans, looked after him until he recovered enough strength to face the long journey out to India.

Ed was keen that the rest of the party still do some climbing. Their surveying had been successful and Makalu was a tantalising challenge. The Americans attempting the difficult southern ridge had not reached the summit and they were happy for the New Zealanders to try to reach the North Col of Makalu (7560 m; 24,800 ft) and from there maybe attempt Makalu II, the lower summit. Ed was becoming bored with inactivity. He was convinced his chest was healing well, could not resist going along, and the initial forays went well. Charles Evans, Geoff Harrow and Bill Beaven established a high camp at 6700 metres (22,000 ft) and George Lowe and Norman Hardie reached the same height reconnoitring the route. But as they were about to push on, disaster struck. Ed collapsed and fell face down in the snow. When he recovered consciousness, George Lowe was tying him to a makeshift stretcher. He was

85

severely dehydrated, with lung damage caused by his cracked ribs. Everybody was needed to help carry him down. The Makalu attempt was off, and the expedition had another invalid.

With careful nursing from Charles Evans, who also diagnosed a recurrence of the malaria Ed had contracted in the Pacific during the war, he gradually recovered, and after ten days could walk down to Base Camp. He then accompanied Jim McFarlane out to India. Porters carried McFarlane in twenty-minute relays, in a packing-case seat strapped to their backs – heroic work. It was twenty days' walk to Dharan, and then by truck to Jogbani and rail to Calcutta. McFarlane flew home to New Zealand and spent months in hospital, eventually losing half of each foot and both his little fingers. Ed greatly admired his courage in the years after Makalu: 'He carried on his profession as a successful engineer and re-established himself as a competent sportsman. He was a strong and brave man.'[38]

Hillary's illness made headlines, of course. The American expedition sent out a report, and John Hunt was asked to produce an obituary for *The Times* – just in case. But Ed survived to acknowledge the efforts of his team and analyse his own errors. Of the injury from that first desperate rescue bid, he wrote: 'I immediately realised I had made a mistake, I had tied the ropes around my waist instead of taking most of the weight around my thighs or feet. Already the rope was cutting into me, crushing my chest and restricting my breathing…'[39] And he later described his decision to push on with the climbing group as 'unbelievably stupid'.[40] But he took great delight and pride in the successes of the other members of the expedition. Wilkins, Ball and Hardie climbed Pethangtse (6730 m; 22,080 ft); Hardie did an outstanding job surveying the head of the Barun Glacier and making the first crossing of a dangerous pass into the top of the Imja Glacier; and Todd, Harrow, Lowe and Beavan all climbed the expedition's major objective: Baruntse. In all, twenty-three peaks were climbed for the first time, nineteen of them over 6000 metres. Hillary's report to the New Zealand Alpine Club analysed all aspects of the expedition and concluded that despite the two rescue operations

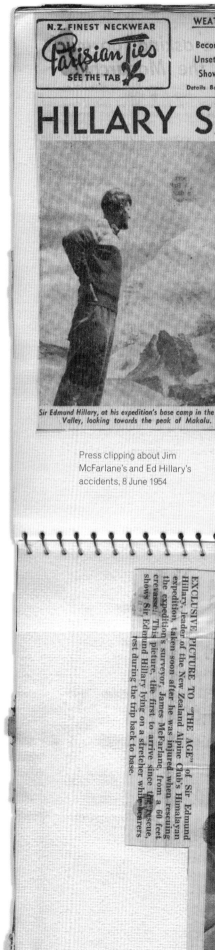

Press clipping about Jim McFarlane's and Ed Hillary's accidents, 8 June 1954

a lot had been achieved. 'We have produced a group of New Zealand climbers who have proved that, temperamentally and physically, they can climb to considerable heights, with every prospect of going a great deal higher.'[41] He was right. This pattern of New Zealand expeditions making first ascents of Himalayan peaks would continue with Ed Hillary's building expeditions to Sherpa villages in the 1960s. But Ed himself would undertake no more Himalayan climbs.

Back in New Zealand Ed was reunited with Louise who had been staying with her parents for four months. They needed somewhere to live, and the Roses had offered to sell them some land adjacent to their own home in Remuera, not far from Ed's parents' home. It was steeply sloping, covered in old fruit trees and looked out across Auckland Harbour. Gummer and Ford Architects designed a modest house which they both loved. Ed went back to working on the bees with Rex, and wrote his first book *High Adventure*. The book was enthusiastically received, sold well and paid for their new house, so finances were not such a worry. In an interview before his wedding Ed had said: 'One could spend a lifetime climbing mountains in New Zealand without running out of new ones to try', and he was back in the Southern Alps before long, making a first ascent of Mount Magellan.[42] But he turned down an invitation to lecture in Japan because he was so enjoying life at home with Louise and their new baby Peter, who was born in December 1954. Louise was well aware that marrying Ed Hillary would mean 'being a grass widow for 50 per cent of the time'.[43] Her resilience, independence and good humour carried her through the challenges with style. And her charm and social ease were a blessing for her husband who was now such a public figure. They were a contented new family.

87

Top and middle: Ed and Louise Hillary with their son, Peter

Left: Harry Ayres and Ed Hillary after the first ascent of Mount Magellan in the Southern Alps, 6 February 1955

Like most people of my generation I had read the absorbing stories of Scott and Shackleton and felt enormous respect and admiration for their deeds. My ideas of Antarctica were hazy in the extreme and, if I thought about it at all, I imagined a sombre land of bitter cold and heroic suffering, of serious men dedicated to impossible ideals, and of lonely crosses out in the snowy wastes – not really my cup of tea at all.
EDMUND HILLARY

Dog teams and sastrugi on the Polar Plateau. December 1957
Roy Carlyon

06
TO THE
ICE-FIELDS

Reading about exploration in remote places always whetted Ed Hillary's appetite for adventure. In 1945 two books transported him from the boiling heat of the Solomon Islands across thousands of kilometres to the frozen expanse of Antarctica. *The Worst Journey in the World* by Apsley Cherry Garrard tells the story of Robert Falcon Scott's *Terra Nova* expedition from 1910 to 1913. *The Home of the Blizzard* is Australian scientist Sir Douglas Mawson's account of two years in Antarctica at about the same time. These are gripping tales of battles with the elements, of comradeship, of triumph and of wrenching tragedy. Apsley Cherry Garrard's dearest friends, Bill Wilson and Birdie Bowers, both perished with Scott on the return journey from the South Pole. Mawson lost two sledging companions: Ninnis vanished into a crevasse and Mertz succumbed to frostbite and starvation as they struggled across nearly 400 kilometres of icy waste to their camp. Ed wrote home to his parents: 'I wouldn't mind a trip to the Antarctic, though I'd much prefer going to the Himalayas.'[1]

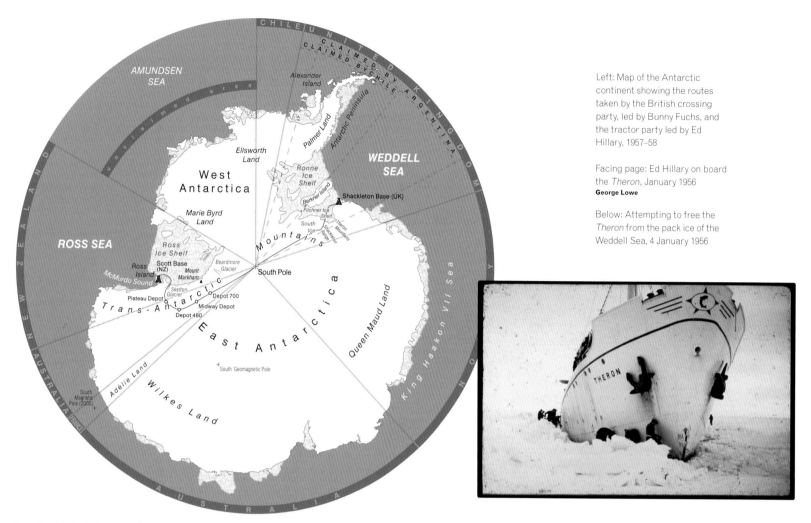

AMUNDSEN
SEA

West
Antarctica

WEDDELL
SEA

ROSS SEA

Ellsworth
Land

Alexander
Island

Palmer Land

Antarctic Peninsula

Ronne
Ice
Shelf

Shackleton Base (UK)

Berkner Island

Filchner Ice
Shelf

Marie Byrd
Land

South
Ice

Mountains

Ross
Ice Shelf

Scott Base
(NZ)

Ross
Island

Beardmore
Glacier

Mount
Markham

McMurdo Sound

Skelton
Glacier

Plateau Depot

Depot 700

Midway Depot

Depot 480

Trans-Antarctic

East Antarctica

Queen Maud Land

South Geomagnetic Pole

Adélie Land

Wilkes Land

King Haakon VII Sea

South
Magnetic
Pole (2000)

CHILE
UNITED KINGDOM
CLAIMED BY ARGENTINA
CLAIMED BY CHILE

unclaimed area

NEW ZEALAND

AUSTRALIA

NORWAY

Left: Map of the Antarctic
continent showing the routes
taken by the British crossing
party, led by Bunny Fuchs, and
the tractor party led by Ed
Hillary, 1957–58

Facing page: Ed Hillary on board
the *Theron*, January 1956
George Lowe

Below: Attempting to free the
Theron from the pack ice of the
Weddell Sea, 4 January 1956

90 By 1955 he had been on four expeditions to the Himalayas, and Antarctica was at last in sight. In London, after Everest, he had met British scientist and explorer Dr Vivian Fuchs, known as 'Bunny'. Fuchs hoped to cross Antarctica from one side to the other – Ernest Shackleton's original plan for the 1915 *Endurance* expedition. Since he was now a public figure and national hero, Hillary's involvement could help Fuchs gain the New Zealand Government's support. Hillary did endorse the scheme, and Louise's father, Jim Rose, was in the Antarctic Society's deputation to the minister of defence in January 1955. The society requested government support for both the International Geophysical Year and the Commonwealth Trans-Antarctic Expedition. Apart from the obvious benefits to scientific knowledge there was wide-spread public enthusiasm for the adventurous nature of the project.

International Geophysical Year (IGY) lasted from July 1957 to December 1958. In a cooperative effort to increase scientific knowledge of the Earth's surface, climate and atmosphere, twelve countries built more than forty scientific stations on the Antarctic

mainland. The Ross Sea Committee was formed in Wellington in May 1955, and in June they sent a telegram to Ed Hillary in Johannesburg, where he was lecturing with George Lowe. It was an official invitation to lead the New Zealand part of the Commonwealth Trans-Antarctic Expedition.

Bunny Fuchs and Ed Hillary had little in common except Antarctica. While Hillary's main drive was his love for adventure, Fuchs was primarily a scientist, and colleagues saw their personalities as poles apart. But the expedition was too exciting to turn down. Hillary went from Johannesburg to the International Antarctic Conference in Paris, and then to London to work with Fuchs on the plans.

Britain would set up Shackleton Base on the Weddell Sea. New Zealand's Scott Base was to be across the other side of Antarctica on the Ross Sea, near the United States base at Hut Point on McMurdo Sound. The Americans were also planning to build the Amundsen–Scott Station at the South Pole itself. Rear Admiral George Dufek of America's Antarctic programme, Operation Deepfreeze – who was to be one of Ed

Hillary's key friends and supporters in Antarctica – made the first landing at the South Pole in a Skymaster plane on 31 October 1956, before building equipment, fuel and supplies were flown in. New Zealand's task was to establish food and fuel depots for the British crossing party between the South Pole and Scott Base, but as soon as he was appointed Hillary began imagining a larger adventure. In July 1955 he wrote from London to Arthur Helm, secretary of the Ross Sea Committee: 'Although the journey objective of the New Zealand end must be the establishment of a dump at Mount Albert Markham, we should plan to have sufficient supplies and equipment so that if organisation and time permits, or an emergency occurs, the Party could travel out as far as the South Pole.'[2] To reach the South Pole overland – the aim of Roald Amundsen, Robert Scott and Hillary's great hero Ernest Shackleton: the challenge was irresistible.

Preparations began immediately. Four New Zealanders travelled with Bunny Fuchs to Antarctica in December 1955 on the *Theron*, a Canadian sealer. They were Ed Hillary, leader

Above: 'Plan N.Z.' in Ed
Hillary's *Theron* diary

of the New Zealand party; Bob Miller, senior surveyor and deputy leader; Squadron Leader John Claydon, in charge of the RNZAF Antarctic flight; and George Lowe, who was invited by Fuchs to join the British crossing party. Lowe was employed as its official photographer, and Fuchs also made the wry request that he help with interpreting New Zealand messages. Ed was primarily an observer on this voyage, but he was surprised not to be included in Bunny Fuchs's regular executive meetings: 'I don't think Bunny had any concept of how irritating I found this.'[3]

The establishment of Shackleton Base was fraught with difficulties. After trying unsuccessfully to find a new route through the frozen Weddell Sea, the *Theron* spent three weeks stuck in the ice. It finally arrived at Vahsel Bay on 30 January, very late in the season, and the men had to unload supplies for the wintering-over team directly on to the sea ice. When a tractor broke down, it was discovered that all the spare parts were buried under other cargo in the second hold. Several of the men had never driven cars before, let alone tractors. After

a severe storm, supplies waiting to be transported to the base site froze solid to the ice shelf; and when winter sea ice forced the *Theron* to leave on 6 February, they had not had time to move everything. A few weeks later all the coal, 300 drums of fuel, a Ferguson tractor, the timber for the workshop, a heavy wooden rowboat and the boat gear all floated out to sea in a storm which broke part of the ice shelf away. The six men who remained at Shackleton for the winter lived in a converted Sno-cat packing case, after relentless wind and blizzards prevented them from finishing their hut.

Hillary noted all this and determined to make the New Zealand team as efficient – and self-reliant – as possible. They had one year to get everything ready. He noted in his diary: 'Stow cargo with efficient unloading in mind; get a vehicle off the ship early on to avoid leaving supplies on the ice; get a heated shelter up fast for men unloading sledges and vehicle mechanics; bring tradesmen down with the ship to work on hut building.'[4] On the voyage back to Britain he drew up a firm outline of the New Zealand expedition. And before returning to New Zealand

he went to Norway with Bob Miller and Fuchs's engineer David Pratt to see how the Norwegians had adapted the Ferguson tractors to work on snow and ice. He had driven Fergusons at Shackleton Base and thought they could be used as more than just workhorses around the base. An idea was forming in Ed's mind.

The usual pattern for Antarctic expeditions was to travel south in the summer, build a base, spend the winter making preparations, and set out into the field the following spring. The Scott Base wintering-over team of twenty-three men included the field party, base personnel, the two pilots and the IGY scientists. Harry Ayres was one of the dog-team drivers – Ed was determined to include him in this adventure after the Everest debacle. A team of builders would also come down for the first summer to assist with unloading the ships, and then construct the base. The huts had been pre-fabricated from insulated panels and the construction team practised assembling them at Rongotai College in Wellington. Hut layout is always a battle to cram everything into the minimum of space. Bunny Fuchs believed that

Right: Louise and Peter Hillary, Mount Cook National Park village, August 1956
Edmund Hillary

Below: Ed Hillary, Mount Cook, August 1956
Louise Hillary

Below: Families visit the New Zealand Antarctic team's training camp at Mount Cook, August 1956. (L–R) Louise Hillary, Peter Hillary, Helen Cranfield, Helen Claydon, Noela Claydon, Richard Claydon, Jan Miller, Marjorie Miller, Roger Miller, Graeme Ayres, Jeanne Ayres, Jane Ayres

92 everyone should sleep in the same room to prevent cliques forming, but Hillary thought every man should have his own cubicle and some privacy. 'I therefore designed what we jokingly called the "Hillary Bunk"…It was merely a two-tier bunk with the bottom bunk opening out on to one side and the top bunk on to the other.'[5]

The whole expedition team spent August 1956 based at the Malte Brun Hut, beside the twenty-eight-kilometre Tasman Glacier near Mount Cook. There they improved their skiing and sledging with the dog teams, and tested the ski-planes. Driving practice with the Fergusons was part of the training too. 'I finished up the training period feeling that it had been well worth while. We had found weaknesses in equipment and even in men, and these we set to work to eradicate, but in general my confidence in the party had been strengthened. I realised that it was impossible to create an experienced band of Antarctic explorers in a month on an alpine glacier…but at least I had witnessed the transformation of a group of excellent individuals into the basis of a strong and united party.'[6]

Above: The view from National Park village, August 1956
Louise Hillary

Right: Louise Hillary and Jeanne Ayres with the Beaver aircraft
Edmund Hillary

Four years after Everest, Hillary was now thirty-seven years old, a husband and father (though often absent from home), and proving himself a leader of men.

Despite public fascination with the venture, there was not enough money, and New Zealanders seemed to think the government should supply all the funds. In desperation, Hillary, Lowe, Trevor Hatherton, Arthur Helm and other team members raced around the country giving inspiring lectures and whipping up support any way they could. On one particularly long day Ed flew 800 kilometres and gave four lectures. It was exhausting, but it worked. Soon schools were adopting huskies; 'Share in Adventure' Antarctic bonds were sold; and cake stalls, auctions, concerts, film evenings, raffles and dances were held to raise money. Many towns exceeded their fundraising target. Companies donated food, blankets, supplies and equipment of every kind; the Eastbourne Knitters made special pullovers for all the team; and a member of the Wellington Mountaineering Club knitted personalised scarves for them as well. The Scott Base Library would have 1000

donated books, including Sir Winston Churchill's *The History of the English Speaking Peoples* – sent by the author with his good wishes. The town of Feilding donated funds for an entire set of the *Encyclopaedia Britannica*. In the end, over £58,000 was raised from a population of two million – almost £35 for each New Zealander. There was not enough money for the 200-horsepower Tucker Sno-cats, but five twenty-eight-horsepower Ferguson tractors were lent by the British manufacturers. The Americans helped with two Weasels, with tracks for use on snow.

Meantime, Ed and Louise's second child, Sarah, was born in June 1956. With two small children, and a husband away organising and fundraising a good deal of the time, Louise Hillary's sterling qualities soon became evident. The family were still settling into their new house and working to get the garden established but Louise spoke to the media when called upon and accepted that she was a public figure now too. Not long before Sarah was born, Louise had unveiled a portrait of her husband by Edward Halliday RA at the Auckland War Memorial Museum. The painting was commissioned by

Sir Ernest Davis, who said: 'I want it to inspire the rising generation to emulate Sir Edmund's deeds. I view him as the excelsior of Auckland.' Excelsior or not, he was a busy man.

There was one more unexpected hurdle. When the *Endeavour* arrived in Wellington in early November, packed with expedition supplies from London, the lower hold had been flooded with sea water and almost everything was ruined. The casualties ranged from rations for men and dogs to wireless equipment, a washing machine, a sewing machine, electrical tools, tractor spares and much more. Frantic telephoning to companies around New Zealand resulted in a massive influx of goods to a Wellington warehouse, where everything was sorted, labelled and repacked by volunteers working around the clock. Finally there were the last few fundraising speeches and an official civil ceremony: the prime minister and the governor-general appointed Sir Edmund Hillary magistrate and postmaster, Dr Trevor

Hatherton coroner, and the *Endeavour*'s captain, Harry Kirkwood, assistant magistrate of the Ross Sea Dependency. On 15 December 1956, with her 500 tons of cargo packed in carefully thought-out order, the *Endeavour* sailed south. In Christchurch the team were farewelled again, this time by the Duke of Edinburgh, who invited them to dine 'dressed as they stood' on the Royal Yacht *Britannia*. Then on 21 December at Dunedin the band played 'Now is the Hour', and the *Endeavour* pulled away from the wharf. The mad rush was over, and Ed Hillary remembers tears welling up as he faced separation from Louise, Sarah and Peter. He would not see them again until March 1958 – almost sixteen months later.

The original plan was to build Scott Base at Butter Point on the Antarctic mainland. This would give direct access to the Ferrar Glacier – a potential route up to the Polar Plateau. The *Endeavour* arrived at the ice edge near Butter Point after two weeks at sea, and tractors were unloaded to reconnoitre the route to the site. But soft, slushy ice made progress slow, and there was a huge tidal crack to cross near the

foot of the glacier. Pilot John Claydon suggested looking at Ross Island itself. The Americans were already there, near Captain Scott's *Discovery* hut, and Admiral Dufek was keen to have New Zealand neighbours. Hillary went to have a look at Pram Point, about three kilometres from the American base. 'The more we walked around Pram Point the more my enthusiasm for it grew…To the north of us were the great volcanoes Erebus and Terror. To the south stretched the Ross Ice Shelf broken only by the low outlines of White and Black Islands. And to the west were the lovely mountains of Victoria Land. It had all the advantages of close proximity to the American Base and yet was still fresh and untouched.'[7] Scott Base is there to this day, a little green village, just over the hill from the scientific township that has mushroomed at McMurdo.

They set to work to unload the *Endeavour* and get building under way. All the components for each hut were removed together, and construction went speedily. 'On the morning of January 14th the floor of the large mess hut was laid down and by 9pm the same evening the hut was

Left: Unloading the
Endeavour, January 1957.
Tracks have been fitted over
the tractor tyres

Below: Scott Base covered
walkway under construction,
January 1957

Bottom: Scott Base after the
winter with drift snow
between the buildings and
the covered walkway,
September 1957

externally complete and we now had satisfactory
shelter...It looked a fine solid building and
we were very proud of it.'⁸ This hut, known as
'A' hut, was in regular use for more than forty
years. Other buildings swiftly followed, connected by corrugated-iron-covered walkways,
which allowed the inhabitants to move between
buildings without venturing outside.

Meanwhile, the dog drivers had found
that the Ferrar Glacier was no good as an entry
to the Polar Plateau. Hillary had to find another
way up to the plateau before winter set in. He
flew across the ice shelf to look at the Skelton
Glacier further south. It looked promising, so
again the dog teams were sent to reconnoitre.
They climbed 2400 metres to the Polar Plateau
and established the Skelton route; aircraft flew
in food and fuel; and by 12 February, only four
weeks after arriving in Antarctica, Hillary had
established a depot 470 kilometres from his
new base. The *Endeavour* sailed away on
22 February, taking the construction crew home
and leaving a very well-accommodated team
ready for the long winter.

Before winter closed in, Ed wanted
to test the tractors on a long trip. He decided
to retrace a journey made by Apsley Cherry
Garrard, Birdie Bowers and Bill Wilson in the

95

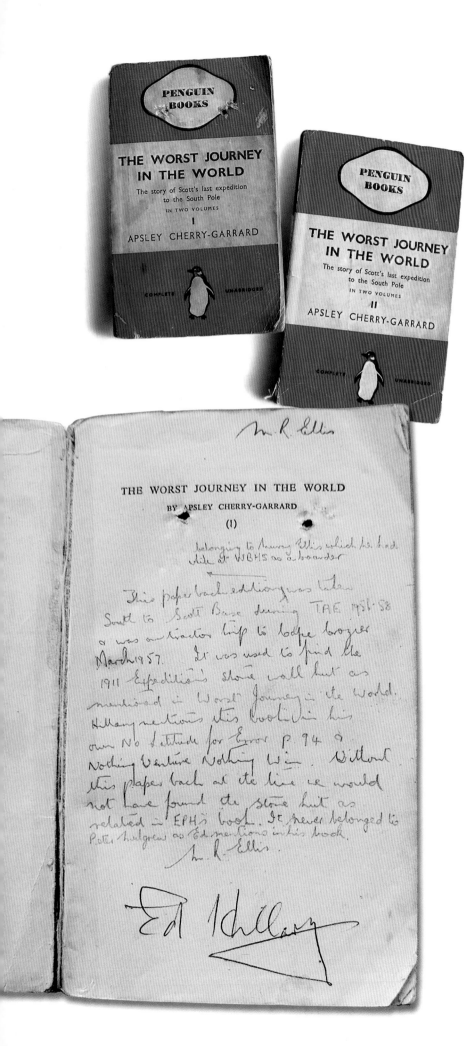

winter of 1911. They had trudged 100 kilometres through the polar night, hauling heavy sledges in soft snow and through blizzards across crevasses to reach the emperor penguin colony at Cape Crozier. Their aim was to gather some penguin eggs which Wilson hoped would prove a link between reptiles and birds. They got the eggs, although it nearly killed them, and were filled with admiration for the penguins themselves. Cherry Garrard, who described polar exploration as 'the cleanest and most isolated way of having a bad time', also wrote: 'I do not believe anybody on earth has a worse time than an Emperor penguin.'[9]

Retracing the trio's journey in tractors, while daylight still held, was less of a 'bad time', but posed its own challenges for Hillary, Murray Ellis, Peter Mulgrew and Jim Bates. After ploughing through soft snow in strong winds and freezing temperatures, they reached Mount Terror and The Knoll above the penguin colony where Wilson and the others had camped. Then, using Murray Ellis's rather battered copy of *The Worst Journey in the World* – appropriately enough a double Penguin – they succeeded in locating the abandoned campsite: 'four rock walls half filled with snow and ice, and the sledge peeping over the top with its wood polished white by forty-five years of this rigorous climate'.[10] It was a tangible link with brave men of the heroic era of Antarctica. 'Simmering with excitement', the New Zealanders carefully excavated

Above: Scott Base and the
Ross Ice Shelf, 1957
Edmund Hillary

the camp. The relics included a nine-foot man-hauling sledge, which had been the roof beam of the hut, and rolls of film marked, 'To be developed before May 1st, 1911'. They are now in New Zealand museum collections.

The return journey took fourteen long and miserable hours. When a tractor would not start at one refuelling stop, ice was discovered in the petrol line: 'Jim and Murray weren't in the mood for dilly-dallying and took drastic action. They lit a powerful blowlamp and played the flame on the fuel lines and petrol tank, and were successful in warming the fuel up sufficiently to melt the blockage out…Peter Mulgrew and I stood well back…waiting for the explosion.'[11] But all was well. 'The Old Firm' comprising Hillary, Ellis, Bates and Mulgrew was constituted on this trip. These four men now had experience in travelling and working with the tractors, and although there was still some work to be done on adapting their unusual vehicles, they were a good team. But for the spring journey Ed wanted them to have a heatable, windproof shelter in addition to the tents, and they worked on this over the winter.

Murray Ellis and Jim Bates had constructed a garage at the base from leftover building materials. Through the dark winter months the Ferguson tractors were adapted for the long journey ahead; the shelter or 'caboose' was built; and dog sledges were worked on. When there was enough moonlight, dogs were taken out for exercise on short trips. The scientists were hard at work too, and had all their equipment up and running for the start of IGY on 1 July 1957.

Winter routine at the base included lessons in navigation and in Morse code, but the lectures on Tuesdays at 4 p.m. were particularly informative. Topics included: '"Bull fighting – blood and tequila in Mexico City" by Don Roberto Miller; "The art of sacking" by Murray Ellis (Why *you* should buy an Ellis sleeping bag); "Thin sectioning" by Guy Warren (Probably about hardboard); and "Climbing in the Southern Alps" by Harry Ayres (The thrilling story of the man who accompanied Sir Edmund Hillary on some of his great climbs).'[12] They had the library and 500 donated gramophone records, and there were some cut-throat games of Bridge and Ludo. Americans visited occasionally and the

New Zealanders could watch movies over at Hut Point. A huge Marcus King painting of a sunny day on a Canterbury sheep station was a reminder of home, filling most of one wall of the mess hut, and another rural New Zealand landscape brightened up the radio room. Both paintings are still there.

The first radio-telephone service from Antarctica connected Scott Base with New Zealand, so the men could telephone home twice a week, but this was sometimes a trial when circuits cut out or conversations stalled. Ed recalls men retreating to the solitude of their bunks after radio misunderstandings. On one occasion he had to wait a week to discover that the loud scream and crash which had terminated his call to Louise was two-year-old Peter dropping his plate of cereal on the floor. On Sundays they had a church service, and because it was also the cook's rest day they were exposed to a range of cooking skills. Early on Hillary and Ayres attempted a particularly ambitious menu which left them exhausted and their 'distended victims' in some discomfort, but overall it was a congenial group.

Far right: Ed Hillary sent regular telegrams to Louise while he was in Antarctica

Below and right: Sarah and Peter Hillary at home. Ed was in Antarctica for Sarah's first birthday, but home again for her second
Louise Hillary

Above and right: Peter and Sarah collecting mussels at Anawhata Beach and the view from the Roses' bach on the cliffs above the beach
Louise Hillary

A740 66 SCOTTBASE CK61 3RD 0730 +
278A
LADY HILLARY REMUERA AUCKLAND +
278A REMUERA RD.
REMUERA.
Rec'd
By
INLAND TELEGRAM
DATE-STAMP
3620
Sent 9/5
To 23169
By
Checked
Tele

RADIO COMMUNICATION HAS BEEN VERY POOR FOR SOME DAYS STOP
WILL TRY AND RING YOU AS SOON AS CONDITIONS PERMIT STOP
TEMPERATURE MINUS TWENTY THREE WITH WIND AND SNOW SO RATHER
MISERABLE OUTSIDE HOWEVER WE ARE VERY COMFORTABLE STOP HOPE
YOU HAVE PLANTED SOME CREEPERS OVER THE TRELLIS STOP THINKING
OF YOU ALL THE TIME LOVE + EDMUND ++

B 27 71/69 SCOTT BASE 21ST 1000Z +
LADY HILLARY REMUERA AUCKLAND +
278 REMUERA RD ZZ
Rec'd 10/57a
By
INLAND TELEGRAM
Tel. 142. 25,000 pads, 4/56—62379-749
DATE-STAMP
AUCKLAND N.Z.
22 APR 1957
TELEGRAPH
OFFICE
294
Sent 140
To 23169
By
Telephoned
Checked

· TRIED TO RING YOU ON SATURDAY NIGHT BUT PIHA EXCHANGE
WOULDNT REPLY STOP THRILLED WITH BROADCAST AND IVE CHANGED
MY MIND ABOUT YOUR BROADCASTING ABILITY STOP IT WAS
PERFECTLY CLEAR AND I HEARD EVERY WORD STOP GREAT FUN
HEARING PETER AND HE REALLY IS GROWING UP IT MADE ME FEEL
SORRY TO BE MISSING IT ALL STOP HOPE YOU HAD A PLEASANT
WEEKEND LOVE + EDMUND +

A3136 38 SCOTT BASE 28TH 0230
+ LADY HILLARY REMUERA
Rec'd 5/20
By
INLAND TELEGRAM
Tel. 142. 25,000 pads, 4/56—62379-749
DATE-STAMP
28 JUN 1957
Sent
To
By
Serial No.
Checked

+ WILL TRY AND RING YOU TOMORROW NIGHT BUT IN CASE CIRCUIT
IS UNSATISFACTORY PLEASE WISH SARAH A HAPPY BIRTHDAY STOPP
WILL LOOK FORSWARD TO GETTING SOME PHOTOGRAPHS OF HER ON
THE FIRST PLANE LOVE + LOVE EDMUND +

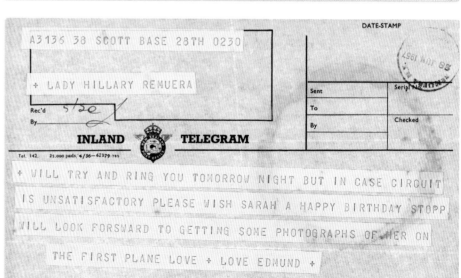

The Wintering Party in the mess room at Scott Base, 1956

Hillary's planning of the base accommodation helped reduce the inevitable tension that comes from seeing the same faces day after day and he knew he was fortunate in having the perfect deputy leader. Bob Miller, the senior surveyor in the New Zealand party, was described by Murray Ellis as having an understanding of human nature that could prevent small problems from escalating. 'People took their worries to him. If he thought they were important he would pass them on to Ed.'[13] But Ed's primary source of irritation was his communication with the executive of the Ross Sea Committee. The committee cabled in March 1957, suggesting that Hillary stick to the basic depot-laying plan and not attempt to reach the South Pole. When he replied with alternative ideas for mapping and geological exploration around the South Geomagnetic Pole, these were also rejected as too ambitious. Hillary, who saw the depot-laying as a fairly routine task, was convinced that the committee's caution was 'largely motivated by their fears of the unknown'.[14] He would keep all his options open and if he could get to the South Pole, he would.

The tractors head south
across the Ross Ice Shelf
away from Scott Base and
Mount Erebus
Edmund Hillary

07
TO THE POLE

We are heading hell-bent for the Pole – God willing and crevasses permitting.
EDMUND HILLARY

Winter eased eventually, the red sun returned, and everything was ready. On 14 October 1957 the three tractors and the Weasel set off, towing the caboose and sledges laden with fuel and equipment. Admiral Dufek and other well-wishers from Hut Point came to see them off, and a smoke bomb planted by Roy Carlyon under the Weasel added drama to the occasion – a portent of the problems ahead with that vehicle. Behind them were Scott Base, Observation Hill and Mount Erebus; ahead the vast expanse of the Ross Ice Shelf.

On Everest Ed Hillary had thought about the courage of past explorers. In Antarctica that awareness was even more acute. Scott and Shackleton had set out across here too, past White Island, Black Island and Minna Bluff – unchanging landmarks in the shimmering whiteness. After failures with vehicles and ponies on those earlier expeditions, men hauled sledges over huge distances – through crevasse fields, across craggy sastrugi (wind-carved ridges on the polar surface) and deep snow, and against biting, icy winds in the thin air of the Polar Plateau. Hillary had tractors to do the hauling, but like his hero Shackleton he knew the vital importance of an harmonious team – the South Pole was more than 1900 kilometres away. Grim determination would be needed for this journey, and a good dose of the usual expedition mixture – dry humour and practical resourcefulness.

102

The initial group was Ed Hillary, leader; Murray Ellis, engineer; Peter Mulgrew, radio operator; and Ron Balham, meteorologist and biologist. Jim Bates would join them once another mechanic arrived from New Zealand to take over his duties at Scott Base. The others in the Old Firm knew that Hillary hoped to go all the way to the South Pole, but they also knew there was a lot of ground to cover before it would become an issue. In the meantime, their first priority was to get out of sight of Scott Base. All eyes were on their progress.

Scott Base to the Skelton Glacier, 14–20 October 1957

Towing loads weighing almost eleven tons, the sturdy little Ferguson tractors coped well over the firm ice below the base. But only a few kilometres out, they struck soft snow. Ed Hillary's lead tractor began to labour, and then stalled. He looked back to see his front sledge, loaded with fuel drums, tipped over and disappearing into a crevasse. Antarctic crevasses are cracks in the ice surface, anything from a

few centimetres to metres across. Snow bridges form across the cracks, and once they freeze over the crevasse becomes an invisible trap, waiting to swallow the unsuspecting sledger, dog team – or motorist. This was a real blow. He hadn't expected crevasses until they reached White Island, fifty kilometres ahead. They unloaded the sled, hauled twelve 350-pound fuel drums to the surface, and then reloaded. 'We moved off again, keeping a close watch for crevasses … my nerves were jumping around'.[1] The surface continued to be heavy going, and by nine p.m. on the first day they had travelled only thirteen kilometres. Many more crevasses and many kilometres of deep soft snow lay before them, so Hillary decided to unload eight drums of fuel, cutting his margins very tight. At the South Pole, over two months later, he had only half a drum left.

Accurate navigation was vital for the success of their primary task: laying depots of fuel and food at agreed points for the British crossing party. The previous autumn Hillary's team had set several depots for themselves and at these they would rendezvous with the drivers of the New Zealand dog teams, who were mapping unexplored areas around their route. The aircraft operating from Scott Base, bringing

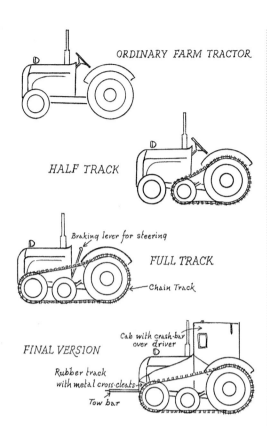

Right: Tractor adaptations made by the New Zealand team at Scott Base

ORDINARY FARM TRACTOR

HALF TRACK

Braking lever for steering

FULL TRACK

Chain Track

FINAL VERSION

Cab with crash-bar over driver

Rubber track with metal cross-cleats

Tow bar

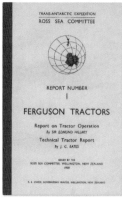

The Ferguson Tractor

Vehicle specification:

Model	TE 20
Horsepower	28.2 at 2000 rpm
No. of cylinders	4
Petrol tank capacity	9 gallons (34 litres)
Maximum speed	10 mph (16 kph) on snow – depending on load
Miles per gallon	1.1 to 1.8 (on the polar journey)
Turning radius	20 ft (6m)
Overall width	6 ft 1 in. (1.8m)
Overall length	10 ft (3m)
Overall height	4 ft 4 in. (1.3m) without the cab
Weight (dry)	3370 lb (1528kg) with full tracks

The New Zealand team led by Ed Hillary drove three of these adapted farm tractors 2000 kilometres across Antarctica from Scott Base to the South Pole. Ed Hillary wrote a report for the Ross Sea Committee on the tractors' performance. 'The Ferguson tractors used by the New Zealand Antarctic Expedition gave excellent service. Their dependability, ruggedness and ease of maintenance were outstanding features. On the Southern Journey the modified tractors were given a thorough testing and operated at maximum throttle throughout. On firm surfaces they performed admirably, even if the going was rough, but in soft snow they were a constant worry. In crevasse country they were something of a risk as their heavily weighted rear wheel punched holes in snow bridges that would easily support a Weasel or a Sno-Cat. For rugged economical base operation they are excellent, but I would not recommend their further use on long polar journeys where soft snow or crevasses may be expected.'' Two of the tractors are now in New Zealand museums.

Murray Ellis 1924–2005

In November 1955 a young Dunedin engineer, Murray Ellis, learned that he had been selected for the New Zealand team to go to Antarctica. By the time he returned home in March 1958 he had travelled overland to the South Pole, an indispensable member of Ed Hillary's tractor party.

With Jim Bates, the expedition's inventive and highly skilled mechanic, Ellis built a garage at Scott Base from leftover building materials; worked through the winter adapting the tractors for long-distance travel; was a key driver in the team; and kept the vehicles going in often appalling conditions. 'Murray and Jim attacked the problem with courage and determination and once again I thanked my lucky stars for having such a pair.'* So wrote Ed Hillary after Ellis and Bates worked for hours in fifty degrees of frost replacing a broken tractor track. Huge crevasses yawned on either side of them. There were many such occasions during their ten-week journey to the South Pole. Murray Ellis attended Waitaki Boys' High School in Oamaru where he was taught by Dan Bryant who had been on the 1935 Everest expedition with Eric Shipton. His father, Roland Ellis, was president of the New Zealand Alpine Club and Murray was a keen climber from his youth. During World War II he was a Fleet Air Arm pilot, flying American naval Corsair fighter aircraft, and after the war he completed an engineering degree at the University of Canterbury. The Ellis family has many connections with Ed Hillary. Roland Ellis was the initiator of the New Zealand Alpine Club's approach to the Himalayan Committee in London, which led to Ed Hillary and Earle Riddiford joining the 1951 Everest Reconnaissance Expedition. Murray Ellis's great-grandfather established Arthur Ellis & Co.

which supplied the sleeping bags for the Everest expedition. The British climbers were impressed. At Camp III Wilfrid Noyce observed: 'I don't need to wear the down coat in bed yet, these New Zealand bags are warmth itself.'† And cameraman Tom Stobart wrote: 'The sleeping bags are superb. Some genius has made them of a nylon which slips, so you can turn over without an exhausting struggle.'‡ Murray Ellis was a founding member of the Himalayan Trust, travelled to Nepal to help with the school-building projects, and with his wife Shirley became firm friends and supporters of several Sherpa families. He died in February 2005 after a short illness. Jim Strang said of him: 'The Sherpas respected Murray's strength, his old-fashioned values and high standards. Sherpas are very good judges of character and they quickly detect inconsistency and patronisation. Murray scored top marks with them.'§ Ed was grateful for Murray's many sterling qualities too: his intelligence, skill, integrity and determination – and his dry sense of humour.

Top left: Murray Ellis in Antarctica in 1967

Top right: Murray Ellis wearing his Antarctic scarf, outside the Otago Museum, 14 October 2004. Behind him is an Antarctic tractor on loan from Auckland's Museum of Transport and Technology for the exhibition *Sir Edmund Hillary: Everest and Beyond*

Above: In August 1971, when Tenzing Norgay visited the Arthur Ellis & Co. factory in Dunedin, Ed Hillary presented Roland Ellis with his copy of John Hunt's book *The Ascent of Everest*, signed by all the climbers. Ed wrote: 'To Roland Ellis, who kept me warm (almost) at 28,000 ft! With deepest regards.'
Stephen Goodenough

supplies and mail and providing a lifeline in case of accident or illness, would also need to find the tiny depots in the vast expanse of the Antarctic Plateau. Drawing on his experience in the air force, Hillary decided to use an astro-compass for navigation – it was accurate, but time consuming. He had 'forty minutes struggle each morning with my Astronomical tables' in order to calculate the results of the half-hourly observations made by the driver of the lead tractor.[2] Careful navigation would also help the party avoid the crevassed areas that Ed had noted on reconnaissance flights in the summer. Several lay near the base of the Skelton Glacier – the route he hoped to pioneer to the Polar Plateau, and the first major challenge for the tractors. It was the crux of the tractor party's southern journey, and sceptics at Scott Base and McMurdo believed it would be their nemesis.

After seven days travelling towards
the Trans-Antarctic Mountains, crumpled like
blue tissue against the translucent sky, they
approached the Skelton Depot at the foot of the
glacier. 'To the south of us the sun was a molten
ball of fire on the horizon and its low rays
brought into sharp relief the jagged sastrugi
and transformed the hills and hollows into a
mottled patchwork of flame and shadow. The
whole sky glowed with a delicate purple while
the great peaks standing all around us were
dressed in crimson robes. We were swimming
along in a sea of glorious colour and for a moment
I forgot even the cold and the discomfort.'[3]
The tractor drivers could stand up on the seats
for an excellent, if chilly, view – their vehicles
had windshields but no roofs. They were driving
across Antarctica in convertibles.

Skelton Glacier to Polar Plateau, 20–31 October 1957

After a final twelve hours' continuous driving,
they were met at the Skelton Depot by George
Marsh and Bob Miller and their dog teams,
flown in from Scott Base and raring to go. Jim
Bates, whom Hillary described as a 'mechanical
genius', was there too, but stricken with the flu
that had arrived at Scott Base with his replace-
ment mechanic. Murray Ellis had already spent
a day on repairs to the Weasel, and despite his
weakened state Bates worked on with him for
three more days. They rigged a bipod using two
crevasse-bridging timbers, cut a hole in the
vehicle's roof, winched out the motor, repaired
the distributor drive and replaced worn springs.
All in the wilds of Antarctica, in temperatures
of –36°C. No wonder Hillary was proud of his
mechanics.

Accommodation was fairly minimal,
particularly for Ellis and Bates, who slept in
a British polar tent with a calico ground sheet
and sheepskins under their sleeping bags. To
cook or brew up they followed a routine familiar
to any polar traveller: pots-and-pans box at the
top of the two sleeping bags, food box at the
foot, and the primus stove hissing in the middle.
The cook, 'enveloped as far as possible in his
sleeping bag for warmth, was obliged to lie
on one elbow as he tortuously moved steaming
water and food about on eye level at the very
edge of two beds'.[4] Ed and Peter Mulgrew were
relatively comfortable in the 'caboose', their
camp headquarters. With primus stoves, radio
equipment and a heater, it was a warm retreat
for the whole team at the end of the day.

Twice a week they sent telegrams
home to wives who were coping alone. Louise's
parents Phyl and Jim Rose lived next door
and played a large part in the family's life, but
Louise had to deal with the regular attentions
of the media, as well as look after her two
children and the concerns of her absent
husband. He needed reassurance that everything was in hand at home – including the
maintenance of the new garden. Ed relied
heavily on Louise's energy, intelligence and
good humour.

The original idea had been to rendezvous
with the British crossing party in November
1957, about 400 kilometres south of Scott Base,
near Mount Markham on the Polar Plateau. Ed
viewed this as a fairly modest requirement,
and decided to aim for a depot at least
800 kilometres south – or maybe further still.
He had calculated how many miles a day he
would need to travel to get to the South Pole
before escorting the British party back to Scott
Base, and diligently recorded every mile they
covered. Good days and bad days were defined
by their mileage, and moods swung accordingly.
Although they often woke to appalling weather
and nil visibility, as soon as the weather cleared,
even if the improvement was likely to be brief,
everyone would be out breaking camp and
getting the vehicles ready to roll.

On 22 October they left the Skelton Depot
to start the 160-kilometre climb up the glacier.
The dog teams raced off too, their drivers clinging
to the sledges and standing hard on the brakes.
Roped together, the tractors made good progress
over the icy surface, and by 9.15 p.m. the day's
total was a respectable thirty kilometres. The

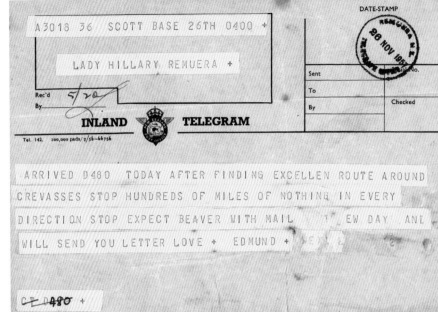

A3018 36 SCOTT BASE 26TH 0400 +

LADY HILLARY REMUERA +

INLAND ✠ TELEGRAM

ARRIVED D480 TODAY AFTER FINDING EXCELLEN ROUTE AROUND
CREVASSES STOP HUNDREDS OF MILES OF NOTHING IN EVERY
DIRECTION STOP EXPECT BEAVER WITH MAIL   EW DAY AND
WILL SEND YOU LETTER LOVE + EDMUND +

CT D480 +

dog drivers had had a tough day, with thirteen toss-outs. Each time they had to unload the sledge, right it, then reload and relash everything – a long and tedious business. Men and dogs were exhausted, but the next day a total white-out gave them all a chance to rest.

On 24 October they set off through a wall of whirling snow and in an hour covered eight kilometres 'more or less in the right direction'. But they lost the dog teams. Hillary unhitched the lead tractor and raced back down the glacier to try to find them, but Marsh and Miller had camped to weather out the storm. So the tractors clattered on over the ice into the teeth of the gale, sledges waving about behind them like flags in the breeze, and into a large crevasse field. They made good progress, but the snow bridges gave way regularly: 'it was rather unpleasant to look back and see a series of black gaping holes'.[5] And so they careered along, a grimly determined crew, while all around them the ground collapsed away.

The glacier grew steeper, so they began relaying, grinding up in low gear with the smaller sledges, then roaring back to get the others. Clawing their way up, 'like flies clinging to the wall', they reached 815 metres above the ice shelf, and the dog teams joined them safely. Visibility was not good, but the dogs could move quite well in the flat Antarctic light, so Hillary began following their tracks, peering over the top of the cab and steering the vehicle with his feet. Then he resorted to walking ahead of the tractors, bent double to make out the dogs' faint marks and testing snow bridges with his ice-axe – nervously tiring work. The journey up to the Skelton nevé – an expanse of granular snow at the top of a glacier – and across to the Plateau Depot took another six days.

On 29 October John Claydon dropped a mail bag from the Beaver aircraft. He had just ferried Harry Ayres, Roy Carlyon and their dogs to set up camp at the Plateau Depot. Antarctica faded away as the party read letters from home, but reasserted itself with bad headaches brought on by altitude, eye strain from driving and the fumes from their primus stoves. When more foul weather turned the cabs into 'a vortex of wind currents and drift', the drivers became miserably cold on the metal tractor seats and had to

crawl into the caboose to warm up. Murray Ellis and Jim Bates had to preheat the Ferguson motors with a hot-air blower to make them start: the altitude was a struggle for vehicles as well as men. But at last, on 31 October, Ed saw a black triangle in the distance. It was the Plateau Depot camp. He was enormously relieved that his navigation had worked. 'To see our four battered vehicles and the laden sledges at the Plateau Depot seemed to be the fulfilment of an impossible dream. I don't think that ever before, even on the summit of Everest, had I felt a greater sense of achievement.'[6]

Across the Polar Plateau to Depot 480, 1–25 November 1957

Ed Hillary was certain now that the tractors should lay the depots, and that the dog teams should be left for surveying and reconnaissance, backed by the aircraft. But their twelve days at the Plateau Depot were beset with problems. They were all getting headaches and had to install a ventilator in the caboose to extract carbon monoxide fumes. Then Murray Ellis and Peter Mulgrew had to be evacuated to Scott Base – Ellis with a strained back after battling with a tractor's automatic hitch and Mulgrew with two broken ribs. He had fallen from the roof of the caboose while installing a radio aerial. While Jim Bates soldiered on with vehicle maintenance, Ed made a quick flight

Above: Jim Bates dealing
with tractor problems on the
Polar Plateau, November 1957
Roy Carlyon

back to Scott Base to check that all was well. It
was, but he was trapped for several days when
low cloud grounded the aircraft. John Claydon
and Bill Cranfield showed daredevil dash and
real flying skill in this crisis. They sneaked
along under the clouds that blanketed the ice
shelf, flew up glaciers and found holes in the
cloud layer through which they could ascend to
the plateau. By 12 November they had the depot
fully stocked; the dog teams had headed off;
and there were two new drivers to stand in for
Mulgrew and Ellis: radio operator Ted Gawn
and cameraman Derek Wright. Ed himself was
a shivering wreck from the Scott Base flu, but
they went on anyway. When they almost missed
a snow cairn built by the dog drivers, they
realised that the astro-compass was giving
erroneous readings. Its fixing plate had worked
loose, and Ed's calculations were out as well.
He was appalled and furious with himself.
Navigation was his responsibility.

On 20 November, five weeks after they had left Scott Base, they had their first news from the other side of the continent. Bunny Fuchs's party, in the huge Sno-cats, was only now preparing to leave Shackleton Base. They were well behind schedule, but Fuchs was confident they would make up the time. He congratulated Hillary on getting his vehicles to the plateau. And there was a surprising message from Arthur Helm. The key sentence was: 'If you are prepared to go for Pole Committee will give you every encouragement and full support following formal approval from London.'[7] Ed was astonished – this was in direct contrast to their usual messages. That he had misunderstood the meaning of 'following formal approval from London' emerged only later. He began reviewing his plans, and working out what he would need to stock all the depots and get the tractors to the Pole.

They had been averaging over thirty kilometres a day, with Ed and Jim Bates alternating in the cold and uncomfortable job of driving the lead tractor. The terrain varied from rock-hard slippery ice with large sastrugi to crevassed areas and dense soft snow – and they had another blizzard to contend with. It took five more days to reach the next depot, driving at night when the sun was clearer for navigation. On one occasion they extracted a tractor from a crevasse, then looked back to see a black hole the size of

a house. 'We crept over to the edge and looked in…sheer ice walls dropping away to vast depths and enough room to put a hundred Fergusons.'[8] They had been extraordinarily lucky in striking the crevasse at a narrow spot. More exhausting extrications and lucky escapes from crevasses followed before, on 25 November, they reached a basin suitable for landing aircraft. Hillary decided it would be the site of Depot 480 – the end of the second long stage in their journey.

To Depot 700, 25 November– 15 December 1957

At Depot 480 they needed good weather for the aircraft to drop the depot supplies. The indefatigable engineers were at work on the Weasel – this time it was worn sprockets on the drive wheels. Nursing the ailing vehicle would swallow up many more hours. Hillary sorted out the food – boxes to stay at the depot, boxes for the dog teams, boxes for Depot 700 and beyond – and mused about his lack of appetite. Altitude and tension tend to make food uninteresting, as climbers know, but Ed's cooking technique probably didn't help. 'I started up the primuses

A Ferguson well wedged down into a crevasse just before Depot 700, November 1957. It took some hours to get it back to the surface. Peter Mulgrew is on the right
Edmund Hillary

Far right: Peter Mulgrew
in Antarctica, 1957

Right: Chief Petty Officer
Peter Mulgrew, RNZN, and
June Mulgrew in London in
1958. Peter had been awarded
the Polar Medal for his work
in Antarctica

108

and put a pot of snow on one of them. On the
other I placed the frying pan and fried up some
bacon. When the bacon was cooked I took it out
and threw in a few handfuls of dried onions and
fried these until they were crisp and hard.
By now the water was hot so I stirred in some
potato powder and produced mashed potato.
I poured the mashed potato into the frying pan
and mixed it up with the bacon fat and fried
onions. I then ladled this glorious mess out
on to two enamel plates, added the bacon and
dinner was ready. It needed a stomach of iron
to absorb much of this fare.'[9]

A day later there was a message from
Admiral Dufek, offering to fly any of them who
made it to the Pole back to Scott Base. The dog
teams had all arrived safely after a cold,
miserable trip, and the planes began to get
through. On 29 November John Claydon's voice
came over the radio: he had sighted the depot.
Ed recalled: 'To see our gallant little orange
plane again brought a lump to my throat. John
made a couple of low runs over the strip we
had marked out for him and then came in for
a perfect landing.'[10]

With Claydon came Murray Ellis, fit and
strong again, half a ton of supplies and a bag
of mail. On 1 December Peter Mulgrew flew in
with Bill Cranfield, bringing the Old Firm back
to full strength. Miller and Marsh headed south
with their dog teams for more surveying and
geologising, while Harry Ayres and Roy Carlyon
decided to explore the Darwin Glacier on their
way back to Scott Base. The pilots operated
a shuttle service stocking the depot, and on
6 December it was done. 'Our fliers had done
an extraordinarily good job under difficult
conditions, and I said goodbye to John with a
considerable feeling of affectionate appreciation...I watched him disappear, and then
turned back to the caboose with a feeling of
loneliness and isolation. Once again we were
consigning ourselves to the wide wastes of the
Antarctic, and heaven knew how many crevasses
and difficulties lay ahead of us.'[11]

On the journey to Depot 700 Hillary
again thanked his lucky stars for Murray Ellis
and Jim Bates. They worked for six hours
changing the clutch on the Weasel one night,
replaced the track on a tractor teetering in a
crevasse field, and spent eight hours fashioning
a new bearing for the Weasel from a welding

Peter Mulgrew
1927–79

'For our senior radio
expert we inter-
viewed two very
experienced naval
chief petty officers.
One of them persist-
ed in calling me Sir,
while the other, Peter
Mulgrew, did not. I
chose Peter Mulgrew
and this was the be-
ginning of a long and
fruitful friendship.'*
After the overland
journey to the South
Pole in 1957–58, Peter
Mulgrew returned
to the navy, but
organised leave
to take part in the
Himalayan Scientific
and Mountaineering
Expedition in 1960–61.
During the attempt
on Makalu, some
105 metres below the
summit he suffered
a pulmonary oedema
in his right lung. He
was extremely ill,
weak and often
unconscious, but
over ten days was
heroically assisted
down by Sherpas and
fellow climbers, and
helicoptered back
to Kathmandu. He
suffered severe

frostbite. Back in
New Zealand both
his legs were ampu-
tated below the knee,
and he lost several
fingers. He fought his
way back to health
with the support of
his wife June, event-
ually walking again
on artificial legs.
Peter Mulgrew
returned to the
Himalayas on
building expeditions
with Sir Ed in 1963
and 1964, and pub-
lished a book, *No
Place for Men*. He
also became a
leading skipper of
one-ton ocean-racing
yachts. In 1979 Peter
Mulgrew was killed
when an Air New
Zealand sightseeing
flight over Antarctica,
on which he was the
commentator,
crashed into Mount
Erebus. By then his
wit, determination
and bravery in the
face of disaster had
made him a New
Zealand legend.
Ed Hillary wrote:
'I felt great sadness
at Peter's death.
We had shared so
much together...
Peter had tremen-
dous determination
and for many years
had been a good and
loyal friend.'†

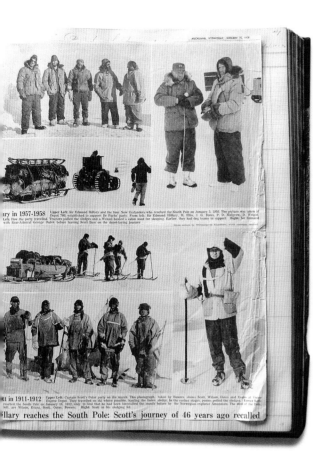

Left: A page from the
Weekly News in Shirley
Ellis's Antarctic scrapbook,
15 January 1958
Alexa Johnston

Soft snow was the other nightmare, constantly bogging them down. Then to top it all, a telegram from the Ross Sea Committee reversed the previous message, insisting that Hillary wait at Depot 700 until Fuchs had at least reached South Ice. This was the first British depot, more than 800 kilometres from the Pole. Ed Hillary certainly didn't intend sitting still for weeks waiting for Bunny Fuchs to travel 1600 kilometres to meet him. When they finally arrived at Depot 700 on 15 December they were a worn, exhausted but triumphant team. The big question now had to be faced: should they, could they, drive on to the South Pole?

The men slept and relaxed a little, built the usual lines of snow cairns to mark the depot for the pilots, and waited for the weather to clear. A message came from Fuchs on 17 December. He expected to be at the Pole between Christmas and New Year. This was surprising, since his progress so far had been very slow, but Hillary calculated that his own team could reach the Pole within a day or two of New Year and would meet Fuchs there. He sent a message that once Depot 700 was fully stocked he intended to head south-west with three Fergusons to avoid crevasse areas and get clear running towards the Pole. 'I don't know how far we will get but will keep you advised of progress.'[12]

To the Pole, 20 December 1957 – 4 January 1958

Although Jim Bates and Murray Ellis were dubious about keeping the tractors going for another 800 kilometres, Ed was determined to go on and Mulgrew agreed. Obviously the team had to stay together, so Bates and Ellis bowed to the inevitable and prepared themselves for more repair work. They set off at 8.30 p.m. on 20 December, leaving a well-stocked depot behind. They had twenty forty-four-gallon drums of fuel and would have to average 1.7 miles (2.7 km) to the gallon all the way – with no reserves. They took a man-hauling sled in case the tractors didn't make it.

All that first night they were weaving among enormous sastrugi, cursing the steering system in the tractors which required constant heaving on the brakes to change course. By six a.m., having covered forty-four kilometres, and going without sleep for twenty-four hours, they stopped to make camp. And Mulgrew took another radio message from the Ross Sea Committee telling Hillary to remain at Depot 700 and wait for Fuchs. Feeling totally exasperated, Ed telegrammed Fuchs, asking if he thought he needed any further assistance. The depot-stocking was complete and Ed had fulfilled all his tasks to the letter. There was no reply for four days while they pushed on south. Crevasse areas caused more problems, but they made good progress across the desolate plateau, climbing gradually towards 2740 metres above sea level, still travelling at night and sleeping through the day – though there was constant daylight of course. On Christmas Eve Bunny Fuchs replied. He had arrived at South Ice on 21 December after severe crevasse trouble and expected to leave for the Pole on the 25th. He wished them all a happy Christmas.

Pleased that Fuchs had not objected to their southern journey, Hillary replied: 'Glad to hear of your arrival at South Ice and hope your troubles are over. We are 390 miles [630 km] from the Pole. Have cairned two areas of crevasses since D700 but last fifty miles has been clear going. Waiting one day here then will push on … Best of luck, happy Christmas and an early New Year at the Pole. Ed Hillary.'[13] They crowded into the caboose that night to hear the special Christmas broadcast from home, and had their 'sumptuous' Christmas dinner at

rod. Unfortunately, the metal they had available was too soft, and the Weasel overheated badly on its test run. Refusing to give up, Ellis and Bates drilled a hole in the bearing and piped a continuous supply of oil to it. Only when the cab filled with smoke and the bearing was red-hot did they reluctantly decide to abandon the little vehicle to the Antarctic wastes. The three red Fergusons trundled on.

They tried to avoid the worst crevasse areas, but were often forced to find a route through them, with Ed usually out in front testing the snow bridges with his ice-axe. Nevertheless, on one occasion Jim Bates felt his whole vehicle sink backwards, then shudder to a stop. He scrambled out, shaken but unhurt, commenting that he didn't like the view: it was an enormously deep, sheer-sided crevasse. After the usual photographing and peering into the blue depths, they shovelled snow to make a kind of ramp for the tractor. Peter Mulgrew nobly climbed down to put it out of gear and, with some careful coordinated driving, the other two tractors jerked it free.

seven a.m. the next day. Murray Ellis had brought brandy for the occasion; Peter Mulgrew cooked salmon fishcakes; and dessert was tinned peaches, a cup of cocoa and a piece of fruit cake. Derek Wright was initiated as a fully fledged member of the Old Firm and was the recipient of much well-intentioned advice from his married companions about a romance he was conducting via telegrams home. 'It was a relief to us all when things took a decided turn for the better and true love had its just reward'.[14]

Many kilometres away, across the frozen landscape, the dog-team drivers were also celebrating Christmas. On the Darwin Glacier Roy Carlyon was treated to a Harry Ayres special – Ayres had a reputation as an outstanding camp

cook. Anchovies on biscuit were followed by boiled chicken roasted in butter – Ayres had been saving the frozen chicken for weeks. 'The result was beyond all expectation ... The next occupant of the primus was a squat Christmas pudding which was subjected to two hours steaming before consumption with our version of cream made from dried milk powder. Extended stomachs by this time were issuing warnings but we pressed on grimly with Christmas cake, muscatels, etc. A rather dessicated [sic] cigar was then smoked with all appearances of enjoyment.'[15] Their Christmas cake, made by Harry's wife Jeanne, had survived falling into a twenty-metre crevasse ten days earlier, when Harry's entire dog team and sledge broke through a fragile snow bridge and disappeared.

The sledge was jammed three metres down but 'there was no sign of the dogs save an occasional whimper from the deep blue depths'.[16] The two men worked for many hours and succeeded in rescuing all the dogs but one: 'Skinny' or Bristles, a gift of Waimate High School, had been killed in the fall. They retrieved essential camping gear from the precariously balanced sledge, then hauled the sledge itself to the surface the next day. In one last trip, right to the bottom, Harry Ayres triumphantly retrieved the Christmas cake.

Back on the Plateau the tractor team felt that the Pole was within their grasp. They were making good progress but were very tired. 'Even though we spent up to twelve hours at a camp site a large proportion of this was taken up

with pitching and unpitching camp, with cooking meals, radio schedules, maintenance on the vehicles and navigation. We were lucky if we got five or six hours' good sleep a night.'[17] On 28 December Bunny Fuchs telegrammed again. He was about to leave South Ice and, for the first time, was expressing concern about fuel for his vehicles: 'I must accept your offer to clear present crevasse area then establish additional fuel depot…thus abandoning your idea of reaching the Pole.'[18] Hillary considered their position. 'We had enough fuel to go either to the Pole or back to D700. The only place we could establish a depot was where we were, and we didn't have the food to sit around for a month or more until the crossing party reached us – and there was always the chance they wouldn't reach us.'[19] He telegrammed back:

'Your message has arrived too late as we are now 240 miles [384 kilometres] from the Pole with only ten drums left. Have neither the food nor fuel to sit here and await your arrival… Expect to arrive at Pole in six days and will commence operations to increase fuel supply to D700.'[20] Hillary did arrange for eight more drums of fuel to be flown to Depot 700, but they were not needed. Of the fifty drums of fuel the New Zealand party placed at the depots, only twenty were used by the crossing party.

Navigation was still a tense matter for the New Zealanders. They couldn't afford to miss the Pole Station, and now the bubble sextant was playing up. But they pressed on. On 31 December they ran into masses of soft snow. 'This was heartbreaking stuff, loose and bottomless, and the Fergies were almost helpless…In six frightful hours we only travelled

six miles and our fuel supplies were shrinking before our eyes. I have rarely felt a greater sense of helplessness.'[21] They had no choice but to reduce the loads, leaving behind sledges, bottles of oxygen and acetylene, food, kerosene, a large tarpaulin and their emergency camping gear. They were cutting it very fine now. But by roping together the tractors, caboose and single remaining sledge, they allowed each vehicle to cut a fresh path. This suited the tractors, and they began making progress again.

Their first direct radio contact with Bunny Fuchs came at nine a.m. on 3 January 1958. He was battling very bad sastrugi, was still some 600 kilometres from the Pole, and hoped to be there in sixteen days. Ed was seriously alarmed now. If the crossing party continued so slowly, they might not reach Scott Base before the last ship had to leave for New Zealand. Everyone would have to spend another

Between the Plateau Depot and Depot 480 the weather was consistently bad. The team encountered poor visibility, strong wind, drifting snow and cold temperatures, but they kept plugging on.
Derek Wright

Left: Pages from Shirley Ellis's Antarctic scrapbook
Alexa Johnston

Right: The Old Firm before leaving Depot 700,
16 December 1957.
(L–R) Ed Hillary, Murray Ellis,
Jim Bates, Peter Mulgrew,
Derek Wright

winter in Antarctica. He suggested that Fuchs consider flying out from the Pole and returning the following year to complete the crossing.

The New Zealanders had been driving since eight the previous evening, but decided to keep going until they saw the Pole Station. On they went. At two p.m. they stopped for a meal and a sun sight, then, deadly tired, climbed back into the gloomy canvas cabs and drove on. 'Only the Antarctic chill creeping up our backbones and freezing our extremities kept us from falling asleep.'[22] Six gruelling hours later they were about to change drivers when Hillary thought he saw a black speck in the far distance. He dashed back to the caboose for the binoculars and – yes, it was a whole line of flags stretching out to left and right. The Pole Station. They had made it. The relief was overwhelming. All Ed's worries about navigation and fuel consumption were over. Before they collapsed into their beds for the last night of the journey, Peter Mulgrew radioed a message through Scott Base to the Ross Sea Committee and thence to the BBC and *The Times*, sponsors of the expedition. The single word which told the world of their arrival at the South Pole was 'Rhubarb'.

At 12.30 p.m. on 4 January 1958, after four hours' driving 'like three tiny black ants across the snowfields of eternity', they rolled into the Pole Station. Admiral Dufek and other friendly American faces, along with dozens of cameras, were there to greet them. 'I turned off my motor for the last time and scrambled wearily out of the seat. I was swept into a confusion of congratulations, photographs and questions, and then led off by friendly hands towards the warmth and fresh food of the Pole Station. But before I descended underground I took a last glance at our tractor train – the three farm tractors, tilted over like hip-shot horses, looked lonely and neglected like broken toys cast aside after playtime; the caboose which had been a haven of warmth and rest to us now seemed more like a horse-box than ever; and the two sledges had only the meagre load of a half-full drum of fuel.'[23]

The Old Firm relaxed with the Americans at the Pole Station, and watched a cowboy movie which had them in fits of laughter, but beyond Antarctica many observers were not amused. A storm was raging. On 26 December, when he headed for the South Pole, Hillary had radioed

his intentions to Scott Base and from there they went out to the world. British and New Zealand media tracking the progress of the two parties had relied on Hillary's regular reports to Scott Base to keep up with the expedition, since Bunny Fuchs, also facing very difficult terrain, was less forthcoming. As a result Fuchs's location and progress were often a matter for conjecture. Ed Hillary's Boxing Day message with its nicely turned, vigorous wording was perfect front-page fodder: 'We are heading hell-bent for the Pole – God willing and crevasses permitting'. This set off the media uproar. Some British papers saw a race between an upstart New Zealander, whose function was merely to assist, and a serious British scientist making an historic and scientifically useful crossing of the whole continent. Ed's suggestion that Fuchs stop at the Pole and come back the next year to finish the crossing was viewed as the final impertinence.

But as John Claydon said many years later, how could it have been a race? There was never a race in it – the tractors were always miles ahead. They set off five weeks before the crossing party and made excellent progress despite constant mechanical setbacks.[24] And Hillary's suggestion that Fuchs delay the crossing

Above and facing page: The tractors arrived at the South Pole on 4 January 1958. Ed Hillary and his team were the first to reach the Pole overland since Robert Falcon Scott's expedition on 17 January 1912

Left: The British crossing party, led by Bunny Fuchs, arrived at the South Pole Station in their Tucker Sno-cats on 20 January 1958. George Lowe is at the left rear of this group, Bunny Fuchs at the back and Ed Hillary on the far right

had been prompted by his real concern that Fuchs might not make it before the next winter. The Americans, of course, were delighted with it all, and Hillary only later saw a report from New Zealand's Department of Foreign Affairs to the New Zealand prime minister describing his drive to the Pole as logical, appropriate – as he had fulfilled all his obligations to Fuchs 'with notable success' – and newsworthy. 'If Fuchs makes no faster progress, and if a successful crossing becomes impossible, the Trans-Antarctic Expedition may be glad of the prestige arising from Hillary's own achievement.'[25]

A photo of the five members of the Old Firm was taken at Depot 700, and has come to symbolise their historic journey to the Pole. In this line-up of thickly clad men, there is a passing resemblance to the photograph of Robert Scott and his companions at the Pole on 17 January 1912. Scott knew he had been in a race with Amundsen, and that he had lost. But Hillary was not racing – he was tracing famous footsteps, he was fulfilling youthful ambitions, he was being an adventurer. On 20 January 1958, when Fuchs's huge orange flag-bedecked Sno-cats swept into the Pole, 'Bunny jumped out of the leading Sno-cat and we shook hands and exchanged a warm greeting…I was mighty pleased to see him.'[26]

The crossing party travelled on from the Pole along the tracks left by the tractors to Depot 700, and Ed flew back from Scott Base to join them there. Fuchs called on Ed's knowledge of the terrain whenever the going was difficult and asked him to arrange some assistance from the Americans flying the British dogs out from the Pole to Scott Base, and bringing in oxygen when one of the Sno-cat drivers was affected by carbon monoxide in his cab. Ed did not enjoy the transformation from leader of his own party to general fixer and factotum for Fuchs's. Nevertheless, he guided the Sno-cats through crevassed areas and down the Skelton Glacier through screaming white wind-drift. Once on the ice shelf, they roared across the 300 kilometres to Scott Base, rolling in there on Sunday 2 March. They were cutting it very fine for the boats, but were one day under the 100 days that Bunny Fuchs, now Sir Vivian Fuchs, had estimated for the crossing. It was a triumph for him too.

As well as making historic journeys, both the New Zealand and British parties contributed to Antarctic knowledge. New Zealand survey parties explored over 103,600 square kilometres of uncharted continent while the IGY scientists at Scott Base kept meteorological records and monitored seismic activity, geomagnetic field

changes, fish levels, and tide and current changes. The teams sailed for New Zealand in HMNZS *Endeavour*, arriving in Wellington to rapturous welcomes on 17 March 1958. Despite the earlier furore, there were many positive comments. Sir John Hunt said: 'Before he even left New Zealand, I was sure Ed would go to the Pole and that nothing would stop him. So I am not surprised, but I am absolutely delighted about it.'[27] The *Sydney Morning Herald* noted: 'By pushing on to the South Pole, Sir Edmund Hillary has added his own particular touch of panache to the drama of the Commonwealth Trans-Antarctic Expedition.'[28]

In 1961 the British *Alpine Journal* reviewed Hillary's book about the expedition, *No Latitude for Error*, and concluded: 'In this book we learn for the first time how the original concept was transcended, by Hillary's vision and thrustfulness, from a mere depot-laying chore into an ambitious and mettlesome exploit of which the New Zealanders can be justly proud; and this despite the misgivings of the over-cautious Ross Sea Expedition Committee. Ed Hillary turned out to be nobody's stooge.'[29]

We planned to winter a party at a height of over 19,000 feet, something that had never been done before, and finally, as a test for the party's standard of acclimatization, to attempt to climb Makalu's 27,790 feet without using oxygen equipment.
EDMUND HILLARY

08 SCIENTISTS AND YETIS

Building a school was not the primary objective of the 1961 Himalayan Scientific and Mountaineering Expedition, nor was hunting for the yeti. Both projects were grafted on to the original idea, which was to carry out a sustained, scientific study of the effects of high altitude on the human body. But public interest would be aroused by the news of Sir Edmund Hillary's leading a search for the mysterious yeti, and this helped to attract expedition funding. And although building the little school in the village of Khumjung was almost an afterthought, it was the beginning of a whole new phase in Ed Hillary's life – and the lives of his friends and family.

The Silver Hut at night, 1961
Mike Gill

Left: Ed Hillary in his
study at home, c. 1964
Louise Hillary

x

116   The high-altitude plan took shape in Antarctica, in conversations between Ed Hillary and the 1953 Everest expedition's physiologist, Dr Griffith Pugh, who was with the British Medical Research Council and spent the summer of 1956–57 at McMurdo Base. Both men had further Himalayan projects in mind: Ed hoped to mount an attempt on Everest without supplementary oxygen equipment and Pugh was keen to test a theory for improving acclimatisation. Was it possible that if men spent a longer period acclimatising, preferably six months at 7000 metres (20,000 ft), they might develop what so many Sherpas clearly had: 'lungs and legs at home in high altitudes'?[1] A fully equipped on-site laboratory to monitor their physical and mental changes would provide invaluable data for medical research. This would be followed by an oxygen-less attempt on a high peak, with new arrivals joining the fully acclimatised men, so that fitness levels could be compared. Their two plans could be happily combined, but only if the money could be found.[2]

After Antarctica, Ed spent eighteen months at home with Louise and the children – Belinda was born in January 1959. Working at the typewriter in his small study was now a normal part of every day, and although Ed professed to find writing hard work, he produced a lot. Expeditions had usually involved writing reports for newspapers; he was still an occasional contributor to the *New Zealand Alpine Journal* and other magazines; his book about the New Zealand part of the trans-Antarctic expedition was published in 1961; and requests to speak at charitable events or write forewords for books had become a steady stream – its flow unabated almost fifty years later. Gertrude Hillary was delighted with this development. Louise was very pleased to have Ed back at home; Peter and Sarah got to know their father again; and like many youngest children, Belinda, who was blessed with a sunny and outgoing nature, became everyone's pet. Family holidays usually involved camping, often with Louise's parents. Ed did some climbing and worked solidly with Rex on beekeeping. He was unsure what the direction of his life would be.

Then in mid-1959 *Argosy* magazine flew Ed and Louise to New York, where Ed was presented with the magazine's 'Explorer of the Year' award. While they were in New York an invitation came to fly on to Chicago and make a short educational film with Field Enterprises Educational Corporation, publishers of *World Book Encyclopedia*. The filming went well. John Dienhart, the company's public-relations director, was charmed by Ed's personality and his enthusiastic account of his 'dream expedition' – combining science with mountaineering and with a search for the yeti thrown in. Dienhart thought Field Enterprises might be able to help, so asked Ed to send a detailed report about his plans. Back in New Zealand Ed decided he had probably exaggerated the American enthusiasm and let the idea lapse, but a phone call from Chicago galvanised him into action. Detailed plans were concocted at the typewriter and posted off, and a week later a cable arrived. He was invited to fly to Chicago and talk to the board of directors of Field Enterprises – at their expense.

Michael Gill

Above: Mike Gill, 1961

'If an Antarctic blizzard is trying to demolish your tent or you're camped on an uncomfortable ledge at 20,000 ft and don't know whether to go up or down ... then Mike Gill is a magnificent companion. He'll cook any meal, do any miserable job that needs doing, and if you feel like mental stimulation he'll argue any abstruse point you want – then drop off to sleep like a baby and let the blizzard rage on.'*

A twenty-two-year-old graduate in physiology, and a keen climber, Mike Gill answered an advertisement in the *Auckland Star* of 23 December 1959: 'Sir Edmund Hillary is looking for two young New Zealand climbers to accompany him on his forthcoming Himalayan expedition ... ' Thus began a long friendship, and over forty years of expeditions and projects, several of them with Gill's wife Linda and their children Tom and Caitlin. Mike Gill made first ascents of two major peaks near Everest: Ama Dablam and Kantega, as well as Mount Herschel in Antarctica – all on Hillary-led expeditions. After the Ama Dablam climb Michael Ward wrote: 'Mike was a very graceful climber and he did everything with ease. Step cutting seemed effortless to him and he moved with a fluid motion from step to step.'[†]

Mike Gill was one of the men who spent the winter of 1960–61 living in the Silver Hut on the Mingbo Glacier. He was a founding member of the Himalayan Trust, gave early medical assistance to the Sherpa people, and worked on the successful programme to combat iodine deficiency. As secretary of the trust's medical committee, he recruited and supported the New Zealand volunteer doctors working at Kunde Hospital. He also worked on the trust's building projects and made films of several Hillary expeditions. A medical professional, he recently retired from his position as clinical biochemist at Diagnostic Laboratory in New Zealand. His retirement activities range from trekking at altitude to yachting – at sea level.

Of Ed Hillary he wrote: 'Ed is more than just a good leader, someone who can organise well and push an expedition through difficulties to a successful conclusion. There are other qualities less easy to define: a real humility, blunt honesty, a spontaneous generosity and warmth of spirit – a combination of qualities that gives him stature above those around and inspires loyalty.'[‡]

The Himalayan Scientific and Mountaineering Expedition 1960–61

ROSTER OF THE EXPEDITION*

Sir Edmund Hillary	Leader, Auckland, New Zealand
Bhanu Bannerjee	Assistant to Desmond Doig, Official Reporter of the Expedition
Pat Barcham	Electrical Engineer, New Zealand Electricity Department, Dunedin, New Zealand
Barry Bishop	National Geographic Society, Washington, DC
John Dienhart	Director of Public Relations, Field Enterprises Educational Corporation
Desmond Doig	Assistant Editor, The Statesman, Calcutta and New Delhi, India
Michael Gill	Physiologist, Otago University, New Zealand
Norman Hardie	Structural Engineer, Christchurch, New Zealand
John Harrison	J. Inglis Wright Ltd, Advertising Agents, Christchurch, New Zealand
Dr S. Lahiri	President College, Calcutta; assigned to expedition by Indian Government
George Lowe	Repton School, England
Dr Jim Milledge	Physiologist, British Medical Research Council
Capt. B. S. Motwani	Indian Army Medical Corps
Peter Mulgrew	Sub-Lieutenant, Royal New Zealand Navy
Dr Tom Nevison Jr	Medical Examiner, US Air Force School of Aviation Medicine, Brooks Air Force Base, Texas
Leigh Ortenburger	Mathematician, Los Altos Hills, Calif.
Marlin Perkins	Director, Lincoln Park Zoo, Chicago, Ill.
Dr Griffith Pugh	Physiologist, Department of Human Physiology, British Medical Research Council
Wally Romanes	Building Contractor, Hastings, New Zealand
Dr Larry Swan	Associate Professor of Biology, San Francisco State College
Dr Michael Ward	Surgeon, London Hospital, London, England
Dr John West	Scientific Officer, Postgraduate Medical School of London, British Medical Research Council

117

Right: Norman and Enid
Hardie, December 1974
N. L. Macbeth

Below: Cartoon by Hal
Eyre Jnr, *Sydney Morning
Herald*, 1961

"Stop worrying. After all, how do we know that Sir Edmund Hillary really exists?"

The company contributed a very generous $US125,000 towards the expedition, to be used at Ed's discretion, and a year later John Dienhart found himself trekking out of Kathmandu at the end of a long stream of porters carrying several tons of supplies for an eight-week yeti hunt in the Rolwaling Valley west of Everest. Mike Gill, a young New Zealand climber with the expedition, recalled Dienhart's description of Ed meeting his firm's directors. They had fully expected the world-famous mountaineering knight to sweep in flanked by lawyers and accountants, but Ed arrived on his own: 'hair all over the place, and carrying an old briefcase held together with string. Well that threw us right from the start. And then we came to the bit where we asked how much would he like for himself and he says, "Well, on an expedition we don't usually take any money for ourselves"…
Up till then I'd never been able to understand why he hadn't made a million bucks out of Everest…I think Ed's the most honest guy I've ever met…I'm not sure he's not the only honest guy I've ever met.' Gill later inherited the briefcase: after its third appearance, Field Enterprises presented Ed with a new one.[3]

And so began a year of frantic planning for and organising the biggest and most complex undertaking Hillary had yet led. The expedition members, who would be in the Himalayas for a total of nine months, comprised twenty-one scientists, climbers and other specialists from New Zealand, Australia, India, Britain, the USA and Nepal. They would need several hundred local porters, and scores of Sherpas to carry loads and work alongside the climbers at altitude. All Ed Hillary's organising skills would be tested, as well as his selection of personnel, his flexibility in responding to opportunities when they arose, his skill in delegating, his stamina – both mental and physical – and his sense of humour when the going got really tough. Through all these challenges he would need to hold on to his vision for the expedition, and exhibit the generous spirit and strength of character which would secure the commitment of all the varied participants, even when he could not be with them in person. Ed had seen these qualities in John Hunt, and he had long admired Shackleton's leadership of men. Now he would find out if he was made of similar stuff.

Norman Hardie

'Norman Hardie is something of a legend, having just emerged as the author of a book on Sherpas; besides, it is no mean person who battles up a peak like Kangchenjunga, the world's third highest mountain and long considered impossible, and then in respect of local sentiment leaves the last few tantalizing feet unscaled.'[*]
Norman Hardie completed a degree in civil engineering at the University of Canterbury, where he began a lifelong involvement with tramping and climbing. In 1948 while working on a hydroelectric project on Lake Pukaki, he employed another young climber, Ed Hillary, as a surveyor's assistant and this was the beginning of a long association. After the successful 1955 ascent of Kangchenjunga (8586m; 28,169ft), on which Dawa Tenzing was sirdar,

Norman trekked to Solu Khumbu and spent several months living among the Sherpas and climbing and surveying the valleys around Everest. His wife Enid was one of the first European women to spend time in a Sherpa village. Hardie's book, *In Highest Nepal*, is a fascinating account of Sherpa life and customs. He noted the attitude of Sherpa families to mountaineering: 'These people are aware, more than most Europeans, how much the ascent of a high mountain is the result of team work. Here the men who did the spade work and opened the routes to the highest camps received as much glamour as those chosen for the summit, and it was a proud mother who knew her son had been as high as Camp VI at 26,900 feet.'[†]
Norman Hardie was a member of the Himalayan Trust for twenty-two years, and served on a committee advising on the establishment of the Sagarmatha National Park. The Hardies were energetic fundraisers for Himalayan Trust projects and welcoming hosts for the many young Sherpas who came to New Zealand for a national-park management course, and to study forestry.

118

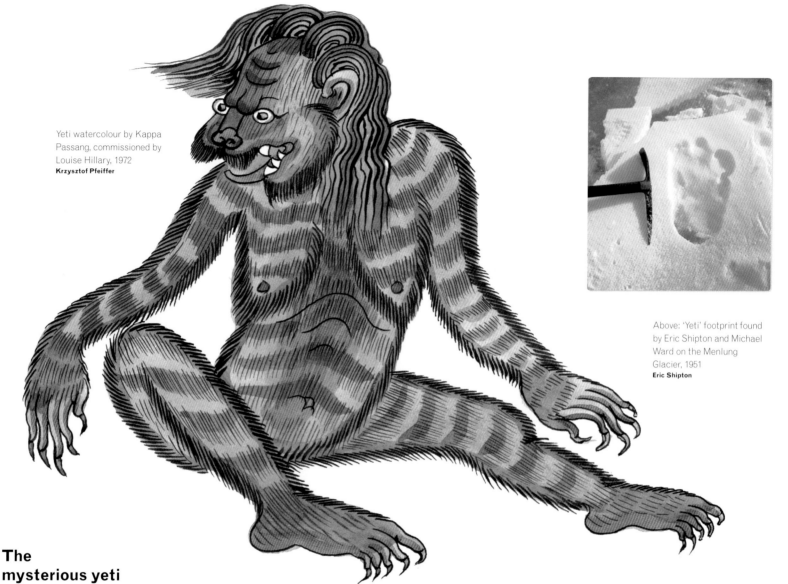

Yeti watercolour by Kappa Passang, commissioned by Louise Hillary, 1972
Krzysztof Pfeiffer

Above: 'Yeti' footprint found by Eric Shipton and Michael Ward on the Menlung Glacier, 1951
Eric Shipton

The mysterious yeti

Ed Hillary's 1960 search for evidence of the yeti, or abominable snowman, was not simply a scheme to attract sponsorship for other more legitimately scientific expedition objectives. Ed had spent many years reading about and climbing in the Himalayas, and had heard about these fabled creatures from Sherpas and from sahibs.

Tenzing Norgay said that his father had twice seen a yeti, and Sherpas told many stories of people attacked by yetis, or of yak herders hearing their frightening high-pitched whistle. But seeing a yeti was thought to bring bad luck, ill health or death, so

Sherpas were not particularly keen to encounter them.

Among sahibs the yeti tradition stretches back into the nineteenth century. Hairy creatures were reported to have attacked servants of the British government's Nepal representative in 1832, and large footprints were seen on a high peak in Sikkim in 1889 and again in 1914. In 1921 members of a British Everest expedition led by Colonel Howard-Bury saw dark figures on the snow above them at about 5335 metres (17,500 ft). When the climbers reached the spot they found huge, human-like footprints. Major Alan Cameron with the 1923 Everest

expedition saw similar creatures and took photographs of their tracks. On later expeditions H. W. Tilman and Frank Smythe both reported seeing unexplained tracks in the snow.

The most celebrated evidence came on the 1951 Everest Reconnaissance Expedition when Eric Shipton and Dr Michael Ward photographed a line of tracks at 5490 metres (18,000 ft) on the Menlung Glacier. The tracks continued for two kilometres before disappearing on hard ice. In the published account of the expedition Shipton wrote: 'When the tracks crossed a crevasse we could see clearly how the creature,

in jumping across, had dug its toes in to prevent itself from slipping back.' Shipton took photographs of Ward standing beside the line of tracks and of a footprint with the head of an ice-axe to show the size.

After the 1960 expedition Ed Hillary and other expedition members decided the yeti was imaginary and the footprints had been made by other animals. But Desmond Doig commented later that theirs was a large and noisy group, likely to frighten away any timid animal. They hadn't seen snow leopards either, though they were in their habitat. The yeti question remains open.

This was the plan. During September 1960, one party would carry tons of expedition stores, equipment and building supplies to the Mingbo Valley above Tengboche and find sites for the two high-altitude huts. Norman Hardie led this group. Ed, meanwhile, would lead another party into Rolwaling Valley west of the Khumbu to search for evidence of the yeti. In late October Ed and his group would cross the Tesi Lapcha Pass into the Khumbu, meet up with the others, and assist with siting and assembling the huts. Scientific director Dr Griffith Pugh and his team would arrive from the UK and America in late October, and spend the winter studying human acclimatisation while Ed returned to New Zealand for more supplies. He would be back in March, bringing Louise with him for the walk in from Kathmandu – her first visit to Nepal. The final part of the expedition was the attempt on a peak – probably Makalu – with the high-altitude team joined by Ed and two other climbers.

Ed was delighted and relieved when Norman Hardie agreed to take on the leadership of the building group. He was the perfect man for the job, a civil engineer and experienced Himalayan climber who had spent six months living in the Sherpa region and spoke the language. He did outstanding work managing the straggling lines of 310 heavily laden porters through torrential monsoon rains to Tengboche, and by the time the yeti-hunting 'playboys' (Hardie's description) arrived in Khumjung on

30 October the 'workers' had plenty to show them. All the prefabricated parts for the cylindrical Silver Hut were on the Mingbo Glacier, while the Green Hut, more like a New Zealand mountain hut, was already complete, thanks to Wally Romanes, a New Zealand climber and builder working with Hardie. This became a staging post and rest stop between Mingbo and the Silver Hut.

The yeti-hunters might have been 'Hillary's playboys' when they set out, but after eight weeks trekking in high valleys and glaciers and crossing a snowy mountain pass as winter set in, they arrived in Khumjung a hardened crew, although yeti-less. Several of them wrote accounts of their experiences, and one of the most entertaining was by Desmond Doig, the expedition's reporter, linguist and enthusiastic Orientalist who earned the affection and respect of the Sherpas and of all his companions. Doig described the last manic

days of preparation before the two parts of the expedition left Kathmandu. While Ed sorted through the fourteen tons of expedition equipment and stores, which had to be made into sixty-pound porter loads – many of them extremely clumsy shapes and sizes – the novices were left to sort out their own requirements: 'whether to sacrifice foot sprays and bath salts for cans of beer, and custom-built boots for the expedition clodhoppers…or take the lot and die under the load. Does one ever know what a load is like until one is under it? And has walked with it a mile, five miles, eight, fifteen?'[4] Doig's description of the reality of trekking in remote parts of Nepal still rings true today. The agony of the first day: 'It never seemed to end; the track would go on forever, always around one more bend, and another and another…'[5] And at the end of that day, although you are numb with exhaustion, every muscle is burning and you are convinced that the worst *must* be

Right: The Silver Hut taking shape – Ed Hillary and Mike Gill, November 1960
George Lowe

Below: Porters carrying the prefabricated sections of the Silver Hut
Jim Milledge

over, your leader surges into camp with a cheering comment: 'Not a bad day. Tomorrow is a real bugger.'[6]

Ed left Kathmandu hours after the rest of the group and, having ensured that everyone got the right footwear, had managed to leave only a pair of size ten sand shoes for himself. His feet are size twelve. Slit in strategic places, the shoes saw him through nonetheless. His fellow yeti-hunters included Dr Marlin Perkins, director of Chicago's Lincoln Park Zoo; Dr Larry Swan, an associate professor of biology from San Francisco; Dr Tom Nevison from the US Air Force School of Aviation Medicine in Texas; the New Zealanders George Lowe, Peter Mulgrew, Pat Barcham and Mike Gill; and Bhanu Bannerjee from Calcutta, who helped Desmond Doig with media reports.

They found several sets of footprints on the Ripimu Glacier at the head of the Rolwaling Valley, but hidden microphones and cameras enmeshed in trip wires failed to capture a yeti's likeness – or record its famous high-pitched whistle. The rifle with the tranquilliser darts was not required. They concluded eventually that the footprints they had found were the tracks of a smaller animal which had melted out in the sun. Michael Ward and Eric Shipton had photographed similar tracks near here on the 1951 Everest Reconnaissance, but those two climbers were far less conspicuous than this large party. Peter Mulgrew recorded the comment of their sirdar Urkien: 'How can the sahibs expect to see a Yeti when they parade around the countryside like a herd of lumbering multi-coloured Yaks?'[7]

But the weeks in the Rolwaling Valley did have a significant outcome: the emergence of the idea of a school. As Ed has often recounted, he was sitting by the campfire one night, thinking about all that mountaineers owed to the Sherpas, and asked Urkien, 'If there was one thing we could do for your people what would it be?' Urkien replied, 'We would like our children to go to school, sahib…Knowledge for our children – that we would like to see.'[8]

The final straw on the abortive yeti hunt seems to have been Peter Mulgrew's fishcakes, made from tinned Canadian salmon – a recipe Ed and Peter had enjoyed on Christmas Day 1957 in Antarctica. Desmond Doig wrote: 'It was never ascertained whether they or the altitude, or both, were responsible for Ed, George, Tom Nevison and Peter himself having a miserable night following the feast. Whatever it was, Ed was prompted by his immediate misery to pull out…To search for tracks on the Menlung glacier, he argued, would be futile. The snow conditions were plainly bad…Besides, sitting around at 19,000 feet might tempt Peter to cook again.'[9] They headed over to Khumjung, making the hazardous crossing of the 5755-metre (18,881 ft) Tesi Lapcha Pass on 28 October with the help of sixty Sherpas who came over to meet them. This was Ed's first time back in Sherpa country since 1954. Doig recalled: 'Ed Hillary sat

Above: The ski run outside the Silver Hut
Mike Gill

Right: 'Yeti' tracks on the Ripimu Glacier, October 1960
Mike Gill

at the top of the pass, his shaggy mane riding a near gale and icicles forming in his beard. For the rugged, unemotional character we considered him to be he was suddenly unexpectedly nostalgic. He confessed to being moved, excited, experiencing a feeling of "coming home".'[10]

Ed had been in regular radio contact with Norman Hardie, but for a few days their frequency was jammed by loud recordings of Chinese opera. This led to an outbreak of jokes about the 'Hillary International Spying Expedition', but was an indicator of the nervousness of the Chinese about their border with Nepal. As the expedition walked down through the village of Thami, they found it surrounded by a sea of black yak-hair tents. The population had swelled with an influx of Tibetan refugees who had crossed the Nangpa La, the high pass from Tibet, bringing their yaks, sheep and goats with them. Norman Hardie walked up to meet Ed's group at Thami and they reached Khumjung on 30 October. Griffith Pugh had arrived with most of the scientific equipment two days before. The next two weeks saw the Silver Hut assembled on a magnificent site at 5940 metres (19,500 ft) with a dramatic fluted ridge behind, a ski slope

at its front door, and Rakpa, an ebullient little Tibetan puppy, in residence. The scientists began their work as winter set in.

Desmond Doig, meanwhile, had been on the track of yeti relics. He had managed to purchase a yeti skin, and Urkien had told him that some monasteries and *gompas* – Sherpa temples – had yeti scalps and skeletal hands. Doig alerted Ed, and after several false starts they began negotiations to borrow a yeti scalp from Khumjung *Gompa* and take it to America and Europe to be looked at by scientists. Village elders were extremely reluctant to part with the precious relic which brought prestige to their village and good luck with weather and crops. Ed brought to the negotiating table an offer to build a school at Khumjung and pay the salary of its first teacher. He didn't have the money to pay for it, but hoped that he might convince Field Enterprises to help both with this and

with airfares for those accompanying the yeti scalp. Unfortunately, John Dienhart wasn't on the spot to confirm this possibility – he had walked back to Kathmandu when his tape recorders refused to work and, after deciding that trekking at altitude was not for him, had not returned. Urgent cables were sent to Chicago and word spread quickly around Kunde and Khumjung. A fifteen-year-old boy, Kalden, presented Ed with a petition signed by sixty village children, asking him to build them a school.

An agreement was eventually reached, signed – and sealed with appropriate ceremony. Ed would contribute 8000 Nepali rupees for *gompa* repairs, and in return Ed and Desmond

Below left: Ed Hillary holding what was said to be a yeti skin, obtained in the village of Beding and later identified as a blue bear from Eastern Tibet
Mike Gill

Below: Khumjung's yeti scalp
Mike Gill

Above: Khunjo Chumbi wearing the yeti scalp
Mike Gill

Right: Filming the yeti scalp – Ed Hillary and Desmond Doig
Mike Gill

Expedition sirdars 1960–61

DAWA TENZING FROM KHUMJUNG – OVERALL EXPEDITION SIRDAR

'Dawa Tenzing is old-school Sherpa, with plaited hair and attempting mandarin whiskers. With a fine record of mountaineering – he was with General Bruce on Everest and has been on some great mountain every year since 1952 – Dawa is on the verge of retirement, possibly into a lamasery . . . As benign as he is wise he can become something of a terror when his authority is even remotely questioned, and I have seen many a hard-boiled Sherpa become jelly before the wrath of the old sirdar.'* The brother of Ang Tharkay, Dawa Tenzing carried loads to the South Col on the 1953 Everest expedition, and was sirdar for many expeditions, including the 1955 ascent of Kangchenjunga (8586 m; 28,169 ft). In his later years Dawa Tenzing lived in a cottage he built beside the nunnery at Daweche where his two daughters were nuns. A devout Buddhist he always upheld the traditions and values of his people.

URKIEN FROM KHUMJUNG – SIRDAR FOR THE YETI HUNT

'Dawa Tenzing's deputy and stepson and leader of our Yeti-hunting Sherpas is Urkien, who has an engaging habit of widening his eyes when he laughs, and he laughs often. Urkien is tougher than the proverbial horse and a very experienced climber. But he has one unfortunate failing, an incapacitating temper . . . The fiery local brew called chang is generally fuel to his rage. But Urkien is a lovable, intelligent person when he's sober, and I've enjoyed his company, discussing religion and reincarnations and Sherpa education, by the hour.'† Urkien was the first to suggest that a school for Sherpa children was the best way for Ed Hillary to help the Sherpas.

Photo: Mike Gill

ANNULLU FROM KHUMJUNG – SIRDAR FOR THE MAKALU CLIMB

An excellent climber, Annullu was on Everest in 1953, carrying to the South Col; he also helped with the rescue of Peter Mulgrew from Makalu, having led Mike Gill on their autumn ascent of Island Peak (6096 m; 20,000 ft). In 1964 he was foreman on the difficult Dudh Kosi Bridge project. 'It had been a dangerous job building the bridge over fierce rapids, but Annulu had employed all his friends and relations on the project, for, as he said, "Working with Burra Sahib, everybody always very lucky." There had been quite a few disasters during bridge-building activities, but Ed had insisted on following normal safety procedures and nobody had been hurt.'‡

In January 1972 Ed and Louise Hillary were shocked to learn that Annullu had died in a climbing accident. As more climbing expeditions came to Nepal there was a marked increase in the number of Sherpa deaths – devastating for the small Sherpa communities. Louise wrote: 'Compensation for the next-of-kin of a dead Sherpa climber is 3,000 American dollars, and this is a very large sum in Nepal, but of course it never compensates for the loss of a young man at the height of his working capacity – or for the blow that his death is to his wife and young children.'§

Photo: Edmund Hillary

From the top of the world's tallest building
EMPIRE STATE
I was photographed in LIFE Color 1472 feet above the street and looking out over the most fabulous skyline of the world.

Right: A souvenir of Khunjo Chumbi's visit to New York from his scrapbook – Desmond Doig, Khunjo Chumbi and Ed Hillary, 17 December 1960

124 Doig were permitted to take the yeti scalp away for exactly six weeks. Khunjo Chumbi, a village elder, would go with them and be with the scalp at all times. Ed would attempt to find funds for a school for Khumjung while he was away, but if they were late back then Ed's three sirdars, Dawa Tenzing, Urkien and Annullu, would forfeit their houses and yaks to the village and monastery. These three were the real heroes of the deal, risking everything on their trust in Ed's ability to return on time. It was a tall order.

Griffith Pugh and his team were less than enthusiastic about Ed's departure for six weeks, but keeping the sponsors happy is a leader's job, and without a live animal to show for the trip this was the next best thing. (And the publicity that Ed, Khunjo and the yeti relics engendered ensured Field Enterprises's continuing support for Sherpa aid projects for over a decade.) On 25 November Ed, Doig and Khunjo Chumbi set off to walk at double pace to Kathmandu, covering the fifteen-day walk in nine. They could just make their deadline if they could get a helicopter to fly them back – though this was by no means guaranteed.

Khunjo had prepared for his trip by getting together blocks of Tibetan tea, *tankas* (sacred scroll paintings), yak-tail fly whisks and bags of *tsampa* (roasted barley flour) to present to the King of Nepal, Queen Elizabeth and President Eisenhower. In Kathmandu they had an audience with King Mahendra Bir Bikram Shah, then they flew to Bangkok and on to Honolulu – Khunjo Chumbi's first sight of the ocean. They arrived in Chicago on 11 December 1960.

Khunjo was a handsome, laughing man and a brilliant dancer, who wore his Tibetan clothes with great swagger and charm. All this, along with the fame of Sir Edmund Hillary and the mysterious yeti relics, contributed to a triumphant progress through New York, Chicago, Paris and London. In the end scientists pronounced the skin to be from a blue bear. The yeti 'scalp' had been made from the hide of the serow antelope – probably intended as a ceremonial hat but gradually acquiring the status of an actual scalp. The scalp might not have been the real thing, but as Mike Gill noted: 'Khunjo Chumbi was declared genuine and as an exponent of Tibetan dancing was asked to perform wherever he went, from the Merchandise Mart in Chicago to the night clubs of Paris.'[11] Khunjo also gave a winning response to Professor J. Millot of the Musée de l'Homme in Paris when he suggested that yetis did not exist: 'In Nepal we have neither giraffes nor kangaroos so we know nothing about them. In France there are no Yetis so I sympathize with your ignorance.'[12]

Khunjo was anxious to spare Ed the embarrassment of having to concede that he could not produce scientific evidence of a yeti. He offered to find a real one for him on their return to the Khumbu, but in the end Ed concluded the yeti's existence was cultural rather than physical. Mike Gill summed up the view of the sahibs: 'What is the yeti? In Sherpa mythology, it seems, the yeti is an evil spirit. To the Sherpas, spirits are as real as atoms, or angels, are to us – though to prove they are there is not easy … the few of us who believe in angels must trust in hearsay or faith, and though we accept atoms without question, there are not many of us who can prove our belief. So if a Sherpa finds unknown tracks in the snow, or catches a glimpse of a vague shape at dusk, or when by himself in a lonely hut on a stormy night hears strange noises – why then it is a yeti.'[13]

On 4 January 1961, exactly six weeks after they had left, they arrived back in a chartered helicopter, the first ever to land at Khumjung, giving an appropriately dramatic entrance for the precious scalp. It was returned safely to the *gompa*; Dawa Tenzing, Annullu and Urkien relaxed; and the main business of the expedition could continue. After visiting the team at the Silver Hut, Ed left with Peter Mulgrew for Kathmandu and New Zealand to get together the supplies for the climbing expedition in the spring. The winter team would go through a lot of food. 'The quantities involved in such an expedition as ours were large. We had a thousand pounds of tinned fruit, three hundred and eighty pounds of bacon, eleven hundred pounds of butter, a thousand pounds of chocolate, three thousand pounds of sugar. We had to feed our Sherpas as well as ourselves, and although in general we purchased local food for their requirements, we also supplied them with freeze-dried meats, butter, dried milk, chocolate, tea and sugar.'[14] Ed avoided the 'common expedition burdens' of rancid butter and melted-down chocolate by having these foods shipped as refrigerated cargo to Calcutta and then flown to Kathmandu. And he was very grateful for the generosity of their sponsors.

While they were in Chicago, Field Enterprises, no doubt impressed by the real Sherpa in their midst (Khunjo received a 900-woman ovation from the typists at their Merchandise Mart), had agreed to contribute more funds to build and furnish the school and pay a teacher's salary. The Indian Aluminium Company would donate a prefabricated building, so the establishment of the school was now added to the list of expedition objectives. Ed just had to get the building to the site and find a teacher.

The wintering party's experiments and physiological monitoring programmes were progressing well. Most of them lived permanently at the Silver Hut, but their scientific leader Griffith Pugh was based at Mingbo, a Sherpa summer settlement at 4570 metres (15,000 ft). In this pretty valley they had hired a Sherpa house as a mess hut, and Wally Romanes fitted out a large Arctic tent with laboratory benches –

Above: Khunjo Chumbi arriving at Chicago, 11 December 1960

Right: Khunjo Chumbi and his wife Pali waiting by the path to welcome Louise Hillary, May 1963. On the right is Thukten Philip Sherpa
Mike Gill

the tent was erected on low stone walls to give extra headroom. Water was not plentiful, but Mingbo had a Finnish-style sauna for a weekly steam bath – a technique introduced by Tom Nevison early in the expedition, much to the sahibs' delight and the amusement of the Sherpas.

Meanwhile, up at the Silver Hut the daily routine included sessions on the bicycle ergometer for each man, while readings were made of heart and lung function, and blood samples were taken every few minutes. The subject pedalled furiously and sweated profusely while balancing the numerous wires and needles attached to his body and breathing into a bag. Physical examinations were made after each session on the machine, and the blood and exhaled air were analysed. It was hard work. The mind also functions more sluggishly at altitude and Mike Gill's primary responsibility was to monitor mental acuteness. Despite the stresses of the bicycle ergometer, these were the most unpopular tests of all. Gill described one of them as diabolic: 'The subject performed two tasks concurrently, one a visual recognition and marking of number sequences on a typed sheet, the other a memory test: in this, a woman's voice on a tape recorder read out ten letters of the alphabet, one of which was repeated. At the end of each sequence of ten, the voice would ask, cynically, accusingly or jeeringly, according to one's mood, "Which letter was repeated?"'[15]

Scientific investigations were taking place outside the Silver Hut too. Barry Bishop, a glaciologist with the National Geographic Society, spent the winter studying the composition and movement of the glacier on which they were living; surveyed the entire Mingbo Valley; and kept regular meteorological readings.

The Silver Hut was a comfortable home. It had been designed by Ed and Griffith Pugh to ensure that the men who lived there were not stressed by difficult living conditions as well as by the altitude. There were bunks at one end, laboratory equipment at the other and a slightly temperamental stove in between. The hut was very well insulated and always warm – and some men chose to sleep in tents outside when the heat and the snoring got too much. Food supplies were excellent and Sherpas were rostered to cook for them.

On Christmas Day 1960, Ed was in Norwich with his sister June and her family, Khunjo Chumbi was with Desmond Doig's family in Kent, and the scientists all gathered in the Silver Hut. That morning Griffith Pugh came up from Mingbo with the last group of recently arrived physiologists: Dr Michael Ward,

Dr Larry Lahiri, Captain Motwani and Dr John West. As they staggered towards the hut, feeling the altitude, they were welcomed by Rakpa, who was galloping about, delirious with excitement, and the five residents lined up outside singing, appropriately, 'God Rest Ye Merry Gentlemen'. After a spot of skiing they sat down amidst silver and red streamers and an array of Christmas cards, and ate a Christmas dinner that included freeze-dried shrimp, roast Sherpa sheep, fried yak, canned Christmas pudding, fresh oranges and cherry brandy.[16] Outside the hut the mountains sparkled and inside it the whisky flowed freely, bringing goodwill to all.

They were a compatible group and the winter passed without friction. Skiing every day was a treat which helped keep the men fit, although they dreamed of a ski-tow at the end of the run. At the beginning they lost weight and their work capacity dropped by half, but this had improved to about two-thirds by the end of the winter. The younger Dawa Tenzing agreed to undergo the same trial by bicycle, and his results showed that a Sherpa, 'strengthened by generations of living at heights above 12,000 feet, lost little of his efficiency at 19,000 feet and could

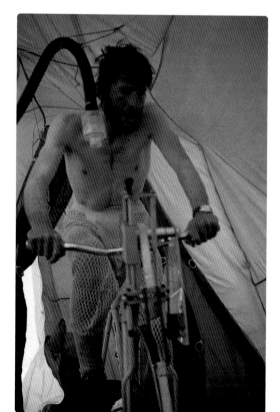

Left: Jim Milledge on the bicycle ergometer in the Silver Hut
Mike Gill

126

still produce an almost sea-level performance'.[17] And that was not his maximum strength, since Sherpas had no experience of riding bicycles. After the expedition Griffith Pugh, Michael Ward and John West all continued their investigations into high-altitude medicine and physiology, and the information from the Silver Hut experiments remains scientifically significant. It has also been practically useful, since more than 150 million people in the world live at high altitude, and many visit these areas for sport and recreation.[18]

There was another winter project too. The International Red Cross was anxious to get food to the Tibetan refugees and had asked Ed to help. 'The Red Cross had a Pilatus Porter aircraft with an outstanding high altitude performance and the ability to operate off very small airstrips – but there was nowhere in the Khumbu for it to land. Could I recommend a suitable area? I remembered the long slopes in the little valley above Mingbo and we agreed to co-operate on building a strip there.'[19] The expedition would organise the building of the strip using Sherpa labour, in return for use of the aircraft to help bring in expedition supplies and the prefabricated school building – in parts.

This became the highest airstrip in Nepal – 4750 metres (15,000 ft) – and the first of the three airstrips in the region, all built by Hillary-led expeditions. The Mingbo airstrip was later condemned as unsafe by Civil Aviation, but for this expedition it would be a lifeline.

Most of the scientists were climbers and Wally Romanes, their indispensable maintenance expert, was one of New Zealand's best. The weather was clear most of the winter, with very little snow, and as they sweated on the stationary bicycle the magnificent peaks around them beckoned. The most spectacular of these, Ama Dablam, was directly above the hut. Like most people, Mike Gill caught his breath in awe at the first sight of this glittering beauty, and wrote: 'Demons dwell on other peaks but Ama Dablam is too lovely a mountain to be the home of an evil spirit.'[20]

Ed Hillary knew perfectly well what makes mountaineers tick. 'Both Pugh and I believed that it was essential for the success of the physiological programme that the mountaineering enthusiasm of the party be maintained at high pitch – otherwise some of the incentive for living at these uncomfortable

heights would be lost.'[21] In mid-February Griffith Pugh decided four of them should do a climb, and leave the other scientists with space and time to catch up with some of their work. Wally Romanes made the initial recce of Ama Dablam with Pemba Tensing and drily noted on his return: 'she'd be a good climb in New Zealand'.[22] And so four Silver Hut residents, Ward, Gill, Bishop and Romanes, after a technically and physically challenging climb, achieved the first successful ascent of this formidable peak. They reached the 6856-metre (22,494 ft) summit on 13 March 1961.

The descent was nerve-wracking and after two days they were greatly relieved to be almost down. Then disaster struck: Gumi Dorje fell badly and broke his leg. Gill and Ward splinted the leg and gave him morphine, then took it in turns to carry Gumi down on their backs while Barry Bishop helped the other Sherpas with the loads and Wally Romanes was on belay. Mike Gill wrote: 'Seldom have I felt so keenly my dependence on a piece of rope as I did then, leaning out from the rock wall with nothing beneath me, feet pressed against the rock, while the whole of my weight, and Gumi's, passed through that thin, taut piece of nylon to Wally's belay.'[23] Two days later they were back at the hut and Gumi was carried down to Griffith Pugh at Mingbo. But this was not the end of the problems created by Ama Dablam.

127

Right: Collecting exhaled air for analysis after a session on the bicycle – Tom Nevison
Mike Gill

Far right: Christmas 1960 in the Silver Hut. (L–R) Tom Nevison, Barry Bishop, Wally Romanes, Mike Gill, Jim Milledge
Mike Gill

On that summit day Ed and Peter Mulgrew were en route from Kathmandu with 230 porters and two new climbers – John Harrison from New Zealand and Californian Leigh Ortenburger. Ed had spent a brief summer at home in Auckland with his family, organising all the supplies for the spring expedition. Among their excited companions were Louise Hillary and June Mulgrew on their first visit to Nepal, and the wives of several other expedition members: Irene Ortenburger, Betty Milledge, Lila Bishop and Gitta Bannerjee. The women would walk the 290 kilometres to Mingbo and then fly back. This would be Louise's first holiday without the children, who spent the four weeks in the care of Louise's parents and the family's mainstay Lillian MacCormack, or 'Mrs Mac'. Sherpa children would be the beneficiaries of this trip, and Louise's enthusiasm for the school idea was immediate and lasting. Thanks to Desmond Doig's contacts, their party also included the first teacher for the Khumjung School. 'We were fortunate in obtaining an excellent man from Darjeeling, Tem Dorji Sherpa, a school teacher of long experience, ex junior army officer, Buddhist religion, born in Darjeeling of Sherpa parents and with a competent grasp of the Nepali, Sherpa, Hindustani and English languages.'[24] This was an inspired appointment, and Tem Dorji went on to lead the school for nine fruitful years.

The Hillarys' short stay in Kathmandu coincided with a state visit to Nepal by Queen Elizabeth II and the Duke of Edinburgh. At a reception at the British Embassy they were delighted to find Khunjo Chumbi and his wife among the guests. The Queen had been away when Khunjo brought his gifts to Buckingham Palace. She wanted to thank him in person, and his wife Pali was invited too. Khunjo had not long returned from his travels and Pali was nine months' pregnant with her sixth child, but without hesitation the couple set out on the fifteen-day walk from Khumjung. Four days out of Kathmandu, Pali gave birth to her third son. She told the Queen, 'I did not want to miss you, so I wasted no time about having the child and decided to keep up with the men when they walked on after their food. That was only five days ago.'[25] The baby was named Thukten Philip Sherpa in honour of the Duke.

Louise's presence offered a new slant for the media covering Ed's Himalayan activities. One French newspaper announced 'Lady Hillary to Climb Everest' and described Louise as 'both gracious and sporting. [She] will climb with three specially chosen companions, without any male, to prove she is as good as her husband.'[26] Ed himself was delighted at last to be showing Louise the country he had come to love. 'This was an old familiar route to me, but now I was seeing it through the eyes of the newcomers … We were constantly climbing or descending over great mountain ridges, crossing tumbling streams, and exclaiming at barely credible views of the snow-clad Himalayan giants … But it was the flowers that really made our days so wonderful. The crimson rhododendrons were in full bloom; our path clung to hillsides which were a blaze of colour in every direction. And as we climbed up to each saddle or pass the air would be heavy with the scent of daphne and the grassy sward hidden by a thick carpet of primulas. The magnolias were just coming in to bloom, and in every shady spot and on every second tree, it seemed, were clusters of graceful orchids.'[27] Louise fell in love with Nepal too.

Ed, Louise and their party visited Tengboche, then walked on up to Chanmitang, a small settlement where the expedition had hired an empty Sherpa house as its main supply store. There on 18 March Ed met the victorious climbers and the rest of the winter team and listened to their stories, while Griffith Pugh flew back to Kathmandu, taking Gumi Dorje to hospital to have his leg treated. Ed set about his usual tasks of paying off porters and sorting supplies. Then 'On March 20th we moved up to our 15,000-foot Mingbo Base Camp and I started the ball rolling for the final major stage of the expedition – the Makalu assault.'[28] He signed on and equipped more Sherpas, sorted food and equipment into loads, and purchased supplies of local food. Meanwhile at Khumjung, Louise and the other women trekkers befriended Sherpa children and socialised with Sherpa families, and Tem Dorji began taking outdoor lessons on the grassy plot where the school would be built. The talk was all of the school, a prefabricated aluminium building which would soon be flown in by the Red Cross. Everything looked bright.

But newspapers in New Zealand, England and America had devised thrilling headlines to report the climb of 'the terrible tooth' and 'killer peak' of Ama Dablam, and the Nepalese authorities took note. Pugh flew back to Mingbo on 22 March with grim news. His Majesty's Government of Nepal was most displeased –

Facing page, left: Ama Dablam (6856 m; 22,494 ft) from Khumjung.

Most spectacular of the lot is Ama Dablam… Its first impact on the senses is disbelief. 'It isn't true! It can't possibly exist!' was the reaction of one member of our party…in 1951.
Edmund Hillary, *High in the Thin Cold Air*
Edmund Hillary

Facing page, right: The first ascent of Ama Dablam, 13 March 1962. (L–R) Mike Gill, Wally Romanes, Michael Ward, Barry Bishop
Mike Gill

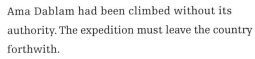

Ama Dablam had been climbed without its authority. The expedition must leave the country forthwith.

And so Ed had to drop everything, just as they were about to set off towards Makalu, and fly back to Kathmandu with Louise and the wives who were due to leave. With them went Kalden, presenter of the Khumjung school petition, who was sent to school in Kathmandu on the understanding that after three years he would return to Khumjung to assist Tem Dorji. Ed was determined to keep the expedition on track. He would fight to prevent the final part of their scientific programme from being undermined – and after all the long months of fundraising and organising he wanted to do some climbing himself. 'For nine days I trudged around Government buildings seeing officials and ministers and trying desperately to change the decision. If it had served any useful purpose I was ready to crawl through the Government offices on my hands and knees. It was an enormous relief when the Government finally relented and allowed us to continue after the payment of a modest fine – but I had spent the worst nine days I can remember and I was emotionally exhausted.'[29] He had won the battle, but his unplanned return to low altitude, and consequent loss of mountain fitness would have severe repercussions for them all.

129

Himalayan
Flowers

Ed and Louise
x Pearl while
e Khumbu

the flowers
made our
derful. The
dodendrons
l bloom;
ng to
hich were
colour in
tion.

Cold Air

'63

EPH

JUL 63N

MADE IN U.S.A.

EPH

JUL 63N

MADE IN U.S.A.

Louise

JUL 63N

MADE IN U.S.A.

VIEW FROM THIS SIDE

MOUNT MADE IN ENGLAND

MADE IN U.S.A.

JUL 63N

EPH/M35/11.

MADE IN AUSTRALIA

MAY 70NZ3

No.

DATE:

TITLE:

JUN 73NZ6

JUN 73NZ5

It was like a fairyland with
half-frozen streams dashing
down story valleys and
graceful waving bamboos
clustered beneath tall,
gnarled trees. Through this
lovely foreground we caught
glimpses of towering mountains while all around us the
little daphne bushes carpeted
the forest floor with dainty
star-like blossoms. We picked
great bunches of the flowers
and drank in their perfume.

Louise Hillary, *A Yak for Christmas*

Perhaps the view was most spectacular to the east, for here the giants Makalu and Kanchenjunga dominated the horizon and gave some idea of the vast scale of the Himalayas. Makalu in particular, with its soaring rock ridges, was a remarkable sight; it was only a few miles away from us. From our exalted viewpoint I could see all the northern slopes of the mountain and was immediately struck by the possibility of a feasible route to its summit. With a growing feeling of excitement, I took another photograph to study at leisure on our return to civilisation.
EDMUND HILLARY

Ed had originally considered a closer peak, Lhotse Shar (8340 m; 27,550 ft) for the high-altitude climb required by the physiological programme, and before winter set in Norman Hardie led a team to investigate its suitability. But he returned to report that the summit approach was too exposed and dangerous for the long line of camps they would need. So Makalu it would be – a mountain which George Leigh Mallory described as 'incomparable for its spectacular and rugged grandeur'[1] and on which Ed's last Himalayan expedition had suffered accident and illness. Their journey from Mingbo to the base of Makalu lay through a high-altitude maze of ridges, glaciers and valleys south and east of Everest – a direct, but technically demanding route. Previous Makalu expeditions had come up the Barun Valley from the south, an approach pioneered by Eric Shipton, George Lowe and Ed Hillary in 1952.

09 MAKALU, GODDESS OF DESTRUCTION

'By going from the Mingbo over the 19,600 foot [5975 m] Amadablam Col, then across the Hongu Glacier, over 20,000 feet [6095 m] passes on either side of the high Barun Plateau and finally down to the Barun Glacier we could cover the distance in three or four days. It was a formidable route over which to take 200 loads of sixty lbs each but certainly a feasible one.'[2] Formidable indeed – and the three to four days was for unencumbered men; Sherpa porters would be working in relays carrying delicate and often clumsily shaped loads over those high passes in uncertain weather. Their bemusement at carrying the stationary bicycle up a mountain can be imagined, but the scientists needed it taken as high as possible on Makalu to obtain data from both the winter party and the new chums. The first party set off on 2 April.

Climbers prepared the route, putting in hundreds of metres of fixed ropes; Sherpas relayed the loads; and by 25 April all the supplies were safely at Camp I in the Barun Valley below the mountain. Everyone was issued with their high-altitude gear. They had supplies of oxygen, but it would be kept for emergencies: they intended, if possible, to climb without it. By an immense effort they had made up the lost days. Assessing the fitness of his team, Ed noted that the winter party were still looking fresh and the new arrivals were in fine form but that their leader was not. During the trek over to the Barun, Ed was called on to sort out some expedition problems. With Mingma Tsering, he raced back over to the Green Hut, met with Desmond Doig, sent cables to Kathmandu from the Silver Hut and hurried back, reorganising loads and leaving stores at an intermediate camp in the Hongu Valley on the way through. By the time he rejoined the main group, Ed was feeling tired and below par, but he kept on going.

The plan for the ascent involved alternating relays of men making the route, carrying supplies and establishing camps. They could then descend to a lower camp for a couple of days to recover their strength, return to the assault and relieve others. The idea of this

sort of climbing is to keep a continuous push upwards and not lose valuable time, so groups of climbers and Sherpas are spread across the camps. Radio contact keeps the leader informed of progress and able to change plans if there is an accident – or if altitude gets the better of someone. Although Sherpas are naturally more acclimatised than sahibs, even their strength and stamina are reduced at extreme heights.

A week later they had set up Camp III at 6460 metres (21,200 ft). The weather was difficult – cloudy and snowy – but Ed and Wally Romanes pushed on with Mingma Tsering and Ang Temba to complete the route to Camp IV (7010 m; 23,000 ft), which Leigh Ortenburger, Peter Mulgrew and Annullu had begun. They returned to Camp III where the physiologists had rigged up a laboratory tent. The plan was to have Camp IV in place by 3 May and it was now the 2nd, but Ed was not feeling well, he had a headache and had lost his appetite – classic symptoms of altitude sickness. He stayed at Camp III while Jim Milledge, Peter Mulgrew, Michael Ward and Mike Gill set off with Urkien, Nima Dorje and five other Sherpas, and the next day Tom Nevison and Leigh Ortenburger left with eight Sherpas. There were now a lot of men high on the mountain.

Left: Ed Hillary at Chanmitang, paying porters who had carried loads from Kathmandu for the Makalu expedition, 18 March 1961
Mike Gill

By 6 May they had a fixed rope almost up to Camp V, but Ward and Gill were tired after two days above 7010 metres, and Ed still had a pain in his forehead and the left side of his face. All three descended to Camp II, and the next day Jim Milledge and John West arrived in a snowstorm, bringing down one of the Sherpas, Aila. He had developed pulmonary oedema and needed oxygen. Things were beginning to unravel.

On Sunday 7 May, after sleeping in the morning, Ed woke and found he couldn't talk properly. He called out to Michael Ward who administered painkillers and oxygen. Ward took turns with Jim Milledge to stay with Ed all through that night, and he was aware of and comforted by their candlelit watch. By the following afternoon he had recovered a little and could speak again, but Ward's instructions were vehement and most unwelcome: Ed must descend immediately and stay below 4570 metres (15,000 ft). He seemed to have suffered a cerebral thrombosis: if he stayed at this height the consequences could be dire. Although he was extremely reluctant to leave, Ed could not

disregard the advice of the two medical officers. As Mike Gill noted, he would be surrendering control of the expedition by going down but would still feel responsibility for the party. It was a galling development. And Ed was feeling pretty wretched: 'I had a terrible urge to see Louise again and also my mother; I suppose I wanted consolation of some sort.'[3] Griffith Pugh had radioed his opinion that Ed should be helicoptered out to Kathmandu, but this he refused. He was determined to go back to Khumjung, at the relatively comfortable altitude of 3800 metres, for the completion and opening of the school.

Peter Mulgrew and Mingma Tsering came down to Camp II and offered to accompany him out. He was pleased to see them and touched by their concern, but he knew they were keen to go higher and he wanted to retain their strength for the assault. He refused their offer. Jim Milledge insisted on coming down with Ed, Aila, Dawa Tenzing and four other Sherpas, generously giving up his chances to get high on the mountain. On Monday 8 May they set off to walk back by a low-level route, resting for a

week at 4660 metres in the Barun Valley and then making the long trek back to expedition base at Chanmitang. They arrived on 29 May to be met with bad news. Makalu had beaten yet another expedition.

Ed had had high hopes of success when he left: 'The camps and route were established to Makalu Col [a saddle at 7300 metres]; there were ample supplies up and down the mountain; the assault necessities and the majority of the scientific equipment were already on the col; and we had an excellent group of Sherpas obviously ready to go anywhere. With a bit of luck and a marked improvement in the weather I felt we could confidently hope for success.'[4] He had delegated leadership of the Makalu assault to Michael Ward, who was extremely capable and had more Himalayan experience than anyone. Ward was confident too: 'The other members of the party were pretty shaken by Ed's illness and his rapid departure. But they were all very experienced mountaineers, and we had some excellent Sherpas with us. I could see no reason why, if we were given reasonable luck, we should not get to the top.'[5]

Above: John West and Michael Ward setting up the bicycle at Camp V, 7406 metres (24,300 ft)
Mike Gill

Right: Camp V on the Makalu Col; Camps VI and VII are on the glacier behind
Mike Gill

Determination they had in abundance, but luck and good weather they did not get. By 17 May the team had established Camp VII (8320 m; 27,000 ft), some 145 metres below the summit, but that day, six roped-together Sherpas fell, leaving Mingma Tsering badly cut in the face and Ang Temba with a possibly broken ankle. They managed to get back down to Camp VI while Peter Mulgrew, Tom Nevison and Annullu remained at VII to try for the top the next day. The wind was relentless.

On 18 May it was still very windy but the sky was clear. They were all moving very slowly but somehow got themselves going and pushed on until the altimeter read 27,400 feet (8350 m). Only 400 feet (120 m) to the summit: they were almost there. And then the worst happened. Peter Mulgrew collapsed, face down in the soft snow. 'The pain gave no warning. It came like a giant knife, plunged into my right side... For several seconds I lay gasping in agony, fighting for breath... For a moment I was unable to comprehend what had happened.'[6] He had suffered a pulmonary embolism – a blood clot in the lung. Above them the wind roared

thunderously past the summit, making it impossible for them to hear one another, but somehow they helped each other crawl and stagger back down to Camp VII and into the tent. They had no radio contact with the lower camps and Annullu was also unwell – it emerged later that he had cracked a rib in the fall the previous day. Tom Nevison managed to get Mulgrew and Annullu into sleeping bags and gave them some soup, but their situation was desperate.

On 19 May they made a little progress down, with Mulgrew collapsing every few minutes, but they had to stop before they reached Camp VI. They were still at 8077 metres (26,500 ft) and Mulgrew could not continue. Annullu volunteered to go for help and a few hours later Pemba Tenzing and Pasang Tenzing climbed up to them, bringing a tent, water and oxygen. Word of Mulgrew's accident was out, and over the next days more climbers and Sherpas joined the rescue efforts, but others were ill too. Michael Ward had come up to Camp VI to look at Ang Temba's ankle; Sherpas carried Ang Temba down and Ward returned to V, but

was himself overcome by the altitude. 'Even a six-inch step upwards needed infinite thought and concentration. Muscles just would not work. There is nothing that I have ever encountered that is anything like the fatigue of high altitude. It is relentless, inescapable and all embracing. No other mental or physical stress has anything in common with it. The feeling of impending dissolution is indescribable.'[7] He was unable to help anyone else and on 20 May, as he later described it, an overview of the camps revealed a grim picture:

At 26,500 feet Peter was unconscious and near to death, and with him was Leigh who was pretty exhausted.

At Camp VI, 26,000 feet was Tom, in no fit state to carry out any rescue operations.

At Camp V, 24,000 feet, on the Makalu Col, I was delirious.

At Camp IV, 23,000 feet was Angtemba with a badly sprained or broken ankle.

At Camp III, 22,000 feet were Mike and Wally, still tired out, plus John West who was not a mountaineer.[8]

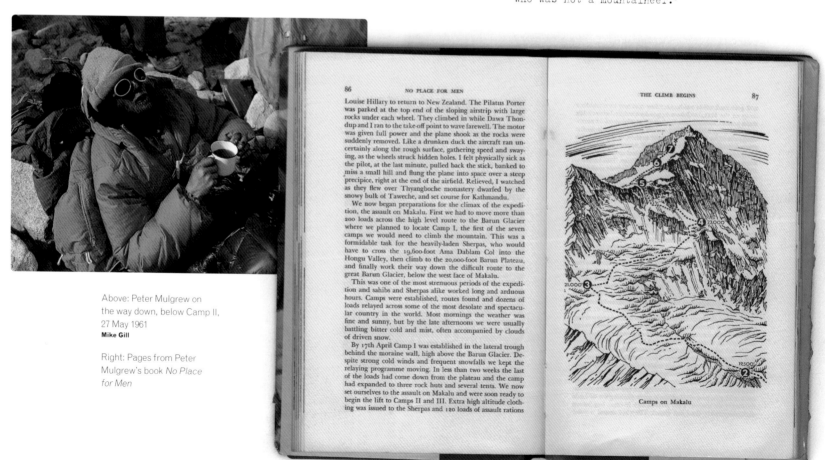

Above: Peter Mulgrew on the way down, below Camp II, 27 May 1961
Mike Gill

Right: Pages from Peter Mulgrew's book *No Place for Men*

In the end, thanks to incredible determination and push from the whole team – including John West who went with John Harrison up to Camp V and whose medical care helped Mulgrew through the journey – Mulgrew was carried all the way down to the Barun Valley. Ed wrote: 'How Peter Mulgrew managed to survive the trip down the mountain is hard to know. It was a nightmarish operation with desperate efforts by many men, spearheaded by Leigh Ortenburger and John Harrison, a New Zealand mountaineer. Urkien and his Sherpas were absolutely magnificent.'[9] On 29 May Peter Mulgrew, Michael Ward and Ang Temba were evacuated to Kathmandu, with John West accompanying them. An American helicopter ferried them out in relays since the thin air at 4660 metres reduced its load-bearing capacity. It was organised by Desmond Doig who had been stationed at the Silver Hut – the contact point between Camp I on Makalu, Khumjung and Kathmandu. On the way down the mountain Peter Mulgrew's feet and fingers had become severely frostbitten, but after a lengthy stay at Shantah Bhawan United Mission Hospital in

Kathmandu he travelled safely back to New Zealand. He lost several fingers, and both his legs were amputated below the knee.

At Chanmitang Ed Hillary was fully recovered after an energetic fifteen-day walk from the Barun Valley. He and Jim Milledge had plenty to do, managing the evacuation of the assault parties and the dismantling and removal of the Silver Hut. The hut was given to the Himalayan Mountaineering Institute in Darjeeling, where Tenzing Norgay was now director of field training, and became a useful expedition hut. But the question was inescapable: what had gone wrong?

Ed's assessment of the setbacks that had led to their defeat began with his own illness and culminated in the Sherpa fall which left a weakened party for the summit. And instead of toughening the climbers, the long stay at 5790 metres had reduced their stamina. 'Pugh had always stressed the dangers of our non-oxygen assault, pointing out that all the organs of the body were working at the limits of their capacity at these heights and there was no margin of reserve … Only some remarkable efforts – notably by Ortenburger and by the Sherpas – had brought everyone out alive … Only Harrison and Ortenburger, the two newcomers to the team, showed the expected reserves of strength.' Ed still believed that with perfect weather and a fit party, Makalu could be

climbed without oxygen, and this has since been demonstrated. But climbers working without oxygen today do not subject themselves to the 'slow and insidious sapping of weight and vitality' undergone by the men who spent that long, and memorable, winter in the Silver Hut.[10]

Still, all was not lost. 'Much had been achieved by the expedition. We had failed to climb Makalu without oxygen – but only just. We had carried out the best high-altitude physiological programme undertaken to that time, and maybe even to this day. In a lighter vein, we had certainly formed an opinion on the possible existence of the yeti.'[11] With the help of his wife June, Peter Mulgrew fought his way back to health and overcame addiction to the painkilling drug pethidine which he developed after the accident. He learned to walk on artificial legs, was successful in business and in competitive yachting, and was back in the Himalayas four years later. But not as a mountaineer. And for Ed Hillary, this second illness on Makalu signalled the end of his career as a high-altitude climber.

In addition to Ed's record of this long expedition, there are accounts by four other members of the team. How did Mike Gill, Peter Mulgrew, Michael Ward and Desmond Doig assess their leader? Did Ed Hillary measure up against his exemplars, Ernest Shackleton and John Hunt?

Right: Peter Mulgrew, June Mulgrew and Ed Hillary in an ambulance travelling from Whenuapai Airport to Devonport Naval Hospital in Auckland, July 1961
Barbara Tipping

Mike Gill, physiologist, mountaineer and filmmaker, comments particularly on Ed Hillary's imagination: his flair for thinking up great ideas for expeditions and his ability to advance from that first creative spark through the relentless detail of planning, fundraising and implementation. He has many images of Ed: the disciplined project manager, clipboard in hand, keeping track of enormous piles of supplies and equipment; the flexible leader, prepared to switch plans quickly if circumstances altered; the entertaining raconteur, relaxing with others at the end of a long day; the load carrier, shouldering a tremendously heavy pack and carrying it doggedly over great distances. And mountaineers know what a heavy pack feels like. After the Ama Dablam climb Mike Gill wrote: 'Carrying forty pounds on steep rock is bad enough at sea-level, but at 20,000 feet it defies description.'[12]

Ed Hillary is competitive by instinct and Mike Gill had first-hand experience of his 'dash and determination' at the steering wheel in the summer of 1960. Gill was in Britain familiarising himself with the expedition's medical programme and the Hillarys were also there for a few weeks. They invited Gill to come with them to Chamonix for a short mountain holiday. 'We shot across France as if we were the Triumph Herald entry in the Monte Carlo road race. Porsche, Citroën, Jaguar – if they were doing two miles an hour less than our maximum speed we passed them. We would draw in close to some sleek limousine and hang on grimly like a terrier chasing a racehorse. On the first clear straight Ed, with set jaw, would put his foot down and with a shaking and whining the car would inch ahead, Ed gripping the wheel, Louise watching tensely, while I leaned forward from my cramped position behind.'[13]

Ed liked being in the lead. He led the expedition, and he was usually out in front on the trail as well. Peter Mulgrew, another competitive man, noted this aspect of Ed's personality – setting a fast pace and pushing

himself hard on the track, hating to be overtaken. But Mulgrew also compared Ed directly with Shackleton and Hunt, and saw him as having similar leadership qualities and inspiring intense loyalty and commitment from his team. He wrote of Ed's love of adventure; his practicality and his romanticism; his tendency to self-criticism and his ability to take criticism from others without resentment; his genuine friendliness, but also the emotional reserve which could make him unaware of the feelings of others. Mulgrew also noted the Sherpas' respect for Ed: 'Hillary is very popular with all the Sherpa people, held in great awe by many of the villagers and regarded with unbounded affection by our senior Sherpas, many of whom had climbed with him on other expeditions.'[14] And on the night before the attempt on the summit of Makalu, he blessed Ed's attention to practical details: 'Insinuating oneself into a tightly fitting bag at high altitudes is no joke, and Hillary had designed ours especially with this in mind.'[15] The sleeping bags were double-sized.

138

Left: Ed Hillary in
lower Nepal, 1960
Mike Gill

Michael Ward had been on several expeditions with Ed before, and was not inclined to be awed by his stature as the climber of Everest. Like Griffith Pugh, he saw the medical-research objectives of the expedition as paramount, and was exasperated at times by Ed's absence during the winter, and by the introduction of the yeti hunt to the programme. But as members of the victorious Ama Dablam team, he and Mike Gill were both aware that their climb had led to Ed's unscheduled nine days in Kathmandu – and his consequent loss of fitness. Ward noted: 'Despite the annoyance and stress that our ascent had caused Ed, at no time did he castigate me or anyone else.'[16] It was not Ed's style to recriminate with people who had climbed well, spurred on by the challenge and excitement of doing something that had never been done before. And he also knew that good publicity helps any project.

Desmond Doig, not a climber, but a very witty writer, reporter, entertainer and linguist, who became a designer and builder of schools and a good friend, warmly praised Ed's character, his charisma as a leader and his acceptance of the weaknesses and foibles of others. He had reason to be grateful. He had been interviewed by the great Sir Edmund Hillary at the Royal Geographical Society. Doig was fresh off the plane from a Parisian holiday, 'full of free champagne and in French sports clothes completely inadequate for the English weather… I weighed something near sixteen stone and found talking and at the same time holding my breath to keep a sagging stomach in reasonable shape difficult. Sir Edmund was magnificent. He ignored alcoholic fumes and obesity in what may have been a personal save-a-soul-through-mountaineering campaign.'[17] Ed appointed Doig as the expedition's correspondent – a decision he never regretted.

One of Ernest Shackleton's men on the *Endurance*, Leonard Hussey, wrote to a friend about the character of 'The Boss' whom he described as 'always cheerful, confident and resourceful, and at his best when things look blackest'. He spoke of the loyalty Shackleton inspired and of his men's appreciation of his human qualities: 'For us he had faults, but no vices…'[18] Ed Hillary's team felt the same way.

By early June the last drama was over. Most members of the expedition headed off back to their own lives, and the monsoon showers began. At Chanmitang Ed stowed 120 loads of the Silver Hut and its equipment for collection later, and walked up to Tengboche across a hillside covered in flowers. There he met the monastery's new Rimpoche, Ngawang Tenzin Zangbu, the first reincarnate Sherpa to hold this position. Ed was impressed. 'He is only a young man – not much over thirty – but his quick, intelligent eyes and air of calmness and knowledge invest him with a cloak of spiritual authority.'[19] After a tour of the buildings, Ed was presented with gifts and assured that his return to the Khumbu would be very welcome. The monastery's new roof was showing signs of rust and Ed agreed to find some paint for it. He still had one more task – to build the school for Khumjung.

Right: Crevasses opened up in the glacier around the Silver Hut during the summer. It was dismantled by Jim Milledge and Mingma Tsering with a small team of Sherpas, and carried back to Chanmitang. Ed offered the hut to the Himalayan Mountaineering Institute in Darjeeling, where Tenzing Norgay was director of field training. It is still in use
Mike Gill

Below: Ed Hillary, 1970
Mike Gill

The dedication of Thami
School by the Head Lama
of Tengboche Monastery,
28 May 1963
Edmund Hillary

Inside the school courtyard the Head Lama sat on a raised seat cross-legged with bright Tibetan rugs around. The senior dignitaries sat on these. First of all the Head Lama said some prayers, then as the villagers and schoolchildren trooped before him and gave offerings of maize and rice, he blessed them ... Then Ed made a speech ... The Head Lama gave a good, forceful speech and he and I together cut the ribbon at the door of the schoolhouse.
LOUISE HILLARY

10 SCHOOLHOUSE IN THE CLOUDS

The Indian Aluminium Company's donated building was very shiny indeed. A box-like structure, it had a pitched roof made from the same corrugated aluminium as the walls, and two six-metre-square classrooms. It is still there today, the smallest of the impressive group of buildings which clusters along the edge of the valley below Khumjung. 'For six days we worked like madmen on the job – putting in rock foundations and wooden floors; assembling walls and trusses; attaching the roof sheets; fitting doors and windows; and bolting and screwing the whole thing down to the foundations. Our task was made more difficult by our inability to follow the assembly instructions. We were rather shaken, late one evening, to complete the roof and find we had three sheets of corrugated aluminium left over.'[1] These were doubtless put to good use by the Sherpas, whose recycling skills are legendary. At 3800 metres above sea level, Khumjung's school is probably the highest in the world.

The school team comprised Desmond Doig, Wally Romanes, Bhanu Bannerjee and Ed – and a crowd of willing assistants from Khumjung and Kunde. The sahibs were entertained by a different family each night, and arrived in the mornings bleary eyed from the after-effects of the ubiquitous *chang* but nourished by Sherpa food and friendship. Desmond Doig built two see-saws inside the yak-deterrent fence and these novelties produced shrieks of enjoyment from both children and adults. There was a lot of excitement and laughter on this building site: although expeditions had been passing through the Khumbu for a decade, it was the first time a climbing party had made a permanent addition to the community. The school opening on Sunday 11 June 1961 was a landmark occasion.

Monsoon rain fell steadily, but the official ceremonies went without a hitch. Ed cut the red ribbons that Tem Dorji had stretched across the classroom doors; the crowd cheered; the monastery trumpets emitted loud blasts; the new Head Lama of Tengboche entered the building chanting prayers, blessed the two classrooms and draped a ceremonial *karta*, a white silk scarf, around the photograph of the King of Nepal. More *kartas* were exchanged on the verandah which, much to Ed's relief, showed no signs of leaking. The culmination of the event was the blessing by the lamas, a ceremony for which the Sherpas formed a long queue. 'The head lama touched them on the crown with a silver emblem and chanted a blessing; the next lama flicked them with a little silver-mounted

brush; the third lama gave them a morsel of food which they quickly ate; the fourth lama spilled a little chang into their palm and they swallowed this; and the last lama poured some Tibetan tea into their cupped hands…It was an astonishing scene with its background of rain and fog, and perhaps the most touching feature was the eagerness with which fathers and mothers brought their tiny babies to be blessed…'[2]

The school team left Khumjung the next morning, farewelling friends and making a final visit to the school where Tem Dorji was taking his first indoor class of 'bright eyed children sitting cross-legged on the dry wooden floor, writing Nepalese characters on their slates with white chalk. Despite the steady rain outside the classroom was warm and comfortable.'[3] They climbed up the path and stopped on the ridge above the village. 'From here we could look back and see the houses of Khumjung, the green potato fields, the giant Chortens and

Left and far left: Khumjung School under construction, May 1961
Edmund Hillary

142

Mane Walls flanking the village, the gleaming wet rock precipices climbing up into the mist, and our little school, with the children waving at us from the verandah.'[4] A photograph of those first forty-five pupils standing solemnly with their new teacher on the leak-free verandah still has pride of place in the Hillary home in Auckland. Ed set off down towards Namche with a lump in his throat.

Although the school had been built in response to Sherpa requests, the children still had to carry out their usual family tasks. They looked after yaks, carried water long distances from springs high above the villages, helped with the potato harvest, and collected great baskets of leaves for the composting toilets which are found in every Sherpa house. They were already very busy, but even so, some walked several hours each day, just to go to school. Many Sherpas did not want their children to have to work as porters and Ed Hillary hoped that education could help them improve their health and their agriculture. 'As fewer people die of smallpox, malaria and TB and more mothers and babies come safely

through childbirth, so the population will rise. And as the population rises so does the need for food. It is not easy to teach people to adopt new methods and ways of living if they are unable to read and write, so this seemed to us a first priority.'[5]

Talk spread around the valleys to other Sherpa communities of the fine work done by Tem Dorji – of the children's enjoyment of their lessons and their progress in reading and writing. Reports came through to Ed Hillary in New Zealand, and before long requests began to arrive from other villages, asking Ed to build schools for them too. This was an unexpected and gratifying development. And a challenge – Ed had to find the money somehow. Fortunately, his American sponsors, Field Enterprises, who had given $US 9000 towards the transport of the Khumjung School building and the teacher's salary, were keen to stay involved.

In return for its sponsorship, Field Enterprises asked Ed to return to Chicago after the expedition and spend a year lecturing for World Book Encyclopedia. The Hillarys changed their first-class return tickets from Auckland to Chicago into economy-class round-the-world tickets, and the whole family flew out of Auckland on New Year's Eve 1961. This was their

first big adventure together, and Louise Hillary described it as 'undoubtedly the happiest experience of my life'.[6] Her book about their year away, *Keep Calm if You Can*, gives an engaging picture of the family dynamic: Ed's intense enjoyment of travel and his excellent organisation; the liveliness of the children – Peter was seven, Sarah five and a half and Belinda three; and Louise's own sparkle and resourcefulness. Like all good travel writers, she managed to find humour in exasperating situations. She recorded her encounters with unfamiliar American supermarkets and laundrettes; the trials of being recognised and photographed – which she avoided whenever possible; the inevitability of untameable piles of luggage; and the children's problems with strange food, upset stomachs and boring airport delays. The indignities of family travel are magnified when you are married to a very famous man and have three very normal children. A passenger sitting in front of the Hillary ménage on one flight commented drily: 'Climbing Everest must have been nothing to this.'

The opening chapter of Louise's book included some advice 'to all would-be wives of mountaineers or explorers. Before saying that final, fateful "Yes", stop and think. Do you want

143

Facing page, right: Collecting leaves for the composting toilets was a regular task for Sherpa children
Edmund Hillary

Facing page, bottom left: Khumjung School students and teachers, 1963
Edmund Hillary

Far right: The Hillary family's Christmas card, 1961

to get up at 5 o'clock in the morning whether it is cold or rainy? Do you want to live under canvas for two months with three young children? What about the thought of being a grass widow for 50 per cent of the time? Well, just for the record I didn't think about any of these things when I took the plunge. Now, ten years later, I am well and truly embroiled in this sort of life and year by year I am finding it more possible to overcome the minor crises of life when they rear their ugly heads. My battle-cry before travelling is, "How many extraordinary and perhaps dreadful adventures will there be before we are all together again at home?"[7]

In their first six months in America Ed was away from Chicago almost every week. He delivered 106 lectures in eighty cities, shook hands with 17,000 World Book employees, and gave innumerable television, radio and press interviews. Field Enterprises were delighted. Early in the year Ed also began another important business relationship. Sears Roebuck and Company invited him to join their sports advisory staff as an expert on camping equipment. It was a connection that lasted more than thirty-five years, so the Hillarys always had excellent tents. Ed took his product-testing responsibilities seriously, and Louise later wrote about waking up on one Himalayan trip to find the corner cut out of their sleeping tent: Ed had sent it back to Sears Roebuck – an attachment needed improving.

In July 1962 the Hillarys set off to drive right across America to San Francisco, then up to Alaska and back to Chicago through Canada. This was not just a get-away-from-it-all family adventure. It was organised in association with the Conservation Education Branch of the Forest Service in the US Department of Agriculture. The chief of the branch, Dr Matthew Brennan, had spent time in Antarctica, and he and his family travelled with the Hillarys, staying in National Forest Service camp grounds across the country. Ed would comment on the parks' suitability for foreign tourists, whom the US was keen to attract, and make himself available for press photographs and interviews en route. The Hillarys would also use Sears Roebuck camping equipment, including the small camper trailer which they towed behind a large Ford station wagon, and Sears would film their travels in Alaska. The mascot for the National Forest Service went with them in the form of two much-loved

Smokey Bear toys, given by the Brennans to Sarah and Belinda.

Louise made wry comments on their progress. On the first day they discovered that a map had been left behind: 'When you are a famous explorer you go in fear and trembling of ever losing your way, because if you do, no one will ever let you forget it.' After a horse-riding excursion they were all saddle sore and Ed had to give more interviews: 'I can't imagine what appeared in the press the following day, perhaps something like this: "Ageing explorer has tiring holiday with family".'[8] Ed wrote to John Claydon, who was in Washington: 'It's something of a strain on one's patience to complete a 460-mile drive over the hot desert and then have three TV cameras record every move as you pitch your tent...Yesterday morning I interviewed two radio stations and three newspapers as I was packing up for our day's drive. They rolled in as we were halfway

Left and below: Photographs from the Hillarys' camping holiday travelling across America, July and August 1962

Colorado

Nevada

Echo

through breakfast.'[9] His temper did fray occasionally, as did Louise's – Ed described her as 'pretty fiery when provoked' – but their spats were quickly resolved. And he was happy – as his family always knew from his piercing whistle around their campsites. The tune was invariably 'On Top of Old Smoky'. In the evenings they all crowded onto the bed in the trailer and Ed continued Percy Hillary's tradition – entertaining his children with gripping stories of the adventures of Jimmy Job. On one memorable occasion Jimmy escaped from a ferocious, roaring grizzly bear by tying mosquitoes to the hairs on his head – they flew him gently into the safety of Belinda's sleeping bag.[10] Ed wrote later: 'It was really Louise who kept us going as a successful and tight little team.'[11] They were travelling through magnificent country and they loved it.

Ed was working hard on Himalayan plans too. His letter to John Claydon included a request for help in ascertaining the Nepalese Customs charges for camping equipment, food, medical stores, construction tools and materials, clothing, radio and photographic gear, since expedition equipment was no longer free of

duty. In May 1962 the *New York Times* had reported that Sir Edmund Hillary, who looked 'somewhat Lincolnesque', was 'starting a five-year program for education for the Sherpas'.[12] Ed was making progress with fundraising – World Book Encyclopedia intended to contribute $50,000, enough to maintain a school for five years. He also applied for grants to help with a medical programme, for he hoped to arrange some elementary health care for the Sherpas.

In November 1962 Gertrude Hillary flew to Chicago to join them, and the whole family packed up and headed off for New York and then London. The round-the-world tickets expired on 31 December and Ed wanted them all to go to India and Nepal before they flew home to New Zealand. He had meetings to attend everywhere, so Gertrude and the children went up to Norwich to be with June and Jimmy and their cousins for a few days while Ed and Louise stayed in London. There was a question mark over the next leg of the journey until the border tensions between India and China eased, but eventually the situation seemed calmer and Ed decided to press on to New Delhi, where Louise enjoyed their stay at the New Zealand High Commission. 'Peter, Sarah and Belinda easily adapted themselves to a life of being idolized by the Residency servants. All my domestic duties were taken over immediately

by the willing staff and I concentrated on such civilized tasks as taking an intelligent interest in my husband's work, and sitting in the warm winter sun in the spacious Residency garden.'[13]

From New Delhi they flew across to Calcutta, where Ed had to sort out the freight and Customs arrangements for the next year's supplies, then north-east to Bagdogra, the airport that serves Darjeeling. It is a long drive up a narrow winding road to the famous hill town, past tiny villages and spreading green tea plantations up into the clouds, until at last the horizon fills with the jagged white outlines of the Himalayas, stretching far into the distance. Having Louise and the children with him greatly increased Ed's delight in being back near the mountains, and it was good to see Tenzing Norgay and his wife and daughters, who welcomed them all warmly. Ed was invited to present the awards to graduating students at the Himalayan Mountaineering Institute. Louise wrote: 'Tenzing looked magnificent in handwoven off-white jodhpurs, made in his home village of Thami near Everest, and a bright scarlet pullover with the Institute badge on it.'[14] Tem Dorji had come across from Khumjung at the end of a year's teaching with three potential new teachers for Ed to interview. Two of them were appointed for the schools to be built the following year.

Far right: Ed Hillary between Da Namgyal and Tenzing Norgay with graduating students at the Himalayan Mountaineering Institute in Darjeeling, December 1962. At the far right is Tenzing's nephew, Nawang Gombu, who would climb Everest in 1963 and again in 1965, becoming the first person to reach the summit twice
Louise Hillary

Above: Belinda and Sarah Hillary at the New Zealand High Commission in New Delhi, December 1962

Right: Jim Wilson on the
Ocean to the Sky expedition
in 1977
Mike Gill

Below: Ann and Jim Wilson
in the Khumbu, 1963
Edmund Hillary

Jim Wilson

**Jim Wilson pinpoints
the start of his
passion for climbing
as a pre-natal ascent
of Mount Pilatus in
Switzerland (2132 m;
6994 ft) aged about
minus four months.
Twenty-six years
later, having con-
firmed his climbing
credentials in New
Zealand and Antarc-
tica – on his own feet
– Jim was invited to
join one of Ed Hillary's
Himalayan expedi-
tions. Ed and Jim hit
it off immediately,
and have been firm
friends ever since.
From 1963 to 1965 Jim
and his wife Ann lived
in India. Jim studied
Indian philosophy
and religion; subjects
he later taught at the
University of Canter-
bury. Jim became a
founding member of
the Himalayan Trust
and has joined Ed
Hillary on expeditions,
films and adventures
for more than forty
years, frequently
with Ann and later
with their three sons.
Ed described Jim as
'a forceful climber
and canoeist, fit and
powerfully built,
completely irrepress-
ible when presented
with any crazy
scheme.'**[*]

**In 2004 Jim Wilson
wrote: 'Ed is a
meticulous organiser,
so all his trips went
without a hitch – we
took it for granted,
but in retrospect,
reading and thinking
about other expedi-
tions with less than
perfect organisation
and resulting disas-
ters, I realise what an
attractive boon this
aspect of Ed is.
Because, while
probably some
meticulous organisers
are fusspots and a
pain to be with, Ed
combines meticulosity
with a wonderfully
free and easy flexibil-
ity in the field . . . Ed is
amazingly loyal, once
you've won his trust,
and providing he is
sure you've done your
best, he never
criticises if you don't
succeed in whatever
task is at hand . . .
He is, and always has
been, in my experi-
ence, a leader Kiwi
style. While there
is never any doubt
who is the ultimate
boss, this is because
of our respect for
him, not because he
demands it. Always
decisions are made
by discussion . . .
Ed loves a laugh, and
a sing-song round a
camp fire . . . his
exuberant love of life
and laughter, with a
spice of danger for
good measure, is
perhaps the strong-
est reason of all for
us leaping at any
opportunity to go
adventuring with
him. He is just
rattling good
company.'**[†]

146   With just a few days left, they drove
back down the winding road and flew across
to Kathmandu where Colonel Charles Wylie was
now the military attaché at the British Embassy.
The Hillary entourage descended on the Wylies,
tents went up on the lawn and the children got
to know more Sherpas, including Mingma Tsering
who had come down from Kunde. Mingma would
be sirdar for the big 1963 expedition, and Ed
gave him money to pay for the timber and rocks
to be taken to the school sites at Pangboche and
Thami. Mingma was also responsible for buying
four yaks and twelve sheep and for feeding
them up over the winter to provide food for the
expedition in the spring. Then at last Ed and
Louise headed home to New Zealand with three
children who had learned to love travelling.
Louise recorded Peter's comment as they
boarded their last plane from Sydney to Auckland on 31 December 1962: 'Mum . . . let's do a
world trip again next year!'[15]

    In 1963, as his involvement in aid
projects with the Sherpas grew, Ed set down
his thoughts about the best ways to help small
communities. This was about to become the

primary focus of his life. 'Over the years I
have observed foreign aid programs in India,
Nepal and elsewhere. Massive aid projects are
essential where there are massive problems
to be overcome. Yet too often they do little to
create goodwill among the local people and
frequently lead to an increase in cynicism,
corruption and all the less desirable habits . . .
The importance of goodwill is frequently overlooked or ignored. We should not expect people
to be continuously grateful for what is being
done for them – the giver–receiver relationship
is always a tricky and a dangerous one, and
most aid is strongly flavoured with self-interest.
Whereas gratitude has something of inequality
about it, goodwill is an active and growing idea
that a proud man need not feel ashamed to
entertain . . . The basic fact is that *people* create
goodwill – money cannot do it on its own.'[16]

    Raising money would be Ed's overriding
concern for four more decades, but from 1963
the picture fills up with the people who worked
alongside him – both Sherpas and visitors –
whose skills, enthusiasm, hard work and
commitment made the aid projects possible.

147

There were climbers, doctors, nurses, engineers, builders and enthusiastic helpers from New Zealand, Canada and other countries. They came to build schools, run clinics, replace bridges, install water pipelines, build airstrips, repair monastery roofs, teach in schools and help with myriad projects. They raised money in their own communities as well, and many returned year after year, developing lasting relationships with Sherpa friends. Horizons were expanded and lives enriched by this long-sustained project of goodwill.

Of course not everybody who wanted to help could drop their normal lives and go to Nepal with Ed Hillary for several months. World Book Encyclopedia had 50,000 employees, and many had met Ed or heard him speak on his travels around America. Their individual donations swelled the budget appreciably and meant that Ed could guarantee operational funds for the schools for at least another three years. He noted: 'Those people who casually brush aside American generosity by saying, "Oh well, they can afford it," have little real experience of the ordinary American…He may have his weaknesses, but lack of sympathy for a worthy cause or reluctance to give freely are not among them.'[17] This expedition was the least financially worrying he had led – and he planned to do a lot.

The programme included building new schools in Thami and Pangboche, both within a day's walk of Khumjung; piping fresh water to Kunde and Khumjung; and setting up a six-month health clinic. The doctors were Phillip Houghton and Mike Gill who, in addition to undertaking his medical duties, was filming the expedition for Sears Roebuck. The programme would be shown on BBC Television and, it was hoped, might attract more supporters for Sherpa projects.

As well as the construction work, Ed wanted the mountaineers in the party to tackle two of the unclimbed peaks that tower above the upper Khumbu villages: Taweche (6367 m; 20,888 ft) and Kantega (6779 m; 22,240 ft). His team comprised four New Zealanders: Murray Ellis, Mike Gill, Phil Houghton and Jim Wilson; two Americans, Tom Frost and Dave Dornan; and the 1960 expedition stalwarts, Desmond Doig and Bhanu Bannerjee. All except Doig were mountaineers – and Bhanu was recovering from being frostbitten on a 6400-metre (21,000 ft) climb with a Bengali expedition.

The usual expedition dramas of clearing goods through Indian Customs and sorting loads for carrying were at last completed. Ed always enjoyed this part. 'The process is rather like all your Christmases coming at once – box after box of new clothing, shiny, unused equipment, enough groceries to fill a country store, plus the pleasure of meeting so many old friends again: Sirdar Mingmatsering, Ang Temba, Pemba Tarkay, Pangboche Tenzing, Siku, Lhakpa Norbu Kunde, Phu Dorje – as redoubtable a group of Sherpas as you'd ever find together.'[18] He was proud of his team.

Ed had thought about the possibility of building an airstrip at Chaunrikarka, a day's walk below Khumjung, remembering what a help it had been to have the temporary airstrip at Mingbo. He approached an American airline suggesting that they might like to lend an aircraft to the expedition, and was turned down; but he appreciated the wit of the rejection letter. 'There is a saying in our country that everyone knows the name of Paul Revere, but no one knows the name of his horse. I feel this describes our position in regard to furnishing an airplane from our publicity budget.'[19]

The trek to the Khumbu with 200 porters began on 12 March 1963. Two weeks later they walked over the ridge into Khumjung. Ed was delighted to see the school still gleaming brightly, and to find it working extremely well. Students were reading and writing Nepali and English – including children who had previously spoken only the Sherpa language, a dialect of Tibetan. Mike Gill remembered that some sceptics had predicted that the school would become a stable for yaks, but the opposite was true. The yaks were kept well outside the school fence and 'The initial burst of enthusiasm grew into a deep-rooted faith in education.'[20] The team set up their encampment of blue and orange Sears Roebuck tents and were quickly ready to start work. But first they had to help with an outbreak of smallpox. The disease came in with a Sherpa porter who had gone to Kathmandu to

find work with the American Everest expedition. He contracted smallpox there, fell ill on the march but staggered on helped by other Sherpa porters and his family. By the time he died everyone who had helped him was infected. Although Sherpas usually cremate the dead, they believed that the smoke from cremating smallpox victims would infect the air, and they consigned the bodies of victims to the rivers. And when people are poor, clothes are too valuable to burn, so a good wash prepares them for someone else to wear. Such practices exacerbated the spread of the disease.

Hillary's party had some vaccine but sent urgently for more and carried out a massive vaccination programme, training Sherpas to give the scratch vaccinations and travelling to the many surrounding villages when people asked for help. For some it was too

Above: Dr Max Pearl giving a smallpox vaccination, 1964
Edmund Hillary

Top middle: Kantega and Thamserku from Thami *Gompa*, 1968
John McKinnon

Left: The welcoming table for Ed Hillary at Khumjung School, 1968
Max Pearl

148

Left: Ed Hillary connecting
the last section of hose for the
water tank at Khumjung, 1963
Louise Hillary

Below left: Sherpa porter with
a roll of alkathene pipe, 1963
Max Pearl

Below: Filling wooden water
buckets from the new tanks
Edmund Hillary

Above: Collecting water
was a daily task in Sherpa
villages. Ed Hillary and his
team made the job less tiring
and time consuming by
piping water from high
springs down to village
holding tanks
Edmund Hillary

late, and there were at least twenty-five deaths, but the expedition vaccinated over 7000 people. Reflecting later, Ed wrote: 'Of all the programs we carried out on the expedition – schools, waterworks, medical clinics and the like – the one most widely appreciated was undoubtedly the vaccination, and this hadn't been part of my original plans.'[21]

There are several villages within a day's walk of Khumjung, and over the three months of the expedition, sahibs and Sherpas seem to have been scattered around most of them, meeting with local people, working on the many projects – and, on one busy day at Thami, vaccinating 200 people before breakfast. Murray Ellis's first engineering and construction task was to replace the sagging ridge beam of Khumjung School, affected by particularly heavy winter snow. Next on the list was water. Sherpa villages are built near the potato fields and the nearest water could be an hour's climb away. Women and children would carry heavy wooden buckets to the nearest source – often only a trickle – and walk back home under a forty-kilogram load. Ed had brought in supplies of

alkathene pipe and paid the porters extra for managing the unwieldy 1.5-metre coils. The best water supply for Khumjung was some 240 metres above the village. The party built a small dam, fitted the end of the pipe with a wire-netting cage, anchored it to the bottom of the pool and worked their way back down, carefully connecting lengths of pipe as they went. 'Murray joined the last roll and we yelled with joy as the water rushed out in a fine stream – 6 gallons a minute or more.'[22] They spent ten days observing and fine-tuning the pipe, which froze each night, though water was usually flowing by ten the following morning after the sun melted the ice. Mike Gill described completion day when a stone course was constructed for the pipe to rest on. 'More than 400 people turned out…Most of the day there appeared to be chaos: small children staggered about under loads of rocks, ex-expedition Sherpas were grubbing out a ledge round the hillside with ice-axes, schoolboys were cutting juniper scrub with *kukris*, groups of pretty young Sherpanis giggled and chattered…lost babies were crying for their mothers and a group of village strongmen were striding purposefully about, shifting apparently immovable boulders. Directing operations in a set of startling blue windproofs was Murray Ellis.'[23] They went on to build two 1200-gallon tanks to hold the water, and put in another pipeline for Kunde.

Ed's next task was to talk to the people at Pangboche about their request for a school. A site had to be found, and local labour and materials organised, so Ed, Desmond Doig and Murray Ellis set off on 1 April. Heavy snow was falling and 'the long rising track clung to the side of the steep spur leading up to the Monastery of Thyangboche [Tengboche]; we puffed our way up this slope which never seems to get any shorter or any easier.'[24] After viewing the Head Lama's new guest house, constructed with timber from the 1961 Green Hut, they pressed on, met with Pangboche village elders, and after rejecting one potential site, reached agreement on another. 'I would purchase the land and donate it to the village for the school,' Ed recalled. 'The village in return must reaffirm its intention of giving free labour for the clearing of the land, the assembling of rocks and the carrying of timber from the forest. The foresters, carpenters and stone-masons would be employed by us. The elders accepted this offer with enthusiasm.'[25] This arrangement set the pattern for the collaborative approach that Ed took to each of the projects.

Progress was fitful at first, with the labour force depleted by the demands of the potatoes and the yaks, and in desperation Ed recalled Murray Ellis, Jim Wilson, Mike Gill, Dave Dornan and Tom Frost from their attempt on Taweche. Eventually the school was completed with stone side walls, wooden floor and front wall, American sliding windows and an aluminium roof with corrugated fibreglass skylights – the first in the Khumbu. On 29 April it was opened, and the school and its fifty-four eager pupils were ceremonially blessed by the Head Lama of Tengboche. Finally Ed leased and renovated another building to house the new teacher and provide a weekly hostel for children from the neighbouring village, Phortse. One more project was satisfactorily complete.

Jim Wilson was impressed by the Buddhist ceremony to propitiate Taweche – the peak that towers over Pangboche and is also the village god – but this was to ensure their safe return from the mountain, not their success in climbing it. Taweche is represented in the Pangboche *Gompa* by a ferocious painted mask and 'Fearsome though the mask is, the reality behind it is worse.'[26] Ed had led the initial reconnaissance with Ellis, Dornan and Wilson, and reached 5180 metres (17,000 ft) – at a pace which Wilson acknowledged was trying at that altitude. Despite the Makalu experience, and his repeated references to his advancing age, Ed was still a physical as well as an organisational leader. After the school opened the mountaineers returned to Taweche and struggled at first to find a feasible route – the most important part of any climb. But they climbed to within thirty metres of a summit which was a huge and precarious-looking cornice. 'On the one side the snarling cornices overhung the plateau; on the other, steep soft snow itching to avalanche; then nothing but remote yak pastures 6000 feet below…We were quite sure there were only one-way tickets available for that stretch of ridge.'[27] Deciding that discretion was the better part of valour, they left the prayer flags given to them by the Head Lama and returned to camp – there was another school to be built. Mike Gill's comment eased their disappointment: 'You know, I think in some ways it's better – and safer – not to have violated so beautiful a summit.'[28]

'By May 20 Thami School was almost completed…Pupils had been signed on some two weeks before and the two schoolmasters, Phu Tsering and Kalden, had been conducting classes out in the open fields.'[29] Kalden had given Ed the petition on behalf of Khumjung and, as agreed, had returned from his schooling in Kathmandu to teach. On 26 May, parents and children trooped over to Khumjung from Thami and Pangboche for a combined school sports day. Louise Hillary and Ann Wilson had arrived the day before, after walking from Kathmandu. Several hundred Sherpas gathered at the school on the big day, and Desmond Doig had organised an energetic programme. There were thirty-two events, from potato races and obstacle races to

Above: Ed Hillary building the swing at Pangboche School, 1963
Mike Gill

Right: Pangboche School began with a roll of fifty-four pupils, including two men whose six- and seven-year-old daughters were also enrolled. The swing in the playground was a great success
Edmund Hillary

Bottom right: The Head Lama of Tengboche arriving to bless Pangboche School, 29 April 1963.

shot-put, sprints and a tug-of-war championship for the adults. 'For the young ones there was a race to eat a chappatty suspended from a string and liberally plastered with sticky honey – and I have rarely seen such determination or such sticky faces.'[30] The prizes were gathered from everyone's backpacks. Louise presented ballpoint pens, key-rings, crayons, hairclips, soap and rupees to the winners, including the victors in the tug-of-war: despite confidence in their superior body weight, the sahibs were outmanoeuvred in the last stage.

Thami School was opened by Louise Hillary and the Head Lama of Tengboche on 28 May, after appropriate ceremonies had been carried out at the *gompa* above the village. Louise described the building: 'The architecture of the schoolhouse is quite brilliant…a perfect blend of Sherpa, Tibetan and Western…The front wall is made of wood with small, Sherpa-type window frames – but glass instead of rice paper. The beams holding up the roof come out under the eaves in traditional *langdy pangdy* pattern. Desmond painted the front wall bright, traditional red and the *langdy pangdy* [a decorative cornice] red and green. The bottom panel of the wall was painted with the eight lucky signs of the Buddhist religion…'[31] The Head Lama blessed

the building, and the more than 500 people who had come for the event. Kalden had a struggle with his conscience as he had been educated at a Jesuit school and now regarded himself as a Christian. But he came forward in the end, after watching Ed and his entire party join the line. As Jim Wilson said: 'The blessing of a good man is worth having, whatever his religion.'[32]

On 29 May there was an impromptu celebration to mark the tenth anniversary of the first Everest climb. The Head Lama arrived at the Hillary tent with gifts; Mingma, Dawa Tenzing and Annullu made speeches; and Desmond Doig produced a cake with a flag on top and a note saying, 'Many happy ten years of mountains'.[33] Ed had forgotten the date. That day the climbing team set off again, this time for an attempt on the unclimbed Kantega, which towers above Tengboche. Mike Gill, Jim Wilson, Dave Dornan and Tom Frost were accompanied by Ang Temba and four other excellent Sherpas. They had just eight days for the climb and there was no possible route from the Khumjung side, so they made a long trek down to 2750 metres and across into the Hinkhu

151

Below top: Louise Hillary was with Ed in the Khumbu villages for two weeks in 1963
Ed Hillary

Below middle: Louise Hillary with Blackie, May 1963
Edmund Hillary

Below bottom: Watching the Combined Schools Sports Day, Khumjung School, 26 May 1963
Mike Gill

Left: The chappati-eating race at the sports day
Jim Wilson

Below: Louise Hillary presenting the prizes
Jim Wilson

Valley to approach the mountain. This time they were successful. Gill and Wilson barely escaped avalanching snow near the top, but Dave Dornan made the last few metres to the summit: climbers in Hillary-led expeditions had now made first ascents of three of the four major peaks that form an inner ring around the Khumbu villages. The fourth, Thamserku, was still to come.

The expedition was almost over, and there were farewell visits to be made, much *chang* to be drunk and wonderful meals to be eaten before they could leave. At Tengboche they were served a range of American delicacies that seemed to have migrated from the successful American Everest expedition, and at Mingma's house in Kunde, Mingma's wife Ang Dooli gave them a Tibetan meal. 'Piles of *tukpa* (handmade noodles) and a lovely thin soup were handed to us in dainty Chinese bowls. We put the *tukpa* into the soup and added a mixture of chopped yak, spring onion and butter...a very tasty

repast, and it was washed down most pleasantly with Mingma's good home brew.'[34] There was vigorous dancing at Khunjo Chumbi's house and Annullu made a short speech: 'We had, he said, lightened their darkness, saved their lives and eased their domestic problems. We were indeed the father and mother of the village. Even allowing for a lot of exaggeration, it was clear that our expedition efforts had been well appreciated.'[35] On 7 June their last visit was to Khumjung School where Ang Rita, the class leader, made a speech and Louise felt the emotional tension beginning to build. Outside the school gate she said goodbye to Ang Dooli and her two boys with tears and long embraces, then walked up the hill, hardly able to breathe. 'I tried to talk to Ed and Desmond but they were having their own problems and wouldn't look at me.'[36] Then below them the children started cheering and the tension broke. They would be back.

Phil Houghton and Mike Gill stayed in Khumjung for three more months, running their clinic from a refurbished room in the Khumjung *Gompa*. They faced a wide range of medical problems: heart and lung disease, pneumonia, boils, ear and nose infections, broken limbs, even one case of leprosy. Most common of all was tuberculosis, which affected not only the lungs but also the spine, joints, eyes and skin. As the Sherpas had no previous exposure to antibiotics, some of the cures seemed almost miraculous, but not every problem could be helped by a temporary clinic. Like many mountain people, the Sherpas suffered from problems associated with iodine deficiency. Every woman had goitre – a swelling of the thyroid gland in the neck – and some of these were extremely large and disfiguring. The men were less affected. Infant mortality was high and a large number of children born to iodine-deficient women suffered from cretinism, a particularly severe form of intellectual and physical handicap. A method of introducing iodine into the Sherpa diet was sorely needed, and Ed left the Khumbu with a definite ambition: to build a small cottage hospital for the Sherpas. Achieving this was his next big challenge.

152

Above: *Namaste* from a child at Thami School, 1966
John McKinnon

Right: The foundation stone for Thami School, 1963
Phil Houghton

Far right: The village of Thami, altitude 4115 metres (13,500 ft)
Edmund Hillary

Below: The tenth anniversary of the first ascent of Chomolungma/Mount Everest, 29 May 1963. (L–R) Annullu, Desmond Doig, Mingma Tsering, Dawa Tenzing, Louise Hillary, Ed Hillary; the Head Lama of Tengboche Monastery is seated in the front

The Venerable Ngawang Tenzin Zangbu
HEAD LAMA AND RINPOCHE OF TENGBOCHE MONASTERY, SOLU KHUMBU

'Lama Gulu founded Tengboche monastery in 1916... In 1935, on the same day the Dalai Lama was born, a Sherpa family from Namche Bazar had a son. When this boy was still very small he insisted he had a home and possessions in Tengboche. His family went to visit Ngawang Tenzin Norbu in Rongbuk and this high lama, who had always been closely connected with Tengboche, recognized him as the Tulku or reincarnation of Lama Gulu. He was given the name of Ngawang Tenzin Zangbu... He spent many years in Tibet studying with the great masters there. In 1956 he returned to Tengboche as the Abbot of the monastery and is known as Tengboche Rinpoche.'[*]
Ed Hillary responded to the wisdom and spiritual authority of the young Tengboche Rinpoche when they met in 1961, and the Rinpoche welcomes the work of the Himalayan Trust. 'Sir Edmund's humanitarian support has brought positive changes, through education and health-care services. His vision, kindness and dedication have directly served the upliftment of the people of Solu Khumbu, as well as inspiring other charitable agencies.'[†] The Tengboche Rinpoche is a leader of the conservation movement in Solu Khumbu, applauding the formation of Sagarmatha National Park and the establishment of nurseries to promote reforestation.
'In my own monastery, Tengboche, in the Khumbu region, we are working to promote environmental conservation, reduce pollution and waste, and raise awareness of the relationship between spirituality and nature in the face of increased tourism, rapid development and pressure on the environment. Great potential exists in dialogue and partnership between the Buddhist community and the modern conservationists, both in promoting environmental conservation and ethical living. The world we live in today is not the same as yesterday's: today we have a bigger population, new and increased needs and therefore more effort is needed to promote the wellbeing of the environment which ultimately ensures our own. In my own local environment of Tengboche monastery, I have been planting trees, cultivating medicinal plants, raising awareness to reduce pollution and waste and promoting environmental conservation. Please try to do the same in your own home, wherever that may be.'[‡]

Left: The Venerable Ngawang Tenzin Zangbu, 1966
John McKinnon

Below: This book is a *Ha Sutra*, the highest Buddhist teaching which Buddhist monks learn by heart. Written in Tibetan script, it is a teaching given by the Lord Buddha to poor students at Varanasi. It takes about ten years to learn. In *Schoolhouse in the Clouds* Ed Hillary wrote: 'We said goodbye to the head lama in his exquisite room in the Thyangboche Monastery. I was overwhelmed to receive an ancient monastery book – in raised gold script on dark-green paper – and a long silk scarf blessed by the lama himself. "You will come back," he said, nodding his head with firm conviction. "You have seen the sun rise on the sacred summit of Khumbila. You will come back!"'
Edmund Hillary

153

11 THE BURRA SAHIB

'Burra Sahib, Burra Sahib, you are the saviour of the people of Khumbu,' said the head man of the village in full poetic flight. We all laughed and he laughed also at the satisfying effect of his oratory. 'Please say you can help us,' he pleaded. 'What can you do with these people,' said Ed to the room at large. 'They're so delightful that it is almost impossible to turn them down.'
LOUISE HILLARY

The Burra Sahib is an informal title given to Ed Hillary by the Sherpas. They translate it as 'Big in Heart'. On 29 May 2003 at the Hyatt Regency Hotel in Kathmandu, hundreds of excited people gathered to celebrate the fiftieth anniversary of the first Everest ascent. The evening had been organised by the Sherpa community with Sir Edmund and Lady Hillary the guests of honour. In the Hyatt ballroom guests wore the colourful 'Triumph on Everest' sashes given to them as they arrived, but all were eclipsed by the brilliantly dressed Sherpas: men in long Tibetan coats and wide hats, women wearing traditional striped aprons over their silk *ingis* and with heavy gold jewellery gleaming. There were heartfelt speeches of thanks; presentations of awards; an impressive dance by Sherpas over the age of fifty – all friends of the Burra Sahib – and polished performances of Sherpa music and song. Then Sir Edmund cut a huge Everest cake and made a short speech. Everyone waited expectantly on his words.

He thanked all those who had spoken and performed. He was pleased to see Jamling and Tashi Tenzing Norgay, son and grandson of Tenzing Norgay. He was delighted to be sharing this anniversary with his closest friends, the Sherpa people of the Himalayas. And looking back over his life, the eighty-three-year-old adventurer said: 'I am not a strongly religious man, but I believe in the Buddhist philosophy that each man or woman must choose his or her own path in life. I have chosen mine. It is not only to take part in exciting challenges, but to work with my Sherpa friends to achieve the things that they want.' Many of the guests that evening had attended Himalayan Trust schools; and standing beside Sir Edmund as he spoke was Ang Rita Sherpa from Khumjung, leader of the first class at Khumjung School, recipient of scholarships for further study, and now chief administrator for the Himalayan Trust's aid work in Nepal. The wheel had come full circle.

By 1964 Ed Hillary could see that the work he had begun with the Sherpas was likely to involve more than a 'five-year plan'. The way ahead was not totally clear, but with each step,

each project, each visit to the Khumbu, Ed and Louise Hillary became more committed to the work they had begun. They were taking on a challenge which had considerable practical implications. Nepal and New Zealand are anything but close geographically, so travel and transport of goods would always be expensive and time consuming; Ed would be away from home for several months each year; the main burden of fundraising would fall upon him, and this would entail more travel; he would have to maintain a high public visibility through appearances and articles to keep the money flowing – and his own family still had to survive and flourish. Without Louise's strong support it would have been an impossible task.

Jim Rose suggested that Ed and Louise form a trust with some interested supporters who had useful expertise to bring to the projects. This would reduce the pressure on Ed a little and would look better for the fundraising – sponsors always want to know who is on your board. It was known at first as the Sherpa Trust Board. And although Ed remained, in Mike Gill's phrase, 'both the infrastructure and the superstructure' of the Himalayan Trust, he had a group of knowledgeable and experi-

enced friends around him to work with.[1] 'There was Max Pearl and Mike Gill, Jim Wilson and Murray Ellis, Peter and June Mulgrew, John and Diane McKinnon, Norm and Enid Hardie, my brother Rex, Neville Wooderson and Wally Romanes. Most of all I had Louise who enjoyed the Himalayas enormously…'[2]

Ed's life assumed a pattern that would continue for four decades, despite occasional setbacks and wrenching personal loss. He gave lectures to raise funds for Sherpa projects, and regularly visited Australia where he was on the board of Field Enterprises's Australian operation. He tested equipment for Sears in America, New Zealand and in Nepal, and spent several months in the Himalayas every year. There were other expeditions in the Pacific, Antarctica and around New Zealand, and he made films, gave interviews and was involved with many organisations. He travelled tourist class, with his clipboard at hand, and his travel schedule was punishing, even in today's long-haul jets.

For each Nepal expedition there were funds to be raised, people to be invited, and negotiations with Her Majesty's Government of Nepal for permission to carry out aid projects, and to climb mountains. There were endless

Above and far left: Ed Hillary wrote books and articles, and gave many slide lectures to raise funds for the aid projects in Nepal
Edmund Hillary

Left: Ed in the Naya Kota – the room that Mingma Tsering and Ang Dooli built on to their house for the Hillary family to use. Louise commissioned Pasang Norbu Sherpa, one of Kappa Kalden's sons, to decorate the room with the Eight Auspicious Symbols of Buddhism
Mike Gill

schedules of supplies, tools, materials and equipment to be prepared; travel bookings to be made and confirmed; myriad details to be checked and double-checked. Ed's correspondence and paperwork were done in a small office at home, with the help of his trusted part-time secretary, Betty Joplin. All across New Zealand, America, Canada, Nepal and further afield, there were networks of people to be kept informed, enthused, positive and generous, without email to speed the process. And the incoming letters never stopped – a stream of requests to speak, or to write, or to lend his support to good causes.

In Nepal Mingma Tsering was Ed's alter ego: manager of labour, materials and porters, adviser on Sherpa etiquette, and generally indispensable right-hand man. He and his wife Ang Dooli provided a home away from home, even adding an extra room on to their house for the Hillarys to use when they were in Kunde. In Ed's and Louise's books about work and adventures in the Himalayas there are many references to Mingma's skills and efficiency, and his good heart.

In New Zealand the Hillary home was in a constant state of flux as expedition necessities and aid materials were checked and dispatched. In 1972 Louise wrote to the Claydons: 'We've just got rid of 11 tons of goods for Nepal. They were all in our garage & a terrible mess.'³ But Ed never forgot the lessons he had learned planning for solo expeditions as a young man – or his astonishment, when a tractor was languishing crippled on the Antarctic ice, to find that spare tractor parts were buried in the *Theron*'s hold. On Hillary expeditions the leader worked relentlessly to make sure that everything would be exactly where it was most needed. Expedition members regularly photographed a rumpled-looking Ed Hillary standing amid piles of crates and cartons in Kathmandu, or beside tents in a rocky valley, personally making sure that all the boxes had the right contents and were in the right place.

In 1964, with the hospital idea still simmering, Ed returned to the Khumbu to build schools in Namche Bazar, Chaunrikarka and Junbesi, as well as two bridges – and an airstrip. If he could fly building materials and equipment into the Khumbu, he could bring a fifteen-day

walk with porters down to three days, reducing potential damage to equipment and allowing more time to get the hospital established. He looked at a possible site near Chaunrikarka, but the area was very fertile – too good to remove from productive use – and there was no other obvious site. It is very steep country.

Then Jim Wilson was approached by some farmers at Lukla. They had six acres of land that might be suitable. It rose over thirty metres from top to bottom, and was divided into terraces with drops of two metres or more between them. Shovels were all they had for earth moving, but with a team of more than 100 Sherpas on the job for two solid weeks the airfield began to take shape. 'Don Mackay [the expedition's engineer] obtained a colossal piece of timber, twenty feet long and one foot square, to be used as a grader. He attached a rope to each end and then had two cows hitched onto each rope. Alas for his grand ideas of mechanization – the cows persistently headed off in opposite directions and the timber remained stationary. Men had to take the place of the cows and this was much more satisfactory. With a dozen laughing and cheering Sherpas pulling at each end of the timber it was dragged backwards and forwards, and up and down the field compacting and leveling at the same time.'⁴

157

Middle left: Some of the Sherpa workers levelling the airstrip
Lynn Crawford

Left: Coming in to land at Lukla, 1964
Dick Stewart

Far left: The tents of the 1964 Himalayan Schoolhouse expedition at Lukla, with Kwangde behind
Don Mackay

Two days of vigorous Sherpa dancing, fuelled by quantities of *chang*, further compacted the earth. 'We were now ready for the first landing. We had an airfield 1,150 feet long and 100 feet wide clearly marked by painted boards. The grade was one in ten – quite steep for an airfield – but the surface was excellent.'[5] The airstrip was extended three years later, sown with grass and recently tar-sealed. It is suitable for helicopters and for small STOL (short takeoff and landing) aircraft, but has one of the world's most terrifying approaches. The small plane drones along like a tiny mosquito, climbing up the Dudh Kosi valley while massive forested mountainsides close in, and it seems impossible that there can be an airstrip anywhere. Then, far below, a tiny patch of grey appears, sloping down a hillside. The plane comes in towards it; the passengers grip their seats, grinning with terror; and suddenly the plane is on the ground and racing up the hill to stop just before hitting the stone wall at the top. You climb out with shaking knees and take deep breaths of the thin, clear air. Pilot John Claydon described Lukla as a '"do or die" strip with a 1,000' drop at the approach

and a 20,000' mountain at the other end!'[6] It is the gateway to the Khumbu and the second busiest airport in Nepal. Over the years, thousands of tourists, trekkers and expedition members, as well as many Nepalese and vast quantities of freight, have flown in to it.

It was still a two-day walk for porters carrying loads from Lukla up to Kunde, and the route included some dangerous river crossings. Ed later noted: 'In the ten years before 1964 eighteen men and women died on bridges over the turbulent mountain rivers of the Khumbu region. Some died in the construction of new bridges, others when old ones collapsed … We could not afford the finance for an elaborate western suspension bridge, but I was convinced we could use the basic Sherpa wooden cantilevered type and extend its practicable length by suspending the central portion from two light stranded steel wire ropes.'[7] They began work on two bridges in mid-October. The larger one was across the thirty-metre-wide Dudh Kosi (Milk River), which tumbles down from the Khumbu Glacier, and the other across the smaller Bhote Kosi (Tibetan River). The two rivers meet

at the bottom of the steep Namche Hill, and traders must cross them before toiling up to the weekly market at Namche Bazar. On the first bridge Don Mackay and his helpers used both mountaineering and engineering skills to close the final gap. 'High above the river on the east bank holes were laboriously drilled into the solid rock and steel bolts concreted firmly in. It became a familiar sight to see Mackay's group festooned with ropes and equipment swinging like a group of agile monkeys across the vertical face.'[8] Both bridges were completed by early December and being used by hundreds of heavily laden travellers every day, but they still had to be blessed. On 7 December the Head Lama arrived from Tengboche to perform the ceremony. 'Clad in glorious silks and brocades and seemingly unaffected by the freezing weather he intoned prayers and cast handfuls of rice into the waters as he strode vigorously across the bridges in a swirl of flapping garments and smoke from ceremonial fires … "When the rains come," said Annullu, a tough Sherpa of vast experience, "the floods will listen to the voice of the Head Lama and leave the bridge alone."'[9]

The mountain on this expedition was Thamserku (6608 m; 21,679 ft). Again Ed led the team to base camp, but left the climb to a group of keen young New Zealanders – Lynn Crawford, Peter Farrell, Don Mackay, John McKinnon, Dick Stewart and Jim Wilson. Mingma Tsering led the Sherpas. They made it to the top. 'It was a

Below and left: Building the cantilevered bridge across the Dudh Kosi, October 1964
Jim Wilson

classic summit with room for only one man at a time – a fitting apex to an "impossible" mountain.'[10] John McKinnon, a fifth-year medical student and a keen climber, would be back in Kunde two years later with his new wife Diane to help build the hospital and be the first doctor in charge. But Ed had two more years of planning and fundraising before then, and his stalwart supporters would be his wife Louise and Dr Max Pearl, who in 1964 was on his first Hillary expedition. Max was the expedition's medical officer and not a climber, but after dealing with some urgent medical problems, he nonetheless decided to follow the group up Thamserku and see how far he could get. At 5180 metres (17,000 ft) the team were astonished to see Max appear over a ridge, having climbed alone to that height. Beginner's luck, combined with the Pearl energy, optimism and tenacity that would prove so invaluable to Ed Hillary, no doubt contributed to this memorable feat.

For Ed building the hospital was 'one of my greatest ambitions' and Max Pearl was equally determined to make it a reality. By October 1966 everything was under way. 'Twelve tons of supplies were shipped to Kathmandu, flown in small aircraft to Lukla airfield and then carried on porters' backs up the hill to Khumjung. Our selected location for the hospital was in the neighbouring village of Kunde at 12,700 feet.'[11] Max's family were involved too. In December Lois Pearl and their three daughters, Ann, Lynn and Susan, travelled to Nepal with Louise, Peter, Sarah and Belinda Hillary, to be there for the hospital opening.

Louise wrote *A Yak for Christmas* about their trip, and her account of the hospital fund-raising programme will ring bells with many who have undertaken such daunting tasks.

The Thamserku climb, December 1964. Don Mackay took the main photograph, which shows the lower summit of Thamserku and Lynn Crawford took the view of Everest from the summit itself

159

On the Thamserku climb –
Jim Wilson's boot
Don Mackay

Far left: The village of Kunde
from the hospital, winter 1967
John McKinnon

Left: Porters carrying
building materials and
supplies for the hospital,
November 1966
Kaye Ibbertson

'The raising of money for the Sherpa hospital had dominated our lives for a year... It was a worrying time for all of us. What if we received no money? or not enough money? or even worse – what if we lost some of the public's money? Money started to trickle in – first a few pounds from the wife and children of a local member of Parliament, then a few precious shillings from an old age pensioner. We organised a business house appeal with me making the appointments and Ed calling on the business-men...the response was terrific and we collected £4,500.

'The turning point came when the forty Lions Clubs in the Auckland provincial district decided to back the project. They organised lectures and sold tickets. Ed, Max and I did as many as five lectures a day and travelled thousands of miles in the process. But the Lions' support brought in handsome results in a cheque for over £8,000. Thousands of pounds worth of building materials, food, drugs, and equipment were donated by business concerns in New Zealand and we received much generous help from World Book Encyclopedia and Sears, Roebuck and Co, both of Chicago, USA. The sale of the expedition Press rights helped too

Above: The Kunde Hospital
construction team.
(L–R) Phu Dorje, Brian
Ahern, Tenzing Niendra,
Ed Hillary, Stuart King,
Mingma Tsering, Pemba
Tarkay, Neville Wooderson
Louise Hillary

Left: Sherpani porters with
corrugated aluminium for the
hospital roof
Jim Wilson

161

although his companions claimed that Ed was pretty hard to live with during the couple of days it took him to write each of the eight despatches he sent out from the field.

'You will understand therefore, that to see the hospital now completed after all our talking and writing and worrying was a wonderful experience.

'I should hasten to add that our family trips weren't being financed out of these generous donations – we were paying for the trip ourselves. I'm sure that Max had mortgaged everything to raise the necessary funds and Ed had taken *his* normal approach...

'"Well, if you and the kids are coming to the Himalayas," he said, "you'll just have to write a book about it to pay the fares."'[12]

The official opening of Kunde Hospital took place on 18 December 1966. Floors were mercilessly scrubbed and windows cleaned, and the children made illustrated signs for the doors of each department – Susan Pearl's gruesome drawing of an operation for the surgery door was greatly admired. Everything was tidy and everybody dressed in their unaccustomed best, ready for the VIPs who were flying in from Kathmandu by helicopter. Only Ed and Max Pearl were still busy 'making hasty

162

last minute changes to their well organized programme for the day. There was Plan A, Plan B and Plan C. One for bad weather, one for good weather and one for the non arrival of some of our important guests . . .'[13] But they all arrived safely: the very elderly Lama from Thamo came on horseback; the Burra Hakim walked up the steep hill from Namche Bazar; the Head Lama from Tengboche swept in with his retinue; and, only one hour behind schedule, the helicopters landed in a potato field, covering the excited throng with clouds of dust. Out climbed the British, American and New Zealand ambassadors to Nepal and Nepal's deputy Minister of Education.

After a cup of tea and Lois Pearl's date scones and Christmas cake, the opening ceremony began. 'The speech making was enjoyed by everyone. To start the function Ed made a short speech introducing his guests and explaining that the three Ambassadors represented the three countries that had helped finance all the Hillary aid work in the area. Many of the audience had not the slightest idea what an Ambassador was, or where England, New Zealand and America were to be found in the great wide world outside the Khumbu. Nevertheless it all sounded frightfully impressive and added a certain dignity to the proceedings.'[14] Mingma translated for Ed and the other English speakers, and then the New Zealand ambassador, Mr Farrell, cut the ribbon – a red dyed bandage across the surgery door. Finally the building was ceremonially blessed by the Thamo Lama. After walking three times around the outside of the building he entered each room, chanting prayers and sprinkling rice as he went. The Thamo Lama did not often visit Kunde, so he was besieged by long lines of Sherpas coming for his blessing.

Max Pearl had invited Professor Kaye Ibbertson, thyroid specialist at the Auckland University School of Medicine, to come to the Khumbu and tackle the iodine problem. All mountain areas of the world are deficient in iodine, and in the developed world iodine has been added to salt, but as the Sherpas use Tibetan rock salt this was not practical. Kaye Ibbertson suggested an alternative approach used for the mountain peoples of New Guinea: injections of lipiodol. This is a medium used in X-rays which was found, by chance, to be a highly effective slow-release source of iodine. John McKinnon described the impact on the community. 'The results were astounding. Huge goitres – imagine a necklace of three craggy grapefruit – gradually melted away. The women, and indeed their spouses, were delighted. When these benefits became obvious, so many people

Above: Kancha and Nima Yangjen using the thyroid scanner.

Left: a Sherpa man with a large goitre.
Richard Evans

Top right: the iodine team at Phortse. (L–R) Standing: Nima Yangjen, Jack Tait, Professor Kaye Ibbertson, Dr Max Pearl, Kancha and Dr Mike Gill. Dr John McKinnon is seated in front with Sherpa children, some of whom are cretins as a result of iodine deficiency
Mike Gill

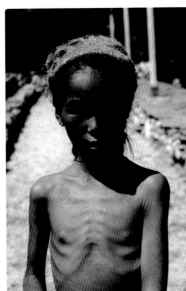

Left: John McKinnon trained Sherpa health workers to inform people of the signs of tuberculosis.
John McKinnon

Below: These three photographs of Tsamje Puti from Khumjung show her complete recovery from tuberculosis after treatment with antibiotics
John McKinnon

163

flocked to the hospital...that I got blisters on my fingers from giving the injection. Cretins – although not made "normal" – certainly perked up.'[15] Only one cretin has been born in the district since the programme began – to a woman who refused the iodine treatment – and the human and economic benefits have been dramatic. When Kaye Ibbertson returned to Solu Khumbu in 1968 and 1972 to study the results of the programme, he found that even those who had not been injected had increased iodine levels. He was puzzled by this at first, but eventually settled on a convincing explanation. The Sherpas' use of composting toilets to make fertiliser for their potato fields had introduced iodine into the food chain, an effect described as environmental cycling. Forty years later, the Himalayan Trust's iodine programme remains a success story for everyone.

John and Diane McKinnon

Dr John McKinnon was chairman of the Himalayan Trust's medical sub-committee.

'I first went to Nepal in 1964 as a climber on one of Sir Edmund Hillary's expeditions. I was a fifth-year medical student and had never been out of New Zealand. The experience changed my life, and at the end of 1966 I was back. Diane and I had been married a few months. We had been selected by New Zealand Volunteer Service Abroad to staff the new Hillary hospital. When the hospital was finished Ed and all his team went home. Diane and I were on our own –

the only foreigners for six days' walk. There was no telephone or two-way radio, the mail came by runner from Kathmandu twelve days' walk down the hill, and email was several decades into the future. It was marvellous!

'The two and a half years we spent at Kunde were very special. Far from being lonely, we were overwhelmed with hospitality and kindness. The generosity and open-hearted nature of the Sherpa people is legendary. We were made welcome, loved, cosseted and cared for in ways which bring tears to my eyes even today. And to live in Kunde was

great fun. The year was punctuated with a series of parties and events, mostly religious, that we were expected to attend. All age groups, from newborns to ancients, went to every event. Diane and I required no encouragement, as what events they were! There was always dancing – in long lines. Men facing women with arms linked, all singing and stamping the melody with complex foot movements – which I loved, and never mastered. There were parties for weddings, parties for deaths, parties for name-giving and celebrations for returning climbers. There was a lot of drinking, rare drunkenness and much good humour.

'The good nature expressed at these festivals mirrored the Sherpa character. It was obvious that these people enjoyed their lives. Superficially, when measured by then-western standards the Sherpas seemed to have very little to feel good about. Their lives by any standards were grindingly hard: their food and housing simple; the climate and terrain, though of great beauty, harsh; and the possibility of disease and death were very immediate. Despite, and as I gradually came to realise, because of these things, the Sherpas were happy, were tolerant and were accepting of life as it happened in a way that challenged my own interpretation of how to live.

'To be the first resident doctor in the region was an astonishing and rewarding experience. The Sherpa people were peasant farmers and traders, living as all our ancestors once did. Theirs was a 'natural' life in magnificent surroundings, but with a great deal of hardship and disease. Almost without exception the Sherpa people accepted and dealt with the adversities of disease and environment without rancour and with notable humour. These qualities have endeared

them to generations of mountaineers. When our son Dorje was born, in Kathmandu, our Sherpa friends never doubted that he would have a local name. A *dorje* represents the "thunderbolt of enlightenment" that abrupt change in human consciousness recognised by all the great religions as a pivotal episode in the lives of mystics and saints. It is a common Sherpa name and seemed appropriate for our newborn. When the time came for us to leave, it was heart wrenching. We had become part of the scene. We belonged.

'I trained as an ophthalmologist in New Zealand and England and have returned to Nepal every year or so to work with Sir Edmund on his various aid projects, and to assist with eye surgery and other medical matters at the Himalayan Trust hospitals. Since I first went to Nepal I have been rewarded and enriched with an intensity of experience, of friendships – and of life. It is rare to be so fortunate. Thanks Ed!'[*]

Diane McKinnon is a member of the Himalayan Trust.

'The inhabitants of the twin villages of Kunde/Khumjung provided the most enriching moments of our lives. The enduring realities lie not so much in challenges met, or the nourishing of your own development by participating in the development of others, but in the wonderfully warm and lasting relationships built up between the people with whom you live, work, laugh and cry. In sharing our common humanity we came to acknowledge and respond to the Sherpa qualities of unconditional acceptance, resourcefulness, psychological and physical robustness, sense of humour, openness, and a non-violent approach to the problems of the world.'[†]

Photos: John McKinnon and Mike Gill

The McKinnons were rapidly accepted into the Sherpa community: John ran the hospital with a Kathmandu-trained nurse, Yangjen, the daughter of Khunjo Chumbi and Pali; and Diane taught at Khumjung School. Their work at Kunde was an affirmation of Ed Hillary's aim to encourage goodwill among people in his aid projects, and he was in Kunde when they left, two and a half years later. 'The contribution by the McKinnons to the welfare of the Sherpas was quite remarkable...Those last few days of farewell are something I will always remember – and it wasn't me that was being farewelled. There were dignified speeches, simple gifts to the McKinnons, and expressions of thanks from the many who believed that their lives had been saved. More than anything it was the tears from these rugged people – floods of tears. I wonder how many of us will have a whole community weep in sorrow at our departure?'[16]

The hospital was a success, but much fundraising and generosity from many quarters would still be needed to keep it staffed and supplied. John and Diane McKinnon were supported by New Zealand's Volunteer Service Abroad (VSA), a non-governmental organisation of which Ed had become the founding president in 1963. Louise was 'the guiding light in VSA's Auckland Branch and its president for eight years...one of VSA's greatest advocates'.[17] Diane McKinnon later chaired the VSA Council, which supported the Kunde volunteer doctors for more than a decade. Max Pearl was tireless in soliciting donations of drugs and medical supplies, and there is a cottage-industry atmosphere about many stories of the hospital's early days. Max's daughters remember hours spent in their bathroom at home, repackaging donated drugs from small sample packs into larger ones more convenient for transport to Kunde.[18] Other unexpected donations came too: in 1971 in Kathmandu John Claydon sought a Nepalese import licence and Customs clearance for a package of toothbrushes donated by some Japanese dental nurses for distribution by the hospital.[19] Forty years on, the hospital remains a key community focus for Kunde, Khumjung

and the other villages in the Khumbu area. Its medical superintendent, Dr Kami Temba, was one of the first children to attend Thami School. He worked for many years as a health assistant at the hospital, and clearly had the intelligence and aptitude to be a doctor himself. In 1997 the Himalayan Trust gave financial support for Kami to study at the Fiji School of Medicine. He graduated at the end of 2000 and returned to Kunde after an internship at Patan Hospital in Kathmandu. And so, rather than being run by foreign volunteer doctors with Sherpa assistants, the hospital is now run by a Sherpa doctor assisted by volunteers.

The Hillary children loved being in Nepal, despite the discomforts of trekking at high altitude. They were welcomed and cared for with great affection, and developed warm relationships with many Sherpas. Siku, who looked after them in 1966, Phu Dorje and Pemba Tarkay were all good friends; and Peter Hillary described Mingma and Ang Dooli as his 'Sherpa parents'. Belinda had a particularly close bond with Ang Dooli who often held her hand and encouraged her to keep walking when the trekking day seemed too long. Cuddles from her father helped too.

In 1962 when the Hillarys were in Darjeeling meeting Tenzing Norgay and his family, Ed took Peter and Sarah on an overnight adventure. After a hair-raising drive over narrow roads to 3660 metres, they camped on Singalila Ridge and had dinner sitting in their sleeping bags, feeling cosy together despite the snow outside. When they woke the tent was lined with frost and all around them mountains sparkled in the dawn. A chilly breakfast was followed by a two-hour walk along the snowy ridge, and the trio were rewarded by a perfect view across Nepal to Mount Everest. The return journey was a highlight of the trip. Tucked into their sleeping bags, Peter and Sarah were carried along in baskets by two Sherpa porters, and arrived back full of excitement and stories for Louise and Belinda.[20]

There were vigorous holidays in New Zealand too. This was not a family that spent its summers lying around. In 1965 Ed and Louise bought some land overlooking the Clutha River in the South Island, near Lake Wanaka, where they spent several Christmases camping. Sarah Hillary remembers her father carrying most of the gear and food on family tramping trips, but 'his strength was also useful for more entertaining pursuits. Not only did the Sears Roebuck dinghy get used on the Clutha River, but it was also well and truly tested on Ed's back…trying to stay on the dinghy was a favourite game for my brother, my sister and me during our early holidays in Wanaka. With the upturned dinghy on his back, Ed would buck like a horse while we bounced on top, squealing with laughter as we slid about before throwing ourselves back on for more.'[21] The children loved living in the open air, just as their parents hoped they would. Ed wrote: 'I was very fond of my children but I was not a demonstrative father. Belinda refused to put up with this. Urged on by Peter and Sarah she would throw her arms around my neck and kiss me furiously while I wriggled in discomfort. But I really loved it. Those camping holidays with my young family were some of the happiest days of my life.'[22]

Peter's first climb – when he was ten years old and Mingma visited New Zealand – stands out clearly in his memory. 'Because the weather was wonderful in the Southern Alps, Dad decided that Mingma and he would take me on a climb of Mount Fog, an eight thousand foot peak at the base of the magnificent Matuki Valley on the west side of Lake Wanaka.' The whole family drove on dusty roads up the valley, fording streams as they went. 'You could tell Dad loved being up there. The more glimpses of craggy peaks capped with snowfields and creased glaciers, the happier he seemed to be. He started to whistle with his lips pursed and his cheeks flexing as he breathed. He liked to whistle cowboy songs, and he was whistling "There's a Bridle Hanging on the Wall."' After a barbecue dinner at the Raspberry Hut, the climbers left Louise and the girls, and walked up through the tussock to spend a night sleeping under the stars. The next morning they climbed up to a rocky ridge and on to the snow which led to the summit. 'We had roped up with a white nylon rope, and I was in the middle. Dad moved steadily forward across the steep snow face, and I followed, stretching my legs from one great boot print to the next. Occasionally… I would lose my footing. With a howl I would rocket down the slope on my side toward the valley thousands of feet below. With just a momentary delay the rope around my waist would draw tight and my father and Mingma would hoist me back up the slope and into the line of footprints. I will never forget the confidence that they exuded up there on Mount Fog. It was a strange and exciting world and they belonged in it.'[23]

Right: Peter Hillary and Mingma Tsering in the South Island of New Zealand, 1964
Edmund Hillary

Below: Peter and Sarah Hillary in *dokas* (Sherpa baskets), Singalila Ridge, December 1962
Edmund Hillary

Left: Ed Hillary, Peter, Belinda and Sarah with Ang Dooli under a Tibetan awning in the grounds of the Himalayan Hotel, Kalimpong, January 1967. The children are wearing new Tibetan outfits purchased at Kalimpong market
Louise Hillary

Some Hillary family holidays. 167
Upper row: Lake Wanaka,
January 1964
Second row: Kennedy Bay,
Coromandel Peninsula,
February 1959; South
Australia, May 1968;
at home, 1968
Third row: Great Barrier, the
outermost island of Auckland's
Hauraki Gulf, 1970
Bottom row: Trekking in
Nepal, December 1971–
January 1972
**Edmund Hillary, Louise Hillary
and Peter Hillary**

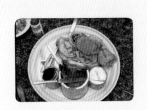

As the children grew, Ed's lengthy absences from home came at a cost. Looking back on her childhood Sarah Hillary said: 'My mother was central to the family. She was the person who was always around and who talked to us and understood what was happening to us. Whereas Ed was away a lot and although we did lots of things with him – it was a different kind of relationship.'[24] School holidays became the important times for the family to be together. In May 1968 the Hillarys set out for the Australian outback with Louise's parents. They drove 1600 kilometres from Sydney to Adelaide, then up into the dramatic Flinders Ranges to the beginning of the Birdsville Track – a famously difficult outback cattle route. Some 110 kilometres out they encountered rainstorms, then flooding, and the holiday became a sometimes hilarious, sometimes nerve-wracking series of river fords, with everyone pushing and covered in mud and wild with the fun of it all.[25]

They were all back in the Himalayas in December 1971, making a long trek into the Khumbu and visiting some of Ed's more far-flung projects. In her book *High Time,* Louise Hillary wrote: 'I always find that when we are in high places our spirits seem to rise accordingly.

Trekking in Nepal is like a long musical composition which crescendos to an exciting fortissimo and then fades to a soft slow interlude before the next summit.'[26] One of the penalties of having Sherpas to carry your gear, however, is the need to be up early to avoid having the tent collapsed around you. The pre-dawn attempts of teenage daughters to be ready in time, involving much frenzied jingling of the glass bangles they'd bought in Kathmandu, proved a little trying for their parents in the next tent. But Louise delighted in a life which consisted of 'hard exercise, sleep and wonderful scenery. Usually at some stage of the day you wonder if you have the power to take another breath or the energy to make one more tottering step. To compensate for this there is the absolute relaxation when your day's walk is finished. There are no telephones, no appointments to be kept, no social life, no television – nothing to do but fix the blisters on your feet, mend a sock, sit and talk and dream, and eventually snuggle into the warmth of a soft sleeping bag. After about a week of this type of life you learn the new and priceless art of being able to sit and do nothing – just looking at the view or watching the sparks flying out of an evening fire.'[27]

Louise saw their close association with the Sherpas as reward in itself. 'Few people are fortunate enough to be wholeheartedly accepted by the inhabitants of a village in a distant land, and I suppose this feeling of unity can only be achieved by working together and then playing together.'[28] Ed was always good at relaxing round the campfire with stories and singing and general hilarity, but he had constant demands on his time. At each village they visited there would be requests for help – and petitions were always accompanied by the legendary Sherpa hospitality. There was much giving of *kartas* and plying the Burra Sahib with *chang* or *arak* – a fiery alcohol distilled from rice or potatoes. Mingma's help on these occasions was invaluable. When the customary drinking of three glasses of *arak* got too much, Mingma would ensure Ed's were quietly passed on to others, avoiding the possibility of giving offence. Then he would glance at his watch, the cue for Ed to ask, 'Is it time to go, Mingma?' The two men talked about climbing too – spending time one morning in cheerful debate over possible routes on Gauri Sankar (7130 m; 23,400 ft) which was glowing above them in the pink dawn. Louise wrote: 'All mountaineers love these discussions; it doesn't really matter whether the mountain is climbable or not, it's just a pleasant pastime, like talking about catching the biggest fish or about scoring a winning goal.'[29]

Left: *The Four Harmonious Brothers* by Kappa Kalden, 1971. Louise Hillary commissioned Kappa Kalden to paint this famous story from Lamaistic Buddhism, after seeing a similar painting at Tengboche Monastery. It shows the elephant, monkey, rabbit and partridge living happily together after agreeing to help each other respect the five laws: never take life, never steal, never commit adultery, never lie and never take stimulating drink. The legend tells that the resulting harmony brought great peace and prosperity to the kingdom
Louise Hillary

Far left: Ed Hillary at the opening of Bakanje School, 1970
Louise Hillary

Below: A silver and jade *tarkye* given to Ed Hillary by Mingma Tsering
Krzysztof Pfeiffer

168

Mingma Tsering
and Ang Dooli
from Kunde

Ed Hillary first met Mingma Tsering when he was a young porter on the 1953 Everest expedition. Mingma was an assistant sirdar on the 1960–61 Silver Hut expedition and the Makalu climb. 'In 1963, the first of my many expeditions devoted primarily to school or hospital-building, I asked Mingma to be sirdar. This involved organising all the load-carrying from Kathmandu to the Khumbu, all the expedition Sherpas and all the labour and local materials on the projects. He and I would negotiate rates of pay and assign loads in the midst of a seeming chaos of up to 200 porters... Though his English was fairly basic and my Nepali and Sherpa even more so, we seemed to be able to communicate with ease and fluency. However, newcomers to the scene, whatever their native tongue, often had difficulty understanding either of us. 'As projects increased in number and complexity, I would often send Mingma from New Zealand lists of local materials needed for the next expedition, rock and timber on the site, nails and other hardware from Kathmandu. Always he would have the materials bought and assembled and be able to tell me where they all were and how much they had

cost. All this required formidable organisational skill, in which Mingma certainly excelled. But even more impressive to me was his prodigious memory. I would be armed with endless written lists and plans... Mingma kept it all in his memory, writing nothing down – indeed not able to – yet I never knew him to make a mistake... Mingma, and the other Sherpas he recruited to build and climb with us, tough and competent themselves in their mountain environment, never really believed we could cope on our own. They would try and ensure we "sahibs" carried only light loads, and would worry if we were going any distance without Sherpa guidance.'* Louise Hillary observed: 'We called Mingma the "boss" – Ed was just the "leader".'† Mingma and Ang Dooli's house in Kunde holds many happy memories for the Hillary family – of talking, eating, drinking, singing, dancing, and celebration as projects were completed and new ones planned. Mingma Tsering died in 1993 and Ang Dooli remains one of Kunde's lively and respected matriarchs. Their sons grew up with the Hillary family. Temba is a painter and lives with Ang Dooli, and Ang Rita lives in Kathmandu.

In 1967 Ed returned to Antarctica to lead a mountaineering and geology expedition. 'On the north-west shore of the Ross Sea were a group of steep and slender summits with ice-fluted faces and narrow soaring ridges. Queen of the area was Mount Herschel, rising 11,000 feet [3350 m] out of the sea across the bay from Cape Hallett and surely one of the most beautiful mountains in the world.'[30] His team included three 'climbing tigers', Bruce Jenkinson, Peter Strang and Mike White, as well as old friends Murray Ellis, Mike Gill and Jim Wilson. After adventures with Sears snowmobiles and an abandonded Weasel vehicle which Murray Ellis characteristically nursed back to life, they established a base camp; everyone accompanied Gill and Jenkinson to 1035 metres (3400 ft), then left them to try for the summit. It was a long climb, but they made it to the top and back in what Ed described as 'a remarkable display of skill and endurance'.[31] Strang and White climbed to the summit the following day. Ed could always enjoy the achievements of others, but when he turned fifty in July 1969 he made

some resolutions for himself. He would build a family bach at Anawhata on Auckland's west coast, where Jim and Phyl Rose had some land; he would improve his skiing; and he would make a Grand Traverse of Mount Cook. He did all three.

The Grand Traverse was first accomplished by Australian mountaineer Freda du Faur in 1912. She credited her New Zealand guides with the real triumph, but in his book *Aorangi: The Story of Mount Cook* Jim Wilson wrote: 'she too deserves the highest praise. With or without guides, and even with crampons, which she did not have, the Grand Traverse of Cook was then, and has remained, a remarkable feat of climbing.'[32]

Climbers on the Grand
Traverse of Aoraki/Mount
Cook

It involves crossing all three summits of the mountain which stretch along a magnificent airy ridge. Ed had wanted to attempt it ever since his first ascent of the South Ridge with Harry Ayres, Ruth Watson and Mick Sullivan. Twenty-two years later his companions on this 'jewel of a climb' were Harry Ayres, Mike Gill, Jim Wilson and Graeme Dingle – old and new friends together in the Southern Alps where Ed Hillary's climbing career began. But Ed had some doubts. The Grand Traverse was a 'glorious route enjoyed even by the "hot shots" of the younger generation – possibly it was now beyond my capacity?'[33] Ed did find it hard work, but they completed the climb in superb weather. It was an exhilarating day.

Below left and middle: The Hillary family bach at Anawhata on Auckland's west coast, 1971
Edmund and Louise Hillary

Below right: Tenzing Norgay and his wife Daku with Ed Hillary on the Tasman Glacier, August 1971

Ed's Everest climbing companion Tenzing Norgay, and his wife Daku, made a whirlwind tour of New Zealand in August 1971 as guests of the Himalayan Trust. Tenzing's presence at fundraising evenings was a great incentive to give generously, but Ed's primary aim was for Tenzing to get to know New Zealand. They went sailing, jet boating and skiing; toured a sheep station; met the prime minister; lunched with the Indian High Commissioner; and visited the Arthur Ellis factory where the 1953 Everest sleeping bags were made. Tenzing wrote: 'We always stayed, wherever we went, in the homes of people who had been on expeditions with Sherpas and we felt very much at home', and he described the Hillarys' house in Auckland as 'not like all the other New Zealand homes, but more like a Tibetan gompa'.[34] Many of the Sherpa and Nepali items in the Hillarys' house were purchased, but there were also numerous gifts from Sherpa friends. And because Louise was raising funds by organising sales of goods from Nepal, both for the Himalayan Trust and for a Tibetan children's aid group, the house was a clearing station for beautiful Tibetan carpets and myriad decorative crafts. Ed wrote: 'We were working together as a very energetic team.'[35]

Each year, after working out the next group of projects with the Sherpa communities, Ed would write to the Nepalese Government to seek its approval for his plans. He hoped that at some stage it would step in to help with the running of the schools, since the Sherpa villages had received little government support. In 1964 Ed had invited the Crown Prince of Nepal to fly to Lukla for the opening of Chaunrikarka School – the first time a member of the Royal Family had visited the Khumbu. This strategically successful move helped pave the way for a three-year agreement between the trust and the government. Ed had stalwart help from

Elizabeth Hawley, New Zealand's honorary consul in Kathmandu, and from John Claydon who was on a posting there for the Asian Development Bank. Claydon devoted a great deal of time and effort to pursuing the document through several drafts until at last all was agreed. On 20 January 1972 Ed and Louise Hillary, Mingma Tsering and Ang Tsering dressed in their best and climbed into the Himalayan Trust's battered jeep to drive to Singhar Durbar, the government offices in Kathmandu. There the Agreement was signed by Mr Bharat Raj Bhandary, foreign secretary, and Sir Edmund Hillary, chairman of the Himalayan

Trust. It began by stating the desire of the two parties 'to cooperate in promoting the economic and social welfare and the development of educational and health services...in Eastern Nepal', and it covered the provision of educational assistance and health services by the trust, and the government's agreement to provide visas free of charge for those working on trust projects and to waive Customs duty on equipment and supplies.[36] The two signatories represented 'His Majesty's Government of Nepal' and 'The Himalayan Trust 278A Remuera Road, Auckland, New Zealand'. Sir Edmund Hillary, the Burra Sahib, was in for the long haul.

172

The Head Lama at Thami *Gompa* asked Ed Hillary to help them repair and extend the *gompa* courtyard. They provided the labour and Ed supplied the necessary funds by writing articles. The extension was supported by three huge buttresses of stone – brought by local people in hundreds of basket loads. The new courtyard was ready in time for the annual Mani Rimdu festival early in May, 1970. Young *tawas* (monks) blew long Tibetan horns to announce the festivities. After lengthy prayers to the Buddha of Compassion, for the benefit of all beings, the monks performed the sacred mask dances known as *Cham* – a recreation of the establishment of Buddhism in the Himalayas by the Guru Rinpoche. In the dances, symbolic demons representing hatred, greed and ignorance are overcome through meditation, compassion and wisdom
Mike Gill and Max Pearl

Below left: Ed and Rex
Hillary working on an
extension to Khumjung
School in 1982
Jim Wilson

Below: Khunjo Chumbi
cutting the ribbon to open
two new classrooms for
Khumjung School in 1968.
The roll had grown to 110
pupils
Andrew Quarmby

173

Above: The schools became
centres for the village
communities and a great
source of local pride
Max Pearl

Above left: Inside a new
classroom – Shyam Pradhan,
Ed Hillary and Ann Lang,
whose husband Selwyn was
the doctor at Kunde Hospital,
1970
Mike Gill

March 24th, 1968.

Dr. John McKinnon,
Khunde Sherpa Hospital,
c/o British Embassy,
Kathmandu.

Dear John,

I have more or less finalised arrangements as far as
visit to Nepal is concerned later this year. Because of shipping
difficulties I plan to visit the Khumbu in August and do the
jet boating in September.

July 30th: I plan to arrive in Calcutta and devote aweek to
purchasing food and equipment, airfreighting everything
to Calcutta, and a quick visit to Kalimpong to check
over schools with scholarships in mind.

August 5th: Party arrives in Kathmandu (Jon and Joyce Hamilton,
probably Max Pearl, Dr. and Mrs. Evans if their
selection is finalised, possibly Tenzing and Dahku,
and Neville Wooderson.)

August 9th: complete flying of ourselves and gear to Jiri.

August 10th to 18th: Walk from Jiri to Khunde with visits to
Junbesi and Chaunrikarka schools.....and Lukla airfield.

August 19th to September 8th: Three weeks in Khumbu visiting
schools, working on Khumjung school addition and on
new Khunde pipelines etc. Neville Wooderson will stay
on until these tasks are completed.

September 10th: Fly or helicopter from Lukla to Kathmandu.
(EPH, Jon and Joyce Hamilton, McKinnons etc.)

Left: Ed with clipboard, 1968
John McKinnon

Facing page: Ed Hillary with
John and Diane McKinnon's
son Dorje, who was born at
the end of their time at Kunde
Hospital, Kathmandu, 1973
John McKinnon

On September 9th Mike Gill will arrive in Calcutta, purchase
some food, collect the two jet boats and truck everything up to
the Nepalese border at Biratnagar.

We will all rendezvous at Biratnagar about September 14th.

September 16th to October 6th: Three weeks jet boating up the
Sun kosi, Tamur and Arun rivers and doing a
survey of the high villages re goitre and medical
needs.

October 6th: Arrive at Dologhat and truck boats to Kathmandu.

October 9th: Kathmandu to Delhi or Calcutta.

This is the general plan. If you are keen on doing the
jet boat trip I suggest you plan to come along. Unfortunately
we are going to be very short of room and I can't offer Dianne
a seat but I imagine she would enjoy a couple of weeks in
Kathmandu.

Food, equipment and drugs: These are being accumulated at the
moment. Some will go by RNZAF at the end of next week;
some by ship at the beginning of May; and the remainder w
with the jet boats at the beginning of July.

I am sure that Neville Wooderson will make a considerable
contribution to the construction program. If you have any
suggestions regarding plumbing or the stoves please let us have t
them as soon as possible so we can get the gear on the May boat.
Do chimney pipes need replacing on the stoves ? How are the
44 gallon drums in the kitchen ? Have you other suggestions
for improvements ? I don't know if you can get a reply to us
in time but we'd really need to have it by May 1st. (If you
have any correspondence for me which will arrive after
May 1st please send it to Max as I'll be in Australia for five
weeks).

Sherpas: I hope we can get the chaps we want. I'd like
Mingma to be in Kathmandu by August 1st plus Pembertarkay,
Tenzing Niendra and Phudorje. Dudley Spain said in December
that I could borrow Ang Passang for cook. I am planning to
set up a large tent (very luxurious) in the Embassy compound
and we'll use this as our home base when passing through.

Then I estimate we'll need 80 porters in Jiri by August
8th (unless we can get some gear flown in to Lukla in August
which seems unlikely).

For the walk from Jiri to Khunde we'll need a further three or four useful Sherpas to act as Sahib lookerafterers and cook boys.

In September I'd like Tenzing Niendra and Phudorje to stay on with Neville to complete the construction activities although they should be finished by the end of the month.

Mingma and Pembertarkay I'd like to travel in the Jet boats xikkxxx plus possibly Ang Passang or some other competent cook. We'll also want a few more Sherpas in the preliminary stages of the jet boat operation but we can select these in Khumbu and send them down on foot. They'll have to be reliable rather than exceptional. This would get Pembertarkay back to Kathmanu by October 6th for his work with Jimmy.

I'll leave it to you and Mingma to work this all out as best you can.

Building materials: There should be ample corrugated aluminium at Khunde and plenty of aluminium nails for the Khumjung school building and I won't bring any more in unless you think it might be desirable. However I'll bring corrugated skylights, aluminium frame windows, aluminium ridging, No 8 wire etc. from NZ and plastic pipe, nails etc etc from India and Nepal. Sears are sending over a number of good tarps which should do for the water tanks.

Field Enterprises in Australia are hoping to raise ₤1500 for the Khumjung extension so we could well afford to make it a little bigger if you and Tem Dorje thought desirable - say 50ft x 20 ft ? I'll have to get some plywood in from Kathmandu for partitions.

At a later stage I'll let you have my detailed lists for your comments so that we can purchase extras in Calcutta and Kathmandu.

Thanks for the photos(the black and white pictures of TB kids) and the receipts from the artists. I was very pleased to hear of the progress at Phortse. I'd rather delay any decisions on the stipend for the second teacher until I reach Junbesi in August.

By the way I think it would be a good idea if you could meet us at Lukla or possibly even at Junbesi if you don't think the hospital would suffer.

World Book in Chicago have agreed to supply the funds for four new scholarships each year. Each scholarship would be a four year course at a worthwhile secondary school in Kalimpong, Kathmandu or elsewhere. We'll probably start next year if it seems desirable so you could perhaps tell Tem Dorje to keep his eyes open. I would like the four recipients to be chosen from all our schools if the standard is high enough.

I'd very much like to take a climbing party in with us but don't quite know if anything could be organised at this late stage even if permission were granted. I think I'm just about draining all my sources of funds for the Jet boat trip. I get so fed up with raising funds at times that I feel like retiring to a beachcomers existence in Tahiti - only I'd get bored to tears in two weeks. Our Australian camping trip is definitely under way... the five Hillarys; two grandparent Roses; and Andrew and Dianne Quarmby. We'll go Sydney/Adelaide/ up the Birsdville track to Birdsville/ across cattle tracks to ther Charleville/ then to Brisbane, Gold Coast, Newcastle and Sydney.   3,600 miles in 18 days and some of it damn rough. It sounds good fun but not exactly a holiday.

I've had some very nice letters from the scholarship boys at Gorkha. I hope I can think up some way of seeing them this trip.

I'll keep you advised of progress but do let us have your comments as quickly as possible if there's anything else you feel we need in the construction line.

Regards to Dianne,

Ed

Sherpa friends

Far right: Porters carrying aluminium roofing for Kunde Hospital, 1966
Mike Gill

Clockwise from top: In the Khumbu today: prayer flags, a *chorten*, a summer dwelling for yak herders on a high pasture and burning juniper
Arthur Boyer

Scores of Sherpas from the villages around Solu and Khumbu worked on the Himalayan Trust's building programme. Porters carried unwieldy loads of aluminium roofing, coils of alkathene water pipe, or heavy glass windows over steep, narrow mountain paths. Women and children brought loads of rocks to the building sites in baskets on their backs; men pitsawed timber for framing; builders and stone-masons worked on foundations, walls and roofs – and everyone from the villages joined in the celebrations when projects were completed.

Many of the Sherpa men were experienced climbers. Some had known Ed since the 1951 Everest Reconnaissance. Once a school was completed, a roof repaired or a water pipe safely installed, they would head off with the mountaineers to tackle one of the Khumbu peaks. Others were senior people in the villages who could advise Ed on local issues and needs. During the most intense period of building (1963–75), a number of Sherpas became particular friends to Ed, to his family and to others in the Himalayan Trust. At the centre of everything was Ed's sirdar and close friend, Mingma Tsering.

PEMBA TARKAY FROM PHORTSE

Ed Hillary described Pemba Tarkay as a natural climber and a tower of strength, always ready to help in any capacity. Early on the Makalu climb Ed was tired after having to make a rapid trek back to the Silver Hut, and 'Pemba Tarkay, an enormously powerful man with a spirit as strong and vigorous as his body, came across to me and felt the weight of my twenty-pound pack. He strolled off with it in his hand. It was a few minutes before I realised that he was adding it to his own sixty pounds, making it an eighty-pound load. I knew he would still reach the west col with the leading group, but my pride wouldn't allow it and I took my modest twenty pounds back again – with a deep feeling of appreciation for his kindness.'[*] Pemba Tarkay was an important member of the hospital building team and has produced some talented mountaineering sons. He still herds yaks near Phortse.

Photo: Edmund Hillary

PHU DORJE FROM KUNDE

'One of the most lovable of all the Sherpas was Phu Dorje, a talented but terrifying type of carpenter who threw himself into his work with such vim and vigour that the building shuddered every time he struck a blow.'[†] Phu Dorje's great strength and irrepressible clowning good humour endeared him to everyone. He was born in 1938 after his parents came to Kunde from Tibet. He first worked as a porter for Ed Hillary on the 1961 yeti-hunting expedition and carried to Camp V on Makalu, after which he was a regular worker on Himalayan Trust projects. In the 1970s when June Mulgrew took trekking groups to the Khumbu, Phu Dorje was her sirdar. He has a piercing whistle, perfected when he was a boy herding yaks, which is still useful for rounding up straggling trekkers. He now spends most of his time at his lodge in Kunde 'praying and drinking *chang*'.

Photo: Mike Gill

AILA FROM PHORTSE

'Aila, a sturdy Phortse farmer and an excellent builder in rock was there to give us a warm and enthusiastic welcome ... He is quite tall and craggy in build for a Sherpa, but like so many Nepalese people he has the same gentleness and dignity as Siku. He is aged about forty-eight and has four nearly grown-up children with a handsome wife of great personality. Aila was a member of Ed's industrious and elite building team.'[‡] Aila became Rex Hillary's right-hand man and they worked on Himalayan Trust projects together for more than twenty years. He is now retired and turning his prayer wheel at Phortse.

Photo: Edmund Hillary

177

TENZING NIENDRA

'Tenzing Niendra was the quietest and most serious Sherpa I have met. In appearance he was immaculate, extremely handsome and very tall. As building foreman for the hospital he had proved himself a man of great capabilities.'[§] In his youth Tenzing Niendra spent several years as a monk. He died in a mountaineering accident. This photograph shows him on Thamserku in 1964.

Photo: John McKinnon

SIKU FROM PHORTSE

Siku looked after the Hillary children with great care and affection on their first visit to the Khumbu in 1966. Louise Hillary described him as 'a slow and gentle but immensely powerful man [who] surprises everybody by very occasionally coming out with a wicked or ribald joke'.[¤] A tough mountaineer, Siku was on the Makalu climb in 1961.

Photo: Edmund Hillary

Far left: A traditional
Sherpa kitchen, 1963
Louise Hillary

Below: A yak painted by
Pasang Norbu from Khumjung
for Louise Hillary
Jennifer French

ANG DAWA FROM PHORTSE

Ang Dawa's large house at Phortse was the headquarters for the doctors studying and treating the effects of iodine deficiency among the Sherpas. 'In a village like Phortse a large proportion of the people had their mental faculties a little dulled as a consequence. Ang Dawa and his wife were typical cases of this.'* But Ang Dawa was tremendously strong and willing, and a valued member of Ed's Sherpa team.

Photo: Edmund Hillary

PASSANG TENDI FROM KHUMJUNG

The brother of Ang Tsering. 'They are both handsome lively men who enjoy hard work and adventure ... until about three years ago [c. 1970] they were greatly sought after as high-altitude climbers for expeditions. But they have young families and after the many climbing tragedies in recent years their wives had persuaded them to withdraw from high climbing.'† For many Sherpas, working with Ed on Himalayan Trust projects in their own communities was an enjoyable alternative to employment with climbing expeditions. Passang Tendi is still herding yaks and enjoying his many grandchildren.

Photo: Edmund Hillary

KAPPA KALDEN FROM KHUMJUNG

Kappa Kalden was trained as an artist in Tibet, but came to Khumjung after the Chinese invasion. Louise Hillary described visiting his house in 1966. 'Kappa Kalden was sitting cross legged in a bay window with a canvas in front of him ... I loved to watch him at work. His broad Mongolian face with its inscrutable expression changed rarely – only when something really amused him would he toss back his head and roar with uninhibited laughter. A long thick pigtail stretched down his back and his old and slightly unsteady hands seemed to come to life when he held one of his fine brushes.'‡ Kappa Kalden's son Ang Rita is the chief administrative officer for the Himalayan Trust, based in Kathmandu. Two other sons Pasang Norbu and Gyalgen became artists like their father.

Photo: Rob Riley

ANG TSERING AND DOMA TSAMJE FROM KHUMJUNG, WITH CHERING DOKA AND PHURBA SONA

Ang Tsering was sixteen in 1953 when he carried loads three times to the South Col. He became Mingma Tsering's assistant on Himalayan Trust projects. Louise Hillary described a meal at his house before the Hillary family set off for Everest Base Camp in December 1966. 'His family was one of the oldest and best established in the village and their house was a very large one ... Most of the walls were covered in rice paper with a black design stamped upon it ... There were long shelves covered with copper and brass household implements and comfortable benches with handsome Tibetan rugs ... Plates of the most delicious potato chips were handed to us and tiny slices of liver that had been fried in butter.' The main course was a Sherpa favourite, *momos*: 'A Tibetan dish made of finely chopped meat and herbs wrapped in pasta and then steamed. The Mo Mos were moulded into beautiful shapes and served with a type of green beet or spinach that had been pickled in a cask of salt water and chillies. It was all so good that I asked Ang Tsering for the recipe to try at home.'§

Photo: Rob Riley

Right: Making *momos* at Kunde Hospital, 1992 – Dr Kami Temba and Mingma Temba Sherpa, health worker and hospital administrator
Lynley Cook

Below: A contemporary Sherpa kitchen with a fine array of thermoses. Since fuel is scarce, water is heated in the morning and kept hot in thermoses for tea during the day
Diane McKinnon

Photo: John McKinnon

ANG PASSANG

'Ang Passang is one of the finest cooks in Nepal as well as being a tough man in the mountains, he is neat and tidy and always on the go, with just the trace of a smile on his face. He started as a shy junior cook boy on one of Ed's expeditions... Over the years he gained more and more experience with trekkers and climbers and was well known as being a fine organiser. From this he graduated to cook at the house of **Major Dudley Spain of the British Embassy**... but after three years [there] he accepted the job of hospital cook up in **Kunde**. There his jobs consist of interpreter, medical assistant, cultural adviser and friend as well as cook for the doctors.'[*] On the 1971 trek, Ang Passang made **Peter Hillary's** birthday cake over the camp fire. 'He creamed the shortening and sugar in the normal way and added flour, eggs, baking powder and some of our precious dried fruit that I had brought from home. The mixture was then put in a small greased *decchi* (cooking pot). While this was being done his largest *decchi* with an inch-deep layer of sand in the bottom was being heated over the fire. When the sand was very hot he put the small *decchi* inside the big one, put on the lid, and heaped a pile of coals on top of it all. In less than an hour the cake was baked to perfection.'[†] Ang Passang now lives in Lukla and owns **Paradise Eco-Lodge** with his wife, **Dawa Phuji**, formerly a nurse at **Kunde Hospital**, who is on the **Himalayan Trust Advisory Board**.

Two Sherpa recipes

The Sherpas grow delicious small, yellow-fleshed potatoes and cook them in many ways. This recipe is from **Diane McKinnon**.

RIGI KOOR

Sherpa potato pancakes were traditionally made with buckwheat flour, but wheat flour is now preferred. You could use some wholemeal flour and even add a couple of eggs for a richer mixture.
Finely grate washed raw potatoes – they should be almost a mush – and mix in enough flour to make a thick batter. Use a spatula to spread the mixture on a greased hot griddle or fry pan, pushing it out to about the size of a side plate. When the underside is browned, turn over to cook the other side.
Serve with butter and either a mixture of white castello cheese and buttermilk which is similar to the sharp nak's milk cheese made by the Sherpas (a nak is a female yak), or chives, chilli and rock salt, pounded together to make a coarse, fiery paste. Place the butter and sauce on the pancake. Eat by breaking off pieces and dipping them into the butter and whichever seasoning mixture you prefer.

MOMOS

Crescent-shaped dumplings, stuffed with finely chopped meat, vegetables and seasonings. This recipe is from Kunde Hospital.

For the dough:
Mix 150 g plain flour with enough lukewarm water to make a stiff paste, knead well and set aside, covered.

For the filling, mix together:
100 g finely chopped, minced or ground raw meat (lamb, beef or pork)
2 finely chopped onions
20 ml (4 tsp) vegetable oil
finely chopped coriander
finely chopped root ginger and garlic
soy sauce and extra vegetable oil to bind
salt and pepper
dried or fresh chilli (optional)

On a floured surface, roll the dough out thinly to about 2 mm. (At Kunde Hospital they use a pasta machine when catering for large parties.) Cut into circles about 7.5 cm diameter. Keep the dough circles covered with a cloth as you work.

To make the *momos*: place a circle of dough on your outstretched fingers and put a large teaspoonful of filling in the centre. Make small pleats in one side of the circle of dough, and then fold the other side over to meet it, enclosing the filling in a small semi-circular pouch. Pinch the edges tightly to seal.
Arrange the *momos* in a steamer – after oiling the base to prevent them from sticking – and steam over boiling water for 10–15 minutes. Serve with a soy and chilli dipping sauce.
Vegetarian *momos* can be made with potato, spinach and cheese filling – or any combination of finely chopped vegetables.

Shay Shay! Suma shimbudup!
(Eat Eat! Food with a great taste!)

179

12
FOR EVER TO DEPLORE HER LOSS

Louise and Belinda Hillary were killed on 31 March 1975. They were flying from Kathmandu to Phaphlu, where Ed and Rex Hillary were building a hospital; but their small plane crashed on takeoff. A locking pin had not been removed from one of the wing flaps. There were no survivors among the five people on board.

182

The Hillarys had planned to have the whole year in Nepal. They had rented a house, Belinda was to go to school in Kathmandu, and she and Louise were determined to learn Nepali. Phyl and Jim Rose were there too. On the day of the accident Peter was travelling in India with a friend, and Sarah had returned to university in Auckland. With their father, they now had to face a loss beyond comprehension. The family had been dealt a shattering blow.

Sarah flew back from New Zealand. 'I remember the whole time thinking that I just couldn't wait to see my father and as soon as I saw him everything would be all right. But when I got off the plane Liz Hawley was there, and she warned me that Ed wasn't very good. And then I saw Ed, and he was completely broken down.'[1]

Peter was still on his way to Kathmandu – it had taken several days to locate him in India. Ed meantime wrote a letter to friends and family in New Zealand: 'It is now five days since Louise and Belinda died in the plane crash and I hope you will forgive me if I share some of my pain with you. When the Pilatus failed to arrive at Phaphlu I had a terrible premonition of disaster – when a helicopter approached I knew that something dreadful had occurred...People have been wonderfully kind and good and Phyl and Jim Rose have been unbelievably calm and strong...I think you know how much Louise has meant to me and Belinda was so kind and joyous. The arrival of Sarah with Peter Mulgrew has been a great blessing. She is a dear girl and stronger in spirit than I believed possible... On Monday we go back to Phaphlu for a while to start work going again on the hospital.

Whatever else happens I feel the task must be finished. Sarah, Mingma and I will then walk up to Khumbu and mourn a little with our friends. What will happen then I don't quite know...I only hope I have the courage to carry through what has to be done...God knows if I'll have the courage to go on living. Love to you all. Your friendship has meant everything to Louise and me. Ed'.[2]

Peter arrived in Nepal at last. 'Landing at Kathmandu was an agony...We took a taxi to Baluwatar. The house was deserted, it was eerie and silent. I made a telephone call to locate Dad. Fifteen minutes later our little green car came bumping along the road. Sarah was driving, Phyl was in the passenger seat and Dad and Jim were in the back. The car stopped and the three remnants of the Hillary family reached for each other. We stood there on the road and wept.'[3]

13
NOTHING VENTURE, NOTHING WIN

Several years would pass before Ed Hillary could see hope or joy in a new day. Louise and Belinda were cremated on the shores of the Bagmati River, the holy river of Kathmandu; later their ashes would be spread on the cliffs above Anawhata Beach near the family's much-loved bach. With Peter and Sarah, Ed returned to Phaphlu to continue working on the hospital with Rex. He needed to immerse himself in practical activity, and this was a project that Louise had strongly supported. He remembers walking alone on the Phaphlu airstrip in the evenings and finding some solace in the great mountains all around – but they were days of bleak despair. 'A little altar had been made in the cookhouse with pictures of Louise and Belinda, and every day new ceremonial scarves were draped over the altar, which was strewn with crimson and white rhododendrons, and butter lamps were always alight. I could hardly bear to look at them.'[1]

Left: On the Ocean to the Sky expedition. A jet boat is dwarfed by a *dhow* beating up the river against the current
Jim Wilson

**Slowly the idea grew of taking jet boats up the biggest and holiest river of India, Mother Ganga. Early in the 1970s Louise and I were in New Delhi to get support for the Ganga adventure ... Louise had decided that this was an adventure she could undertake too. Early in 1977 I received positive support from the Indian Government [and] the many tasks to undertake helped shake me out of the depression that had gripped me for the past two years.
EDMUND HILLARY**

Rex Hillary was now in Nepal almost every year, and would work on the Himalayan Trust's projects for two more decades. Ed left him to continue at the hospital, and walked on up to Kunde with Peter and Sarah. 'In Solu and in Khumbu there were ceremonies and sadness; many *kartas* and mountains of flowers. And the "burra sahib" had to act like a "burra sahib", even though his heart was broken.'[2] That Ed had suffered such a loss while working to help the Sherpas further cemented his place in their hearts. On a ridge high above their house in Kunde, Mingma and Ang Dooli built two stone *chortens* in memory of Louise and Belinda, and for many weeks Ang Dooli climbed up to them each day to light a fire of juniper brush, its aromatic smoke drifting upwards to commemorate their lives. Mingma was drinking heavily, something Ed could sympathise with, but unlike Mingma and Ang Dooli and other Sherpa friends, he couldn't cry. Tears seemed to elude him now.

Peter and Sarah kept close to their father during those first weeks. They stayed with old friends in Geneva, travelled to London where Ed had to give interviews about his recently published autobiography, *Nothing Venture, Nothing Win*, and then flew to Canada. 'With our friends from Sears we canoed down the Buffalo river in Arkansas and we were glad for their friendship, and the beauty, and the peace in our tents at night. I still wasn't sleeping well, despite masses of pills, but I wasn't often now having the ghastly nightmares reliving that awful day.'[3] In mid-June they finally had to return to Auckland. 'Our house was just like an empty tomb without Louise's warm presence and Belinda's laughter and I felt the same way – empty and sterile. I didn't stay long.'[4]

In the years ahead Ed would regret his inability to help his children face the loss of their mother and sister at this time. He was deeply depressed, numbing his feelings with several whiskies every evening and taking sleeping pills at night. Sarah recalled: 'It was really a very terrible time. Some families get closer together and that helps, but I think in our family the two people who would probably have dealt with an accident much better had died. And the people who were left really couldn't cope very well, and we all spun off in our own individual directions.'[5]

Ed took refuge in his usual routines of planning and organisation, and in August he went back with Rex and Jim Wilson to complete the Phaphlu Hospital. In Kathmandu, 'I shared a room with Jim Wilson...After a quiet dinner, Jim and I retreated to our room with a bottle of Scotch whisky. Then the dam burst – we drank and talked and wept...I have always appreciated Jim Wilson's friendship on that sad occasion.'[6] But the raw emptiness persisted. More than a year later, George Lowe was shocked when Ed said he couldn't face living like this. And Peter later said that it seemed as if for Ed the meaning in doing anything had evaporated. The change in him left friends wondering if the man they loved – and had laughed and talked and worked and trekked and climbed with – would ever return. June Mulgrew remembered: 'Everybody was very worried for him...They did everything they could to cheer him up and jolly him along and he wasn't having any of it – and that's all there was to it.'[7]

186

Jim and Phyl Rose, also desperately sad, helped Peter and Sarah pull through this wrenchingly difficult time. And Ed did go on living. It wasn't in his character to give up; the determination that had kept him plugging on against cold and weariness and 'sheer misery' when he was climbing was what he called on now. He certainly couldn't bring himself to desert his family and the Sherpas who depended upon him, and this ingrained awareness of his responsibility to others helped carry him through. His parents, Percy and Gertrude, had both died in 1965, but they had encouraged Ed's earliest projects in Nepal, and their values and strong social conscience still motivated him.

For over a decade Ed Hillary had given his support to a number of social, political and environmental causes, and he now had a reputation for speaking out on issues he believed in. In June 1967 his address at an Auckland Rotary Club luncheon for secondary school head prefects had sparked a flurry of headlines and letters to the newspapers. Ed had said he was sad that New Zealand made 'one of the lowest percentage contributions of all the affluent countries toward overseas aid'. He hoped that this new generation of leaders would tackle the growing gap in wealth between nations 'with more courage and generosity than we have done' and that the day would come when 'every young person of conscience would regard it as a duty to devote a couple of years of his life to the constructive betterment of those needing help'.[8] His comments reflected the aims of Volunteer Service Abroad and the United Nations' target for economically developed countries of one per cent of gross national product to be given in overseas aid. The charity Corso was promoting this target in New Zealand. But the media fuss was sparked by his call to young people, as future leaders, to 'bring a little honest-to-God morality into politics and

Sagarmatha Pollution Control Committee

In the late 1980s there was international concern about waste and rubbish in **Sagarmatha National Park**, most of it left behind by trekking and climbing expeditions. A local campaign to clean up the Everest region received initial funding from **Nepal's Ministry of Culture, Tourism and Civil Aviation**, and in 1991 the **World Wildlife Fund** supported the establishment of the **Sagarmatha Pollution Control Committee (SPCC)**, chaired by the Head Lama of Tengboche Monastery. **Ed Hillary** was in **Namche Bazar** for the launch of the **SPCC** and applauded its aims.

The original goal was to manage waste disposal along the main trekking routes of the Khumbu, but the **SPCC's** work now includes educating and helping the local people to be more environmentally conscious, and promotions aimed at visitors to the Khumbu. Its overall goal is a 'pollution-free Khumbu'. Between 1994 and 2003 the **SPCC** disposed of 202,745 kilograms of rubbish, and has initiated a wide range of measures.

These include:

- rescue equipment and a first-aid service
- visitor information centres at Namche Bazar and Lukla
- garbage collection and disposal systems in the villages
- conservation education in local schools
- incinerator installation
- trail improvement
- Everest Base Camp cleaning and monitoring
- a kerosene and LPG depot
- removal of empty oxygen bottles

Each climbing season, expeditions to Mount Everest pay a fee to the Sherpa-run Khumbu Icefall rigging team, which establishes the icefall route and makes it as safe as possible. These fees are a major source of income for the SPCC. With the assistance of individuals and agencies who want to help preserve the beauty of this region, Sherpas believe that the tide of pollution can be turned.

government at all levels nationally and internationally'. He was horrified that governments could 'one moment deny that their countries are carrying out some particular action and then, a couple of days later, and with complete calmness, admit the whole thing'.[9] America's actions in Vietnam were dominating the international news at the time, and at home there had been vehement opposition to hydro-electric power schemes which would flood large areas of countryside. His speech infuriated New Zealand's conservative prime minister Sir Keith Holyoake and the Minister of Electricity, who read Ed's 'insulting remarks' and demanded that he 'substantiate or retract'.[10] Ed Hillary stood by his comments – and received a pronounced snub from the PM the next time they met, at a VSA annual meeting.

Ed had been shocked to witness South Africa's apartheid system in 1955, and in 1970, despite his lifelong enjoyment of a good rugby game, criticised New Zealand's national team, the All Blacks, for touring South Africa with a 'whites only' team. Many staunch rugby supporters were not impressed by his stand. Others may have been surprised to find Ed Hillary supporting the Family Planning Association and becoming an honorary vice-president of the Abortion Law Reform Association, which proposed the liberalisation of New Zealand's abortion laws. But Ed was aware of widespread concern about the world's population growth fast outstripping food production, and reliable and safe methods of contraception were widely seen as vital for both developing and developed countries. At Kunde Hospital Ed had observed for himself that Sherpas were happy to limit the size of their families – once they knew that their children were no longer likely to die from infectious diseases or lack of medical care. Forty years later Michael King noted that Hillary had 'aligned himself with some of the less popular, anti-authoritarian social movements – United Nations groups when they weren't especially popular, the Race Relations Council. People who have a liberal or humanitarian cause in New Zealand have usually been able to go to Ed Hillary and find they had his support.'[11]

The New Zealand general election of 1972 was won by the Labour Party under Norman Kirk. Testing of nuclear weapons in the Pacific was the subject of intense concern in the country and a flotilla of yachts sailed to Mururoa Island, south-east of Tahiti, to protest French nuclear testing. There had been thirty-nine tests since 1966. The new government sent a navy frigate to support the protestors. But Norman Kirk died suddenly and his successor, Bill Rowling, faced a strong opponent at the 1975 election. The National Party's new leader, Robert Muldoon, was a tough, confrontational campaigner whose policies – including welcoming American nuclear-powered and -armed ships back into New Zealand ports – seemed destined to 'exacerbate conflicts in society'.[12] David Exel, a broadcaster and business consultant,

launched the Citizens for Rowling Campaign, and its members included prominent New Zealand educators, church leaders, lawyers, business people and Ed Hillary.

Ed was back at work on the Phaphlu Hospital with Rex, but his letter of support appeared in the campaign booklet, published in October 1975. 'When I first met Bill Rowling I was impressed with the almost unexpected strength of his personality. Remarkably quiet when there was nothing of consequence to say – but always alert – he was firm and forthright when the occasion demanded...I find that Bill Rowling has developed an image overseas that is both moderate and yet individualistic. It is good to once again feel a modest pride in being a New Zealander – Bill Rowling has helped us regain our self-respect as a country that

Facing page: Sagarmatha
National Park, 2003
Arthur Boyer

Left: Juniper seedlings
Anne B. Keiser

Below: Signs at the
entry to the park
Arthur Boyer

wood mainly from dead trees, using dried yak dung as fuel – and putting up with very cold houses. Trees grow slowly at altitude, and deforestation, which had begun with the climbing expeditions, was now obvious, ugly and worrying. At Kunde Hospital in 1972 the Himalayan Trust installed solar heating for the water supply and a kerosene stove for general heating to reduce the consumption of firewood. Louise had written about the pollution problem after spending two days cleaning up around Tengboche. 'Only a tourist with a heart of stone could not be affected by the grandeur that surrounds this little community but unfortunately there are a few who don't care about such things. They cut the rhododendron bushes that surround the Thyangboche meadow for firewood, and leave their litter in careless piles wherever they happen to camp... In the upper Khumbu the dark green, prostrate juniper and the azalea bushes have been hacked away slowly by advancing armies of tourists and climbers as they puff their way towards the foot of Everest...There is probably time for the Everest region to be saved by making it a National Park, patrolled by highly trained rangers. But this must happen soon.'[15]

189

Above: Mingma Norbu
Sherpa in Sagarmatha
National Park
Anne B. Keiser

frequently leads and doesn't always follow blindly.'[13] At a time when it was common to label anyone who spoke about world peace as communist, Muldoon described the campaign members as 'a bunch of cranks and queers and clergy'.[14] And National won the election. It was not until 1984 that New Zealand elected another Labour Government under David Lange, and nuclear ships were again excluded from the country's ports. Nonetheless, Ed Hillary's stand for larger principles, even in the midst of personal distress, would have pleased his parents.

Nuclear contamination of the Pacific was not the only form of environmental destruction that concerned Ed Hillary. He was intensely aware that by building Lukla Airport he had helped increase the flow of tourists to Solu and Khumbu. These visitors brought some economic benefits to the area, but they also brought quantities of rubbish and used huge amounts of firewood. The Sherpas' traditional methods of managing the use of firewood included taking

And it did. The push for a park in the Everest area came from many groups, including the Himalayan Trust. At the World Congress of the World Wildlife Fund at Bonn, on 5 October 1973, His Royal Highness Prince Gyanendra of Nepal announced the decision to create a national park in the Khumbu. Because of Ed Hillary's work in the area, the New Zealand Government was asked to assist, and by 1975 New Zealand was providing advisers experienced in mountain park management to work in the area. Ed was determined that Sherpas should be able to carry on their normal lives inside the park – a first for any national park – and this has happened too. Sagarmatha National Park was declared a UNESCO World Heritage Site in 1979.[16] By 1986 it was being run by the Department of Parks and Wildlife Conservation of the Nepal Government. Its Sherpa workers had trained in New Zealand in the management of national parks and high-altitude forests. It was a successful project.

Ed's regular speaking engagements, his books and articles, and the influx of trekkers to the Khumbu helped increase awareness of the Himalayan Trust's work with the Sherpas, but the primary responsibility for fundraising was always his. Without Louise at his side, it was a heavy burden, and Ed was immensely grateful for Dr Max Pearl's dedicated work as medical director of the trust – and his warm friendship. Max spent several weeks in Nepal each year. He persisted in the face of lengthy bureaucratic delays in Kathmandu, and his energy and drive were legendary.

There was some light on the funding horizon, sparked by Ed's continuing association with Sears Roebuck. In 1972 on a canoe trip with Sears, Ed had met Zeke O'Connor, a former star player for the Toronto Argonauts football team, who was in charge of the Sporting Goods Division of Sears Canada. Ed invited O'Connor to trek to Everest Base Camp for the 1973 reunion of the British Everest expedition, and O'Connor returned from that visit determined to help. He became founding president of the Sir Edmund Hillary Foundation of Canada, established to raise funds for the Himalayan Trust's work. In May 1975 Ed and Max Pearl met with O'Connor in Toronto to discuss the future funding of Kunde Hospital. It was the start of a long and rewarding partnership which would extend into reforestation and health programmes. With many private benefactors and assistance from the Canadian International Development Agency, the Foundation became a key supporter of the work in Nepal in the years ahead. Other partners would follow in the United States, Britain and Germany.

190

Above and right: Phurte Forest Nursery, run by Ang Tarkye and his wife Da Choki (top right), May 2003
Arthur Boyer

Right: Zeke O'Connor and Ed Hillary, 1972

In mid-1977 Ed felt the depression which had dogged him for so long begin to lift. It did not come through fundraising triumphs or building projects completed, but in the midst of his best-loved activity – an adventure. Friends like Mike Gill, Jim Wilson and John McKinnon often commented on Ed's ability not only to think up great ideas for expeditions but also to move them forward into reality. This was a perfect example. Ed wrote later: 'For more than five years I had dreamed of a new adventure – to travel with a group of friends from the mouth of the Ganges River upstream against the current as far as we could go. We would use jet boats,

those lively and speedy craft, and penetrate for 1,500 miles through the centre of the country, seeing a new view of India from the holiest of its rivers. And, when the waters became so violent that even a jet boat couldn't handle them, then we'd travel on foot and climb up into the mountains where the river had its beginnings... and so ultimately we'd reach up to the sky itself...And in the long journey from the ocean we would see and experience the heart of India – for to hundreds of millions of Indians Mother Ganga *is* the heart of India. Our journey would not only be an adventure but a cultural pilgrimage as well – we would learn much of the history and religion of this great country... And at the end

I would meet my old love, the Himalayas...The journey would be full of excitement and variety, and have its share of danger, too – what more could one ask than that?'[17]

In his book about the expedition, Ed Hillary quotes from Jawaharlal Nehru, 'that great Indian statesman who, when I spoke to him in 1953, impressed me more than any other man I have met, before or since'. Nehru wrote: 'The Ganga, especially, is the river of India, beloved of her people, round which are intertwined her racial memories, her hopes and fears,

Ed Hillary and Jim Wilson in the jet boat *Ganga*, with Jim driving, in the rapids above Rishikesh, 1977
Mike Gill

her songs of triumph, her victories and her defeats. She has been a symbol of India's age-long culture and civilisation, ever changing, ever flowing and yet ever the same Ganga.'[18] In the Hindu story Ganga came down from the sky through the intercession of the god Shiva. He stood high on the Himalayas so that the waters could trickle softly down through his long hair, across the plains, bringing life to the earth.

In August 1977 the Ocean to the Sky expedition was under way. The New Zealanders were Ed and Peter Hillary, Mike Gill, Jim Wilson, Max Pearl, Murray Jones, Graeme Dingle, and the jet-boat experts Jon and Michael Hamilton, son and grandson of William Hamilton, the boat's

New Zealand inventor, who always insisted that Archimedes should really take the credit. The Indians were Harish Sarin, president of the Indian Mountaineering Federation; climbers Captain Mohan Kohli, who had been leader of the successful 1965 Indian Everest expedition, and Commander Joginder Singh; and Major Bridhiv Bhatia, who was liaison officer. Captain Kohli was Air India's manager for East Australasia and his enthusiasm ensured major support from the airline, without which the expedition would have foundered. Mingma Tsering, always Ed's right-hand man, was sirdar. 'Without Mingma the party would have been incomplete both to me and to the others, who knew him well.'[19] Their cook was Pemma, another invaluable old friend. 'When we staggered into a

mountain camp at dark, completely done in, we knew that Pemma would have a cup of tea in our hands within an hour, and a three-course meal ready an hour after that.'[20] Such people are the making or breaking of most expeditions. The whole thing was being filmed by Mike Dillon, Waka Attewell, Prem Vaidya and B. G. Dewari, since the sale of book, magazine and film rights would provide essential income. It was a big team, although some would not join them until they arrived at the upper reaches of the river. The jet boats, named *Kiwi*, *Ganga* and *Air India*, were equipped with 250-horsepower V8 engines and collapsible canvas awnings designed by Ed Hillary and provided by Sears Roebuck.

Below middle: Crowds of
people lined the banks of the
river at every *ghat* to greet
Sir Edmund Hillary and the
expedition
Jim Wilson

Below right: The jet boats
arrive at Varanasi, Hinduism's
most important city,
8 September 1977
Mike Gill

Sears also donated and shipped all their camping equipment. Ed was overwhelmed by the enthusiastic support they received from Indian officials at all levels, and Indian oil companies donated fuel for the trip. The secular auspices looked good.

On 24 August 1977 the team drove out into the Bay of Bengal and along the coast to the temple of Ganga Sagar. 'To the people of India, for the past 3,000 years Ganga Sagar has been the place where Ganga meets Sagar, the ocean, the place from which any great pilgrimage must start. If you wish to gain infinite merit by walking, hopping, crawling or measuring your length for the full 1,500 miles of the Ganga to

its source … then this is where you begin.'[21] The boats and the crew were appropriately blessed in a *puja* ceremony which culminated in red *tilak* imprinted on bows and foreheads. Then the *pujare* filled a small copper container with *pani*, Ganga water which they would pour out into the snow at their journey's end. They could begin.

Jet boats are extremely noisy and not the most holy-looking form of transport, but their apparently miraculous ability to skim over very shallow water or up rapids without propellers attracted enormous numbers of people to see them. In Calcutta there were four million packed on to the river bank, and everywhere they stopped they were mobbed by exuberant crowds. It was hard not to be overwhelmed. The party was revered as pilgrims following

a sacred path – the pilgrimage made even more inspiring because their leader was the legendary Sir Hillary, who with Tenzing Norgay had climbed the highest mountain in the Himalayas, home of the gods.

The halfway point of their journey was Varanasi, the holiest city in India. Varanasi is known as a *tirtha* – a crossing point between the physical and spiritual worlds where the barrier between these realities is most permeable – but the secular world wanted Ed. 'Before I'd washed the mud from my legs, I found myself committed to a Lions Club, a Jaycees, a Rotary meeting and a civic reception. I found it difficult to think, surrounded by a milling crowd, and although I had no desire to

193

194

offend people…my Victorian sense of duty was beginning to desert me with the autograph marathons and business receptions.'[22] But he did do his duty and still found time to sit and watch the crowds on the *ghats* performing their ritual ablutions.

Ed Hillary had always been open to the spiritual dimension of human existence. He respected the Buddhist beliefs and religious observances of the Sherpas, and had spent many months working on monastery repairs and additions as well as on schools and bridges. Over the years he and Jim Wilson had enjoyed intense debates over the existence of a creative intelligence behind the universe. Although he was less likely to believe in this than Ed, Jim Wilson's roles on this trip included those of religious and cultural adviser, as well as jet-boat driver. He had spent three years at Benares Hindu University completing a doctorate on 'The grounds of religious belief in Hindu philosophy'. With Ed and Harish Sarin, he took part in the *puja* at Dasasvamedha *ghat* to help to bless them on the second and most dangerous part of their journey. Looking back on this event Ed wrote: 'A large group of smiling Indians gathered around and then the pujare appeared – a tall, slim, muscular young man with tangled hair and a look of wild energy. He started a vigorous chant and a band behind him took up the refrain. It was an incredible scene with flaming butter lamps, the tinkling of bells, and blossoms floating on the water. For half an hour we were transported into a different world, a world of religious fervour, of deafening sound, of the importance of Mother Ganga, and the surprising acceptance of our journey as a sacred pilgrimage. The pujare gestured to us to get down on our knees and then he pressed our foreheads onto

the damp sand. I don't know why, but suddenly my feeling of constant depression began to lift a little. In my tent that night, with the music and chanting still ringing in my ears, I felt stimulated and revived. For a time at least the sadness of the previous two years had vanished from my mind and life was worth living again.'[23]

On 12 September they left Varanasi and two weeks later encountered their first big rapids between Rishikesh and Deoprayag, in the foothills of the Himalayas. With considerable skill and daring Jon and Mike Hamilton and Jim Wilson negotiated the jet boats through difficult rapids, and survived two boat swampings – to the amazement of locals who had never seen *any* boats on that narrow and turbulent stretch

of the river. At Nandaprayag a large waterfall spelled the inevitable end of the journey for the boats. Some of the team finished their journey here. The boats had to be returned to Delhi and Max Pearl was heading off to Nepal to check on Himalayan Trust projects there. The others continued on foot alongside many other pilgrims heading for Badrinath. Ed had not been there since the 1951 New Zealand expedition, before 'the Everest Reconnaissance of that year, an expedition which in the end, was to change my life so completely'.[24]

Below: Going up the 'Chute', the sternest test of boats and drivers, beyond Rudraprayag, 27 September 1977
Mike Gill

195

Facing page: Peter Hillary
on the summit ridge of Akash
Parbat, 18 October 1977
Mike Gill

Left: Ed Hillary and Mingma
Tsering climbing to the High
Camp on a snow plateau at
5500 metres, 12 October 1977
Jim Wilson

They negotiated a steep snow slope and
in less than an hour had dropped 450 metres; 197
Ed's colour was visibly improving, but ahead
lay an icy gully. 'Everything depended on the
belayers now. If one of them failed, Ed would
shoot off down the steep ice, irretrievably. Ding
and Jim worked off good shaft belays where
there were patches of snow, or they climbed
down into crevasses where they could wedge in
firmly – "I could hold a jet boat from down here,"
called Jim from the depths of a crevasse – or
they worked off fragile pick belays with Ding
constructing intricate friction systems through
karabiners . . . At midday we came to a final halt
where the gully plunged over a cliff. We were
down to 16,000 feet [4900 metres] and Ed's
complexion had a healthy pink glow that he'd
not had three hours earlier.'

More nerve-wracking belaying over steep
stone slabs got them down to within 100 metres
of their Base Camp. They had heard the helicopter
above them, but it couldn't get through the
cloud, so they decided to camp for the night
on a rock ledge. Peter Hillary, Mingma, Graeme
Dingle, Waka Attewell and Mike Dillon headed
off for Base Camp. Peter would return with a

From Badrinath they set off on the final
part of the journey, a steep climb up to a snow
plateau at 5500 metres and a final push to the
summit of an unnamed peak which they called
Akash Parbat – Sky Peak. They poured the sacred
Ganga *pani* on to the snow, and Peter Hillary,
Jim Wilson, Graeme Dingle, Murray Jones and
Waka Attewell made it to the top on 18 October.
For Ed the expedition had ended five days earlier.

On 13 October Mike Gill and Mingma
went down to Base Camp. They returned to the
plateau with letters from home for everyone,
including the happy news of the birth of Sarah
Hillary's son, Arthur. Ed was now a grandfather.
But he was feeling too ill to celebrate. The climb
to their High Camp on the plateau had been a
struggle – they were all carrying heavy loads –
and next morning he was clearly in trouble.
Mike Gill described the ensuing hours. 'Whatever it was, cerebral oedema, or pulmonary
oedema, or both, it was high-altitude sickness,
and I felt a panicky sense of urgency . . . the only

way to get better is by taking oxygen, either
from a cylinder, of which we had none, or by
going to a lower altitude. Even a couple of
thousand feet can make a critical difference.
So we had to get lower, and quickly.' Murray
Jones raced off down the mountain to get help.
He reached Badrinath in a record one and three-
quarter hours, alerted the New Zealand High
Commission, arranged for a helicopter, then
climbed back up to Base Camp with a bottle
of oxygen. Meanwhile, the others collapsed
the tent over Ed and improvised a sledge.
'The affection and loyalty we all felt for him
suddenly seemed intensified a hundred times . . .
We grabbed a minimum of gear for ourselves
and set off, hauling Ed, with his tent-sledge
ploughing through the snow like a big seal. Peter
had been distressed beyond words back at camp
– on the verge of tears – now he was out in front
pulling like a huge cart-horse. We were moving
fast, everyone straining at the ropes and panting
in the thin air.'

tent and food. He arrived back 'carrying a huge load, including a can of peaches, Ed's favourite food in the mountains. And what a difference the tent made! Into a small comfortable world of our own we crawled, out of the vast inhospitable darkness outside…The crisis was over.'[25]

The following morning the rest of the team came back up and Graeme Dingle described the reunion: 'At the temporary camp everyone was in good spirits. Ed was vastly improved. We crowded into the small tent – Ed, Mike, Jim, Mingma, Peter, Waka, Murray and me – our arms and legs around each other, and we joked and laughed until the sun hit the tent.'[26]

Ed was grateful when an Indian Army helicopter took him down to Joshimath at 2000 metres, with Mike Gill accompanying him. There he faced the usual media attention. Newspapers had been reporting the failure of the expedition since Nandaprayag, for stories of the jet boats' flying abilities had grown in the telling. Some now imagined that Ed Hillary had intended to drive the boats up waterfalls and across snow fields, and editorials in the *Daily Himachal Times* also suggested that he was tempting the wrath of the gods by trying to climb too high at an inauspicious time of the year. He was flown on to the Indian Air Force base at Bareilly for a full medical check, but it was extremely hot at that low altitude and he refused the offer of transport on to Delhi. 'I couldn't face the publicity and the hullabaloo and television cameras of Delhi. I just wanted to get back to the mountains.'[27] Mike Gill felt the same way.

Ed was recovered and back in Badrinath to meet the returning climbers. The prayers of the *pujare* for the success of the expedition and a safe return for all members had been granted. Ed and Jim Wilson both recorded their feelings at the end of it all. Ed wrote: 'My thoughts turned to the expedition and the amazing

experience it had been – the white sand and breaking waves at Ganga Sagar; the superb tiger in the Sundarbans; the vast cheering crowds in Calcutta; the chaotic welcome at Nabadwip. I could see the sparkling eyes of the high-school children at Farakka; the great *dhow* beating up against the current with their sails billowing in the breeze; the peaceful camp-sites of the plains; the fort at Chunar; the incomparable waterfront of Varanasi. There was the wild water above Rishikesh, the terrifying rapids at Rudraprayag… and the great mountains above Badrinath… It had been a unique experience for all of us – we would never be quite the same again.'[28] Jim Wilson added his perspective: 'Even on our restless minds, Ganga-*mata* worked her magic. As her flow and the life of her people mingled with our lives, though so briefly, almost imperceptibly she imparted to us something of the gentle wisdom of Hinduism, leaving us a memory of a moving alternative to our excited search for adventure, should we ever need one.'[29]

Adventure would never leave Ed Hillary's mind, regardless of physical setbacks, but for the next few years the routine of fundraising and visits to Nepal continued. Zeke O'Connor's Canadian foundation was now supporting Kunde Hospital and alternating Canadian volunteer doctors with the New Zealanders. They were also supporting the reforestation programme in the park. A tree nursery was established below Namche Bazar, others would follow at Teshinga, below Tengboche, Phortse and Phurte. In May 1978 Ed was at Kunde where Rex was leading a team working on a big remodelling of the hospital: lifting floors, building an extra bedroom in the doctors' quarters, replacing all the kitchen plumbing, and strengthening rock walls. But each time Ed slept at over 4000 metres he suffered severe headaches. He was fifty-eight now and his enjoyment of energetic walking up steep hills was waning a little, but he continued working on the trust projects. Bridges were repaired and school hostels and health clinics built, with sterling work from Rex, Murray Jones and others.

Ed was still coping with an undercurrent of depression and personal sadness. Peter Mulgrew was killed on the Air New Zealand flight which crashed on Mount Erebus in Antarctica in November 1979, and the following year he was shocked to lose his close friend and stalwart supporter, Max Pearl. Tragically, Max was drowned while fishing in the Tongariro River. But a close friendship between Ed and June Mulgrew developed at this time, and would be a boon in the years ahead.

Adventure beckoned again in 1981 through Richard (Dick) Blum, a leading American merchant banker who had trekked many times in Nepal. He had asked Ed Hillary's advice about helping with Sherpa children's education, and as a result decided to establish the American Himalayan Foundation. This gave substantial support both to the Himalayan Trust and to the Dalai Lama's projects in Dharamsala. 'Every year they held very large and expensive dinners with distinguished speakers. The Dalai Lama spoke on one occasion which was understandably popular and the Foundation netted a record $150,000.'[30] The following year Ed was prevailed upon to speak and, despite his doubts about his drawing power, $75,000 was raised. 'I felt that being half as good as the Dalai Lama was a reasonable recommendation.'[31]

Dick Blum invited Ed to come on an American Himalayan Foundation expedition to attempt the unclimbed East Face of Everest, 'a prize mountaineering plum', not as a climber but as 'Chairman emeritus'. Dick Blum was overall leader and Lou Reichardt, who had reached the summit of K2 without oxygen, was the climbing leader. It was a big team and Ed was to write media dispatches. 'My task would be to help with publicity and fund raising and maybe a little bit of advice. The temptation was too great – a chance to visit Tibet and its monasteries; and a journey into the remote Karma valley up to the foot of the East Face. I enthusiastically agreed. What did I care that the last few times I had been at high altitude I had been severely affected? This time I would be O.K.'³² He didn't expect to go much above 5000 metres (16,000 ft), but nonetheless he would later reproach himself for not learning from his recent problems at altitude.

As the expedition came together, Ed was this time an observer of the organised chaos – rather than the manager of it. And when they arrived at Lhasa, he was delighted to see Tenzing Norgay again. Tenzing had retired from the Himalayan Mountaineering Institute. He was unfailingly charming and thoughtful to the tour groups he met in Tibet, but he did not really enjoy the work. He and Ed talked about their families and their lives with more ease than in the past: Ed's Nepali had not improved much over

the years, but Tenzing now spoke English well.

On the mountain, although the climbers faced appalling weather and other difficulties, they overcame the buttress – the hardest part of the East Face route. They did not reach the summit of the mountain, but some of the party returned to complete the climb in 1983. Ed's decision to take part had proved foolhardy. He reached the old Everest Base Camp at 5200 metres (17,000 ft), which he and George Lowe had visited in 1951, but there he realised that he was not 'O.K.' at all. He went down to 4500 metres (14,800 ft) for a few days, felt better, and returned to Base Camp, but when the symptoms of altitude sickness reappeared he faced the truth. 'Chairman emeritus or not, my big mountain days were over.'³³

Over the next few years there were other low-altitude adventures: a relaxing family tour around India – 'just looking'; a holiday in Fiji with Mike Gill, Jim Wilson and their families; and a new book, written with his son Peter, *Two Generations*. On 20 July 1984 Ed was in Chicago with his good friends Larry and Joan Witherbee. Like Zeke O'Connor, Larry was a Sears Roebuck man. He had established the Hillary Foundation USA with a group of friends, providing funds which the Himalayan Trust could use wherever they were most needed. Larry Witherbee had been visiting Nepal with Ed since 1980, helping with the building programme. But this was Ed's sixty-fifth birthday, and Joan Witherbee remembers him wondering what lay ahead now that he had reached retirement age. He was not in an optimistic frame of mind.³⁴ In fact, an adventure of a totally different sort was just around the corner. It would mean a return to India, a country he loved, to represent New Zealand, not as an unofficial ambassador but as his country's high commissioner. Ed Hillary was about to become a diplomat.

199

Left: Near Varanasi, September 1977
Jim Wilson

Below: Tenzing Norgay and Ed Hillary at Lukla, 1983
Michael Dillon

Sir Edmund Hillary, Lady Hillary and Junko Tabei in Kathmandu, 27 May 2003. On 16 May 1975 Junko Tabei became the first woman to reach the summit of Mount Everest
Narendra Shrestha.
Kathmandu Post, 28 May 2003

Below right: Children waiting to greet Sir Edmund Hillary, Kathmandu, 27 May 2003
Ares Stein

I have had the world lie beneath my clumsy boots and saw the red sun slip over the horizon after the dark Antarctic winter. I have been given more than my share of excitement, beauty, laughter and friendship.
Each of us has to discover his own path – of that I am sure. Some paths will be spectacular and others peaceful and quiet – who is to say which is the most important? For me the most rewarding moments have not always been the great moments – for what can surpass a tear on your departure, joy on your return, or a trusting hand in yours?
EDMUND HILLARY

14
A NEW DAY IN VIEW

May god give us strength to be like you.

Right: Robyn, June and
Susie Mulgrew, 1984

A few days before Edmund Hillary's sixty-fifth birthday New Zealanders voted in a Labour government under the leadership of Prime Minister David Lange, who was also Minister of Foreign Affairs. In 1982 Lange had been appalled when New Zealand's High Commission in India was unceremoniously closed by then prime minister, Robert Muldoon. On a visit to New Delhi in 1983 he tracked down the former High Commission staff and promised them their jobs back if Labour won the next election.[1] Lange knew he had no mandate to make the promise but, like the man he would send to India to re-open the posting, he had a strong sense of natural justice. And he kept his word.

Soon after the election David Lange met with Ed Hillary to discuss the position of New Zealand High Commissioner to India.[2] Ed was extremely interested – as long as he could continue his fundraising work and be in Nepal for at least a month each year. He wrote to David Lange after their meeting. He would be proud to represent New Zealand in India, but thought he would find it difficult to fulfil his duties if he didn't have access to a car.[3] Lange assured him that the High Commission would have at least two cars and several drivers – and the exchange became a favourite story in New Zealand's Ministry of Foreign Affairs. It neatly sums up Ed Hillary's practicality, his wish to do the job efficiently and his lack of assumptions about his own precedence. These characteristics were often commented upon by those who worked with him in what would be his first nine-to-five job.[4]

Ed Hillary's friendship with June Mulgrew had become more important to him in recent years. 'It wasn't as if I was going to forget Louise and Belinda – I'd never do that – but June had known them too and I started getting great pleasure from her company and companionship.'[5] The position in India was a large responsibility and he was reluctant to

take it on alone, but the Hillary reticence again proved an obstacle. 'The only thing that worried me was what to do about June, as I would certainly miss her if she wasn't with me. I was a little scared to ask her to join me in case she turned me down – June has a very close attachment to her family. Finally it was June herself who made the decision. "Why don't I come too?" she asked me. I was mightily relieved.'[6]

June Mulgrew and Ed Hillary had much to draw them together. They had known each other for almost thirty years, and when Peter and Louise were alive the two couples had been good friends. The Mulgrews were early members of the Himalayan Trust and June was the trust's secretary. She was familiar with Ed's work and with Nepal, having first visited the Khumbu with Louise Hillary in 1961. In 1975 she established June Mulgrew Trekking, taking groups to the Everest region each May and to Kashmir in July. Her daughters Robyn and Susie, like Ed's children, were adults now. Ed enjoyed June's sense of humour and admired her strength of character – her courage and commitment when Peter Mulgrew was recovering from his injuries on Makalu had been exemplary. June was fast becoming indispensable for Ed's happiness, and her energy, practicality and wit would contribute greatly to his success in New Delhi.

David Lange's selection of Ed Hillary was a masterstroke. Hillary was probably the only New Zealander – apart from cricketer Richard Hadlee – whose name was known throughout the sub-continent. And he was certainly the only one whose name has appeared in Indian school textbooks since 1953. Ed noted: 'I think that as Tenzing and I stood on the top of Everest it proved…beyond all doubt that Indians were at least the equal of Westerners.'[7] One of the restored High Commission staff, Mrs Uma Lal, later said that Ed Hillary's appointment 'placed a balm on the wound that had been created by the closure of the post'. New Zealand had sent one of its national treasures to India.[8] The generosity was noticed – and approved of.

Before taking up the appointment Ed was in New Delhi in November 1984 for the funeral of the prime minister of India, Mrs Indira Gandhi. The city had descended into grief and chaos after the assassination and David Lange travelled through turbulent streets to her funeral with Ed Hillary and others. Lange noted that although some official visitors found the atmosphere in Delhi too electric for safety, Ed stayed calm through it all. It was proof of Lange's later comment that although most people coming to India need six months to acclimatise, Ed was acclimatised from the moment he arrived.[9] He knew the country well and felt at home there.

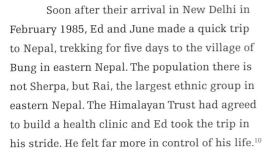

Far left: Ed Hillary and June Mulgrew in the Solu Khumbu, 1984

Left: June Mulgrew QSM with Sir Edmund Hillary, 1987

Soon after their arrival in New Delhi in February 1985, Ed and June made a quick trip to Nepal, trekking for five days to the village of Bung in eastern Nepal. The population there is not Sherpa, but Rai, the largest ethnic group in eastern Nepal. The Himalayan Trust had agreed to build a health clinic and Ed took the trip in his stride. He felt far more in control of his life.[10]

Sir Edmund Hillary presented his credentials to the President of India on 18 April 1985. He was met at the entrance to the grounds of Rashtrapati Bhavan, the presidential palace, by a limousine which drove him, flanked by mounted Indian lancers, to the gates. He then walked slowly into a large open courtyard. 'I think I stood a little straighter as the New Zealand national anthem was played. I'm not a great flag waver by any means, but it made me realise that I was representing New Zealand formally and that I would just have to make sure I handled the job properly.'[11] Sir Ed was now His Excellency. June found her New Delhi title more amusing – she was Ed's Official Companion: June Mulgrew OC.

But to begin with they had no residence and no office. The whole infrastructure of the post had been obliterated and leases had lapsed on the residence, chancery and staff accommodation. Ed and June stayed in a hotel, staff worked in a suite in an adjacent hotel and the restoration of New Zealand's diplomatic presence in India was begun from a suitcase. Ed quickly got to grips with the job while June – a skilled interior decorator – undertook the refurbishment of the former residence. The once-gracious building and its grounds were extremely run down, but after several months the High Commissioner had an elegant residence at 24 Prithviraj Road, with June as his relaxed and accomplished hostess. Ed was again 'mightily relieved': for any ambassador, entertaining guests with ease is vitally important, although it can be one of the more challenging aspects of life in an embassy – or home.

And this was not the High Commissioner's permanent home. It was a rented property, some distance from the main diplomatic area of New Delhi – Chanakyapuri – where New Zealand had been allocated a block of land by the Indian Government. Apart from a caretaker's small dwelling, the land had remained empty, and Ed and June were involved in planning the new High Commission buildings. The High Commissioner's residence, chancery, immigration office and staff accommodation were all designed by New Zealand architect Sir Miles Warren, who at the Hillarys' suggestion incorporated some aspects of the design of Prithviraj Road. June's work earned her a Queen's Service Medal in 1987, and the new High Commission was opened in 1992.

Ed Hillary had important work to do but he still fitted in the odd adventure. He had accepted an invitation to fly to the North Pole with Neil Armstrong, the captain of Apollo XI and the first man to walk on the moon. Peter Hillary went with him. They flew to Edmonton in Canada and then on to the Arctic Circle, landing on an ice runway at Resolute Bay. They continued in small ski-equipped aircraft and Peter described an evening at Ellesmere Island on the last leg of the journey. 'I'd really wanted to ask Neil about his lunar experiences, but I'd seen my father suffer the endless question "What was it like on the top of Mount Everest?" and knew well enough to let the moon man be…But the mountain hut atmosphere brought out the stories as we had all hoped.'[12] When Ed asked Neil Armstrong how he came to be chosen for the moon flight, Neil replied 'Luck! Just luck!' Ed was inclined to think that more than luck was involved.[13]

They landed at the North Pole on 6 April 1985. The temperature was –45°C. 'Someone produced a bottle of champagne and poured a little into glasses for Neil and me. Before we could even wet our lips the champagne froze solid.'[14] They were standing on pack ice four metres thick and all around them ice pressure ridges stretched away to the horizon. After an hour and a half they climbed back into the Twin Otter plane and headed south. 'It had been an exciting experience, if not exactly a great adventure. But I did have a considerable feeling of satisfaction – I believed I was the first person to have stood at both the North and South Poles and on the summit of Mount Everest. As technology had changed, so had my method of travel. I'd used my feet on Everest, a farm tractor to the South Pole, and finally a small aircraft to the North Pole.'[15]

Back at the office Sir Edmund Hillary's arrival in New Delhi was noticed and greatly enhanced New Zealand's profile in a city with 105 diplomatic posts. His name helped open doors that would otherwise have been closed

and his Trade Commissioner, Tony Mildenhall, made excellent use of the opportunities this offered. Deputy High Commissioner Graeme Waters recalled Ed's zeal for the work, his informality, his unfailing good humour; and the patience with which he accepted the Everest questions that came up after almost every meeting, dinner or address – always with politeness and never giving the impression that he might have been asked the same thing once or twice before. The autograph marathons which developed after most public events were undertaken with a smile.[16] The Indian staff at the High Commission enjoyed working with him and Christmas parties in the residence's large gardens, organised by June for everyone's children, were great occasions. India's new prime minister Rajiv Gandhi stayed in regular contact with Ed, and when he visited New Zealand in 1987 was one of the surprise guests – with Mingma Tsering and Ang Dooli – on a Television New Zealand programme: 'Ed Hillary: This is Your Life'. Ed was genuinely surprised and proud to have two prime ministers on the programme. David Lange was involved in the subterfuge needed to get him, unsuspecting, to the television studio.

Part of Ed Hillary's success came from the widespread feeling that he was an Indian too. '"We know you are a New Zealander," they would say, "but you are also one of us." Tenzing Norgay and Everest had tied me irrevocably to India.'[17] In Kathmandu on Himalayan Trust affairs, Ed Hillary often spent time with his old

Top: Ed Hillary and Rajiv Gandhi
Above: Ed Hillary, Mingma Tsering and Ang Dooli

Everest companion, since Tenzing's wife Daku ran trekking groups in Nepal, and they had many long discussions about the way that Everest had shaped their lives. In 1985 Ed heard that Tenzing was in hospital in New Delhi with pneumonia. He wrote: 'I called on him a number of times and was sad to see him looking so frail…He was still proud of the fact that we had been the first on top of Mount Everest but he agreed with me in deploring the growing commercialisation of the mountain.'[18]

Ed Hillary has often voiced his concern that too many people are now climbing Everest. Speaking about the tragic deaths on Everest in 1996 he said: 'With so many climbers on the

mountain, climbers are practically queuing up for the difficult parts ... quite a few don't get to the top till three or later in the afternoon. And then ... the late weather comes sweeping in.'[19] Hillary knew that he and Tenzing had been fortunate. 'I think we were the lucky ones really. We had to do everything, we had to establish the route, we had to carry the gear up, we had to pioneer upper parts of the mountain ... those sorts of challenges simply don't exist any more.'[20]

It was a considerable shock to learn in May 1986 that Tenzing had died at home, suddenly, in his seventy-fourth year. Ed and June were determined to attend the funeral, but there was political unrest in the area and on the road up to Darjeeling they were stopped by a threatening crowd. Ed recalled that the army captain who was escorting them told the people that Hillary Sahib was coming to pay his last respects to his old comrade. 'Tenzing was a famous name in the hills and the crowd parted

and waved us through. At Tenzing's house we were warmly welcomed by his family with cups of tea and biscuits, then we were taken upstairs to Tenzing's beautiful private gompa where he lay in state and I looked for the last time on the still, waxy face of my friend who had shared that great moment with me on Everest some thirty-three years before.'[21]

Tenzing's funeral was held in the grounds of the Himalayan Mountaineering Institute, where the majestic beauty of Kangchenjunga dominates the skyline. The only Europeans present, Ed and June sat with Daku and other family members. As the Buddhist ceremony proceeded, with chanted prayers and clashing cymbals, Tenzing's body lay on the funeral pyre surrounded with green juniper, draped in white *kartas* and piled with golden marigolds. 'In many ways it was a happy occasion with an almost picnic atmosphere of laughter and tea drinking. As Buddhists, they all believed in reincarnation and that ultimately Tenzing would return, but now they must celebrate the departure of a great hero with both joy and sadness.'[22] Then at last, as rain began to fall, Tenzing's eldest son Norbu lit the funeral pyre and 'the chanting rose to a crescendo to symbolise his spirit being released from his body.'[23]

Ed was back at the Himalayan Mountain- eering Institute in April 1997 to unveil a large black marble statue of Tenzing. He said: 'I have never regarded myself as much of a hero, but Tenzing, I believe, undoubtedly was. From humble beginnings he achieved the summit of the world. I think it is appropriate that this magnificent statue should stand here forever in front of the mountains he loved where he introduced so many young people to the joys and challenges of the great outdoors.'[24]

On 19 January 1989 Ed and June were devastated to learn of a disastrous fire at Tengboche Monastery. Ed had known and loved Tengboche for almost forty years. He and Tenzing had been heartened by the sight of the beautiful buildings, far below, on the morning of their climb to the summit and the Incarnate Lama of Tengboche, Ngawang Tenzin Zangbu, was a good friend. Ed and June flew immediately to Nepal and took a helicopter to Tengboche and the still smoking ruins. The Sherpa people were overwhelmed by the destruction of the spiritual centre of their community and Ed and June resolved to help Tengboche rise again. Ed spoke at fundraising events with Zeke O'Connor all across Canada, and Dick Blum and the American Himalayan Foundation were extremely generous. 'Funds poured in from Japan and France and the United Kingdom. The Swiss supplied a magnificent copper roof at great expense and altogether we raised $400,000.'[25] The Sherpas themselves raised US$50,000 – 'a fantastic sum from people who are far from well to do.'[26] The Sir Edmund Hillary Himalayan Trust UK, established that year by Ed's old friend George Lowe and his wife Mary, was the focus for fundraising in Britain. The rebuilding of Tengboche took four years of intense work by skilled local craftsmen and artists, and on 22 September 1993 Ed and June were back at Tengboche for the consecration and inauguration of the new buildings.

Below and right: Edmund Hillary and June Mulgrew were married at Ed's home in Auckland on 30 November 1989

By the time Ed Hillary left India the New Delhi High Commission had become a major New Zealand posting, and the potential for future growth in trade and immigration was firmly established. When Larry and Joan Witherbee visited New Delhi they found Ed totally galvanised – almost a different man.[27] Other friends felt the same – it was as though he had come back to them, revived by the stimulus of a demanding job, by the magic of India and by June Mulgrew's affection. They left India in July 1989. 'We arrived back in Auckland and June returned to her house and I returned to mine. Even though June was only a mile away, it seemed a rather lonely existence. It was our children who solved the problem for us. "Now that you are home, why don't you just get married," they told us.'[28] And so they did.

Sir Edmund Hillary and June Mulgrew were married on 30 November 1989 by their friend Cath Tizard, Mayor of Auckland and soon to be Dame Catherine Tizard, Governor-General of New Zealand. It was a beautiful day and a joyous occasion. Draped with *kartas* and surrounded by their children, their grandchildren, relations and many friends, they happily began the next phase of their lives as Sir Edmund and Lady Hillary. 'I was now seventy years old and June was twelve years younger. My life would have been very empty without Louise and June.

206

Right: Sir Edmund and Lady Hillary with some of their grandchildren: Arthur Boyer, William, Rebecca and Amy Hayman, and Anna Boyer

For the twenty-two years after Everest Louise was responsible for the happiest and most productive period of my middle years. After her death I had five years of depression and misery. When my long friendship with June blossomed into a much warmer relationship, I learned to live and love again.'[29]

Over the ensuing fifteen years the Hillarys have continued a demanding schedule of travel, fundraising, visits to Nepal, and management of the Himalayan Trust's affairs. The trust meets annually in their home in Auckland and there is now an advisory board based in Kathmandu chaired by Ang Rita Sherpa. Inevitably, there have been gains and losses. Births and new beginnings have been celebrated and friends whose lives have ended have been celebrated too, their achievements still fresh in Ed Hillary's mind. Jim Rose, who was such an important mentor and friend to Ed and his children, saw Ed happily married again, but died the following year at the age of ninety-one.

207

Right: Ed Hillary at the October 2002 meeting of the Himalayan Trust in Auckland
Lynley Cook

Rex Hillary 1920–2004

Plans of proposed High School for Khumjung April 1983.

Completed High School at Khumjung May 1983.

Far right: Rex Hillary
in Nepal, 1993
Anne B. Keiser

Above: The New Zealand
$5 note

Right: Rex Hillary's back-
of-an-envelope plans for the
high school at Khumjung
School – and the completed
building, 1983
Rex Hillary

208

That year was New Zealand's sesquicen-
tennial – the commemoration of 150 years since
the signing of the Treaty of Waitangi between
Maori leaders and the British Crown. New bank
notes were issued to mark this milestone in the
history of Aotearoa New Zealand, and after wide
consultation the Reserve Bank decided who
would be depicted on them. In addition to the
Head of State, Her Majesty Queen Elizabeth II,
they were: Lord Ernest Rutherford of Nelson
(1871–1937) chemist and Nobel Prize winner;
Sir Apirana Ngata (1874–1950) renowned
Maori leader and parliamentarian; Kate
Sheppard (1848–1934) leader of the campaign
for universal suffrage in New Zealand; and
Sir Edmund Hillary. In September 1893

New Zealand had become the first country in
the world to extend voting rights to women,
and suffrage campaigners worked hard to ensure
that as many women as possible were on the
electoral roll. Ed's grandmothers, Ida Hillary
and Harriet Clark, both registered to vote and
they would surely have been proud to see
their grandson Edmund – explorer, adventurer
and humanitarian – in such illustrious
company. He appears on the five-dollar note
with images of Aoraki/Mount Cook and a
Ferguson tractor. On the reverse of the note are
a hoiho or yellow-eyed penguin; a subantarctic
lily, *Bulbinella rossi*; a giant alpine daisy,
Pleurophyllum speciosum; and bull kelp,
Durvillea antarctica.

'By the end of
December [1975] the
Paphlu Hospital was
virtually finished. My
brother Rex and his
construction team
had done a remark-
ably good job. There
was 10,000 feet of
floor space in five
buildings: an accom-
modation building
for staff, a kitchen,
bathroom, classroom
complex, a medical
centre, a large building
with several medical
wards, and another
building where the
relations of patients
could stay. We had
good plumbing, with
flush toilets and
showers, two solar
heating systems, and
an excellent X-ray
machine. It was now
up to our volunteer
doctors and the local
staff to make full use
of the hospital.'*
This hospital is just
one of the many
projects that Rex
Hillary worked on in
the Solu Khumbu – his
list covers twenty-five
years of almost annual
visits, working always

with his Sherpa friend
and building assistant
Aila.
As a young married
man and a beekeeper,
Rex Hillary taught
himself to build by
constructing his first
home from scratch
and asking advice
from professional
builders when he
needed it. He became
a full-time builder
after he sold the
bees, and a member
of the Himalayan
Trust. From Pang-
kongma School in
1970, to remodelling
Kunde Hospital in
1978, to a new
classroom block for
the rapidly growing
Khumjung School in
1984, to a new floor for
the staff quarters at
Phaphlu Hospital in
1995 – Rex Hillary
made an outstanding
contribution to the
Himalayan Trust's
projects for the
Sherpa people.
Rex Hillary died in
September 2004 and
is survived by his
wife Ann, his children
John and Su, and his
grandchildren. His
life was character-
ised by personal
charm, cheerfulness,
hard work, good
friends and strong
family affections. Ed
Hillary described him
as 'A delightful man
and the very best
brother anyone could
wish for.' Sherpa
friends lit butter
lamps and offered
prayers in Rex's
memory at Boudha
Nath in Kathmandu,
and at Thami and
Tengboche monas-
teries in the Khumbu.

Left: Mingma Tsering and Ed Hillary in the Khumbu, 1990
Diane McKinnon

Far left and middle: Memorial *chorten* for Mingma Tsering on a ridge above Kunde
Alexa Johnston and Arthur Boyer

Above, bottom left and bottom far left: Ed Hillary being welcomed at Khumjung and the new bridge at Hinkhu, 1993
Lynley Cook

Peter Hillary's experience on Mount Fog as a small boy with his father and Mingma Tsering had started his own lifelong love for climbing. After many climbs in New Zealand and the Himalayas, in May 1990 he went on an expedition to Mount Everest with fellow New Zealanders Rob Hall and Gary Ball. Ed was sitting in his study at home on 10 May when the telephone rang: it was Peter, calling from the summit. He was filled with admiration for his father's courage in first attempting the final rock step, and said later, 'Although it was hard, I knew it could be done – it had been done before – but Dad had no idea if it was even possible.'[30] Ed wrote: 'For some reason you don't expect your son to be impressed by something you've done a long time ago, but I have to admit I experienced a slight glow of pleasure.'[31] Jamling Tenzing Norgay, Tenzing's son, climbed Everest in 1996; his grandson Tashi Tenzing in 1997; and both Tashi and Peter climbed again in 2002.

Since 1991 Ed Hillary's tolerance to altitude has gradually decreased, but he continued to fly into the mountains for several more years and in 1993 he had to farewell Mingma Tsering, his sirdar and closest Sherpa friend. The two men had worked together for over forty years. 'Almost completely illiterate, Mingma had an astonishing memory and an executive ability that was unequalled... All of us in the Himalayan Trust relied on Mingma for his sound judgment. I could certainly have done little without him.'[32] Mingma's death left an enormous gap in Ed's life and in the lives of the Sherpas of the Khumbu. They would miss the familiar sight of the Burra Sahib walking along rocky paths with Mingma close behind, watching his every step. Their rapport was legendary. 'I understood Mingma perfectly well even though his English was rather complicated, and he, of course, understood me. Perhaps I could say I understood Mingma with my heart.'[33] Ang Dooli had Mingma's memorial *chorten* built high on the ridge above Kunde, near the *chortens* for Louise and Belinda. From that ridge prayer flags flutter constantly in the breeze, and Khumbila, Ama Dablam, Kantega and Thamserku form a breathtaking backdrop to the villages of Kunde and Khumjung far below.

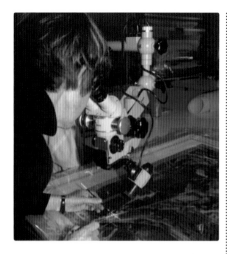

Right: Sarah Hillary working on the restoration of *Still on Top* c. 1873, a painting by James Tissot, at Auckland Art Gallery Toi o Tamaki
John McIver

Below: Sarah Hillary with her two children Anna and Arthur Boyer
Ian Jervis

Below: Peter and Ed Hillary with Peter's younger children, Lily Louise and Alexander, 2000
Yvonne Oomen

Bottom: Peter Hillary on an Everest expedition in 2002
Oscar Kihlborg

Sarah Hillary

'I am extremely proud of Sarah.'* After a childhood spent largely on the move, out of doors or 'huddled inside innumerable tents', Sarah Hillary still enjoys travel, walking, camping and the outdoor life. But her love of art and music, inspired and nurtured by her mother Louise and her grandmother Phyllis Rose, led to a career in the art world. She completed a degree in art history at the University of Auckland and then studied conservation at the University of Canberra, where she graduated with a Masters degree in applied science, specialising in the conservation of paintings. She is now principal conservator at Auckland Art Gallery Toi o Tamaki, where she began working in 1983.
Sarah Hillary's particular field of expertise is the technical examination of paintings. She has

carried out detailed analyses of the materials and techniques used by the Bolognese artist Guido Reni in his painting *Saint Sebastian* (1617–18), held at Auckland Art Gallery, and has undertaken a similar study of the paintings of Frances Hodgkins, of which Auckland Art Gallery has a major collection. She is co-author of *Artcare: The Care of Art and Artefacts in New Zealand* (1986, 1998); *Beneath the Surface: Colin McCahon's materials and techniques 1954–1966* (2000); and *Tissot: Still on Top* (2001). Sarah's son and daughter also spent much of their childhoods in the outdoors. In May 2003 they all trekked into the Khumbu to visit friends in Kunde and Khumjung, and then joined Ed and June for the fiftieth anniversary celebrations of the Everest climb.

Peter Hillary

'Peter is a very effective chip off the old block.'*
'On the day after Christmas 1954 my son Peter was born and I began sharing with Louise the disturbed nights that most parents experience. I had no premonition, or indeed ambition, that my son would one day climb Everest, too.'† Peter Hillary has climbed Mount Everest twice – in 1990 and again in May 2002. The second climb was filmed by National Geographic for a documentary to

celebrate the fiftieth anniversary of his father's ascent with Tenzing Norgay. Sarah Hillary said: 'Peter just loves to climb.'‡ He has faced difficult challenges on over thirty alpine expeditions – to the Himalayas, the Karkoram, the Southern Alps of New Zealand, the Andes, Antarctica and North America – and travelled overland on skis to the South Pole.
Yet some of Peter's best memories are of the trips with his father: 'Dad was able to include me in some extraordinary journeys – from childhood excursions to many parts of New Zealand, America and the Himalayas, to full-scale expeditions like Ocean to the Sky in 1977.'§ Like Ed Hillary, Peter has written many books about his adventures and is an accomplished public speaker. He is married to Yvonne Oomen and has four children: Amelia, George, Alexander and Lily Louise. Peter Hillary runs an adventure travel business, and fundraises for the Himalayan Trust and other aid organisations in Nepal.

In May 1995 Ed and June were at Junbesi village where a Swiss firm had erected a new school building. Junbesi had recently acquired a telephone and late one afternoon a messenger arrived with news of a call for the Burra Sahib. 'It was quite a long way down to the telephone box so, with a groan, I asked June if she would mind answering the call. Very agreeably she descended the hill…it was the British Ambassador with a message from the Secretary to Queen Elizabeth II. Would I be pleased to accept the award of the Order of the Garter?'[34] June had to return the call to make sure it was not a hoax before climbing back up the hill to deliver the news. Ed was similarly amazed. 'I hadn't received many invitations from Her Majesty the Queen and as this was clearly a great honour we agreed I must accept.'[35] This time they both walked back down the hill to telephone the ambassador.

Ed Hillary was about to be admitted to the oldest and highest British Order of Chivalry, founded in 1348 by Edward III. It comprises her Majesty the Queen, who is Sovereign of the Order, His Royal Highness the Prince of Wales and twenty-four Knights Companions. 'The big day was Monday 9th June. It was a beautiful morning as we drove to Windsor…At the castle I met my distinguished fellow Knights of the Garter – mostly Dukes and Earls and Lords – who all welcomed me into the Order in an extremely friendly fashion. Among them was John Hunt who had been a Knight of the Garter for some years and was very proud that now two members of his expedition had achieved this distinguished status.'[36]

There were regular reunions of the 1953 team in North Wales at the Pen-y-Gwyrd Hotel, and a gathering at Everest Base Camp on the fortieth anniversary in 1993. The climbers had all remained friends over the years and the positive outcomes of the expedition did not relate solely to the successful ascent. Griffith

Pugh and Michael Ward's sustained study of humans at high altitude was a medical first, and they did more valuable research in that area. Funded by the proceeds of the team's lectures and John Hunt's best-selling book *The Ascent of Everest*, the Mount Everest Foundation has helped to fund scores of ground-breaking expeditions. Ed Hillary's Himalayan Trust work with the Sherpas was a direct result of the expedition; and George Band and George Lowe are both involved in raising funds for the UK branch of the Himalayan Trust.

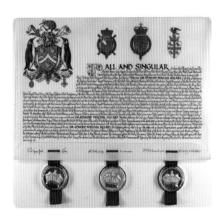

Below: Sir Edmund Hillary, Knight Companion of the Most Noble Order of the Garter, Windsor Castle, 9 June 1995
June Hillary

211

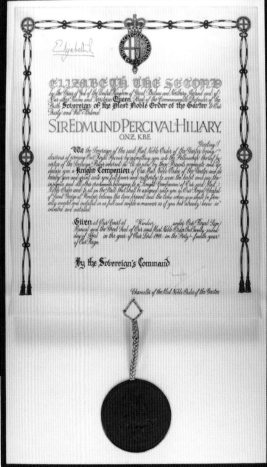

Above: Arms and Crest of Sir Edmund Hillary, KBE, ONZ, KG. The Coat of Arms includes emperor penguins, mountains and prayer wheels, surmounted by 'A Kiwi Azure grasping in the dexter foot an Ice Axe bendwise Or'. His motto is 'Nothing Venture, Nothing Win'
Krzysztof Pfeiffer

Left: Illuminated address presented by Queen Elizabeth II, Sovereign of the Most Noble Order of the Garter, to her 'Trusty and Well Beloved Sir Edmund Percival Hillary', admitting him to the Order
Krzysztof Pfeiffer

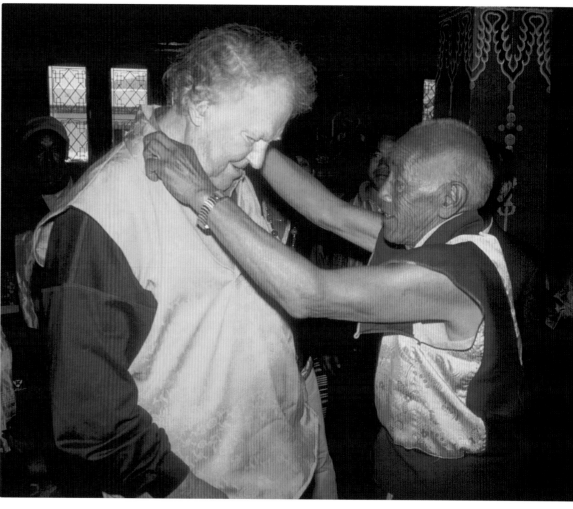

In 1997 Television New Zealand made
a documentary series about Ed Hillary's life,
'Hillary: A View from the Top'. It was written
and directed by Tom Scott – a sharply witty
political commentator and an outstanding
cartoonist. Building a new life with June had
helped restore Ed Hillary's love of laughter and
the two men were both great raconteurs. Ed's
travels around the world with June, Tom and
the television crew, revisiting many of the
landmark places of his life, were marked with
hilarity and good humour. Another film made
around that time, *Beyond Everest*, directed by
Michael Dillon, included the opening of the new
Salleri Monastery which the trust had helped
to fund as a religious and cultural centre for the
local people. After the opening, Ed was installed
as an Honorary Lama, with many smiles and
much applause. Resplendent in crimson robes
and saffron-yellow headgear, he remarked: 'June
will have to take a bit more notice of me now.'[37]

Peter Hillary was at that opening, and so
were George and Mary Lowe, since a new trust
project was beginning in Salleri that year. For
many years the trust had been building schools,
providing books and equipment, and paying
teacher salaries, but the quality of teaching was
becoming a concern. Primary teachers had only
to pass the Nepalese school-leaving certificate
and had no real training, so rote learning was
the norm. In a visionary and cooperative
venture, teachers were offered three weeks
training during their winter holidays at the
trust's Solukhumbu Multiple Training Campus,
Salleri. The programme was funded by the
Grand Circle Foundation (USA), UNICEF (Nepal)
and the Swiss Foundation, with the approval
of the Nepalese Ministry of Education and
National Council for Educational Development.
Jim Strang, a New Zealand teacher and climber

who first came to Nepal with Ed Hillary in 1971,
was the coordinator, and over six years fifteen
New Zealand teacher-training volunteers gave
up their holidays to assist, including Jim's wife
Janette. Ed commented that although they
expected about thirty or forty teachers at the
first training programme, 180 teachers from
forty-seven schools arrived.

Strang also recruited four Nepali primary
teacher trainers to give in-school support, and
they visited schools at least three times each
year. The morale of the teachers, the quality of
the teaching, the atmosphere in the classrooms
and the achievements of the children improved
dramatically, and Solu Khumbu primary schools
became an example of educational excellence
in Nepal. Then secondary teachers requested
a programme too. George and Mary Lowe were
convinced that all teachers needed training, and

that year included Te Arikinui, Dame Te Atairangikaahu, head of the Maori kingship, and Sonja Davies, a leading trade unionist and diligent worker for peace. In July 1999 Ed Hillary reached another milestone when his eightieth birthday was celebrated with a banquet at Government House in Wellington. The evening was hosted by the governor-general Sir Michael Hardie Boys and Lady Hardie Boys. Sir Michael commented: 'Most heroes die young or just fade away, but not this one. It's this enduring quality about Ed Hillary that has carved for him an indelible place in the annals of our nation.' Ed Hillary's autobiography *Sir Edmund Hillary: View from the Summit* was published the same year. Reviewing the book, Jan Morris described Ed Hillary as having 'one of the most marvellous lives of our time'.[38] But for Ed himself, the lives of the children who had attended schools in Solu Khumbu were the real sign of achievement.

On 25 March 2000 it was forty years since Tem Dorji began giving lessons to a small group of children sitting in the grass on the site of the Khumjung School. The original aluminium building is still there, surrounded now by ten other buildings, which serve more than 400 children. Former students of Khumjung School produced a Souvenir Booklet to thank Sir Edmund Hillary, the Himalayan Trust, the teachers and other supporters for their long commitment to the school. It gives a history of the school, records student successes and includes photographs of past and present pupils. The former students' tribute concludes: 'Education helped us to become better farmers, stronger business managers and professionals. Education also helped us to appreciate and

Below: Children in Solu Khumbu schools today
Jim Strang

their commitment led the UK Lotteries Board and the Himalayan Trust UK to fund a three-year (later extended to six-year) secondary programme. With the involvement of secondary teacher trainers from Kathmandu and New Zealand, improvements in classrooms and in student achievement were soon evident. Training for school-board members, community training and assistance with income generation was also offered. Over 300 primary and secondary teachers took part and the Nepalese Government awarded the programme with official accreditation.

In 1987 Ed had been among the first group of people to be awarded his country's highest honour, the Order of New Zealand, instituted to recognise outstanding service to the Crown and people of New Zealand and limited to twenty members. Other recipients

Left: The Buddha Shakya-muni at the moment of enlightenment. An eightieth birthday gift to Ed Hillary from Ang Rita Sherpa and Elizabeth Hawley
Krzysztof Pfeiffer

Above: Sir Michael Hardie Boys and Lady Hardie Boys introducing Sam and Noriko Neill to Sir Edmund and Lady Hillary at a dinner at Government House, Wellington, in celebration of Sir Edmund's eightieth birthday, July 2000

value our own cultural traditions and understand and respect others. Our education, no matter how limited, made every one of us a better and more committed person for the cause of our own community and the country. We wish to thank you for your unyielding support and foresight. The stories of Sir Edmund Hillary schools in the Himalayas, we hope will become an example of goodwill and lasting mutual co-operation between people of different nations and inspire people around the world.'[39]

In the booklet Diane McKinnon recalls mornings teaching conversational English at the school: 'What a joy – teaching children who really wanted to learn…students were thirsty for knowledge and like sponges soaked up everything that fell upon them. To the extent that some students were said to have acquired a New Zealand accent! This was no doubt an advantage for those who later came to New Zealand for further study.' She thanks the first teachers, Tem Dorji and Shyam Pradhan, the parents whose support for every school activity was unfailing, and the students: 'I thank them for using their talent…for being a wonderful part of my life and I thank them for realising their parents' and grandparents' dreams.'[40] One of the many messages to Sir Edmund reads: 'Conquering Everest won you our respect, but with Khumjung School you won our hearts. Deepest thanks to you, Sir Edmund Hillary.'[41]

The fiftieth anniversary of the climbing of Mount Everest on 29 May 2003 was celebrated with events, publications and exhibitions in many parts of the world. On the way to Nepal Ed spent three days back in the heat of New Delhi, his diary packed with interviews and meetings. He officiated at the naming of the street on which the New Zealand High Commission is sited. The Delhi Municipal Authority had decided to call it Sir Edmund Hillary Marg and its adjoining street Tenzing Norgay Marg. Visitors arriving at Kathmandu Airport were greeted by huge posters announcing 'Mount Everest 50th Jubilee Celebrations – Nepal: the Ultimate Nirvana' and lamp posts throughout the city were festooned with banners reading 'Triumph on Everest'. Ed and June Hillary led a street procession of successful Everest climbers including Jamling Tenzing Norgay, Junko Tabei, Reinhold Messner and many others. Dr Lhakpa Norbu gave a lecture on the life and achievements of Tenzing Norgay and His Majesty King Gyanendra Bir Bikram Shah Dev made Sir Edmund Hillary a citizen of Nepal. On the anniversary itself, at the Hyatt Regency, Boudha, the chandeliers sparkled, the marble floors were lined with marigolds and butter lamps, and the air itself seemed to shimmer with excitement. Crowds of international press vied with guests to get close to Sir Edmund and, despite the crush, it was a joyous occasion.

In Kathmandu one of the publications marking the fiftieth anniversary was a tribute to Sir Edmund from the Sherpas of Nepal: *Triumph on Everest*. Compiled and edited by Ang Rita Sherpa and Susan Höivik, the book is filled with Sherpa stories relating to Ed Hillary and his work in Nepal. There is a preface by the Head Lama and Rinpoche of Tengboche Monastery. He recalls being asked to join Sir Edmund in inaugurating the first school in Khumjung and writes: 'Hillary's holistic, grass-roots approach has helped to pave the way for maintaining a healthy natural and cultural heritage in our homeland…We are proud that Sir Edmund has chosen to celebrate the golden jubilee of Everest amidst the Sherpa people of Nepal despite other important engagements. On this auspicious occasion, we would like to express our deep appreciation for all that he has done for the people of Nepal. We are offering a special prayer, to wish there can be peace and happiness for all, that our benefactor Sir Edmund and his family will enjoy a long, healthy and prosperous life and that we will be able to celebrate together many further achievements. Tashi Delek!'[42]

214

Left: Ed Hillary with Ayesha Goel, daughter of Vicky Goel who is on the staff of the New Zealand High Commission, New Delhi, May 2003
Simon Mark

Right: An embroidered congratulatory garland presented to Ed Hillary by the New Delhi Municipal Authority, 29 June 1953
Krzysztof Pfeiffer

Above: Medal presented to Edmund Hillary in 1953 by the Nepal Taxi Drivers' Association of Kathmandu
Krzysztof Pfeiffer

Left: Ed Hillary and Phu Dorje from Kunde in the gardens of the British Embassy at Kathmandu, 28 May 2003
Ares Stein

Below top: Ed Hillary greeting Kancha Sherpa, 28 May 2003
Ares Stein

Below left: Ed and June Hillary's friends Murray Jones and Passang Tendi at the British Embassy, 28 May 2003
Ares Stein

Below middle: Ang Dooli, Doma Tsamje and other Sherpanis, 29 May 2003
Ares Stein

215

Above: Phu Dorje and friends at the Sherpa celebration evening '50th Anniversary of Triumph on Everest', Hyatt Regency Boudha, Kathmandu, 29 May 2003
Ares Stein

Left and above: June Hillary with her granddaughter Rebecca and daughters Susie Hayman and Robyn Mulgrew, Kathmandu, May 2003
Ares Stein

Peter Hillary and his eldest daughter Amelia were guests of honour at the ceremony with the Head Lama at Tengboche Monastery. And as climbers struggled to reach the top of Everest on the actual anniversary, a golden jubilee dinner organised by Peter was held on the meadow in front of the monastery, raising funds to help the Himalayan Trust to continue its work.

In London at the Odeon Theatre, Leicester Square, where the premiere of the expedition's award-winning film had been held in October 1953, Sir David Attenborough compered 'Endeavour on Everest' at which surviving members of the team recalled their experiences. Ed and June were in London for the service at Westminster Abbey and the luncheon for members of the 1953 expedition hosted by the New Zealand High Commission. Several books were published to mark the anniversary, and exhibitions of varying kinds were held all over the world. The Royal Geographical Society exhibited a selection of photographs from all the British Everest expeditions; and in Castlemaine, Victoria, near Alfred Gregory's home, a selection of his 1953 Everest photographs was on show. Explorers Hall, National Geographic's Museum in Washington DC, showed the exhibition *Sir Edmund Hillary: Everest and Beyond* which had been organised by the Auckland War Memorial Museum. Fifty thousand people saw the exhibition in Auckland and 80,000 more in America. The exhibition banners read: 'He took Everest by foot; the world by storm; the South Pole by Massey Ferguson'.

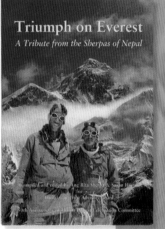

When the Auckland Museum exhibition was about to open in October 2002, Ed and June Hillary came to look through the show. Ed was somewhat surprised in the last exhibition gallery to find nine glass cases filled with his medals, awards and beautifully illuminated parchments. Few are displayed at the Hillarys' home – although there are many cartoons on the walls of Ed's study. He has received dozens of honours from all over the world, honorary doctorates and mountaineering and conservation awards; from a medal especially made by the Kathmandu Taxi Drivers' Association in 1953 to the Patron's Medal of the Royal Geographical Society, UK, and the Hubbard Medal of the National Geographic Society, USA. He has been honoured for his work for UNICEF, the World Wildlife Fund and many other organisations.

Top: Ed and June Hillary, guests of honour at the Sherpa celebration '50th Anniversary of Triumph on Everest', Kathmandu, 29 May 2003
Ares Stein

Above left: Peter and Amelia Hillary with the Head Lama of Tengboche Monastery at the Tengboche celebration of the fiftieth anniversary, 29 May 2003

216

Some Sherpa stories

Right: Ang Rita Sherpa from Khumjung, Lhakpa Norbu Sherpa from Khumjung and Mingma Norbu Sherpa from Kunde: the first three recipients of Himalayan Trust scholarships for further education, 1970
Edmund Hillary

ANG RITA SHERPA, SON OF KAPPA KALDEN OF KHUMJUNG, CHIEF ADMINISTRATOR, HIMALAYAN TRUST

I was eleven years old when I joined the first school built by Sir Edmund Hillary in Khumjung village in 1961 and I was one of the first batches of forty-seven scrubby students of Khumjung School. None of my older brothers and sisters can read and write as they were too old to go to school at that time. After Khumjung, three of us received scholarships from Sir Edmund Hillary's Himalayan Trust and I completed my education at Anandakuti High School, a very reputable school in Kathmandu in those days. I was placed at the top of more than 19,000 students taking the national level of the school-leaving certificate examination throughout the county. It was a great sense of pride to my community as well as for myself to achieve this position.

In 1985, I was invited by Sir Edmund Hillary to work with the Himalayan Trust, which has shaped the lives of hundreds of Sherpa people. Today, I hold the position of the chief administrative officer to oversee the Himalayan Trust projects in the Solu Khumbu and I find this job very gratifying. The photo shows Ang Rita with his wife Ang Zhangbu.

Photo: Edmund Hillary

ANG RITA SHERPA, SON OF MINGMA TSERING AND ANG DOOLI OF KUNDE, SENIOR CONSERVATION OFFICER

I first saw Burra Sahib in 1966, when Sir Edmund Hillary pitched his tent in my mother's field, surrounded by lots of support staff and Sherpas.

After seven years in Khumjung School, I went away to school at Salleri, about three days walk from Khumjung. I was homesick, missing my mother, her daily packed cold lunches and being away from my family. After three years in Salleri,

I took the SLC exam at Okhaldunga and passed with second division marks. Upon graduation from Amrit Science College, I learned that there was a special diploma course in parks and recreation at Lincoln College in New Zealand. I knew that Sir Edmund Hillary had encouraged some of my Sherpa brothers to take this course and they had received excellent training in national park management from New Zealand. I am now senior conservation officer for tourism, culture and information at The Mountain Institute, working to conserve mountain environments and cultural heritage while improving the livelihoods of mountain people.

Photo: Ares Stein

DR KAMI TEMBA

I had my primary schooling at Thami in one of the first primary schools set up by the Himalayan Trust. I then attended Khumjung School for class 5 to 7. Khumjung is three hours' walk from Thami. My friend and I shared a small room in Khumjung and we spent the first two years there. The life was hard as we were only twelve years old and we had to do everything by ourselves – cooking, collecting firewood, carrying food from Thami. So we both felt two years in Khumjung was more than enough and decided to walk every day from Thami for the last year. By then we both were fourteen years old and walked six hours each day but enjoyed

it more than our previous two years. We then received scholarships from the Himalayan Trust to complete our high school at Salleri. After high school, I came home and worked one year in Thami School as a teacher and part-time health worker in the Thami health clinic. Then I worked the last nineteen years (1977–96) at Kunde Hospital before I joined the Fiji School of Medicine in 1997. I graduated at the end of 2000 and came back to Nepal and started my internship in Patan Hospital in Kathmandu. In 2003 I became the superintendent at Kunde Hospital. I am very proud of the fact that my son Tsering Wangdi is now a student at the Nepal Medical School.

Photos: Lynley Cook and Sue Heydon

217

Sherpa friends at the fiftieth anniversary celebrations, Kathmandu, May 2003
Photos: Ares Stein

Gyalzen Sherpa from Kunde who was on the 1953 Everest Expedition

Phu Dorje Sherpa from Kunde, a stalwart friend and worker on Himalayan Trust projects since 1963

Ang Rita Sherpa from Kunde

Kancha Sherpa from Kunde who helped with the Iodine programme and other Himalayan Trust projects

**MINGMA NORBU SHERPA
DIRECTOR OF CONSERVATION, ASIA AND PACIFIC, WORLD WILDLIFE FUND; DIRECTOR, HIMALAYAS AND SOUTH ASIA PROGRAM, WORLD WILDLIFE FUND**

I was born in the village of Kunde. One of my clearest memories growing up is from 1961 when I was six years old. A group of us – all barefooted children dressed in homespun Sherpa clothing – went to greet Sir Edmund Hillary in the village of Khumjung, where he had just completed building the first school for Sherpas. Hillary, better known to us as Burra Sahib, stood like a giant, looking out over a crowd of much shorter Sherpa people as he spoke.

Though I barely knew what a school was, I was excited and eager to become one of the first students. Since my first day of school, Hillary has been a mentor to me and many other Sherpas. With Sir Edmund's help I obtained scholarships to universities in New Zealand and Canada. In 1980, I became the first Sherpa to be appointed chief warden of Sagarmatha National Park after obtaining a degree in parks and recreation from Lincoln University in New Zealand. Again, Hillary was there to help me and the park, providing support for our reforestation and wildlife conservation efforts.

Sir Edmund Hillary has opened the eyes of the Sherpa people and encouraged us to venture out into the world to see and learn for ourselves. Without him, I would likely be herding yaks in my tiny, remote village rather than directing a conservation programme for the Himalayas.

Photo: Anne B. Keiser

**ANG ZHANGBU
PILOT**

Primary school in Thami was quite a unique one since it was the farthest school from my home and Pasang teacher gave me the opportunity to have free accommodation for helping in the house. By the time I joined Khumjung School I was old enough to walk the four-hour round trip to the school. I won a scholarship and sponsorship for high school education in Kathmandu which was a luxury – being in a hostel, not having to do long-distance walks or collect wood and water for daily needs.

I was a part-time trekking guide for about two years before moving on to Europe and the USA. I learned to fly in the States, worked in flight operations at Boeing in Seattle and received B727 ground instructor training. Since 1980 I worked for Royal Nepal Airlines on domestic and international routes. I am very grateful to Sir Ed Hillary and New Zealand volunteers and all the supporters the world over for their dedication and contribution to the Himalayan Trust which has benefited so many Nepalese.

Photo: Anne B. Keiser

**DAWA PHUJI
MEMBER OF THE HIMALAYAN TRUST ADVISORY BOARD**

I went to Khumjung School for six years. I was one of the first girls to go to school in Khumjung. No one went to school in Kathmandu then. I worked at Khumjung School as a volunteer teacher for three months when I first finished schooling, then worked at Kunde Hospital. I worked as a medical assistant for more than one year. I have been very busy for some years running a lodge in Lukla and am a member of the Himalayan Trust Sherpa Advisory Board.

Photo: John McKinnon

Pendo Sherpa from
Khumjung

Phu Larma Sherpa from
Kunde, Ang Rita's wife

Doma Tshering Sherpa from
Kunde, Phu Dorje's wife

NIMA YANGJEN
FIRST SHERPA NURSE AT
KUNDE HOSPITAL

I was born in 1945, the daughter of Mr Khunjo Chumbi Sherpa and Mrs Pali Sherpa, I was brought up in Khumjung and from my childhood helped my father in his business. At the age of eighteen I went to Kathmandu to train as a nurse and later worked as a nurse assistant with Dr Bethel Fleming at Shanta Bhawan Hospital for four years. In 1966 I went back to Kunde and worked with Dr John and Diane McKinnon at Kunde Hospital. I have raised a family, owned and run a carpet factory and supported a busy entrepreneurial husband to establish an airline. I am now busy with my friends, family, grandchildren and the Kathmandu committee for our Sherpa *gompa*.

Photo: John McKinnon

ANG TSHERING
CLIMBER, TOURISM
OPERATOR AND LEADING
BUSINESSMAN

The son of a flamboyant and community-minded father, Khunjo Chumbi, Ang Tshering is a real product of the Khumjung School and Kathmandu scholarship programme. Selected to become a doctor because of his intelligence, he soon discovered that medicine was not his vocation. He went into the trekking business where he demonstrated considerable leadership and business skills. His entrepreneurial abilities and Sherpa–Buddhist compassion have made him an important and respected contributor to both the Sherpa and the wider Nepalese community. Ang Tshering has a Belgian wife, Yo, and two sons.

Photo: John McKinnon

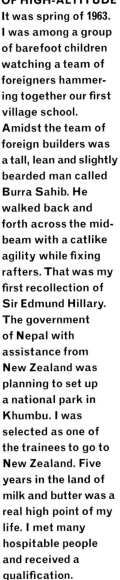

DR LHAKPA NORBU
FIRST SHERPA PhD, MANAGEMENT
OF HIGH-ALTITUDE FOREST

It was spring of 1963. I was among a group of barefoot children watching a team of foreigners hammering together our first village school. Amidst the team of foreign builders was a tall, lean and slightly bearded man called Burra Sahib. He walked back and forth across the mid-beam with a catlike agility while fixing rafters. That was my first recollection of Sir Edmund Hillary. The government of Nepal with assistance from New Zealand was planning to set up a national park in Khumbu. I was selected as one of the trainees to go to New Zealand. Five years in the land of milk and butter was a real high point of my life. I met many hospitable people and received a qualification.

I returned to Nepal to join the Nepalese Park Service. I assisted with the establishment and management of a number of mountain national parks including Sagarmatha National Park. Conserving resources in a resource-limited country was not without challenge. In between, I went to the United States for a Masters course under a Fulbright scholarship, which led to a doctoral degree in forestry. Sir Edmund Hillary's educational programme provided the young people from downtrodden mountain communities the means to overcome social, economic and cultural barriers. Within the hierarchical Nepali society, scaling the socio-cultural barriers is often more

challenging than the slopes of Mount Everest. Sir Edmund Hillary, his friends and supporters deserve to be congratulated for making a difference.*

Photo: Anne B. Keiser

219

The awards keep coming. On 17 June 2004 Sir Edmund was in Poland, a country with a distinguished mountaineering tradition. At the Presidential Palace in Warsaw, President Aleksander Kwasniewski presented him with the Commander's Cross of the Order of Merit of the Republic of Poland. He said: 'You sir, are the representative of the romantic, which is close to the spirit of generations of Polish explorers and pioneers. Without any doubt you have influenced to a great extent the imagination and actions of many youngsters...Your personal achievements and deep humanitarianism will be cherished in our memory forever. Thank you very much Sir Edmund. It is a great honour that you are here with us in Warsaw.'[43]

Tongariro National Park is on the central plateau of the North Island of New Zealand. The road through the western side of the park travels around the foothills of three snow-capped mountains, Ruapehu, Tongariro and Ngauruhoe – the first mountains Ed Hillary ever saw. And near the small National Park village a large sign announces the Sir Edmund Hillary Outdoor Pursuits Centre, the brainchild of New Zealand mountaineer Graeme Dingle, who set up the centre in 1973 in buildings that were originally for workers on a hydro-electric scheme. Now directed by Grant Davidson, it is a magnet for young people keen to test themselves in the outdoors, and Ed Hillary is its proudest supporter. 'It seems only a few years ago that Graeme Dingle with a mass of enthusiasm and precious little else got it all going...and now thousands of young people have been introduced to adventure and the great out-of-doors – certainly in my view one of the most worthwhile undertakings in New Zealand.'[44]

Above and right: One of the three Ferguson tractors that travelled overland from Scott Base to the South Pole in 1957 (now in the collection of Auckland's Museum of Transport and Technology) arrives at the Auckland War Memorial Museum for the exhibition *Sir Edmund Hillary: Everest and Beyond*, October 2002
Krzysztof Pfeiffer

At Tuakau Primary School on 7 August 2003 Ed Hillary unveiled a stone commemorating his time at the school, and entertained the children with memories of his childhood there; on 29 May 2004 he spoke at the opening of Sir Edmund Hillary Collegiate, Otara, an innovative multicultural campus in Manukau city, south of Auckland. At Macleans College in the Auckland suburb of Bucklands Beach, students at Hillary House raise $5000 every year for the Himalayan Trust activities in the Khumbu. Edmund Hillary is threaded through the New Zealand consciousness at every level – from the streets that are named after him (and Tenzing Norgay) in many towns, to the sculptures of him in Orewa, where he spent childhood holidays, and at the Hermitage, Mount Cook. He supports a plethora of groups devoted to conservation and outdoor activities and his name lends credibility to any venture. In 2002 the Government of New Zealand established

Facing page: A French Chamonix ice-axe, purchased by Ed Hillary before the 1951 New Zealand Himalayan expedition and used on his climb to the summit of Mount Everest, 29 May 1953
Krzysztof Pfeiffer

the Sir Edmund Hillary Trust to ensure the future of his work in Nepal and New Zealand.

Like the awards, the adventures keep coming. In November 2004 Antarctica New Zealand invited Ed Hillary to spend a week at Scott Base. He was delighted to accept and made the long flight to Antarctica in an RNZAF Hercules aircraft. His visit was filmed for a documentary which will mark the fiftieth anniversary of the base in 2007. On Sunday 28 November he read 'Erebus Voices' by New Zealand poet Bill Manhire at a memorial service for those killed in 1979. That evening he gave a lecture at the American McMurdo Station and

the next day he opened the new Hillary Field Centre, the largest construction project ever undertaken at Scott Base. An army engineer at the base said: 'He's a living legend. No one else is like him, so having him here is pretty special.'[45] And when he climbed into the helicopter to visit huts built by Robert Scott and by his own hero Ernest Shackleton, he stood on a box made by field support officer Doug Henderson in the base's carpentry workshop. Stencilled onto the box were the words: The Hillary Step.[46]

Right: Chomolungma/Mount Everest/Sagarmatha from Gokyo Ri, 17 May 2003
Arthur Boyer

Below: Ed Hillary's 1953 high-altitude boots, worn on the summit climb of Mount Everest, 29 May 1953
Krzysztof Pfeiffer

The world is proud of Edmund Hillary – determined climber, bold adventurer, practical philanthropist and cheerful friend – a man whose craggy face and broad smile are recognised everywhere. But at the age of eighty-five his own assessment of his life is characteristically simple, and brief: 'What a fortunate person I have been!'[47]

EPILOGUE

As the fiftieth anniversary of the Everest climb approached, Ed Hillary's role as a national symbol was often discussed. Journalist Tim Watkin noted: 'Somehow a beekeeper-turned-mountaineer-turned-fundraiser has come to be regarded as the greatest New Zealander'.[1] National identity is never fixed, but there is some consensus that Ed Hillary embodies qualities central to the way New Zealanders see themselves. A love for the outdoors is a good start. In a recent study researchers observed that New Zealanders immediately take you outside just after inviting you in, and when asked for images that represent their country, both men and women come up with the All Blacks, sheep, tractors and the beach.[2] In 1995 New Zealand-born comedian John Clarke selected his own All Black team to represent New Zealand at the Rugby World Cup in Europe; reading out the players' names in the traditionally sepulchral tones of the All Blacks selectors. The team included: Centre: K. Te Kanawa (Auckland); Second five-eighth: N. S. Neill (Otago); First five-eighth: A. J. Curnow (Auckland); Halfback: R. Hotere (Otago); Number 8: P. Jackson (Middle Earth); and Hooker: J. P. Frame (Horowhenua). And these high-achievers in literature and art were led by a mountaineer – Fullback: E. P. Hillary (Auckland).[3]

Tim Watkin's article included a comment about Ed Hillary from Dr Geoff Watson of Massey University's history department: 'What made him famous was unquestionably physical – he's a very manly man, so even though he's been so humble and a little too liberal, he could not be knocked as a softie. What he did required enormous physical strength, courage and drive, but he made it seem ordinary. Hillary was able to give the impression anyone could do it, that he was one of us.'[4] Historian Michael King spoke of Ed's classic stories about Tenzing's hug on the summit of Everest, or the 'new pair of overalls' response to his knighthood as 'perfect kiwi bloke yarns – self-deprecating, stoic, funny'.[5] Sir Ed's work with the Sherpas is the real clincher, though. Helping your friends to do things – whether concreting a driveway, bottling fruit or building a boat – is fondly thought of as the Kiwi way. And still he lives in New Zealand – that helps too.

For any small country to have a world-recognised citizen is a bonus, and even Australians, New Zealand's long-term rivals, acknowledge Edmund Hillary's qualities. On 20 February 2003 the following appeared in the *Sydney Morning Herald*: 'A humble request to New Zealand: Can we share Sir Edmund Hillary? Without a doubt this man is the Greatest Living Australasian. Since the death of The Don, Australia has been without a citizen of such world standing. Sir Edmund, 83, is here raising funds for the Himalayan Trust, and he spoke for 45 minutes to a rapt audience of 620 at the Star City Ballroom on Tuesday night.'

While working as curator of the exhibition which was the beginning of the idea for this book, I met many New Zealanders who know and love Ed Hillary. I tried to understand what had made him such a magnet for these talented and busy people. There were several theories. All the climbers agreed that you would be mad *not* to go on expeditions to the astonishing places that Ed made available. And those who went to Nepal invariably spoke of their pleasure in getting to know the Sherpas. Diane McKinnon talked about Ed's ability to make everyone feel

they had a useful and important job to do, and that his attractiveness is enhanced by the fact that he is completely unaware of it. In one conversation Linda Gill said: 'Ed doesn't think he's superior to anybody. He really values and respects others for their abilities in a generous way.' Being with Ed Hillary has other benefits too. Linda and Mike Gill's daughter Caitlin, as a ten year old on a family trek in Nepal with Ed, coined the phrase 'The RG Factor' to describe the reflected glory that falls on anyone near him.[6] Proximity to Ed Hillary also builds respect for the way he deals with the fame that has surrounded him for so long. Jim Wilson talked of autograph signings on the Ganges trip that seemed to go on for ever. Others in the group began by joining in but were soon exhausted by the crush and slunk away, while Ed continued, as June Hillary describes it, being 'public property'.

All this affects his family, who love him and are proud of him, but need to retain their separate identities. Sarah Hillary is a leading New Zealand conservator of paintings and head of the conservation department at the Auckland Art Gallery, but Peter has been driven by the same passions as his father – climbing and adventuring. Looking back on his teenage years, Peter Hillary remembers sometimes pretending to be someone else: 'Mainly for a laugh really. When Dad and I were on the jet boat expedition up the Ganges, in seventy-seven, an old man got down on his knees to put his forehead on my toes, because I was the son of "the great Sir Hillary." I was appalled. I was twenty-two years old. I hadn't done anything to deserve this... enthusiasm, beyond being my father's son.' But at the age of fifty Peter can say: 'The "son of" business, I've got used to it. Most of it's pretty harmless, and much of it is kind of nice.'[7] June's daughters Robyn and Susie and their families are an important part of Ed's life too, and between them the Hillarys have ten grandchildren, whose company they greatly enjoy.

At the New Zealand High Commission in New Delhi I talked with staff who had worked for Sir Edmund there. Their recollections focused not on his fame, but on the warmth and kindness that Ed and June displayed as employers. Joseph Gomes, their driver for four years, told me: 'He is a great man, but he is also a good man, with a good heart... his heart is very, very soft for the people. He talks with everyone very politely, he never says, "No, no, no, I don't have time." He meets with people like a friend.' Financial manager Mr D. Majumdar remembered an affectionate and accessible boss, and administration manager Mr A. Rajan wrote: 'His door was always open to any of the local staff and there were many occasions when Sir Edmund Hillary used to come down from his first floor office to meet the school children who came to the High Commission for his autograph and to take photos with him. No matter how busy he was he always gladly fulfilled the children's requests. We noticed that the joy of the children and their cheerfulness was his great strength and happiness.'[8]

In May 2003 I was in Kunde with Sarah Hillary, her children Arthur and Anna, Diane McKinnon and other friends. We visited Ang Dooli and Temba and showed them a videotape of the museum exhibition in which we had recreated part of Ang Dooli's kitchen. When Ed appeared on the video, we joined in Ang Dooli's tears that the Burra Sahib could not come up to Kunde any more – emotion and altitude overwhelmed us all. Peter Hillary and his daughter Amelia were in Kunde too, staying for a few days with Ang Dooli and Temba on their way up to Tengboche for the fiftieth anniversary. Spending time with them I observed the profound and lasting affection the Hillary family have earned through their commitment to their Sherpa friends. Ed Hillary's relationships with the Sherpas, the vigour of the Himalayan Trust schools and the continuing importance of Kunde Hospital for the whole region, are proof that the goodwill he hoped to create has borne fruit. The challenge to those who care about what Sir Edmund Hillary, the Sherpas and others of goodwill have achieved in Solu Khumbu is to continue to support their work.

The exhibition *Sir Edmund Hillary: Everest and Beyond* opened at Auckland War Memorial Museum on 24 October 2002. Sir Hugh Kawharu of the museum's Maori Advisory Committee representing Ngati Whatua, Tainui and Ngati Paoa welcomed Sir Edmund, saying: 'We find it hard to comprehend from here, the scale of the high mountains in the Himalayas and the vast expanses of Antarctica. But we do understand leadership. And we have admired for many years now the way in which you have inspired other New Zealanders to join you in returning the friendship of the Sherpa people of Nepal, through the building of hospitals and schools in that distant land. To us it seems that this is a conquest of another kind – one that will leave its mark in the minds and the spirit of a people. No reira e Koro, tena koe, ka nui nga mihi atu ki a koe, mo to kaha, mo to aroha, mo

to tino rangatiratanga. Tena koe, tena korua ko to hoa rangatira. E rau rangatira ma, tena koutou. Kia ora mai tatau.'[9]

Khumjung School sent a message to Sir Edmund for the exhibition at Auckland War Memorial Museum. It was displayed in the replica schoolhouse, alongside greetings, tributes and classwork from children in other Sherpa schools. It reads:

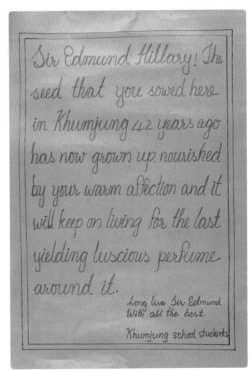

The Himalayan Trust, New Zealand, established 1963

Founded by Sir Edmund and Louise Hillary and some of their friends, the Himalayan Trust is a New Zealand-based non-profit organisation which has assisted the Sherpa people of the Himalayas for more than forty years. Since May 2002 responsibility for the trust's work in Nepal has been shared with the Himalayan Trust Advisory Board, based in Kathmandu. Ang Rita Sherpa, the chief administrative officer, receives petitions from groups, individuals and whole communities, and the board assists Sir Edmund in supervising, guiding and developing the trust's work according to the wishes of the local people.

The Himalayan Trust Advisory Board

Chairman	Ang Rita Sherpa (Himalayan Trust)
Secretary	Pasang Sherpa Lama
Treasurer	Ang Thukten Sherpa
Members	Tashi Jangbu Sherpa
	Pasang Dawa Sherpa
	Pertemba Sherpa
	Dr Kami Temba Sherpa
	Ang Rita Sherpa (The Mountain Institute)
	Ms Dawa Phuji Sherpa
Honorary member	Norbu Tenzing Sherpa (American Himalayan Foundation)

In 2002 Sir Edmund invited Elizabeth Hawley to be chief executive for the Himalayan Trust in Nepal. She has lived in Kathmandu since the 1970s, and has given unstinting support and assistance to the trust. She is now the Honorary New Zealand Consul in Nepal.

The Himalayan Trust
278A Remuera Road
Auckland 5
New Zealand

The Himalayan Trust
Advisory Board
Dilli Bazar
PO Box 224
Kathmandu
Nepal

APPENDIX

224

Himalayan Trust Building Projects in Nepal, 1961–95

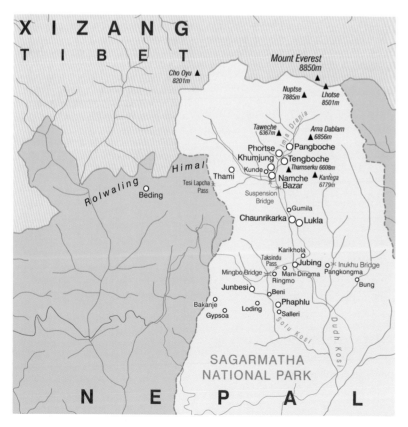

1961 Khumjung School
1963 Schools at Pangboche and Thami; Khumjung water supply
1964 Lukla airstrip; Dudh Kosi and Bhote Kosi bridges; schools at Namche Bazar, Chaunrikarka and Junbesi
1965 Tengboche School; Khumjung School – carpentry training shed
1966 Kunde Hospital; Kunde water supply; bridge below Tengboche; Khumjung *Gompa* – new roof
1967 Junbesi School – new classrooms; Phortse School
1968 Khumjung School – two new classrooms; lengthening Lukla Airstrip; Phortse water supply
1970 Schools at Pangkongma, Beni and Bakanje; Kunde Hospital – public health lecture room, storeroom and bathroom; Khumjung School – Sherpa handicrafts room; Tengboche and Khumjung water supplies; Thami *Gompa* – terrace reconstruction; Ringmo Bridge
1971 Schools at Gypsoa and Loding; Hinkhu Bridge
1972 Rolwaling School and Junbesi Middle School; rebuilding Ringmo Bridge
1975 Phaphlu Hospital and airstrip; Salleri High School
1976 Phaphlu Hospital – workshop and firewood shed; Salleri School Hall – new seating
1977 Kunde Hospital – charcoal store, workshop, tool store, septic tank
1978 Kunde Hospital – major remodelling
1979 Khumjung School – new classroom and student hostel; Thami School – rebuilding and new health clinic; Junbesi health clinic; Junbesi School – student hostel and toilet block

1980 Gumila School and health clinic; Chaunrikarka School – new classrooms and health clinic
1981 Kunde Hospital – rebuild long-stay ward and toilet; Phortse School – maintenance
1982 Khumjung High School
1983 Mani Dingma School – new roof; Junbesi School – new roof; Chaunrikarka School – refurbishment and new classroom; Thami Monastery – new roof on Rinpoche's and tawas' building
1984 Khumjung School – new classrooms
1985 Bung – health clinic
1986 Beni School – additional classrooms; Kharikhola School
1987 Tengboche School – additions
1988 Phaphlu Hospital – complete refurbishment
1991 Kunde water reservoir
1993 Phaphlu Hospital – repairs to plumbing and solar heating; Hinkhu Bridge repairs; Solu Khumbu Multiple Campus at Salleri
1995 Phaphlu Hospital – new floor in staff quarters, workshop and ward roof

The Himalayan Trust's more recent projects do not appear on the above list. Its continuing work, with help from other funding bodies, covers a wide range of activities. These include maintaining and developing existing schools and the hospitals at Kunde and Phaphlu, subsidising teacher salaries, managing tree nurseries, advising on reforestation programmes, funding student scholarships, providing adult literacy classes for women, giving financial help to individuals and responding to local requests for other forms of assistance. A successful six-year programme of in-service teacher training, supported by the Himalayan Trust UK, began in 1997. It reached sixty-five schools in the communities closest to Mount Everest.

Tashi Jangbu Sherpa with Zeke O'Connor, 2003 **Ares Stein**

Sir Edmund Hillary Foundation of Canada, established 1973

The Sir Edmund Hillary Foundation (SEHF) of Canada was founded by W. F. (Zeke) O'Connor. Its first project was to renovate the structure of the Kunde Hospital and to add an extra room and from this the foundation moved on to provide Canadian volunteer doctors for the hospital, who alternate with the New Zealand medical volunteers. The

SEHF established several tree nurseries in Sagarmatha National Park and in 1978 assumed principal responsibility for funding the park's reforestation programme. Over eight years one million seedling trees were planted. The SEHF contributed to tuition fees for the first park warden, Mingma Norbu Sherpa, to complete a Masters degree in national resource management. The SEHF also contributes to the Adult Women Literacy programme in Solu

Khumbu. With considerable support from the Canadian International Development Agency, the SEHF is a major contributor to all the Himalayan Trust's work.

Sir Edmund Hillary Foundation of Canada
222 Jarvis Street
Toronto, Ontario M5B 2B8
Canada

Larry and Joan Witherbee, 2003 **Ares Stein**

The Hillary Foundation, USA, established 1975

Larry Witherbee established the Hillary Foundation, USA as a non-profit organisation to assist the activities of the Himalayan Trust. Witherbee has travelled to Nepal with the Hillarys each year since 1980. He says: 'The Hillary Foundation board members are

friends of Sir Edmund and for the most part are just regular folk dedicated to his projects in Nepal. There are no world-famous people involved with our Foundation…We are a low-overhead operation and are very proud of it.' The Foundation acts as a liaison with Sears, Roebuck and Co., one of Sir Edmund's long-term associations. Many donations are offered by Americans who have been

to Nepal or who have heard or read about the Trust's work.

The Hillary Foundation
814 Saddlewood Drive
Glen Ellyn, IL 60137
USA

Ed Hillary and Richard Blum, c. 1985

The American Himalayan Foundation, San Francisco, established 1981

After meeting Ed Hillary in the late 1970s Richard Blum established the non-profit American Himalayan Foundation (AHF) to help the people and ecology of the Himalayas. A major financial sponsor of the

Himalayan Trust, the American Himalayan Foundation has pledged its support over the next decade. 'We have over a hundred projects now, from Bhutan to Tibet, but the Sherpas and the Himalayan Trust remain our heart's work. Ed is known all over the world, but to the people of the Solu Khumbu he is a living legend who continues to give hope and opportunities to many, many

lives. We are proud to be part of Ed's work and passion.'
Richard C. Blum,
Chairman and Founder

American Himalayan Foundation
909 Montgomery Street, Suite 400
San Francisco, CA 94133
USA

225

George Lowe and Ed Hillary, Solu Khumbu, 1996

Sir Edmund Hillary Himalayan Trust UK, established 1989

The Himalayan Trust UK was established by George and Mary Lowe with other trustees. Its object is to work alongside the New Zealand trust in improving the quality of education in the schools of the Khumbu. The UK trust

has contributed to a wide range of educational projects. It funded the renovation and upgrading of Phaphlu School whose 250 pupils are from very poor families, and most recently a three-year in-service training programme for secondary teachers, which complemented the existing primary teacher training scheme. The UK trust

welcomes donations from people who have visited Nepal and who want to help with its work in Solu Khumbu.

The Sir Edmund Hillary Himalayan Trust UK
Registered Charity No 1000153
Danewood, High Lane
Upper Holloway, Matlock, DE4 5AW
United Kingdom

Ed Hillary, Ingrid Versen and the Mayor of Bad Wiesse, Lukla, 1993

Sir Edmund Hillary Foundation, Germany, established 1991

Ingrid Versen went to Nepal with Sir Edmund and Lady Hillary in 1990. She was impressed by the Himalayan Trust's schools and hospitals, and decided to set up the Hillary Foundation, Germany. The following year Ed Hillary began

giving annual fundraising lectures in Versen's home town of Bad Wiessee, near Munich. Since 1998 Peter Hillary has also delivered lectures for the foundation. With a working membership of just fifty people, the Hillary Foundation, Germany has contributed generously to Phaphlu Hospital.

Sir Edmund Hillary Stiftung Deutschland eV
Altwiesseer Weg 6,
D-83707 Bed Wiessee am Tegernsee
Germany

ACKNOWLEDGEMENTS

In August 2001 the exhibitions manager at Auckland Museum, John Haydn, called to ask if I was interested in putting together an exhibition about Sir Edmund Hillary. It would celebrate both the museum's 150th birthday and the fiftieth anniversary of Hillary's ascent of Mount Everest. As a freelance art curator I was not an obvious choice for the job, so I am grateful to John for offering it to me, and to the museum's director Dr Rodney Wilson – my former boss at Auckland Art Gallery – for believing I could do it. Over the next year I spent many enjoyable hours with Ed and June Hillary, and met most of their Himalayan Trust friends. I was welcomed into houses, fed and entertained, and given free access to memories, to slide collections, and to thoughts and insights about Ed's life and achievements. I am deeply grateful to them all for their warm generosity.

My study was fairly rapidly taken over by a library of second-hand books – Ed and Louise Hillary's own books; books about climbing and climbers, about Everest, Nepal and Antarctica. I immersed myself in them, and my fascination with the subject grew. After the exhibition opened, a friend and curator at the museum, Louis Le Vaillant, asked me when the book was coming out. I hadn't thought of adding to the line-up on my bookshelves, but nonetheless the idea took root. It would be a book for the people who were spending time in the exhibition, who wrote in the visitors' book that they were surprised, impressed and moved by Ed Hillary's achievements – and who felt proud that he is a New Zealander. I asked Ed and June Hillary what they thought, and was very pleased when they approved.

And so my primary thanks are to Sir Edmund and Lady Hillary, and to their families. Ed and June Hillary, Sarah Hillary, Peter Hillary and Yvonne Oomen, and June and Alistair Carlile all read and commented on the text, and Hilary Carlile, Rex and Ann Hillary, and Robyn Mulgrew were unfailingly helpful and encouraging. I am particularly grateful for permission to quote freely from Ed's own writing and from Louise Hillary's books; and to Mike and Linda Gill, Jim and Ann Wilson, John and Diane McKinnon, George Lowe and Peter Hillary for allowing me to use their words – their voices are the threads that bind this story. Mike Gill's and Peter Hillary's first-hand experience of Himalayan climbing and geography was invaluable to me, as was Mike's medical knowledge and his experience on many Hillary expeditions. Warmest thanks also to John and Noela Claydon, to Lindsay and Genevieve Strang, and to Jim and Janette Strang. If there are errors in the book they are mine alone.

Chris Mace and Dayle Mace offered their support at an early stage. Chris was then chairman of Antarctica New Zealand and is now a trustee of the Antarctic Heritage Trust. He arranged for me to visit Scott Base on one memorable weekend in February 2003, and for that astonishing experience alone I would be eternally grateful; but it was the Maces' vision and generosity that enabled me to spend eighteen months researching and writing this book.

Since it all started with the exhibition, I want to acknowledge the whole exhibition team, particularly Andrew Thomas, Louis Le Vaillant, Steve McCraith, Shaun Higgins, Arch McDonnell, Alan Deare, Wilma van Heeswijk, Max Riksen, Julia Gresson, Merv Hutchinson, Laura Vodanovich, Nicola Jennings, Lucinda Blackley, Richard Smith, Hayden Chambers, Nick Eagle, Hannah Kerr and Workshop E. Thanks also to Susan Norton and her staff at National Geographic's Explorers Hall in Washington DC who joined Auckland Museum as partners in the exhibition. Diane McKinnon created a richly textured Sherpa kitchen; Jim Strang, Ang Rita Sherpa and the children of Solu Khumbu schools made our replica of Thami School feel like the real thing; Michael Dillon's film took visitors up the River Ganges with Ed; and Bill Sykes's botanical photographs took them on a walk towards Everest. And to all the others who lent objects and film and photographs, and contributed in countless ways, my thanks.

I am grateful to all those who helped with and contributed to the book, and my particular thanks go to the following people. At Antarctica New Zealand and Scott Base: Lou Sanson, Natalie Cadenhead, Emma Reid, Anna Howard, Paul Woodgate, Marie Peters, Doug Bell, Helen Brown, and Kevin Rigarlsford who took me up Observation Hill. In Nepal: Ang Rita Sherpa, Nima Yangjen and her family, all the Footprints Tours group, the staff of Kunde Hospital – Dr Kami Temba, Mingma Temba and Ang Lhamu, Gayse Nuru Sherpa, Nima Yangjen Sherpa, Tsumji, and Canadian volunteer doctors Katie Morgenstern and Simon Pulfrey. For their warm hospitality and friendship during my stay at Kunde: Phu Dorje and Doma Tshering Sherpa, Ang Dooli, Temba and Ang Rita; Kami Tshering, Yangjen, Pemba Doma, Pema Chutin and my daily companion Mingma Kanche. At Lukla: Da Phuti and Ang Passang at Paradise Eco-Lodge, and Lisa Choegyal and Hans Höfer. In India: Caroline McDonald, Simon Mark and the staff of the New Zealand High Commission at New Delhi, Mrs Uma Lal, Captain M. S. Kohli and Mr Gulati. In Darjeeling: Nawang Gombu and Chandranath Das at the Himalayan Mountaineering Institute. In the United Kingdom: Lieutenant Colonel Charles Wylie and Sheila Wylie, George Band, Dr Michael Ward and Jane Ward, Jan Morris and Michael Westmacott. In Australia and New Zealand: Bill Beaven, Arthur and Anna Boyer, John Clarke, Ed Cotter, Lynley Cook, Michael Dillon, Murray, Shirley and David Ellis, Jennifer French, Michael Green, Alfred and Sue Gregory, Norman and Enid Hardie, Sir Hugh Kawharu, Ian Kennedy, David Lange, Thomas Lawn, Hilary Mace, Sue Michelsen-Heath, Colin and Betty Monteath, Johnny Mulheron, Lois, Ann, Lynn and Susan Pearl, Anna Riddiford, Krzysztof Pfeiffer, Tashi and Judy Tenzing, Graeme Waters, Tim Watkin, Dr Geoff Watson, and the Swiss Foundation for Alpine Research.

Thanks to all the librarians and museum staff who helped with my research, especially Bruce Ralston and Heather Stone at Auckland Museum Library; Justin Hobson at the Royal Geographical Society's picture library; Yvonne Sibbald and Kate Miller at the Alpine Club Library, London; Lynda Hilliam at Dargaville Maritime Museum; Janet Pates at Tuakau Museum; and Linda Tyler at the Hocken Library, University of Otago, Dunedin. For permission to quote from his work I thank the estate of A.R.D. Fairburn.

Geoff Walker at Penguin Books was an enthusiast for this book right from the start; Rebecca Lal dealt with a tardy writer with calm and patience; Jane Parkin was the editor all writers dream of; and Alan Deare, Dean Foster and the team at Inhouse made the design of the book all that I had hoped. Deepest thanks to them all.

For their positive and practical support – beds, meals, cups of tea and patient listening to my endless Ed Hillary stories – I thank Bridget Ikin, John Maynard, Billy and Stella Maynard, Leah Andrews, John Haydn and Alison Copland, Paul Cox and Dorothy Fitzgerald, Bronwynne Cornish and Denys Watkins, Julia Gresson, Anna Miles, Ian Jervis, Peter and Coral Shaw, Heather Buchan and Jeremy Anderson, Robert Hancock, Gitta Hancock, Adam Gifford, Judith Thompson and Chiara Corbelletto, Jenny Maidment and Ray McVinnie.

My family have all lived with this project for several years and never failed to be enthusiastic and interested. Warmest thanks and love to Paula, Andrea, Fiona, Ralph, Cato, Aphra, Lara, Paloma and Kirk; to Ingrid, Tim, Jane, Tristan and Lucas in Christchurch; and to Nick, Sally, Eleanor and Anna in London.

I have dedicated this book to four people:

To my father Malcolm Johnston, a Presbyterian minister, a fine scholar and a wise and loving man. He was a high-achiever who took great pleasure in the achievements of others and his 1938 Penguin paperback of *The Worst Journey in the World*, bought when he was a boy dreaming of adventure on a farm in the Rangitikei, went with me to Antarctica.

To my mother Paula Johnston, for her constant encouragement and for a lifelong inspiration of intelligence, humour, love and good sense.

To my husband Malcolm Cheadle, who travelled with me in New Zealand, Nepal, India and England; who put up with my long immersion in another man's life with great patience and good humour – and who kept me smiling.

And to Sarah Hillary, whose confidence and friendship was my strong belay, all through.

ALEXA JOHNSTON
Auckland, April 2005

REFERENCES

Contents page

Quotation: Edmund Hillary, *High Adventure*, Hodder & Stoughton, London, 1955, p. 13.

Prologue

1 James Morris, *Coronation Everest*, Faber & Faber, London, 1958, p. 81.
2 Anne B. Keiser and Cynthia Russ Ramsay, *Sir Edmund Hillary and the People of Everest*, Andrews McMeel Publishing, Kansas City, 2002. Foreword by HRH Prince Philip, Duke of Edinburgh.

Chapter 1

Quotation: Jane Mander, *The Story of a New Zealand River*, 1920. Reprint. Random House, Auckland, 1999, p. 11.
1 Wayne Ryburn, *Tall Spars, Steamers and Gum, A History of the Kaipara from Early European Settlement, 1854–1947*, Kaipara Publications, Auckland, 1999.
2 Thomas Webb, *Reminiscences of Old Wairoa*, Alexander Turnbull Library, Wellington, MS-Papers 4077-1 Peter Mathews.
3 *Northern Wairoa Gazette*, 5 August 1886, Alexander Turnbull Library, Wellington.
4 Account by Leila Sumner (née Hillary), Alexander Turnbull Library, Wellington, MS-Papers 4077-5.
5 June Carlile (née Hillary) in conversation with the author, May 2004.
6 E. K. Bradley, *The Great Northern Wairoa*, 3rd edition, Phoenix Printing Co., Auckland, 1973.
7 June Carlile in conversation with the author, May 2004.
8 In 1918 just over 140 tonnes of honey were exported from New Zealand. By the end of the 1920s, this had risen to more than 1000 tonnes, and beekeeping would eventually become one of the country's important primary industries.
9 Edmund Hillary, *View from the Summit*, Doubleday, London, 1999, p. 40.

Chapter 2

Title: *. . . seeking before all things the honesty of substance/touch of soil and wind and rock,/frost and flower and water* A. R. D. Fairburn, 'Dominion' in Mac Jackson (ed.), *A. R. D. Fairburn, Selected Poems*, Victoria University Press, Wellington, 1995, p. 85.
Quotation: Edmund Hillary and Peter Hillary, *Two Generations*, Hodder & Stoughton, London, 1984, p. 19.
1 Bruce Hamilton, 'Ulric Gaster Williams (1890–1971)', *The Dictionary of New Zealand Biography*, vol. 4, 1921–40, Auckland University Press, Auckland and the Department of Internal Affairs, Wellington, 1998, p. 567.
2 Dr Ulric Williams, *Hints on Healthy Living*, 3rd edition, Wanganui Chronicle, Wanganui, p. 27.
3 I am grateful to Dr Cliff Tasman Jones, scientific director of the New Zealand Nutrition Foundation for his comments on Dr Ulric Williams's career.
4 Sir Edmund Hillary in conversation with the author, May 2004.
5 Edmund Hillary, *Nothing Venture, Nothing Win*, Hodder & Stoughton, London, 1975, p. 20.
6 ibid., p. 22.
7 ibid.
8 Edmund Hillary, *High Adventure*, Hodder & Stoughton, London, 1955, p. 13.
9 L. V. Bryant, *New Zealanders and Everest*, A. H. & A. W. Reed, Wellington, 1953.
10 Rex Hillary in conversation with the author, 9 October 2003.
11 June Carlile in conversation with the author, 16 June 2004.
12 Edmund Hillary and Peter Hillary, *Two Generations*, p. 19.
13 C. G. Scrimgeour, John A. Lee, Tony Simpson, *The Scrim–Lee Papers*, A. H. & A. W. Reed, Wellington, 1979, p. 36.
14 'A Courageous Teacher', *New Zealand Herald*, 1 October 1974.
15 Edmund Hillary, *Nothing Venture, Nothing Win*, p. 26.
16 Robert S. Ellwood, *Islands of the Dawn: The Story of Alternative Spirituality in New Zealand*, University of Hawaii Press, Honolulu, 1993, p. 240.
17 Edmund Hillary, *Nothing Venture, Nothing Win*, p. 27.
18 ibid., p. 25.
'The Friendly Road' on p. 26
* Ray Richards, introduction to *The Scrim–Lee Papers*, p. xi.

Chapter 3

Title: *They went then till they came to the Delectable Mountains, which mountains belong to the Lord.* John Bunyan, *The Pilgrim's Progress*, 1675.
Quotation: Edmund Hillary, *Nothing Venture, Nothing Win*, Hodder & Stoughton, London, 1975, p. 25.
1 Eric Shipton, *Upon that Mountain*, Hodder & Stoughton, London, 1943; Readers Union edition, 1945, p. 30.
2 A 1962 conversation recounted in *Reader's Digest*, December 1976.
3 Edmund Hillary and Peter Hillary, *Two Generations*, Hodder & Stoughton, London, 1984, p. 21.
4 Edmund Hillary, *High Adventure*, Hodder and Stoughton, London, 1955, p. 16; *Nothing Venture, Nothing Win*, pp. 36, 41, 43, 55, 78, 73.
5 Quoted in Edmund Hillary, *Nothing Venture, Nothing Win*, p. 84.
6 Edmund Hillary, *Nothing Venture, Nothing Win*, p. 28.
7 ibid., p. 46.
8 ibid., p. 67
9 Edmund Hillary, *High Adventure*, p. 16.
10 Graham Langton, 'Horace Henry Ayres', *The Dictionary of New Zealand Biography*, vol. 5, Auckland University Press, Auckland and the Department of Internal Affairs, Wellington, 2000, p. 26.
11 Edmund Hillary, *High Adventure*, p. 17.
12 Philip Temple, *The World at Their Feet*, Whitcombe & Tombs, Christchurch, 1969, p. 41.
13 Edmund Hillary, *Nothing Venture, Nothing Win*, p. 92.
14 Norman Hardie, 'Long Haul on La Perouse' in Hamish MacInnes (ed.), *The Mammoth Book of Mountain Disasters*, Carroll & Graf, New York, 2003, p. 266.
15 Edmund Hillary and Peter Hillary, *Two Generations*, p. 24.
16 George Lowe, *Because It Is There*, Cassell & Co., London, 1959, p. 10.
17 ibid., p. 12.
18 Edmund Hillary, *Nothing Venture, Nothing Win*, pp. 98–9.
19 ibid., p. 105.
20 Edmund Hillary, *High Adventure*, p. 18.
21 Edmund Hillary, *Nothing Venture, Nothing Win*, p. 113.
22 Temple, p. 56.
23 Edmund Hillary, *Nothing Venture, Nothing Win*, p. 114.
24 Shipton, *Upon that Mountain*, p. 177.
25 Edmund Hillary, *Nothing Venture, Nothing Win*, p. 126.
26 Peter Steele, *Eric Shipton: Everest and Beyond*, Constable, London, 1998, p. 147.
27 Lowe, p. 18.
28 Telegram to Scott Russell from Harry Stevenson, 9 August 1951, NZ Alpine Club records, Hocken Library, University of Otago, Dunedin.
29 Steele, p. 149.
30 Edmund Hillary, *Nothing Venture, Nothing Win*, p. 130.
31 Lowe, p. 19.
32 Edmund Hillary, *High Adventure*, p. 20.
33 ibid., p. 33.
34 Michael Ward, *In This Short Span*, Victor Gollancz, London, 1972, p. 71.
35 Steele, p. 158.
36 Eric Shipton, *The Mount Everest Reconnaissance Expedition 1951*, Hodder & Stoughton, London, 1952, p. 19.
37 Edmund Hillary, *High Adventure*, p. 38.
38 Shipton, *The Mount Everest Reconnaissance Expedition 1951*, p. 19.
39 Edmund Hillary, *High Adventure*, pp. 46–7.
40 Temple, p. 69.
41 Edmund Hillary, *High Adventure*, p. 95.
Harry Ayres: A master of snow and ice on p. 32
* Jim Wilson, *Aorangi: The Story of Mount Cook*, Whitcombe & Tombs, Christchurch, 1968, p. 174.
† Michael Mahoney, *Harry Ayres: Mountain Guide*, Whitcoulls Publishers, Christchurch, 1982, p. 5.
George Lowe on p. 35
* Edmund Hillary, *High Adventure*, 1955.
† Edmund Hillary, *Nothing Venture, Nothing Win*, p. 112.
‡ Edmund Hillary and George Lowe, *East of Everest: An Account of the New Zealand Alpine Club Himalayan Expedition to the Barun Valley in 1954*, Hodder & Stoughton, London, 1956.
§ Lowe, *Because It Is There*.
Eric Shipton on p. 39
* Steele, p. xiv.
Ang Tharkay on p. 41
* Shipton, *Upon that Mountain*, p. 169.
† Edmund Hillary, *View from the Summit*, p. 82.
A southern route to Everest on p. 42–3
* Michael Ward, *Everest: A Thousand Years of Exploration*, The Ernest Press, Glasgow, 2003, pp. 113–15.
† H. W. Tilman, *Nepal Himalaya*, Cambridge University Press, Cambridge, 1952.
§ Edmund Hillary, *High Adventure*, Hodder & Stoughton, London, 1955, pp. 40, 41.

Chapter 4

Quotation: Edmund Hillary, *High Adventure*, Hodder & Stoughton, London, 1955, p. 115.
1 Letter from Edmund Hillary (EPH) to Harry Ayres, August 1952. Courtesy of John Claydon.
2 Letter from Murray Ellis to Harry Ayres, 12 August 1952. Courtesy of John Claydon.
3 EPH to Harry Ayres, August to November 1952. Courtesy of John Claydon.
4 ibid.
5 ibid.
6 ibid.
7 EPH to Jim Rose, 29 March 1953, NZ Alpine Club Records, Hocken Library, University of Otago, Dunedin.
8 ibid.
9 John Hunt, 'Letters from Everest', *Alpine Journal*, no. 98, 1993, p. 11.
10 EPH to Jim Rose, 18 April 1953, NZ Alpine Club Records.
11 Wilfrid Noyce, *South Col*, William Heinemann, London, 1954, p. 24.
12 Tom Stobart, *Adventurer's Eye*, The Hollen Street Press, London, 1958, p. 239.
13 EPH to Jim Rose, 18 April 1953, NZ Alpine Club Records.
14 ibid.
15 EPH to Mrs P. A. Hillary, 19 April 1953, collection of Edmund Hillary.
16 John Hunt, *The Ascent of Everest*, Hodder & Stoughton, London, 1953, p. 256.
17 Edmund Hillary, *High Adventure*, p. 137.
18 ibid., p. 140.
19 Tenzing Norgay, *Man of Everest, The Autobiography of Tenzing* told to James Ramsay Ullman, George Harrap & Co., London, 1955, p. 245.
20 Frank Smythe, *Camp Six*, The Six Alpine/Himalayan Climbing Books, Bâton Wicks, London, 2000, p. 551.
21 EPH to Mrs P. A. Hillary, 28 April 1953, collection of Edmund Hillary.
22 Edmund Hillary, *High Adventure*, p. 146.
23 Edmund Hillary, *View from the Summit*, Doubleday, London, 1999, p. 116.
24 John Hunt, *Our Everest Adventure*, Brockhampton Press, Leicester, 1954, p. 90.
25 Edmund Hillary, *High Adventure*, p. 169.
26 ibid., p. 179.
27 ibid., pp. 185–6.
28 ibid., p. 174.
29 ibid., p. 196.
30 ibid., p. 197.
31 ibid., p. 201.
32 ibid., p. 203.
33 ibid., p. 204.
34 ibid., p. 206.
35 ibid.
36 ibid., pp. 206–207.
37 ibid., p. 208.
38 ibid.
39 ibid.
40 Tenzing Norgay, *Man of Everest*, p. 269.
Chomolungma/Mount Everest/Sagarmatha: A history on p. 49
* Stephen Venables, *Everest: Summit of Achievement*, Royal Geographical Society and Allen & Unwin, London, 2003, p. 30.
† Michael Ward, *Everest: A Thousand Years of Exploration*, The Ernest Press, Glasgow, 2003, p. 11.
Tenzing Norgay on p. 50
* Edmund Hillary, *Nothing Venture, Nothing Win*, Hodder & Stoughton, London, 1975, p. 145.
† Ed Douglas, *Tenzing: Hero of Everest*, National Geographic Society, Washington DC, 2003, p. 38.
‡ ibid., p. 103.
Sherpas and sahibs on p. 51
* Noyce, *South Col*, p. 23.
† Michael Gill, *Mountain Midsummer*, Hodder & Stoughton, London, 1969, pp. 110–11.
The boots they wore on p. 53
* Noyce, *South Col*, p. 158.
† Hunt, *The Ascent of Everest*, p. 41.
The 1953 team on pp. 54–5
* Hunt, *The Ascent of Everest*, p. 28.
† ibid., p. 158.
The 1953 team on pp. 56–7
* Stobart, p. 235.
† Hunt, *The Ascent of Everest*, p. 61.
Oxygen equipment on Everest in 1953 on p. 62
* T. D. Bourdillon, 'Oxygen Equipment' in Hunt, *The Ascent of Everest*, Appendix V, pp. 257–60.
Three Sherpa climbers on p. 64
* Edmund Hillary, *High Adventure*, p. 164.
Food on the mountain on p. 67
* Hunt, *The Ascent of Everest*, p. 264.
† Noyce, *South Col*, p. 112.

Chapter 5

Quotation: Edmund Hillary in 'Hillary: A View from the Top', TVNZ, 1997, director Tom Scott.
1 Edmund Hillary, *High Adventure*, Hodder & Stoughton, London, 1955, p. 212.
2 John Hunt in 'Hillary: A View from the Top', TVNZ, 1997, director Tom Scott.
3 George Lowe, *Because It Is There*, Cassell & Co., London, 1959, p. 30.
4 Edmund Hillary (EPH) to Gertrude Hillary, 1 June 1953, collection of Edmund Hillary.
5 EPH to Jim Rose, 2 June 1953, NZ Alpine Club Records, Hocken Library, University of Otago, Dunedin.
6 Edmund Hillary, *High Adventure*, p. 210.
7 ibid., p. 16.
8 Lowe, p. 40.
9 Alf Gregory in conversation with the author, 20 February 2004.
10 'Hillary: A View from the Top', TVNZ, 1997, director Tom Scott.
11 Wilfrid Noyce, *South Col*, William Heinemann, London, 1954, p. 238.
12 George Band in conversation with the author, 15 December 2003.
13 EPH to Gertrude Hillary, 19 May 1953, collection of Edmund Hillary.
14 Peter Steele, *Eric Shipton, Everest and Beyond*, Constable, London, 1998, p. 204.
15 Tom Stobart, *Adventurer's Eye*, The Hollen Street Press, London, 1958, p. 250.
16 Tenzing Norgay, *Man of Everest, The Autobiography of Tenzing* told to James Ramsay Ullman, George Harrap & Co., London, 1955, p. 268.
17 Edmund Hillary, *Nothing Venture, Nothing Win*, Hodder & Stoughton, London, 1975, p. 166.
18 Edmund Hillary, *View from the Summit*, Doubleday, London, 1999, p. 25.
19 *Times of India*, 16 June 1953.
20 Noyce, *South Col*, p. 237.
21 George Lowe to Mr and Mrs P. A. Hillary, 17 June 1953, collection of Edmund Hillary.
22 John Hunt to Mr and Mrs P. A. Hillary, 16 June 1953, collection of Edmund Hillary.
23 Wilfrid Noyce, *Climbing the Fish's Tail*, Heinemann, London, 1958, p. 19.
24 Unidentified NZ press clipping dated 4 July, in 'The Ascent of Everest 1953' scrapbook, Alexander Turnbull Library, Wellington, MSY-5508.
25 Romesh C. Kumar, *The Statesman*, Calcutta, 18 June 1953, Jim Rose Papers, Hocken Library, University of Otago, Dunedin, MS 1-11-56.
26 EPH to his parents, 12 July 1953, collection of Edmund Hillary.
27 *New Zealand Herald*, 6 August 1953.
28 Henare Te Ua in conversation with the author, 2003.
29 Arthur's Pass hut book, 2 June 1953, NZ Alpine Club Records.
30 Edmund Hillary, *View from the Summit*, p. 118.
31 EPH to Gertrude Hillary, 27 September 1953, collection of Edmund Hillary.
32 EPH to Jim Rose, 4 May 1953, NZ Alpine Club Records.
33 EPH to Jim Rose, 27 June 1953, NZ Alpine Club Records.
34 Edmund Hillary, *View from the Summit*, p. 118.
35 Frank Smythe, *Camp Six*, The Six Alpine/Himalayan Climbing Books, Bâton Wicks, London, 2000, p. 536.
36 Edmund Hillary and George Lowe, *East of Everest*, Hodder & Stoughton, London, 1956, p. 36.
37 ibid.
38 Edmund Hillary, *View from the Summit*, p. 122.
39 Hillary and Lowe, p. 31.
40 Edmund Hillary, *View from the Summit*, p. 121.
41 Edmund Hillary, 'Report to Members of the Club Committee on the New Zealand Alpine Club Himalayan Expedition 1954', NZ Alpine Club Records.
42 *New Zealand Herald*, 5 September 1953.
43 Louise Hillary, *Keep Calm If You Can*, Hodder & Stoughton, London, 1964, p. 9.
Louise Rose on p. 81
* Edmund Hillary and Peter Hillary, *Two Generations*, Hodder & Stoughton, London, 1984, p. 24.
† Edmund Hillary, *View from the Summit*, p. 29.
‡ ibid., p. 40.

Chapter 6

Title: *But one, in dead of winter, Divine Agape, kindles Morning suns, new moons light start trophies; Says to the waste: rejoice and bring forth roses; To the ice-fields: let here spring thick bright lilies.* Ursula Bethell, 'Warning of Winter' in Ian Wedde and Harvey McQueen (eds), *The Penguin Book of New Zealand Verse*, Penguin, Auckland, 1985, p. 126.
Quotation: Edmund Hillary, *No Latitude for Error*, Hodder & Stoughton, London, 1961, p. 13.
1 Edmund Hillary, *Nothing Venture, Nothing Win*, Hodder & Stoughton, London, 1975, p. 60.
2 Edmund Hillary, *View from the Summit*, Doubleday, London, 1999, p. 128.
3 ibid., p. 129.
4 Edmund Hillary, diary, collection of Edmund Hillary.
5 Edmund Hillary, *No Latitude for Error*, p. 53.
6 ibid., p. 60.
7 ibid., p. 77.
8 ibid., p. 79.
9 Apsley Cherry Garrard, *The Worst Journey in the World*, vol. 1, Penguin, London, 1937, p. 11.
10 Edmund Hillary, *No Latitude for Error*, p. 95.
11 ibid., p. 98.
12 ibid., p. 107.
13 Murray Ellis in conversation with the author, 27 April 2004.
14 Edmund Hillary, *No Latitude for Error*, p. 104.

Chapter 7

Quotation: Telegram from Edmund Hillary to Scott Base, 26 December 1957.
1 Edmund Hillary, *No Latitude for Error*, Hodder & Stoughton, London, 1961, p. 116.
2 ibid., p. 117.
3 Edmund Hillary, *Nothing Venture, Nothing Win*, Hodder & Stoughton, London, 1975, p. 211.
4 Douglas McKenzie, *Opposite Poles*, Robert Hale, London, and Whitcombe & Tombs, New Zealand, 1963, p. 59.
5 ibid., p. 127.
6 ibid., pp. 137–8.
7 Edmund Hillary, *No Latitude for Error*, p. 156.
8 ibid., p. 161.
9 ibid., p. 174.
10 ibid., p. 167.
11 ibid., p. 171.
12 ibid., p. 191.
13 ibid., p. 202.
14 ibid., p. 203.
15 Roy Carlyon, diary, December 1956–February 1958, Antarctica New Zealand.
16 ibid.
17 Edmund Hillary, *No Latitude for Error*, p. 204.
18 ibid., p. 205.
19 ibid., p. 206.
20 ibid.
21 ibid., p. 210.
22 ibid., p. 214.
23 ibid., pp. 215–16.
24 John Claydon in conversation with the author, 3 March 2004.
25 Edmund Hillary, *View from the Summit*, Doubleday, London, 1999, p. 177.
26 ibid., p. 182.

27 Unidentified NZ press clipping, 'All Pleased is London comment', dated 3 January, Shirley Ellis's scrapbook, Dunedin.
28 *Sydney Morning Herald*, 6 January 1958.
29 M. E. B. Banks, *The Alpine Journal*, no. 303, November 1961, p. 402.

The Ferguson Tractor on p. 102

* Edmund Hillary, 'Report to the Ross Sea Committee on the Ferguson Tractors, 1958', collection of the Auckland Museum.

Murray Ellis on p. 103

* Edmund Hillary, *No Latitude for Error*, p. 178.
† Wilfrid Noyce, *South Col*, William Heinemann, London, 1954, p. 128.
‡ Tom Stobart, *Adventurer's Eye*, The Hollen Street Press, London, 1958, p. 225.
§ Jim Strang, tribute at the funeral service for Murray Ellis, 8 February 2005.

Peter Mulgrew on p. 108

* Edmund Hillary, *View from the Summit*, p. 108.
† ibid., p. 257.

Chapter 8

Quotation: Edmund Hillary and Desmond Doig, *High in the Thin Cold Air*, Hodder & Stoughton, London, 1962, p. 156.

1 Desmond Doig, 'Sherpaland, My Shangri-La', *National Geographic*, vol. 130, no. 4, October 1966, p. 562.
2 Michael Gill, *Mountain Midsummer*, Hodder & Stoughton, London, 1969, p. 96.
3 ibid., pp. 93–4.
4 Hillary and Doig, p. 23.
5 ibid., p. 34.
6 ibid.
7 Peter Mulgrew, *No Place for Men*, A. H. & A. W. Reed, Wellington, 1964, p. 49.
8 Edmund Hillary, *Schoolhouse in the Clouds*, Hodder & Stoughton, London, 1964, p. 2.
9 Hillary and Doig, p. 70.
10 ibid., p. 88.
11 Gill, p. 121.
12 Hillary and Doig, p. 120.
13 Gill, p. 121.
14 Hillary and Doig, p. 183.
15 Gill, p. 136.
16 ibid., pp. 133–4.
17 Hillary and Doig, p. 213.
18 Michael Ward in conversation with the author, 10 December 2003.
19 Edmund Hillary, *Nothing Venture, Nothing Win*, Hodder & Stoughton, London, 1975, p. 244.
20 Gill, p. 120.
21 Hillary and Doig, p. 172.
22 Michael Ward, *In this Short Span*, Victor Gollancz, London, 1972, p. 182.
23 Gill, p. 145.
24 Edmund Hillary, 'A School for Khumjung', Official Souvenir of the 40th Anniversary of Khumjung School, 2000.
25 Hillary and Doig, p. 127.
26 Gill, p. 147.
27 Hillary and Doig, pp. 203–4.
28 ibid., p. 204.
29 Edmund Hillary, *Nothing Venture, Nothing Win*, pp. 245–6.

Michael Gill on p. 117

* Edmund Hillary in Gill, foreword.
† Michael Ward, *In This Short Span*, Victor Gollancz, London, 1972, p. 189.
‡ Gill, p. 194.

The Himalayan Scientific and Mountaineering expedition, 1960–61 on p. 117

* Hillary and Doig, pp. 12.

Norman Hardie on p. 118

* Hillary and Doig, p. 26.
† Norman Hardie, *In Highest Nepal*, George Allen & Unwin Ltd, London, 1957, p. 75.

The mysterious yeti on p. 119

* Eric Shipton, *The Mount Everest Reconnaissance Expedition 1951*, Hodder & Stoughton, London, 1952, p. 127.

Expedition sirdars 1960–61 on p. 123

* Hillary and Doig, pp. 29–30.
† ibid., p. 30.
‡ Louise Hillary, *High Time*, Hodder & Stoughton, London, 1973, p. 114.
§ ibid., p. 112.

Chapter 9

Title: This is one of the Sherpa names for Makalu, a mountain that Desmond Doig described as 'hugely formidable, even in the distance, its rock summit dark among the other glittering peaks, as sombre and prophetic as a black veil at a white wedding'. Edmund Hillary and Desmond Doig, *High in the Thin Cold Air*, Hodder & Stoughton, London, 1962, p. 224.
Quotation: Edmund Hillary, *High Adventure*, Hodder & Stoughton, London, 1955, p. 211.

1 Hillary and Doig, p. 223.
2 Edmund Hillary, *Nothing Venture, Nothing Win*, Hodder & Stoughton, London, 1975, p. 246.
3 ibid., p. 248.
4 Hillary and Doig, p. 237.
5 Michael Ward, *In This Short Span*, Victor Gollancz, London, 1972, p. 202.
6 Peter Mulgrew, *No Place for Men*, A. H. & A. W. Reed, Wellington, 1964, p. 114.
7 Ward, *In This Short Span*, p. 210.
8 ibid., p. 208.
9 Edmund Hillary, *View from the Summit*, Doubleday, London, 1999, p. 207.
10 Hillary and Doig, pp. 263–4.
11 Edmund Hillary, *View from the Summit*, p. 207.
12 Michael Gill, *Mountain Midsummer*, Hodder & Stoughton, London, 1969, p. 142.
13 ibid., p. 102.
14 Mulgrew, p. 111.
15 ibid., p. 110.
16 Ward, *In This Short Span*, p. 195.
17 Hillary and Doig, p. 22.
18 Roland Huntford and Julie Summers, *The Shackleton Voyages*, Weidenfeld & Nicholson, London, 2002, p. 274.
19 Hillary and Doig, p. 269.

Chapter 10

Quotation: Louise Hillary in Edmund Hillary, *Schoolhouse in the Clouds*, Hodder & Stoughton, London, 1964, pp. 138–9.

1 Edmund Hillary and Desmond Doig, *High in the Thin Cold Air*, Hodder & Stoughton, London, 1962, p. 272.
2 ibid., p. 274.
3 ibid.
4 ibid., p. 275.
5 Edmund Hillary, *Schoolhouse in the Clouds*, p. 23.
6 Louise Hillary, *Keep Calm If You Can*, Hodder & Stoughton, London, 1964, p. 158.
7 ibid., p. 9.
8 ibid., pp. 24, 36.
9 Letter from Edmund Hillary (EPH) to John Claydon, 25 July 1962, Claydon collection.
10 Louise Hillary, *Keep Calm If You Can*, p. 42.
11 Edmund Hillary, *View from the Summit*, Doubleday, London, 1999, p. 236.
12 *New York Times*, 23 May 1962.
13 Louise Hillary, *Keep Calm If You Can*, p. 139.
14 ibid., p. 149.
15 ibid., p. 159.
16 Edmund Hillary, *Schoolhouse in the Clouds*, pp. 3, 6.
17 ibid., p. 9.
18 ibid., p. 17.
19 ibid., p. 15.
20 Michael Gill, *Mountain Midsummer*, Hodder & Stoughton, London, 1969, p. 168.
21 Edmund Hillary, *Schoolhouse in the Clouds*, p. 49.
22 ibid., p. 30.
23 Gill, p. 174.
24 Edmund Hillary, *Schoolhouse in the Clouds*, p. 50.
25 ibid., p. 53.
26 Jim Wilson in Edmund Hillary, *Schoolhouse in the Clouds*, p. 72
27 ibid., p. 97.
28 ibid.
29 ibid., p. 135.
30 Louise Hillary in Edmund Hillary, *Schoolhouse in the Clouds*, p. 124.
31 Edmund Hillary, *Schoolhouse in the Clouds*, p. 140.
32 Louise Hillary in ibid., p. 139.
33 ibid., p. 142.
34 ibid., pp. 164–5.
35 Edmund Hillary, *Schoolhouse in the Clouds*, p. 163.
36 Louise Hillary in ibid., p. 171.

Jim Wilson on p. 146

* Edmund Hillary, *From the Ocean to the Sky*, Hodder & Stoughton, London, 1979, p. 33.
† Letter from Jim Wilson to the author, 5 May 2004.

The Venerable Ngawang Tenzin Zangbu on p. 153

* Tengboche Monastery Development Project, www.tengboche.org
† Ang Rita Sherpa and Susan Höivik (eds), *Triumph on Everest: A Tribute from the Sherpas of Nepal*, Mandala Book Point, Kathmandu, 2003, p. ix.
‡ Tengboche Monastery Development Project, www.tengboche.org

Chapter 11

Quotation: Louise Hillary, *High Time*, Hodder & Stoughton, London, 1973, p. 113.

1 Mike Gill in conversation with the author, 15 April 2004.
2 Edmund Hillary, *View from the Summit*, Doubleday, London, 1999, p. 226.
3 Letter from Louise Hillary to John and Noela Claydon, 27 October 1972, Claydon collection.
4 Edmund Hillary, *Nothing Venture, Nothing Win*, Hodder & Stoughton, London, 1975, pp. 260–1.
5 ibid., p. 262.
6 Letter from John Claydon to David Anderson, Rotary Club of Linwood-Woolston, Christchurch, 8 April 1971, Claydon collection.
7 Edmund Hillary, *Nothing Venture, Nothing Win*, p. 264.
8 ibid., p. 265.
9 ibid., p. 266.
10 ibid., p. 269.
11 ibid.
12 Louise Hillary, *A Yak for Christmas*, Hodder & Stoughton, London, 1968, pp. 47–8.
13 ibid., p. 79.
14 ibid., pp. 82–3.
15 John McKinnon, 'Some Thoughts on my Nepal Experience', 26 September 2002, unpublished.
16 Edmund Hillary, *Nothing Venture, Nothing Win*, p. 272.
17 Neville Peat, *The VSA Way: 25 Years of Volunteering Overseas*, Compatriot Press, Wellington, 1987, p. 19.
18 Lois, Ann, Lynn and Susan Pearl in conversation with the author, 3 April 2004.
19 Letter from John Claydon to the Foreign Secretary, Singh Durbar, Kathmandu, 30 December 1971, Claydon collection.
20 Louise Hillary, *Keep Calm If You Can*, Hodder & Stoughton, London, 1964, pp. 145–6.
21 Sarah Hillary, *Metro*, Auckland, May 2003, p. 33.
22 Edmund Hillary, *View from the Summit*, p. 232.
23 Peter Hillary and John E. Elder, *In the Ghost Country*, Free Press, New York, 2003, pp. 199–202.
24 Sarah Hillary in 'Hillary: A View from the Top', TVNZ, 1997, director Tom Scott.
25 Edmund Hillary, *Nothing Venture, Nothing Win*, pp. 278–82.
26 Louise Hillary, *High Time*, p. 75.
27 ibid., p. 47.
28 ibid., p. 133.
29 ibid., p. 63.
30 Edmund Hillary, *Nothing Venture, Nothing Win*, p. 284.
31 ibid., p. 289.
32 Jim Wilson, *Aorangi: The Story of Mount Cook*, Whitcombe & Tombs, Christchurch, 1968, p. 131.
33 Edmund Hillary, *Nothing Venture, Nothing Win*, p. 303.
34 Tenzing Norgay Sherpa, *After Everest: An Autobiography*, George Allen & Unwin, London, 1977, p. 150.
35 Edmund Hillary, *View from the Summit*, p. 237.
36 Louise Hillary, *High Time*, p. 182.

John and Diane McKinnon on p. 164

* John McKinnon, 'Some thoughts on my Nepal experience', 25 September 2002, unpublished.
† Diane McKinnon in Peat, p. x.

Mingma Tsering and Ang Dooli from Kunde on p. 169.

* Louise Hillary, *High Time*, p. 53.
† Edmund Hillary, *View from the Summit*, pp. 226–27.

Sherpa friends on p. 177

* Louise Hillary, *A Yak for Christmas*, p. 45.
† Edmund Hillary and Desmond Doig, *High in the Thin Cold Air*, Hodder & Stoughton, London, 1962, p. 220.
‡ Louise Hillary, *High Time*, p. 32.
§ Louise Hillary, *A Yak for Christmas*, p. 45.
¤ Louise Hillary, *High Time*, p. 32.

Sherpa friends on p. 178

* Louise Hillary, *A Yak for Christmas*, p. 67.
† Louise Hillary, *High Time*, p. 43.
‡ Louise Hillary, *A Yak for Christmas*, p. 56.
§ ibid., p.88

Sherpa friends on p. 179

* Louise Hillary, *High Time*, p. 43.
† ibid., p. 47.

Chapter 12

Title: *I waked To find her. or for ever to deplore Her loss. and other pleasures all abjure.* John Milton, *Paradise Lost*, 1668, line 478.

1 Sarah Hillary in 'Hillary: A View from the Top', TVNZ, 1997, director Tom Scott.
2 Edmund Hillary and Peter Hillary, *Two Generations*, Hodder & Stoughton, London, 1984, pp. 43–4.
3 ibid., p. 140.

Chapter 13

Quotation: Edmund Hillary and Peter Hillary, *Two Generations*, Hodder & Stoughton, London, 1984, pp. 53–4.

1 Edmund Hillary, *View from the Summit*, Doubleday, London, 1999, p. 240.
2 ibid.
3 ibid.
4 Edmund Hillary, *View from the Summit*, p. 241.
5 Sarah Hillary in 'Hillary: A View from the Top', TVNZ, 1997, director Tom Scott.
6 Edmund Hillary, *View from the Summit*, p. 241.
7 June Hillary in *Hillary: A View from the Top*.
8 *New Zealand Herald*, 27 June 1967.
9 ibid.
10 *New Zealand Herald*, 30 June 1967.
11 Philip Matthews, 'Michael King', *New Zealand Listener*, 18–24 October 2003.
12 David Exel, Citizens for Rowling Campaign, quoted in *New Zealand Herald*, 24 October 1975.
13 David Exel et al, 'Citizens for Rowling', Wellington, October 1975.
14 John Hinchcliff quoted in Philip Matthews, 'Ask that Philosopher', *New Zealand Listener*, 1–7 May 2004.
15 Louise Hillary, *High Time*, Hodder & Stoughton, London, 1973, pp. 169–70.
16 Margaret Jefferies, Margaret Clarborough et al, *Sagamartha, Mother of the Universe: The Story of Mount Everest National Park*, Cobb/Horwood Publications, Auckland, 1986.
17 Edmund Hillary, *From the Ocean to the Sky*, Hodder & Stoughton, London, 1979, pp. 13–14.
18 ibid., p. 15.
19 ibid., p. 40.
20 ibid.
21 ibid., p. 19.
22 ibid., p. 106.
23 Edmund Hillary, *View from the Summit*, p. 248.
24 Edmund Hillary, *From the Ocean to the Sky*, p. 18.
25 Mike Gill in ibid., pp. 217–21.
26 Graeme Dingle in ibid., p. 223.
27 Edmund Hillary, ibid., p. 226.
28 ibid., pp. 236–7.
29 Jim Wilson in ibid., p. 258.
30 Edmund Hillary, *View from the Summit*, p. 270.
31 ibid.
32 Edmund Hillary and Peter Hillary, *Two Generations*, p. 89.
33 ibid., p. 111.
34 Joan Witherbee in conversation with the author, 4 October 2003.

Chapter 14

Quotation: Edmund Hillary, *Nothing Venture, Nothing Win*, Hodder & Stoughton, London, 1975, foreword, p. 308.

1 David Lange in conversation with the author, 17 October 2003.
2 A High Commissioner is an ambassador between countries in the British Commonwealth.
3 David Lange in conversation with the author, 17 October 2003.
4 Graeme Waters, Deputy High Commissioner to Sir Edmund Hillary, in conversation with the author, 15 October 2003.
5 Edmund Hillary, *View from the Summit*, Doubleday, London, 1991, p. 268.
6 ibid., p. 272.
7 'A different kind of challenge', interview with Louise Guerin, *New Zealand Listener*, 8 December 1984, p. 22.
8 Mrs Uma Lal in conversation with the author, 28 November 2003.
9 David Lange in conversation with the author, 17 October 2003.
10 Edmund Hillary, *View from the Summit*, p. 273.
11 'Ambassador Ed', 'Close Up', TVNZ, 18 April 1985.
12 Peter Hillary and John E. Elder, *In the Ghost Country*, Free Press, New York, 2003, p. 143.
13 Edmund Hillary, *View from the Summit*, p. 274.
14 ibid., p. 275.
15 ibid.
16 Graeme Waters in conversation with the author, 15 October 2003.
17 Edmund Hillary, *View from the Summit*, p. 276.
18 ibid., pp. 277–8.
19 Robert Sullivan and Robert Andreas (eds), *The Greatest Adventures of All Time*, Life Books, Iowa, 2000, p. 104.
20 ibid., p. 105.
21 Edmund Hillary, *View from the Summit*, pp. 278–9.
22 ibid., p. 279.
23 ibid.
24 ibid., p. 280.
25 ibid., p. 284.
26 ibid., p. 283.
27 Joan Witherbee in conversation with the author, 4 October 2003.
28 Edmund Hillary, *View from the Summit*, p. 285.
29 ibid., p. 285.
30 Peter Hillary in conversation with the author, 29 November 2001.
31 Edmund Hillary, *View from the Summit*, p. 287.
32 ibid., p. 289.
33 Anne B. Keiser and Cynthia Russ Ramsay, *Sir Edmund Hillary and the People of Everest*, Andrews McMeel Publishing, Kansas City, 2002, p. 108.
34 Edmund Hillary, *View from the Summit*, p. 293.
35 ibid.
36 ibid., p. 294.
37 Edmund Hillary in *Beyond Everest*, a film by Michael Dillon, 1997.
38 Jan Morris, 'Impossible not to be a bit pleased with himself', www.users.dircon.co.uk/litrev/reviews/1990/07/Morris-on-Hillary.html
39 Official souvenir of the 40th Anniversary of Khumjung School, 2000.
40 ibid.
41 ibid. From Atalante Mountaineering and Trekking Pvt. Ltd, Kathmandu, Nepal.
42 Ang Rita Sherpa and Susan Höivik (eds), *Triumph on Everest: A Tribute from the Sherpas of Nepal*, Mandala Book Point, Kathmandu, 2003, p. ix.
43 *Agence-France Presse*, Warsaw, 17 June 2004.
44 Sir Edmund Hillary Outdoor Pursuits Centre website, 1998, www.opc.org.nz
45 'ONE News', TVNZ, 29 November 2004.
46 Kylie Pinker and Tim Pankhurst, 'Sir Ed makes commemoration trip to Antarctica', www.stuff.co.nz, 25 November 2004.
47 Edmund Hillary, *View from the Summit*, p. 285.

Rex Hillary on p. 208

* Edmund Hillary, *View from the Summit*, p. 242.

Sarah Hillary on p. 210

* Ed Hillary in conversation with the author, May 2002.

Peter Hillary on p. 210

* Edmund Hillary, book inscription, 1999.
† Edmund Hillary, *View from the Summit*, p. 125.
‡ Sarah Hillary in conversation with the author, September 2002.
§ Peter Hillary in conversation with the author, September 2002.

Some Sherpa stories on pp. 217–219

* All stories sent to the author in August 2002 for the exhibition *Sir Edmund Hillary: Everest and Beyond* at the Auckland War Memorial Musuem.

Epilogue

1 Tim Watkin, 'Just a gutsy bloke', *New Zealand Herald*, 28 May 2003.
2 Chris Barton, 'Where women are real men', *Weekend Herald*, 5 February 2005.
3 Frederick Dagg, *Fred Dagg Anthology*, sound recording, Columbia, 1998.
4 Tim Watkin, 'Just a gutsy bloke'.
5 ibid.
6 Linda Gill, *Living High*, Hodder & Stoughton, Auckland, 1983, p. 76.
7 Peter Hillary and John E. Elder, *In the Ghost Country*, Free Press, New York, 2003, p. 206.
8 Joseph Gomes, D. Majundar and A. Rajan in conversation with the author, New Delhi, November 2003.
9 And so congratulations to you Sir, for your strength, for your compassion and for your superb leadership. Welcome and warmest greetings to you and to your wife. Ladies and gentlemen, welcome and good evening.

Select bibliography

Band, George, *Everest: 50 Years on Top of the World*, HarperCollins, London, 2003.

Douglas, Ed, *Tenzing: Hero of Everest*, National Geographic Society, Washington DC, 2003.

Gill, Michael, *Mountain Midsummer*, Hodder & Stoughton, London, 1969.

Hardie, Norman, *In Highest Nepal*, George Allen & Unwin Ltd, London, 1957.

Hillary, Edmund, *High Adventure*, Hodder & Stoughton, London, 1955.

—— *No Latitude for Error*, Hodder & Stoughton, London, 1961.

—— *Schoolhouse in the Clouds*, Hodder & Stoughton, London, 1964.

—— *Nothing Venture, Nothing Win*, Hodder & Stoughton, London, 1975.

—— *From the Ocean to the Sky*, Hodder & Stoughton, London, 1979.

—— *View from the Summit*, Doubleday, London, 1999.

Hillary, Edmund, and Desmond Doig, *High in the Thin Cold Air*, Hodder & Stoughton, London, 1962.

Hillary, Edmund, and Peter Hillary, *Two Generations*, Hodder & Stoughton, London, 1984.

Hillary, Edmund, and George Lowe, *East of Everest*, Hodder & Stoughton, London, 1956.

Hillary, Louise, *Keep Calm If You Can*, Hodder & Stoughton, London, 1964.

—— *A Yak for Christmas*, Hodder & Stoughton, London, 1968.

—— *High Time*, Hodder & Stoughton, London, 1973.

Hillary, Peter, and John E. Elder, *In the Ghost Country*, Free Press, New York, 2003.

Hunt, John, *The Ascent of Everest*, Hodder & Stoughton, London, 1953.

—— *Our Everest Adventure*, Brockhampton Press, Leicester, 1954.

Keiser, Anne B., and Cynthia Russ Ramsay, *Sir Edmund Hillary and the People of Everest*, Andrews McMeel, Kansas City, MO, 2002.

Lowe, George, *Because It Is There*, Cassell & Co., London, 1959.

Morris, James, *Coronation Everest*, Faber & Faber, London, 1958.

Mulgrew, Peter, *No Place for Men*, A. H. & A. W. Reed, Wellington, 1964.

Noyce, Wilfrid, *South Col*, William Heinemann, London, 1954.

Shipton, Eric, *Upon that Mountain*, Hodder & Stoughton, London, 1943; Readers Union edition, 1945.

—— *The Mount Everest Reconnaissance Expedition 1951*, Hodder & Stoughton, London, 1952.

Smythe, Frank, *Camp Six*, The Six Alpine/Himalayan Climbing books, London, 2000.

Stobart, Tom, *Adventurer's Eye*, The Hollen Street Press, London, 1958.

Tenzing Norgay, *Man of Everest, The Autobiography of Tenzing* told to James Ramsay Ullman, George Harrap & Co., London, 1955.

Tenzing Norgay Sherpa, *After Everest: An Autobiography*, George Allen & Unwin, London, 1977.

Venables, Stephen, et al., *Everest: Summit of Achievement*, Royal Geographical Society and Allen & Unwin, London, 2003.

Ward, Michael, *In This Short Span*, Victor Gollancz, London, 1972.

—— *Everest: A Thousand Years of Exploration*, The Ernest Press, Glasgow, 2003.

Photographic acknowledgements

The author and publisher would like to thank the following for their kind permission to reproduce the photographs in this book.

Photographers' names appear at the end of each caption. Every effort has been made to identify photographers, but where this has not been possible photographers have been left unattributed.

All photographs are from Sir Edmund Hillary's collection, apart from the copyright holders listed below.

Abbreviations key: t = top, b = bottom, l = left, fl = far left, c = centre, m = main

Antarctica New Zealand: 93tl, 95tl, 95cr, 95b, 96r, 97l, 108r, 110tl, 110–11m, 112, 113l, 113r; **Auckland War Memorial Museum:** 32l, 33tr; **June Carlile:** 27tl; © **Chivas Bros:** 201br, 215tc, 215c, 215bc, 215tr, 215cr, 215br, 216tl, 217bc, 224cl, 224r, 232tl, 232tr, 232bl; © **Dominion Post:** 232br; **Ellis Family Archive:** 103l, 109; **Peter Hillary:** 49r; **Hulton Archive, Getty Images:** 1–2; **Kathmandu Post:** 200–201; **Captain M. S. Kohli:** 75l; **Thomas Lawn:** 27tr; **New Zealand Herald:** endpapers, 77, 79tl, 79cl, 79bl; **Otago Museum:** 103tr; © **Royal Geographical Society:** 39br, 40bl, 42–3, 46, 47, 48, 50l, 51, 52–3m, 52tr, 53b, 54–7 (all), 58bl, 58cl, 58–9, 59l, 59r, 60, 61tl, 61tr, 61cl, 61bl, 63tl, 63m, 63r, 64fl, 64cl, 64l, 65r, 66–7b, 67tl, 67tr, 68–9, 70, 72t, 72b, 73cl, 74tl, 119r; © **Royal Geographical Society, Courtesy of Nick Bryant:** 49l; **Courtesy of Mick Sullivan:** 33bl, 33br; **Swiss Foundation for Alpine Research:** 50r; **Tashi and Judy Tenzing:** 76c; **Tuakau Museum:** 20, 21l, 21r; **Alexander Turnbull Library:** 12l, 13tl, 13bl; **Weekly News:** 38br.

INDEX

Pages in **bold** indicate profiles

229

230

Below and right: Sir
Edmund Hillary in
Kathmandu, May 2003
Ares Stein

Above: Sir Edmund Hillary
at Scott Base, Antarctica,
November 2004
Phil Reid

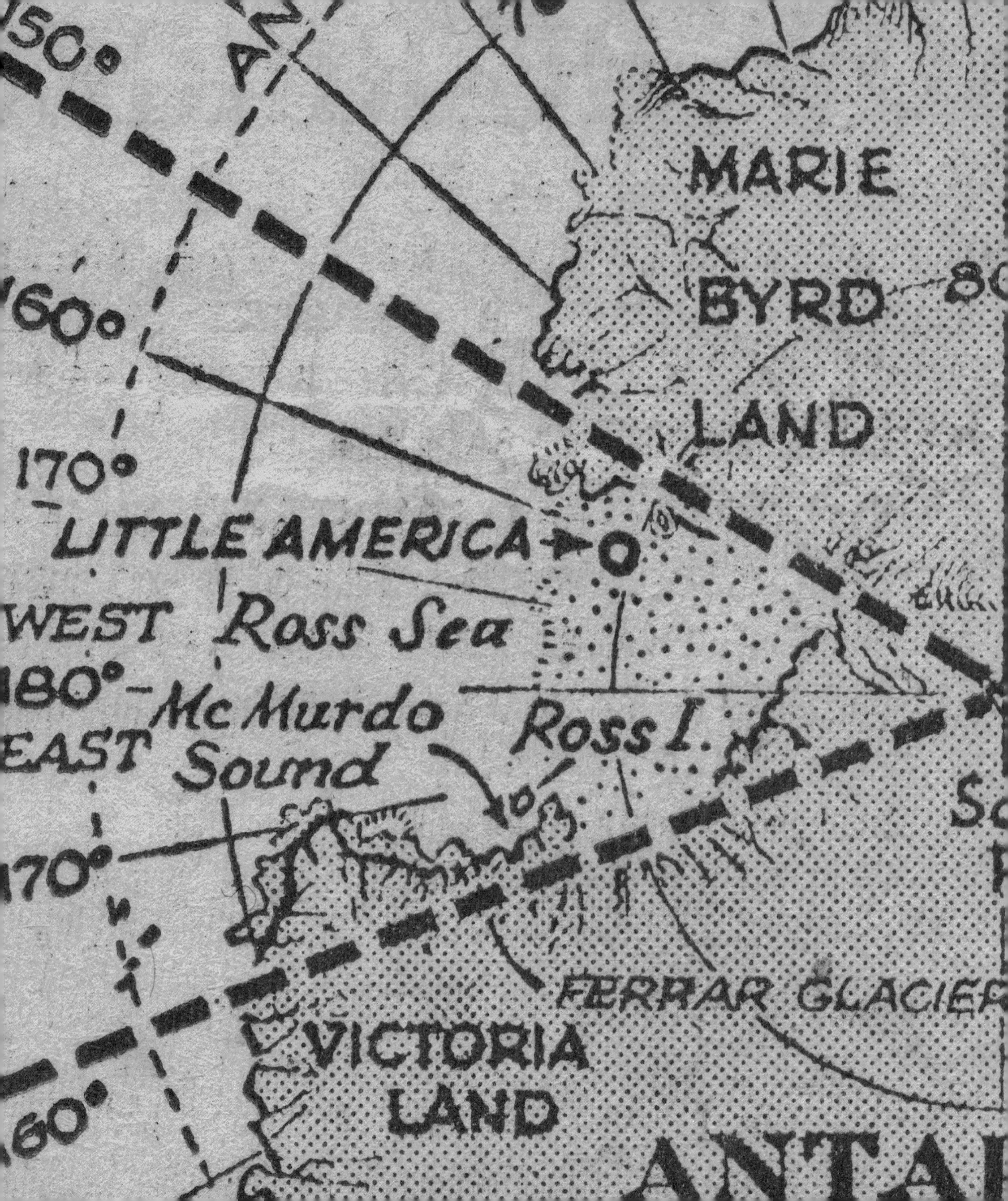

50°

A

160°

170°

MARIE

BYRD 80

LAND

LITTLE AMERICA O

WEST *Ross Sea*

180° *McMurdo*

EAST *Sound* *Ross I.*

170°

FERRAR GLACIER

VICTORIA
LAND

60°

ANTA